Scenario-Based Design

Envisioning Work and Technology in System Development

Edited by:

John M. Carroll

John Wiley & Sons, Inc.

New York • Chichester • Brisbane • Toronto • Singapore

Publisher: Katherine Schowalter
Senior Editor: Diane D. Cerra
Managing Editor: Robert S. Aronds
Editorial Production & Design: Publishers' Design and Production Services, Inc.

This text is printed on acid-free paper.

Library of Congress Cataloging-in-Publication Data:

Scenario-based design : envisioning work and technology in system development / edited by John M. Carroll.
p. cm.
Includes bibliographical references.
ISBN 0-471-07659-7
1. User interfaces (Computer systems) 2. system design.
I. Carroll, John M. (John Millar), 1950–
QA76.9.U83S34 1995
005.1'028—dc20 94-23772
CIP

Printed in the United States of America
10 9 8 7 6 5 4 3 2 1

Contents

Preface

On June 8, 1993, we gathered at the Kittle House Inn near Chappaqua, New York, for three days of discussions on the nature of use-oriented design representations, and the roles they play and could play in the development of computer systems and applications. The topic is broad—how to conceptualize work and activity in a way that can proactively guide design efforts, how to envision designs by envisioning their impacts on work and activity, how to direct empirical evaluation of designed tools and environments toward better designs, how to cumulate what is learned in design work. To my mind, this topic lies at the heart of a new view of human–computer interaction, one that conceives of user tasks, system designs, and even implementations as scenarios of interaction.

This is a deceptively simple idea. It is a sharp departure from traditional concepts and methods in both human–computer interaction and software engineering. Scenarios are not the traditional activity logs of human factors, nor the keystroke-level models of cognitive engineering—they are meaningful to and discussible by users; they are couched at the level at which people understand and experience their own behavior. Scenarios also contrast with traditional functional analysis and specification, and with procedure-based decomposition—developing systems "by scenario" means building object-oriented models of the user's task domain. These two thrusts entrain a fundamental shift in thinking about design: Artifacts *are* the tasks they enable, the understandings and experiences they engender. When we design systems and applications, we are, most essentially, designing scenarios of interaction.

Scenario-based design is not a finished paradigm, a shrinkwrapped methodology, ready for passive consumption. It is, rather, a set of perspectives and approaches, linked by a radical vision of use-oriented design. It is a set of case studies that will, and ought to, raise more questions than they settle. The chapters in this book are not the end state of the project, but I believe they present a substantial beginning. I feel enormously fortunate to have been able to work with this impressive group of thinkers and technicians; I think that what we have produced will be valuable to those now poised to take the next steps in developing a scenario-based design paradigm. One can never, of course, capture all the dynamics of a successful workshop in the static medium of a bound book, but I am very grateful to the authors for their energetic efforts toward capturing some of the discussion and points of contact in revising their chapters.

In organizing this workshop, I had the great good fortune to get excellent advice from many sources. In addition to the participants, I would like to thank Dick Berry, Steve Fickas, Jonathan Grudin, Kim Halskov Madsen, Lewis Johnson, Clayton Lewis, Susanne Maass, Don Norman, John Richards, Danny Sabbah, Lucy Suchman, John Tang, Bill Verplank, and John Woolsey. I got much more good advice than I was able to productively implement. My managers at the IBM Thomas J. Watson Research Center, Danny Sabbah and John Richards, provided generous support at a time when it was a challenge to do so; Bonnie Zingarelli kept all the balls in the air and always knew where each one was; the Kittle House staff provided a beautiful and isolated work environment, with fine food and drink.

JMC
Blacksburg, Virginia

Authors

Tom Carey
Department of Computing and Information Science
University of Guelph
Guelph, Ontario N1G ZW1
Canada

Rebecca Carr
U.S. West Communications
1801 California
Denver, CO 80202
USA

John M. Carroll
Department of Computer Science
562 McBryde Hall
Virginia Polytechnic Institute and State University
Blacksburg, VA 24061
USA

Tom Dayton
Bellcore
444 Hoes Lane
Piscataway, NJ 08854
USA

Barbara Diekmann
U S West Technologies
4001 Discovery Drive
Boulder, CO 80303
USA

Elizabeth Dykstra-Erikson
U S West Technologies
4001 Discovery Drive
Boulder, CO 80303
USA

Thomas Erickson
3136 Irving Avenue South
Minneapolis, MN 55408
USA

Ivar Jacobson
Objectory AB
Torshamnsgatan 39
Box 1128
S-164 22 Kista
Sweden

Hilary Johnson
HCI Laboratory
Department of Computer Science
Queen Mary and Westfield College
University of London
Mile End Road, London, E1 4NS
United Kingdom

Peter Johnson
HCI Laboratory
Department of Computer Science
Queen Mary and Westfield College
University of London
Mile End Road, London, E1 4NS
United Kingdom

John Karat
IBM Watson Research Center
Box 704
Yorktown Heights, NY 10598
USA

Kari Kuutti
University of Oulu
Department of Information Processing Science
Linnanmaa, SF-90570, Oulu
Finland

Morten Kyng
Department of Computer Science
Aarhus University
Building 540, Ny Munkegade
DK-8000 Aarhus C
Denmark

Robert L. Mack
IBM Watson Research Center
30 Saw Mill River Road
Hawthorne, NY 10532
USA

Allan MacLean
Rank Xerox Research Centre
61 Regent Street
Cambridge CB2 1AB
England

Diane McKerlie
Rank Xerox Research Centre
61 Regent Street
Cambridge CB2 1AB
England

Michael Muller
US West Technologies
4001 Discovery Drive
Boulder, CO 80303
USA

Bonnie Nardi
Apple Computer
Advanced Technology Group
Intelligent Systems Program
1 Infinite Loop
Cupertino, CA 95014
USA

Jakob Nielsen
SunSoft
2550 Garcia Avenue
MS MTV 21-225
Mountain View, CA 94043-1100
USA

Scott P. Robertson
Applied Research and Multimedia Services
U S West Technologies
4001 Discovery Drive
Boulder, CO 80303
USA

Robert W. Root
Bellcore
444 Hoes Lane
Piscataway, NJ 08854
USA

Mary Beth Rosson
Department of Computer Science
562 McBryde Hall
Virginia Polytechnic Institute and State University
Blacksburg, VA 24061
USA

Mak Rusli
Department of Computing and Information Science
University of Guelph
Guelph, Ontario
Canada

Leslie G. Tudor
AT&T Bell Laboratories
220 Laurel Avenue
Middletown, NJ 07748
USA

Ellen A. White
Bellcore
444 Hoes Lane
Piscataway, NJ 08854
USA

Daniel M. Wildman
Bellcore
444 Hoes Lane
Piscataway, NJ 08854
USA

Stephanie Wilson
HCI Laboratory
Department of Computer Science
Queen Mary and Westfield College
University of London
Mile End Road, London, E1 4NS
United Kingdom

Rebecca Wirfs-Brock
Digitalk, Inc.
7585 S.W. Mohawk Street
Tualatin, OR 97062
USA

Introduction: The Scenario Perspective on System Development

John M. Carroll

There was a time, not too long ago, when it seemed reasonable to view computers chiefly as electronic devices and circuits, as embodiments of computational algorithms. However, through the 1980s computing broadly permeated nearly all arenas of human activity in most Western societies. Computers were transformed from strictly technological artifacts—the remote, arcane, and unique province of engineers and programmers—into ubiquitous cultural artifacts that are embedded in nearly everything that people do, indispensable, or at least inescapable, to the general public.

There are many facets to this transformation, and many debates have been and should be provoked and focused by it. One of these is a fundamental rethinking of the goals and methods of system design and development: As technological artifacts, computers must produce correct results; they must be reliable, run efficiently, and be easy—or at least possible—to maintain (that is, technicians must be able to understand how they work well enough to diagnose problems and to add or enhance functions). But as artifacts of general culture, computer systems must meet many further requirements: They must be accessible to non-technologists (easy to learn/easy to use); they must smoothly augment human activities, meet people's expectations, and enhance the quality of life by guiding their users to satisfying work experiences, stimulating educational opportunities, and relaxation during leisure time.

These latter requirements are far more difficult to specify and to satisfy. We do not now (and in fact may never) understand human activities in enough detail to merely list the attributes computer systems would have to incorporate in order to meet these requirements: Precisely what kind of computer will help people learn microbiology, choose a new job, or relax? Indeed, human society and psychology develop in part as a consequence of the contemporary state of technology, and technology is precisely what is running ahead of our understanding so rapidly now. Thus, we have little prospect of developing *final* answers to questions about the nature of human activity—certainly not at the level of detail that would provide specific guidance to designers. Our best course is to develop rich and flexible methods and concepts, to directly incorporate descriptions of potential users and the uses they might make of an envisioned computer system into the design reasoning for that system—ideally by involving the users themselves in the design process.

Opening up the design process to intended users and descriptions of their projected use entails many technical issues. We need to develop new vocabularies for discussing and characterizing designs in terms of the projected activities of the intended users. These vocabularies should be accessible to the users themselves, so that they can help to define the technology they will use. We need also to be able to integrate and coordinate such use-oriented design representations with other representations produced in the course of system development. We need to be able to assess design alternatives with use-oriented criteria and to integrate and coordinate such assessments with those we make on traditional grounds, like correctness, reliability, efficiency, and maintainability. We need to develop new sorts of tools and techniques to support the development and use of use-oriented representations and methods in design. We need to produce education to help system developers understand the need for use-oriented approaches and to help them adopt such methods in their work. This is a lot to ask for, but to do anything less is to risk losing sight of the line between human beings using and controlling their technology and its antithesis.

1.1 THE SCENARIO PERSPECTIVE

A substantial amount of current research and development activity is focused on creating a more use-oriented perspective on the design and development of computer systems. One key element in this perspective is the user-interaction scenario, a narrative description of what people do and experience as they try to make use of computer systems and applications. Computer systems and applications can be and should be viewed as transformations of user tasks and their supporting social practices. In this sense, user-interaction scenarios are a particularly pertinent medium for representing, analyzing, and planning how a computer system might impact its users' activities and experiences. They comprise a vocabulary for design and evaluation that is rich and yet evenly accessible to all the stakeholders in a development project.

Figure I.1 presents a simple example, a textual sketch of a situation in which a person interacts with a video information system. The person is browsing a database of video clips in which the individual members of a project team describe episodes and issues that were salient to them at various points in time during the development project. The person is particularly interested in the evolution of the project vision and the choice of a content domain, as these bear on the curriculum design role this person will play in the project team. The person pursues these interests by selecting among control icons to request a series of video clips [5].

The scenario identifies the person as having certain motivations toward the system, describes the actions taken and some reasons why these actions were taken, and characterizes the results in terms of the user's motivations and expectations. In practice, a scenario like that in Figure I.1 might be developed to help envision various further aspects of the user's activity and experience: precisely which controls were selected, just what the user concluded from whatever video was presented, and so forth. The focus of these descriptions, however detailed they might be, is on the user, what the user does, what the user perceives, what it all means to the user.

Scenarios need not be in the form of textual narrative as in Figure I.1. They can be storyboards of annotated cartoon panels, video mockups, scripted prototypes, or physical situations contrived to support certain user activities. Scenarios also can be couched at many different levels of description and many grains of detail. The example in Figure I.1 is a very high-level usage scenario, suggesting the overall motives that prospective users might have when they come to the system and the general kind of interaction they might experience. But that scenario could be articulated at a much finer grain to specify precisely the system's functionality, including the interactions among system components (hardware, software, and user interface elements) that occur in the course of the scenario.

The defining property of a scenario is that it projects a concrete

- Harry, a curriculum designer, has just joined a project developing a multimedia information system for engineering education. He browses the project video history. Sets of clips are categorized under major iconically presented headings; under some of these are further menu-driven subcategories.
- He selects the Lewis icon from the designers, the Vision icon from the issues, and an early point on the project time-line. He then selects Play Clip and views a brief scene in which Lewis describes his vision of the project as enabling a new world of collaborative and experience-based education.
- Harry selects Technical Issues (instead of Vision) and from its menu, he selects Course Topic, and then Play Clip. Lewis explains why bridges and bridge failures is a good choice: It's a concrete problem, accessible to anybody and yet seriously technical; it can be highly visual—as in the Tacoma Narrows film.
- Harry selects a point on the time-line further along in the project history. In the new clip, Lewis explains why nuclear power plants are such a good choice for the course topic: socially urgent and seriously technical.
- Harry selects Walter from the designer icons, and then requests a video clip. Walter appears in a window and explains his reasons why nuclear power plants is a good course topic: lots of good video, lots of popular-press text, and lots of technical debate.
- Harry selects various combinations: other designers besides Walter and Lewis on these same issues and times, and other times and issues for Walter and Lewis. He begins to appreciate the project vision more broadly, attributing some of the differences to individual interests and roles in the project team. He begins to see the course topic issue as a process of discovering and refining new requirements through active consideration of alternatives.

Figure I.1. Browsing project history scenario: A new project member uses a design history system to understand the evolution of the project's vision and content domain.

description of activity that the user engages in when performing a specific task, a description sufficiently detailed so that design implications can be inferred and reasoned about. Using scenarios in system development helps keep the future use of the envisioned system in view as the system is designed and implemented; it makes use concrete—which makes it easier to discuss use and to *design* use.

Empirical studies of system design have frequently noted the spontaneous and informal use of scenarios by system developers [10, 12, 29]. And in the current state-of-the-art, a set of user interaction scenarios is required for designing user training and documentation as well as us-

the scenario perspective:	*the establishment view:*
concrete descriptions	abstract descriptions
focus on particular instances	focus on generic types
work driven	technology driven
open-ended, fragmentary	complete, exhaustive
informal, rough, colloquial	formal, rigorous
envisioned outcomes	specified outcomes

Figure I.2. Contrasting perspectives on system development: the scenario perspective (left-hand side) and the establishment view (right-hand side).

ability tests [18, 27]. These observations raise many questions and possibilities: Can system development occur *without* scenarios? How might the "upstream" creation and use of scenarios be more directly encouraged and supported, and more broadly exploited? What savings might be obtained by generating training, documentation, and testing scenarios relatively early in the development process, and then referring to them continuingly throughout the process?

At a workshop at the Kittle House Inn, the authors of this book explored the implications of such an enhancement of the software development process. Taking scenarios as a focal object for software and system development indeed yields a clearly alternative perspective on the nature and objectives of the system development process relative to the current establishment view in software and systems engineering. Figure I.2 summarizes a set of contrasts that were generated after reflection on the workshop activity.

Scenarios seek to be concrete; they focus on describing particular instances of use, and on a user's view of what happens, how it happens, and why. Scenarios are grounded in the work activities of prospective users; the work users do drives the development of the system intended to augment this work. Thus, scenarios are often open-ended and fragmentary; they help developers and users pose new questions, question new answers, open up possibilities. It's not a problem if one scenario encompasses, extends, or depends upon another; such relations may reveal important aspects of use. They can be informal and rough; since users as well as developers may create and use them, they should be as colloquial and as accessible as possible. They help developers and their users envision the outcomes of design—an integrated description of what the system will do and how it will do it—and thereby better manage and control these outcomes.

Specifications seek to be abstract; they focus on describing generic types of functions, and on the data processing that underlies functions. Specifications are driven by the technology they specify; they are grounded in logic. They are intended to be complete and exhaustive. They do not omit even predictable details; they do not duplicate information. They are rigorous; ideally, they are formal. They specify design outcomes by enumerating conditions that the system must satisfy. They precisely document what is designed.

The scenario perspective is not a call for a Kuhnian *paradigm shift*; the authors of this book do not take the position that the establishment view needs to be overthrown by a scenario-based system development paradigm. Our view is that current system development practice needs to be augmented to include use-oriented system development activities and artifacts. It is simply not enough to enumerate functions that a system will provide; the same function set may augment human work or obstruct it; it may stimulate and enrich the imagination or stifle and overwhelm. We need to be able to specify systems to ensure that they are logically coherent. But we need to envision the use of systems to ensure that they actually can support human activities. Our point is that neither consideration guarantees the other.

I.2 SCENARIOS AS A FULCRUM FOR THE SYSTEM DEVELOPMENT LIFECYCLE

If we agree that the scenario perspective on system development is a potentially valuable enhancement of current development practice, we must ask *how* the use of scenarios in system development can be evoked, supported, and brought to bear on various activities within the system development lifecycle. Our workshop focused on these questions; we were particularly concerned with upstream activities like requirements analysis and design, but we agree that the scenario perspective can play a guiding role throughout the lifecycle. Figure I.3 lists a set of design activities and the roles that scenarios can play in supporting these.

The scenario in Figure I.1 could in principle fill *all* of the roles in Figure I.3. For example, if the scenario were the summary of an observed user interaction, or a hypothesized user interaction, it could be part of a requirements analysis: It epitomizes what people may do with a project video history browser, and therefore what capabilities must be provided. Indeed, many proposals have been made for managing the

Requirements Analysis: People using current technology can be directly observed to build a scenario description of the state-of-the-art and to ground a scenario analysis of what subsequent technology might be appropriate: The requirements scenarios embody the needs apparent in current work practice. A heuristic variant of this approach is to interview users about their practices or to stage a simulated work situation. A supplemental approach is to hypothesize scenario descriptions; this is less responsive to users' immediate needs but may facilitate discovering user needs that are not obvious in actual situations, or even apparent to users.

User-Designer Communication: The intended users of a system can contribute scenarios illustrating design issues that are important to them, specific problems or strengths in the current technology, or the kinds of situations they think they would like to experience or avoid. The system designers and developers can also contribute scenarios to such a discussion, since the users can speak this language. Users and designers together evaluate possibilities for usability and functionality. A heuristic variant is to include user representatives.

Design Rationale: Scenarios can be a unit of analysis for developing a design rationale. The rationale would explain the design with respect to particular scenarios of user interaction. Alternative scenarios can be competitively analyzed to force out new issues and new scenarios. Because such a rationale focuses on particular scenarios, it can be more of a resource for guiding other lifecycle activities with respect to those scenarios.

Envisionment: Scenarios can be a medium for working out what a system being designed should look like and do. The scenarios can be detailed to the point of assigning specific user interface presentations and protocols for user actions. Such scenarios can be embodied in graphical mockups such as storyboards or video-based simulations; they can themselves be early prototypes for the actual system.

Software Design: A set of user scenarios can be analyzed to identify the central problem domain objects that would be required to implement those scenarios. These scenarios can then be developed with respect to articulating the state, behavior, and functional interactions of the design objects. Further scenarios can be run against such a problem domain model to test and refine the design.

Implementation: The problem domain objects identified and defined in software design can be implemented and run as scenarios. Developing the implementation of one scenario at a time can help to keep developers focused on the goal of supporting that specific user activity while at the same time producing code that is more generally useful.

Documentation and Training: There is an unavoidable gap between the system as an artifact presented to users, and the tasks that users want to accomplish using it. This gap is bridged when documentation and training is presented within the framework of scenarios of interaction that are meaningful to the users. Such documentation and training is easier to initially make sense of and to use later on.

Figure I.3. Roles of scenarios in the system development lifecycle.

Evaluation: A system must be evaluated against the specific user tasks it is intended to support. Hence it is important to have identified an appropriate set of such tasks for the evaluation. Of course, it is even more useful to know what these tasks are throughout the development process.

Abstraction: It is often possible to generalize the lessons learned in the design of a given system to design work within a class of domains. Conversely, it is important to develop and evaluate candidate generalizations across a variety of user task domains in order to understand the boundary conditions for a given generalization. Thus, it is important to develop techniques for describing similarities and categorizations among scenarios.

Team Building: Developing and sharing a set of touchstone stories is an important cohesive element in any social system. Design teams tend to do this, and some of the stories they share are the scenarios that motivated and directed their design work. Gathering, discussing, and sharing these stories as a group can be an effective means to team building.

Figure I.3. *(Continued)*

discovery and refinement of requirements through a variety of scenario representations (e.g., [6, 13, 14, 17, 19, 22, 31]). The scenario in Figure I.1 is couched in the lingua franca of end-user action and experience, and therefore it can be a meeting ground for communication and collaboration between developers and users—indeed, it is easy to imagine that this scenario might have been contributed by a developer, by a human factors specialist, or by a user in a participatory design discussion. Ehn and Kyng [11] illustrate this property of scenarios in their discussion of the cooperative use of mockups (see also [21]).

The scenario could be evaluated by users or analyzed by designers to bring to light further issues and perhaps further scenarios. For example, the users and designers might contrast a query scenario with the browsing scenario in Figure I.1 to clarify their assumptions about envisioned use of the system. These discussions would comprise part of a design rationale for the video information system by presenting the capabilities of the system in terms of what users can do with them, and in that sense justifying and explaining why the capabilities are what they are [2, 7, 8].

If the project history browser did not yet exist, then the scenario in Figure I.1 could be part of the envisionment of the system as it was being planned [23, 30]. Envisioning such concrete situations in the problem domain guides the identification of the central computational objects—most clearly in responsibility-driven [32] and use case-driven

[15] approaches to object-oriented analysis and design, though these approaches have now been assimilated into most object-oriented software engineering methods. In turn, such a scenario-based analysis directly supports the implementation of the application functionality [28].

If we assume that the scenario in Figure I.1 describes a typical or critical user task, then the scenario also could provide a template for the development of documentation and training: People better understand and can make better use of documentation and training if it is presented in the context of the tasks they actually want to accomplish (e.g., [3]). Similarly, the scenario provides a framework for evaluation: The functionality, usefulness, and usability of system must be evaluated in the context of the tasks for which the systems will be used (e.g., [18, 24, 27]). These latter applications of scenarios are well-established practice, but often scenarios for documentation, training, and evaluation are constructed very late in the development process—integrating them with the many other roles scenarios can play creates the possibility for highly leveraged scenario-building effort.

Design is more than a work process and an application context. It is a context for inquiry; one learns and one must learn in order to do design work. It is an important though difficult task to try to make what is learned explicit so that others can share in what was learned. One way of doing this is to generalize scenarios. The scenario in Figure I.1 is a *search* scenario, a scenario in which a person is browsing data with a fairly specific objective in mind [1, 8]. Making the generalization of a search type of scenario creates the possibility of mapping whatever might have been learned in designing the project history browser to issues that will arise in any subsequent information system design project. Several approaches to theory-building in human–computer interaction take scenarios as the basis for their empirical taxonomy of phenomena [9, 33, 34].

Design also is a social process; many projects can succeed only if a viable social system is created in which a variety of skills, and an even greater variety of personalities, can achieve a state of mutual respect and commitment [16]. Jointly creating a set of touchstone stories is a powerful factor in this. Some of the stories pertain to how the design project originated, oriented itself, progressed, and finally prevailed; other stories pertain to what the design project is all about or how to work around the shortcomings of current situations. Orr [25] discussed how technicians tell each other stories about usage episodes as a means of mutual learning. Carroll [4] described the role that shared stories played in maintaining the continuity of two long-term design projects. The scenario in Figure I.1 can be seen as a story about the team's mission.

Figure I.3 is not meant to imply that every detail of an effective and efficient scenario-based perspective on system development methodology is now in place. Neither is it meant to imply a prescribed sequence for design activities or even that all the listed activities need occur in a given design process (for example, a project carried out by a single designer does not consider team building). Rather, it is a direction and a possibility suggested by the chapters in this book.

I.3 A SCENARIO VIEW INTO THIS BOOK

The scenario perspective on system development is a touchstone for the various chapters in this book; it is part of the common ground of concerns and methods shared among the various authors. It is an important element in every author's work, but it is not the only important element in any author's work. It provides a framework through which to view the various chapters.

Many of the authors emphasize the variety of roles that scenarios can play in the system development process. John Karat (Chapter 5) describes the development of a speech recognition application from the standpoint of the many roles that scenarios played in the course of that project. Morten Kyng (Chapter 4) provides a taxonomy of scenario roles based on his experiences with cooperative design. Jakob Nielsen (Chapter 3) discusses the variety of roles that scenarios play in his development of usability engineering. Ivar Jacobson (Chapter 12) and Rebecca Wirfs-Brock (Chapter 13) describe the roles that scenarios can play in object-oriented software engineering, particularly in requirements analysis and design. Mary Beth Rosson and Jack Carroll (Chapter 10) describe an approach to more closely integrating specification and implementation by focusing both activities on scenarios.

Some of the authors focus on particular roles for scenarios within their methodological frameworks and practices. Peter Johnson and his collaborators (Chapter 9) use scenarios for requirements gathering in their design work with medical professionals. Scott Robertson (Chapter 11) uses them for design analysis, adapting the systematic questioning methodology he pioneered in cognitive science studies of narratives. Tom Carey and Mark Rusli (Chapter 7) adapt scenarios as a framework for evaluation. Tom Erickson (Chapter 2) describes uses of scenarios in facilitating communication among designers in the early stages of design work. Michael Muller and his collaborators (Chapter 6) design user work flow in participatory exercises. Allan MacLean and Diane McKerlie (Chapter 8) use scenarios in generating and evaluating design rationales. Kari Kuutti (Chapter 1) addresses the overall role of scenarios in designing and understanding interactive systems. He sees scenarios as providing a preliminary vocabulary for describing work processes in the context of system development, noting that scenarios give us a way to discuss systems both as work contexts and as pieces of technology.

The chapters individually address many of the roles that scenarios can play and are now playing throughout the system development lifecycle. Thus, Johnson, Johnson, and Wilson gather requirements by visiting their users' workplace, observing what was done and how it was done, even trying themselves to carry out the domain activities. The designers and the users explicitly negotiate the scenarios and descriptions of the domain. Kyng summarizes initial studies of the work situations of his prospective users with *work situation overviews*, general descriptions of user activities. These are used to develop a set of specific use scenarios, describing how the users' work would be altered and improved with computer support. Erickson describes extracting the underlying stories from requirements interviews in a way that is reminiscent of Propp's classic analysis of the Russian folktale: The material collected in various user interviews is distilled into a set of succinct, evocative stories [26].

Many of the authors emphasize the point that scenarios are representations accessible to both users and designers. Scenarios make communication between designers and users more effective. Erickson notes that stories make it easy to involve people. Johnson and his collaborators stress the point that their early joint work with the users to develop overview scenarios and scenarios for particular tasks established a working relationship that helped throughout the development process. Muller and his collaborators emphasize how low-tech scenario exercises with physical objects like cards can help stakeholders *problematize*, that is, to transform their assumptions into open questions, and thereby better articulate their concerns and ideas. Kyng describes how communication between users and designers can be focused through design workshops in which designers and users jointly explore usage scenarios with a mockup of the system being designed. Rosson and Carroll describe a tool that allows a user and a designer to create a scenario, express it as a partial software design, and immediately render the design as running code.

Several authors are directly concerned with scenarios as means of embodying design rationale, or as tools to help generate design rationale. Rosson and Carroll consider a system being designed as the set of use scenarios that will be supported by the system. Each scenario can be expanded into a set of causal relations between elements of the design and specific consequences for the users' activity and experience, and for the software implementation of the envisioned function. In this approach to design rationale the entities being explained are the scenarios of use. Kyng creates *explanation scenarios* to concretely link elements in a design to hypothesized effects for users and their work; these scenarios become the focus of workshops for users and designers. MacLean and McKerlie use scenarios as means to generate and identify specific issues and tradeoffs in a design. On the one hand, they develop and analyze scenarios to identify new design options or criteria with which to evaluate options. On the other hand, they extract the issues, options, and criteria from particular scenarios to construct a generalized view of the design.

Many of the authors emphasize the open-endedness, incompleteness, or roughness of scenarios as a property that makes them especially suitable for design envisonment. Erickson notes that scenarios often encourage creative thinking by leaving some details out. Nielsen describes his experience working with a group brainstorming electronic presence applications in which a large set of microscenarios were generated. Each scenario was very briefly sketched, just enough to hold its place relative to the other scenario ideas. At a later stage, the group selected a smaller set of scenarios to be envisioned in detail. Kyng makes the point that by couching the requirements, the design rationale, and the envisionment all as scenarios one coordinates design work to avoid developing technical solutions to irrelevant problems.

Scenarios afford a great variety in grain of descriptive detail. Karat stresses the level-switching between overall specification and detail design that occurred as his team first began to enumerate and elaborate their scenarios. Kuutti notes that scenarios encompass both rich work-process-oriented descriptions and simple, computer-oriented descriptions. Muller and his collaborators contrast the task-flow and user cognition descriptions of their CARD technique with the detailed design within a context of task-flow, addressed by their PICTIVE technique. Rosson and Carroll contrast wholistic scenario descriptions with more piecemeal, causal schemas. Kyng distinguishes work situation overviews from detailed scenarios.

Within object-oriented software design, scenarios play a very direct structuring role. Wirfs-Brock's pioneering work on *responsibility-driven design* emphasizes a view of software objects as bearing specific functional responsibilities in user-system interactions. Jacobson develops the notion of a use case as the basic element of requirements analysis for object-oriented software. Jacobson's use cases describe all the possible user action paths for each given area of a system's functionality.

Robertson illustrates a systematic question-asking technique intended to help designers identify and refine problem domain. All three are defining techniques to articulate software designs directly from scenarios of user interaction. Rosson and Carroll describe an environment that supports a highly interleaved relationship between such scenario-based software design and a rapid prototyping approach to implementation.

Many of the authors discuss roles for scenarios in documentation, training, and evaluation. Karat's team used scenarios to direct the design of their documentation and training material, using the early envisionment and specification scenarios. Thus, the same scenario-design effort was leveraged across several system development activities. Nielsen describes scenario-based formative evaluation of systems in which screens are presented to prospective users who are then asked to explain what they think they could do and with what effects from that screen. Muller and Kyng also describe early-stage evaluation through mockups of systems. Carey and Rusli wish to extract underlying scenarios from sets of particular scenarios to reduce actual evaluation data, in their case scenario descriptions of particular usage situations, to *composite scenarios*. Their vision is that a library of such composites could serve as a summary of an evaluation and as a resource to guide further design work. Nielsen also describes his experiences summarizing patterns in data logs for an electronic door application as scenario stereotypes.

Karat describes how his team discovered that speech navigation would be of limited use without general speech input capability: Working through the implications of this evaluation scenario early in the project completely changed its direction. Later, the team conducted workshops with potential customers in which current work practices were queried and discussed, and then future possibilities (envisioned in brief video clips) were presented and discussed. This gave Karat's team detailed information on how the customers perceived speech recognition, what they thought about alternative microphone arrangements, processing delays, error rates, and error correction and enrollment procedures.

Kuutti characterizes scenarios as an abstract vocabulary that allows us to speak about activity, the use of computers within work processes, while still preserving situational complexity—thus avoiding one of the typical pitfalls of abstractions. Kyng's explanation scenarios preserve some of the reasoning from the current context to be engaged in a subsequent discussion. Rosson and Carroll develop a scenario typology for developing applications in their design environment. Jacobson conceives of use cases themselves as design objects in a structural hierarchy, to be refactored into *abstract use cases* for reuse in subsequent software designs. Carey and Rusli's composite scenarios are an abstraction built on top of a set of actual usage scenarios; their *discretionary usage choice graphs* provide an abstract description of the activities in observed user scenarios.

Erickson emphasizes that stories support communication; his discussion focuses on facilitating the communication among various groups within the organization developing a system, particularly in the early stages of exploration and refinement, and at the crucial junction of transition or transfer from an advance technology group to a development group. Karat recalls that at the earliest stage of the speech recognition system design, generating and discussing scenarios helped the team decide what it was that they wanted to do, to articulate a shared understanding of what they were working toward: They imagined the consequences of performing everyday tasks without a keyboard or pointing device.

Bob Mack (Chapter 14) and Bonnie Nardi (Chapter 15) generously agreed to write discussion chapters for this volume. These discussions provide integrative thematic views into the various other chapters. Mack reflects on three themes: the central role that scenarios can play in all facets of development activity, the range of practical, scenario-based techniques for coordinating use-oriented design, and prospects for scenario-based models and concepts of design. Nardi reflects on methodological issues stemming from the empirical nature of scenarios, for example, their cost-effectiveness, representativeness, and the boundary conditions on using them. Both discussions point the way to further developments and extensions of scenario-based design by asking about the bigger picture of design and design knowledge within which scenarios can play their part.

1.4 SCENARIOS AS A MIDDLE-LEVEL ABSTRACTION

In the 1950s, C. Wright Mills [20] complained that social science was failing in its obligation to provide effective guidance for the development of social policies, practices, and institutions. His book, *The Sociological Imagination*, criticized the penchant of social scientists for "grand theory": precise, formal, intellectually awesome, but also low-level, limited in scope, and impossible to apply. Mills was understandably concerned that a grand science, which failed nonetheless to guide practical decision-making, might on balance be worse than no science at all. He called for a new perspective, for the development of "middle-level abstractions" that would be better grounded in social reality and better suited to application in actual social contexts. He suggested that this pursuit be called *social studies* to more clearly differentiate its concrete aspirations from those of its more ambitious and prideful complement.

System development is now in need of a guiding middle-level abstraction, a concept less formal and less grand than specification, but a concept that can be broadly and effectively applied. Scenarios are not formal; they are not scientific in any fancy sense. We know that they can be used because they already do play many roles in the system lifecycle. Perhaps the time has come to consider how a more integrative scenario perspective for system development can be constructed. Design methods must live on a razor's edge between creative intuition and grounded analysis. Perhaps scenarios can help balance the need for flexibility and informality with the need to progress systematically toward creating effective and usable computer systems and applications.

ACKNOWLEDGMENTS

I am grateful to Jurgen Koenenmann-Belliveau, Morten Kyng, Bob Mack, Scott Robertson, Mary Beth Rosson, and Paul van Schaik for guidance with these ideas and for comments on their presentation here.

REFERENCES

[1] Brooks, R. (1991). Comparative task analysis: An alternative direction for human-computer interaction science. In J. M. Carroll (ed.), *Designing Interaction: Psychology at the Human-Computer Interface*. New York: Cambridge University Press, pp. 50–59.

[2] Carey, T., McKerlie, D., Bubie, W. & Wilson, J. (1991). Communicating human factors expertise through design rationales and scenarios. In D. Diaper & N. Hammond (eds.), *People and Computers VI*. Cambridge, U.K.: Cambridge University Press, pp. 117–130.

[3] Carroll, J. M. (1990). *The Nürnberg Funnel: Designing Minimalist Instruction for Practical Computer Skills*. Cambridge, MA: MIT Press.

[4] Carroll, J. M. (1992). Making history by telling stories. In *Proceedings of the CHI'92 Research Symposium*, Monterey, CA, May 1–2. Unpaged.

[5] Carroll, J. M., Alpert, S. R., Karat, J., Van Deusen, M. S. & Rosson, M. B. (1994). Raison d'être: Capturing design history and rationale in multimedia narratives. In *Proceedings of the ACM CHI'94 Conference*, Boston, April 24–28. New York: ACM Press, pp. 192–197, 478.

[6] Carroll, J. M. & Rosson, M. B. (1990). Human-computer interaction scenarios as a design representation. In *Proceedings of the 23rd Annual Hawaii International Conference on Systems Sciences*, Kailua-Kona, HI, January 2–5. Los Alamitos, CA: IEEE Computer Society Press, pp. 555–561.

[7] Carroll, J. M. & Rosson, M. B. (1991). Deliberated evolution: Stalking the View Matcher in design space. *Human-Computer Interaction*, *6*, 281–318.

[8] Carroll, J. M. & Rosson, M. B. (1992). Getting around the task-artifact cycle: How to make claims and design by scenario. *ACM Transactions on Information Systems*, *10*, 181–212.

[9] Carroll, J. M., Singley, M. K. & Rosson, M. B. (1992). Integrating theory development with design evaluation. *Behaviour and Information Technology*, *11*, 247–255.

[10] Carroll, J. M., Thomas, J. C. & Malhotra, A. (1979). A clinical-experimental analysis of design problem solving. *Design Studies*, *1*, 84–92. Reprinted in B. Curtis (ed.), *Human Factors in Software Development*. Washington, DC: IEEE Computer Society Press, pp. 243–251.

[11] Ehn, P. & Kyng, M. (1991). Cardboard computers: Mocking-it-up or hands-on the future. In J. Greenbaum & M. Kyng (eds.), *Design at Work: Cooperative Design of Computer Systems*. Hillsdale, NJ: Lawrence Erlbaum, pp. 169–196.

[12] Guindon, R. (1990). Designing the design process: Exploiting opportunistic thoughts. *Human-Computer Interaction*, *5*, 305–344.

[13] Holbrook, H. (1990). A scenario-based methodology for conducting requirements elicitation. *ACM SIGSOFT Software Engineering Notes*, *15–1* (January): 95–103.

[14] Hooper, J. W. & Hsia, P. (1982). Scenario-based prototyping for requirements identification. *ACM SIGSOFT Software Engineering Notes*, *7–5* (December): 88–93.

[15] Jacobson, I., Christerson, M., Jonsson, P. & Overgaard, G. (1992). *Object-Oriented Software Engineering: A Use-Case Driven Approach*. Reading, MA: Addison-Wesley/ACM Books.

[16] Karat, J. & Bennett, J. B. (1991). Using scenarios in design meetings—A case study example. In J. Karat (ed.), *Taking Design Seriously: Practical Techniques for Human-Computer Interaction Design*. Boston: Academic Press, pp. 63–94.

[17] Kuutti, K. & Arvonen, T. (1992). Identifying potential CSCW applications by means of activity theory concepts: A case example. In *Proceedings of CSCW'92: Conference on Computer-Supported Cooperative Work*, Toronto, October 31–November 4. New York: ACM Press, pp. 233–240.

[18] Mack, R. L., Lewis, C. H. & Carroll, J. M. (1983). Learning to use office systems: Problems and prospects. *ACM Transactions on Office Information Systems*, *1*, 254–271.

[19] Malhotra, A., Thomas, J. C., Carroll, J. M. & Miller, L. A. (1980). Cognitive processes in design. *International Journal of Man-Machine Studies*, *12*, 119–140.

[20] Mills, C. W. (1959). *The Sociological Imagination*. New York: Oxford University Press.

[21] Muller, M. J. (1991). PICTIVE—An exploration in participatory design. In *Proceedings of CHI'91: Conference on Human Factors in Computing*, New Orleans, April 27–May 2. New York: ACM Press, pp. 225–231.

[22] Nardi, B. (1993). *A Small Matter of Programming: Perspectives on End-User Computing*. Cambridge, MA: MIT Press.

[23] Nielsen, J. (1987). Using scenarios to develop user friendly videotex systems. In *Proceedings of NordDATA'89 Joint Scandinavian Computer Conference*, Trondheim, Norway, June 15–18, pp. 133–138.

[24] Nielsen, J. (1990). Paper versus computer implementations as mockup scenarios for heuristic evaluation. In *Proceedings of INTERACT'90: IFIP TC 13 Third International Conference on Human-Computer Interaction*, Cambridge, U.K., August 27–30. Amsterdam: North-Holland, pp. 315–320.

[25] Orr, J. E. (1986). Narratives at work. In *Proceedings of CSCW'86: Conference on Computer-Supported Cooperative Work*, Austin, TX, December 3–5, pp. 62–72.

[26] Propp, V. (1958). *The Morphology of the Folktale*. The Hague: Mouton (originally published 1928).

[27] Roberts, T. L. & Moran, T. P. (1983). The evaluation of text editors: Methodology and empirical results. *Communications of the ACM, 26*, 265–283.

[28] Rosson, M. B. & Carroll, J. M. (1993). Extending the task-artifact framework: Scenario-based design of SmallTalk applications. In H. R. Hartson & D. Hix (eds.), *Advances in Human-Computer Interaction, Volume 4*. Norwood, NJ: Ablex, pp. 31–57.

[29] Rosson, M. B., Maass, S. & Kellogg, W. A. (1988). The designer as user: Building requirements for design tools from design practice. *Communications of the ACM, 31*, 1288–1298.

[30] Vertelney, L. (1989). Using video to prototype user interfaces. *ACM SIGSCHI Bulletin, 21-2*, 57–61.

[31] Wexelblat, A. (1987, May). *Report on Scenario Technology*. Technical Report STP-139-87. Austin, TX: MCC.

[32] Wirfs-Brock, R., Wilerson, B. & Wiener, L. (1990). *Designing Object-Oriented Software*. Englewood Cliffs, NJ: Prentice Hall.

[33] Young, R. M. & Barnard, P. B. (1987). The use of scenarios in human-computer interaction research: Turbocharging the tortoise of cumulative science. In *Proceedings of CHI+GI'87: Conference on Human Factors in Computing Systems and Graphics Interface*. New York: ACM Press, pp. 291–296.

[34] Young, R. M. & Barnard, P. B. (1991). Signature tasks and paradigm tasks: New wrinkles on the scenarios methodology. In D. Diaper & N. Hammond (eds.), *People and Computers VI*. Cambridge, U.K.: Cambridge University Press, pp. 91–101.

CHAPTER 1

Work Processes: Scenarios as a Preliminary Vocabulary

Kari Kuutti
University of Oulu, Department of Information Processing Science
Linnanmaa, SF-90570 Oulu, Finland

1.1 INTRODUCTION

Scenarios have been gaining more and more popularity in both human-computer interaction (HCI) and software engineering (SE) research and design. During 1992, there was within the HCI community a lively debate on scenarios in the pages of *SIGCHI Bulletin* [6, 24, 35, 36]; and a popular tutorial on scenarios took place in the *Interchi'93* conference [33]. In SE, scenarios have not been raising such direct curiosity, but seem more to be tacitly accepted as a normal part of the field both in research [2, 11, 26] and in practice [21]. Scenarios have some interesting features. First, they seem not to have much in the way of roots or history but are mostly taken as given; although less than ten years ago within the same fields hardly anybody was using the term—it has just emerged from somewhere. Second, despite their popularity there is no generally accepted definition of what the term means and its use in different contexts varies widely. For example, Campbell [6] distinguishes four different major types of *scenario*: system illustration, evaluation, design/redesign, and theory testing. Finally, there are also problems in defining the scope of a scenario: How narrow or broad a part of the world should they take into account?

This chapter is an attempt to create some order in the scenario phenomenon and offer some explanations as to why it has become popular just now. It is based on the idea of the historically shifting focus and broadening scope of software development. Scenarios are seen in this chapter as an indication that design has new challenges to cope with, and some possible reasons for these challenges are explored. Scenarios are analyzed using a three-level framework developed within the information system design community, where some of the issues related to scenarios have already been discussed for some time. It is found that on one hand the framework can be used in explaining scenarios and relating the different types to each other, but on the other hand scenarios contain features exceeding those found in the framework, and thus show the way to further conceptual development.

This chapter elaborates on the theme that it is the necessity for dealing with work processes that has made it obligatory to find tools suited for that purpose. Scenarios are filling that role. It might be useful to interpret scenarios as preliminary concepts for dealing with the complexity of the work settings. Although not well-defined, they are rich enough to be practical in design situations. There have been several attempts to conceptualize the field and it is probable and desirable that eventually some progress will be made that will lead to more systematic and generalizable ways to analyze work situations. Meanwhile, we can use scenarios.

1.2 THE NATURE OF SCENARIOS

What are the distinguishing features of scenarios in a broad sense? The definition of scenarios was discussed and questioned in the *SIGCHI Bulletin* debate (1992) without achieving a clear consensus. However, two generally accepted attributes can perhaps be highlighted.

First, a scenario describes a process or a sequence of acts, not individual acts:

> A scenario is a description of an activity, in narrative form [24].
>
> At the most general level, scenario refers to a situation or more precisely (since it has a temporal component), an episode [35].
>
> A scenario is a sequence of actions showing how a transition from one state to another might occur [2].

Second, when scenarios look at a system they do it from outside, from the viewpoint of a user:

> Clients often say "I need a (better) way of getting from point A to point B," where "point A" and "point B" refer to the states of the world [2].
>
> Answering the what-if question by analyzing specific scenarios gives stakeholders insight into general requirements and helps in the refinement process [26].

In contrast to these common views, when it comes to the scope of a scenario there exist two drastically different opinions. The first one sees a scenario as an external description of what a system does:

> More specifically, a scenario is a description of one or more end-to-end transactions involving the required system and its environment [26].
>
> The basic idea is to specify use scenarios that cover all possible pathways through the system functions [29].

The second one proposes a much broader view, looking at the use process as situated in a larger context:

> An important feature of a scenario is that it depicts activities in a full context, describing the social settings, resources, and goals of users. It is not narrowly focused task description, but the "big picture" of how some particular kind of work gets done" [24].
>
> Scenarios embody information about the environment, person, and details of screen and input devices as well as other objects and activities happening. They reflect the complexity of the real-world human interaction with things [33].
>
> The common core, for us, concerns the role of scenarios in concretizing something for the purposes of analysis and communication. . . . The concreteness also enables designers, analysts, and researchers to deal with complicated and rich situations and behaviors in their own terms instead of being restricted to dealing with them one issue at a time [36].

These conceptions seem to sharply contrast each other, and it is not easy to see how they would fit nicely within a common frame of reference. I believe, however, that such a frame exists and that it not only allows but demands the existence of two separate process-oriented levels of description.

1.3 WHY SCENARIOS AND WHERE DO THEY BELONG?

In this section, an attempt is made to locate scenarios within a larger framework consisting of three domains. This framework is studied from three perspectives: as three historically sequential periods, each concentrating on a new problem focus and generating a new problem domain for design; as the resulting three parallel *worlds* for a system; and finally, as an elaborated theoretical three-level model for describing the domains. Each of these perspectives is used in explaining some features of scenarios: The *historical model* is used in explaining the emergence of scenarios; the *parallel-world model* is used in explaining the existing tension between at least some interpretations of scenarios and more formal approaches; and the *theoretical model* is used in explaining the existence and necessity of two different kinds of scenarios.

1.3.1 Historical Development

In his book on the history of information system development, Friedman [10] bases the separation of three phases interestingly on the issues that have been the biggest obstacles of development during each period. The restricting factors have been studied most intensively and corresponding problem-setting has been the prominent one. Eventually former acute problems have been solved or at least alleviated to the extent that the focus has moved toward different topics. The three phases identified by Friedman are as follows:

1. The *cost of hardware and the processing capacity* were the main problems.
2. Due to the intensive research and rapid development of technology it was possible to build acceptable efficient systems on technologies that were reliable enough to serve well in most usual situations. Although technical problems remained, especially when pushing the borders of performance, they were no longer the most commonly restricting ones. The main problem and focus of interest was shifted to *managing the complexity* and *efficiency in developing programs*.
3. Only when enough experience was gained in building systems and when there were advanced tools both for building systems and con-

trolling the process could *the fulfillment of the needs of users* become a major problem focus to be taken seriously.

Friedman expands his argument throughout his whole book. For this chapter we adapt only the idea of the expanding nature of the object of computer systems design and the major phases. It is obvious that the set of problems encountered during each phase has given rise to different approaches in attempting to tackle them: in the first phase—computer science, concentrating on what is needed to make a computer system run better, be it hardware or operating-systems-level software; in the second phase—software engineering, concentrating on the process of producing software in a more controllable and efficient way; in the third phase—a diverse bunch of approaches, such as Management Information Systems (MIS) or HCI, requirements engineering, user-centered design, participatory design, all concentrating on different aspects of *user needs*.

However, the rising importance of user needs and our increasing ability to devote more emphasis to them cannot alone explain the recent interest in scenarios, because user needs have been studied at least in some corners of the research field for much longer than scenarios have been popular. Is there anything happening with the needs that might help in explaining the interest in scenarios?

During the late 1980s and early 1990s there has been indeed more and more discussion on the changing relationship between work and information technology. A vision has emerged and gained popularity that information technology could contribute more if it would *support* whole work processes instead of just *automating* some parts of them (see e.g., [1, 7, 17, 18, 30, 37]). On the other hand, the recent research in HCI and computer-supported cooperative work (or CSCW) (e.g., [4, 27, 32]) has convincingly revealed that supporting work as it is actually done in real life calls for much more intimate understanding and description of work processes than has been usual in system design. It is not far-fetched to think that there is a connection between this heightened emphasis on the process characteristics of work and the fact that scenarios are explicitly process-description tools.

1.3.2 The Three Worlds of System Design

Although the focus of interest has been shifting, the problems and issues central to each of the historical phases have naturally not totally vanished but continue their parallel existence in system analysis and

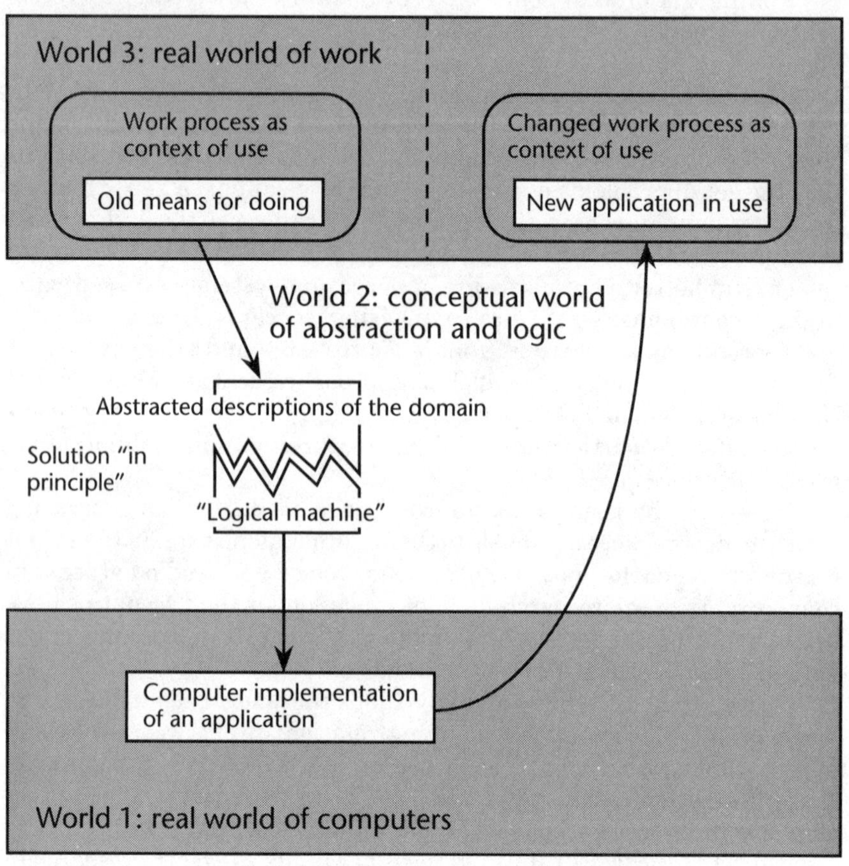

Figure 1.1. The worlds of design and a general, idealized path of a design process through them.

design. We can say that for each historical main phase described before there exists a relatively independent world where the corresponding part of analysis and design has to be done, and distinguishing between these worlds may alleviate some of the confusion and misunderstanding (Figure 1.1).[1]

[1]The idea of three worlds of design is not by any means new or unique in software engineering; for example, Jarke et al. [16] present a very similar perspective.

The worlds are numbered according to their order of appearance. The oldest one is the technical world, which any designer must inevitably often visit in order to make a system run. It consists of both hardware and all the necessary system software available in that particular environment—an operating system, DBMSs, compilers, libraries, and various tools—all having their good properties and defenses that one has to cope with during the design process.

The second world is that of conceptual analysis and design. As said before, it was initially created in order to help designers better master the development by hiding the technical complexity and enabling the search of solutions on a purely logical level. This level has already long been the main focus of interest in software engineering, and correspondingly a huge number of different conceptualizations, formalisms, and tools have been developed for different tasks at this level. Looking (only) at the second world is obviously the perspective against which Carroll (in this volume) is contrasting the use of scenarios.

The third world is real life, where computer systems are used. For the sake of simplicity we call it a world of work processes and leave other contexts of computer use aside. The use of computer systems is never an end in itself; computers are used for something, and the use is always embedded in situations and becomes meaningful through those situations. In Figure 1.1, a box describing a system-in-use is embedded in a lager shape describing the part of all work processes that is impacted by the system and that will change if the system changes. It has long been known that when people start to use a new system, the situations change. However, the fact that the situations—work processes—can and must be explicitly studied and designed is only beginning to be recognized.

One of the indications that the system design community has recognized the necessity to cope also with the world 3 issues has been C. Floyd's seminal "Outline of a paradigm change in software engineering" [9]. In her paper, Floyd contrasts two different perspectives on software engineering: product-oriented and process-oriented:

> The product-oriented perspective regards software as a product standing on its own, consisting of a set of programs and related defining texts. In doing so, the product-oriented perspective abstracts from the characteristics of the given base machine and considers the usage context of the product to be fixed and well understood, thus allowing software requirements to be determined in advance.
>
> The process-oriented perspective, on the other hand, views software in connection with human learning, work, and com-

> munication, taking place in an evolving world and changing needs. Processes of work, learning, and communication occur both in software development and use. During development, we find software to be the object of such processes. In use, software acts both as their support and their constraint [9].

She then continues in criticizing the dominant product-oriented perspective for its inability to allow designers to "treat systematically questions pertaining to the relationship between software and the living human world, which are of paramount importance for the adequacy of software to fulfill human needs", and demands that the product-oriented perspective should be replaced by the process-oriented one, which is more capable in this respect.

Although there is some ambiguity in the text because Floyd subsumes both the design and use of a system under the same process-label, it is clear that she is directly addressing the shift of emphasis from one domain to another. For purposes of this chapter, we can explicate her message as follows: From the product-oriented viewpoint, the end result of design is a system, while from the process-oriented viewpoint, the end result is a process of using the system, ultimately the whole work process where the using is embedded in and will be changed by the system.

Now we can summarize one reason why scenarios have emerged: If the focus of problems is moving toward a better understanding of user needs—to world 3—and those needs reveal themselves truly only in the work processes where a system is going to be used, we clearly need means to describe those processes of work and use. And that is exactly what scenarios do: *Scenarios are a way to describe and discuss world 3 issues in system design.*

It is also quite obvious why there are tensions between scenarios and older, more formal methods of system design. During a period of transition it is not always easy to avoid using old concepts or methods within the new domain although they may no longer be the best possible ones in the present situation. Thus the hardware-oriented, hierarchical model of a database had a long life in software engineering before it was finally replaced by the relational one, which is more elegant and adequate for the purposes of searching out an implementation-independent solution. In a similar vein, widely available and familiar world 2 methods are often used to study world 3 issues. The methods developed for elaboration within world 2 are fully adequate for that purpose, but there is a feature that seriously limits their applicability outside it: They are looking at everything through computerization-eyeglasses. Thus a data-modeling method does not see anything that cannot be put into a database, and so on. In principle, there is nothing wrong with that, but if one has to describe whole work processes it is impossible to limit oneself only to computerization aspects.

1.3.3 A Systematic Approach to Worlds: Iivari's "Levels of Modeling"

The discipline that has the longest record in recognizing the need to separate the three worlds mentioned above can broadly be called *organizational information systems* (IS). Within it, the Scandinavian *infological* school has been the groundbreaker, B. Langefors already pioneering the identification and developing the first system of concepts for it in 1966 [20]. Ten years later the belief that it is necessary to take world 3 explicitly into account in design was already firmly established within the infological school, and the first textbook incorporating special methods for world 3—for designing organizational change—was published in 1978 [22]. Since then the idea of different worlds has gained broader and broader acceptance, but opinions have also become more varied. During the 1980s a lively debate took place within the IS community concentrating especially on the social character of world 3: Because the organizational context where a computer system is embedded is also a social system, a community of practice, to what extent should this social character be taken into account in research and design? How could that be methodologically done? What is the relationship between the social system and the technical one? The ongoing debate—epitomized, for example, in [23] and [25]—has similarities with the discussion currently going on within the HCI community.

One of the researchers continuing the work within the infological tradition is J. Iivari, whose three-level framework model for information systems will be used here to clarify a couple of scenario-related issues. The framework is one of the most elaborate within IS and it integrates much of the work done in the infological system design tradition. Figure 1.2 gives one perspective of the framework.

A basic idea in the framework is that each of the three worlds identified and roughly described in the previous section needs its own level of modeling. Iivari calls these modeling levels *technological* (defining the technical implementation for the information system and thus corresponding to world 1), *conceptual* (defining the implementation-independent specification for the information system—world 2), and *organizational* (defining the organizational role and context of the in-

		Structure abstraction	*Function abstraction*	*Behavior abstraction*
ORGANIZATIONAL LEVEL	**Designed context**	Organizational actors Organizational positions - internal - external Organizational channels	Organizational functions - material/inf. processing Input flows - material/information Output flows - material/information States/stores - material/information Work procedures Instruments Communication relationships - creators/receivers - performative functions	Events Situations Triggering conditions Organizational acts
	Application concept	Users - input users - output users	IS services	IS use acts - input use acts - output use acts (queries/ reception of reports)

Figure 1.2. A conceptual model of an information system using the three-level approach. (Slightly modified from Livari [15].)

CONCEPTUAL LEVEL	**Universe of discourse**	Object types - entity types - event types - time interval types Association types Attributes Consistency rules	Action/operation types	Events States Triggering conditions Actions/operations
	IS specifications	Information base Information types	IS functions Input information types Output information types State information types Derivation rules	Events States - functional states - control states Triggering conditions IS processes Control state transitions
	User interface	Interface object types - application dependent - generic Representations	Interface operation types - application dependent - generic Representations	Interface acts
TECHNICAL LEVEL		Abstract machine Abstract data comm. link	Databases/files Software/program components Input data type Output data type Algorithms Rules	Events Control states Control rules Data processes Control state transitions

Figure 1.2. (Cont'd)

formation systems—world 3). Figure 1.2 simply lists these levels, the main sublevels of the organizational and conceptual level, and the three aspects (structural, functional, and behavioral) pertinent to each level, and names the elements of the corresponding models. There are more accurate descriptions about the relationship between the elements [12], about their use in the design process [13, 14], about possibilities of using them in object identification [15], and so on, but for the purposes of this chapter this rather simple description is good enough.

The model by Iivari will be utilized here in a rather limited way for two purposes: first, in illustrating the difference between domain 2 and domain 3; second, Iivari's conception of organizational level will be used in studying the relationship between the two variations of the scope of scenarios.

1.3.4 The Relationship between "Narrow" and "Rich" Scenarios

The difference between Iivari's conceptual level and organizational level illustrates clearly the needed shift in perspective when moving from world 2 to world 3. While the terms at the conceptual level belong to the vocabulary of most system design methods in describing the structure and functioning of system, the terms at the organizational level are much less familiar. In fact, hardly any system design method still recognizes the need to model the organization or work beyond the immediate use actions of a system. The organizational level—model of world 3—is describing the context of use of a system; system seen only as a black box giving some services. The conceptual level is modeling the internals of the system.

From the scenario perspective it is very interesting to note that Iivari divides the organizational level in his model into two sublevels, *designed organizational context* and *application concept*. This division is not by any means arbitrary but the result of a long development in attempts to cope with problems in conceptualizing systems when they are embedded in organizational context. Iivari explains the distinction as follows:

> The organizational level as a design level is particularly relevant in the case of organizational IS, implying, for instance, that information systems development is always organizational development as well, and that it may not be reasonable to re-

> strict the organizational development to information systems only, but that different types of organizational development should be combined (e.g., IS development, work organization, reward structures, etc.). From the viewpoint of SE, the need for an organizational context can be argued on the basis that the application concept and information requirements related to the system depend on the organizational context and role of the system. Therefore the definition of the organizational context can be seen to be a part of the explication of the application domain knowledge.
>
> The application concept is defined by the IS services provided by the system to support its intended users in their organizational activities (Iivari [13]). The major goal of the application concept is to delineate the application information system and to make its organizational role and context visible. (Iivari [12]).

If one compares the purpose and elements of a designed organizational context and an application concept with the definitions of scenarios given earlier, one is bound to notice a striking parallel between them. The narrow definition of scenarios seems to be explicitly the same as Iivari's application concept, even to the level of terminology used in definitions. And although there are certain differences, at a general level a designed organizational context has much the same flavor as a rich scenario: It is aiming not at a narrowly focused task description, but at the big picture how a work gets done.

Thus the IS experience seems to hint that the narrow and rich scenarios are not conflicting but rather complement each other. According to Iivari's model it is necessary to delineate the system and describe it by the services it is giving to users, but because the system will get its meaning from the situation in which it will be used, it is also necessary to describe this context as well. The copier machine described in Suchman [32] had a well-defined *use case*, but when an external disturbance occurred, the user got lost—and this getting lost had been impossible to detect by looking only at the corresponding use case scenario (as designers surely had done), because anything external is beyond the scope of that type of scenario.

Thus we need both application scenarios, describing the services a system is going to deliver, and context scenarios, describing the work practices where the services are going to be used. To be exact, it would seem we actually need *application scenarios embedded in context scenarios*—something that has not yet been very well explicated.

Let's return to the differences between rich or context scenarios and designed organizational context in Iivari's model. Although their general flavor is comparable, it is doubtful if the proponents of context scenarios would think it possible to describe the "full context . . . social setting, resources, and goals of users" [24] or "complexity of the real-world human interaction with things" [33] using a vocabulary that consists of "organizational actors," "organizational positions," and so on, used in Iivari's model. This selection of elementary concepts reflects the fact that Iivari—like the whole IS tradition—is drawing heavily from organizational theory that is committed to prescribed, formal aspects of organizations, not the emergent features of actual work processes done in these organizations, where the target of most of the users of rich context scenarios lies. This suggests that there might be a reciprocal relationship between Iivari's model and scenarios: While the model is helping in locating the place of scenarios in the big picture, scenarios are pointing to some shortcomings in the model. This becomes especially clear when we look at the behavior abstraction part of the model, which is based on rather atomistic *use acts* connected with *organizational acts*. In fact, Iivari [12] complains about the paucity of well-established behavioral concepts in organizational theory and has based that part of his model on von Cranach's psychological theory of goal-oriented actions. In the discussion below we will return to some recent attempts to find alternatives to organization theory when searching for foundations for analyzing world 3 issues in system design.

1.4 DISCUSSION

From the viewpoint of this chapter, the call for a scenario-based design life cycle (Carroll, introduction to this volume) can be interpreted as an attempt to articulate the importance and independence of the work process level in design, and, to some extent, demand that it should be given a dominant voice in guiding the process. In this stage of affairs both of these goals seem to me very reasonable.

In a stereotypical view on the relationship between theory and practice innovations are made in theoretical research and then applied in practice. The rise of scenarios is a nice example—not the first one in the area of HCI—that this relationship is much more complicated and reciprocal: Sometimes theoretical research must strive to understand something that is already being applied in practice.

This chapter has attempted to position scenarios in the field of system design both historically and conceptually. The main thesis is that for designing today's systems it is necessary to describe the use of systems and work processes where they are embedded in a way that preserves enough situational complexity, and that scenarios seem now to be the best means available for that purpose. Despite a certain fuzziness they form a usable and practical vocabulary that allows designers to describe and discuss work processes relevant to design.

Some researchers (e.g., [31]) consider the transformation from informal to formal to be a crucial point in requirements engineering. It is rather fascinating to find that this crucial transformation is in fact located inside the scenario field, namely between proposed rich contextual scenarios and more systematic application scenarios. This suggests that the embedding of application scenarios into context scenarios—considered to be desirable earlier in this chapter—may not be a trivial task. On the other hand, scenarios themselves may help in making progress in this respect: If one can by exploring and experimenting with them find a way to combine application scenarios with context scenarios that works in practice, we are certainly a step closer toward understanding their relationship.

Although scenarios are now fulfilling an important practical role, they do not fill the undeniable theoretical void. Besides the HCI community, the existence of this void has been felt, as we have seen, within the IS community and, perhaps most acutely, within the CSCW community. System analysis and design is in need of new conceptualizations and theories of work processes, and several attempts to search out new foundations have already been launched during the last few years, exploring the new background in phenomenology [34, 8], in distributed cognition [28], or in activity theory [3, 5, 19]. It is plausible that eventually concepts and constructs will emerge that will help in this transition—providing a more standard language with which to discuss work and computers in a rich way. This does not automatically mean that scenarios would disappear: It is fully possible that scenarios may form a part of that language.

That scenarios have been emerging within practical design and not as a result of theoretical considerations is new evidence of the relationship between theory and practice in the area of HCI. HCI is not a practical field where theories are applied but rather a field where practice leads theory and poses challenges to it. Thus scenarios have a double nature, and this book can have two audiences and two messages. For practical designers, scenarios are useful tools for dealing with acute design problems, while for researchers scenarios are a serious challenge: If our problem is how to describe reality at a rich level but still make the transition to formal design possible and even easy, why do they seem to offer such a good starting point? The superficial answer sketched in this chapter is aimed at no more than whetting the appetite.

ACKNOWLEDGMENTS

This chapter would not have been written without the Kittle House workshop and the variety of its participants—it was there, in the discussions, where different bits and pieces started to fall together and form some sort of a picture. Special thanks goes to John Carroll, Bonnie Nardi, and Mary Beth Rosson for their constructive comments on the first version of this chapter. Financially the work has been supported by the Finnish Centre for Technology Development (TEKES) as a part of CEC ESPRIT Basic Research Project 6225 COMIC.

REFERENCES

[1] Adler, P. A. (1992). Introduction. In P. A. Adler (ed.), *Technology and the Future of Work*. New York: Oxford University Press, pp. 3–14.

[2] Anderson, J. S. & Durney, B. (1992). Using scenarios in deficiency-driven requirements engineering. In *Proceedings of the IEEE International Symposium on Requirements Engineering*. Washington: IEEE Computer Society Press, pp. 134–141.

[3] Bannon, L. & Bødker, S. (1991). Beyond the interface: Encountering artifacts in use. In J. M. Carroll (ed.), *Designing Interaction: Psychology at the Human-Computer Interface*. Cambridge, U.K.: Cambridge University Press.

[4] Bentley, R., Hughes, J. A., Randall, D., Rodden, T., Sawyer, P., Shapiro, D. & Sommerville, I. (1992). Ethnographically-informed systems design for air traffic control. In *Proceedings of CSCW'92*, Toronto, October 31–November 4. New York: ACM Press, pp. 123–129.

[5] Bødker, S. (1989). A human activity approach to user interfaces. *Human Computer Interaction*, *4*(3), 171–195.

[6] Campbell, R. L. (1992). Will the real scenario please stand up? *SIGCHI Bulletin*, *24*(2), 6–8.

[7] Ciborra, C. U. & Schneider, L. S. (1992). Transforming the routines and contexts of management, work, and technology. In P. A. Adler (ed.), *Technology and the Future of Work*. New York: Oxford University Press, pp. 269–291.

[8] Ehn, P. (1988). *Work-Oriented Design of Computer Artifacts*. Stockholm: Arbetslivscentrum.

[9] Floyd, C. (1988). Outline of a paradigm change in software engineering. *ACM SIGSOFT Software Engineering Notes*, *13*(2), 25–38.

[10] Friedman, A. (1989). *Computer Systems Development: History, Organization and Implementation.* Chichester: Wiley.

[11] Hsia, P., Samuel, J., Gao, J., Kung, D., Toyoshima, Y., & Chen, C. (1994). Formal approach to scenario analysis. *IEEE Software* (March); 33–41.

[12] Iivari, J. (1989). Levels of abstraction as a conceptual framework for an information system. In E. D. Falkenberg & P. Lindgren (eds.), *Information System Concepts: An In-depth Analysis.* Amsterdam: North-Holland, pp. 323–352.

[13] Iivari, J. (1990a). Hierarchical spiral model for information system and software development. Part 1: Theoretical background. *Information and Software Technology, 32*(6), 385–399.

[14] Iivari, J. (1990b). Hierarchical spiral model for information system and software development. Part 2: Design process. *Information and Software Technology, 32*(7), 449–458.

[15] Iivari, J. (1991). Object-oriented information systems analysis. In *24th Annual Hawaii International Conference on System Sciences*, II. IEEE Computer Society Press, pp. 205–218.

[16] Jarke, M., Bubenko, J., Rolland, C., Sutcliffe, A. & Vassilou, Y. (1992). Theories underlying requirements engineering: An overview of NATURE at genesis. In *IEEE International Symposium on Requirements Engineering*, San Diego, CA, January 4–6. IEEE Computer Society Press, pp. 19–31.

[17] Kofman, F. & Senge, P. M. (1993). Communities of commitment: The heart of learning organization. *Organizational Dynamics* (Autumm 1993): 5–23.

[18] Kuutti, K. & Bannon, L. J. (1991). Some confusions at the interface: Reconceptualizing the "interface" problem. In Nurminen, M. I. & Weir, G. R. S. (eds.), *Human Jobs and Computer Interfaces.* Amsterdam: North-Holland, pp. 3–19.

[19] Kuutti, K. & Bannon, L. J. (1993). Searching for unity among diversity: Exploring the "interface" concept. In *Proceedings of Interchi'93*, Amsterdam, April 24–29. New York: ACM Press, pp. 263–268.

[20] Langefors, B. (1966). *Theoretical Analysis of Information Systems.* Lund, Sweden: Studentlitteratur.

[21] Lubars, M., Potts, C. & Richter, C. (1992). A review of the state of practice in requirements modeling. In *Proceedings of the IEEE International Symposium on Requirements Engineering.* Washington, DC: IEEE Computer Society Press, pp. 2–14.

[22] Lundeberg, M., Goldkuhl, G. & Nilsson, A. (1978). *Systemering*. Lund, Sweden: Studentlitteratur.

[23] Mumford, E., Hirschheim, R., Fitzgerald, G. & Wood-Harper, A. T. (eds.). (1985). *Research Methods in Information Systems*. Amsterdam: North-Holland.

[24] Nardi, B. A. (1992). The use of scenarios in design. *SIGCHI Bulletin, 24*(4), 13–14.

[25] Nissen, H.-E., Klein, H. K. & Hirschheim, R. (eds.). (1991). *The Information Systems Research Arena of the 1990s: Challenges, Perceptions and Alternative Approaches*. Amsterdam: North-Holland.

[26] Potts, C., Takahashi, K. & Antón, A. I. (1994). Inquiry-based requirements analysis. *IEEE Software* (March): 21–32.

[27] Rogers, Y. (1994). Exploring obstacles: Integrating CSCW in evolving organizations. In *Proceedings of CSCW'94*, Chapel Hill, NC, October 22–26. New York: ACM Press, pp. 67–77.

[28] Rogers, Y. & Ellis, J. (1994). Distributed cognition: An alternative framework for analyzing and explaining collaborative working. *J. Information Technology, 9*(2).

[29] Rubin, K. S. & Goldberg, A. (1992). Object behavior analysis. *Communications of the ACM, 35*(9), 48–62.

[30] Scott Morton, M. (ed.). (1991). *The Corporation of the 1990s: Information Technology and Organizational Transformation*. New York: Oxford University Press.

[31] Siddiqi, J. (1994). Challenging universal truths of requirements engineering. *IEEE Software* (March): 18–19.

[32] Suchman, L. (1987). *Plans and Situated Actions*. Cambridge, U.K.: Cambridge University Press.

[33] Verplank, B., Fulton, J., Black, A. & Moggridge, B. (1993). *Observation and Invention—Use of Scenarios in Interaction Design* (tutorial notes, *Interchi'93*).

[34] Winograd, T. & Flores, F. (1987). *Understanding Computers and Cognition. A New Foundation for Design*. Norwood, NJ: Ablex.

[35] Wright, P. (1992). What's in a scenario? *SIGCHI Bulletin, 24*(4), 11.

[36] Young, R. M. & Barnard, P. J. (1992). Multiple uses of scenarios: A reply to Campbell. *SIGCHI Bulletin, 24*(4), 10.

[37] Zuboff, S. (1988). *In the Age of the Smart Machine: The Future of Work and Power*. New York: Basic Books.

CHAPTER 2

Notes on Design Practice: Stories and Prototypes as Catalysts for Communication

Thomas Erickson
User Experience Architect's Office
Apple Computer, Inc.
Cupertino, CA 95014
USA

Donald Schön [13] has argued eloquently that professional practices like design are more of an art than a science. In much of their daily work designers are not grappling with well-formed problems but with, as Schön puts it, "messy, indeterminate situations." Schön's investigations have been principally directed at design by one or two individuals, with an emphasis on education and the master-apprentice relationship. I want to discuss the design of products that incorporate new technologies. This means that the design process usually involves a team of designers from different disciplines, and that the team must interact with the prospective users of its product and with the much larger organization of which it is a part. In short, the design of technology-based products is inextricably entwined with social and organizational dynamics. This expands the realm of messy, indeterminate situations considerably.

My goal is to talk about some of the informal, practical methods that designers use to grapple with the messy, ill-defined issues that pervade their daily practice. I am concerned with the following issues:

- *Problem setting.* Before designers can solve a problem, they first must define what it is. How do designers of new technologies begin when they are unsure of what they are making, what it should do, or who will use it?
- *Team building.* Technology design is carried out by interdisciplinary teams. Members of the team may not necessarily understand the skills or priorities of others. How can a diverse group of people evolve into a smoothly functioning design team?
- *User involvement.* Designers know too much, and they know too little. Designers who know enough to incorporate a technology into a product know too much to understand how users will perceive it. At the same time, designers know too little about users' lives to understand how the product will mesh with their work practices. How can users be effectively involved in the design process, particularly in the beginning when there is nothing to show them?
- *Collaborative design.* The heart of design is the iterative process of creating a prototype that embodies the design, evaluating it, and then using the feedback to create a new prototype. In the course of this, the members of the design team must work closely with one another, even though they have different working techniques, methods of analysis, and evaluation criteria, and different languages for describing what they do. How can the collective activity of the team be supported? What properties make a prototype useful?
- *Design transfer.* In large organizations, those who design a product are often not the same as those who implement it. A product concept may be developed in a research division and then transferred to a product division. Even when the designers and implementors are the same, many new people—in marketing, manufacturing, documentation—will become involved as the design makes its way from concept to reality. It is important that knowledge about the rationale behind the design be shared with those involved in preparing it for the marketplace. How can that be done?
- *Design evangelism.* Much design occurs in the context of large organizations. Buy-in on the part of executives, managers, and potential collaborators is a necessity if the designed product is to be implemented, manufactured, and marketed. How can those not involved in the design process be convinced of its validity and worth?

An underlying assumption of this chapter is that design is a distributed social process, and that, as such, communication plays a vital role in design. In holding this view, I share common ground with others in this volume who discuss the social and communicative aspects of design. Karat (Chapter 5) discusses the use of scenarios as devices for facilitating communication among members of the design team. The chapters by Kyng (Chapter 4) and by Muller and his colleagues (Chapter 6) focus on ways of enabling users to participate as first-class contributors to the design process, and pay special attention to the use of concrete representations for this purpose. Carey and Rusli (Chapter 7) go beyond the scope of a single design project, and look at ways of reusing design knowledge in the education of new designers and the development of different but related products.

This chapter extends these ideas in two ways. First, it discusses communication within the organization in which design takes place, as well as communication within the design team and between the design team and the users. Second, it examines two concrete artifacts—stories and prototypes—and discusses the properties which make them effective communications catalysts.

2.1 DESIGN AS COMMUNICATION

To begin, I will sketch a simple, communication-oriented model of design. It is useful to think about design as a process of communication among various audiences. Central to this discussion is the notion of design artifacts, material or informational objects that are constructed during the design process. Let's examine this perspective in more detail.

2.1.1 Communication

I am using *communication* in its broadest sense. Talking, telephoning, sending e-mail, writing reports, giving presentations, and showing videos all fall under communication. Thus, communication can be one-to-one or one-to-many, and a conversation may occur in real time, or may be spread out over hours, days, weeks, or longer. Also note that many of these types of conversations occur through, or are facilitated by, the use of some kind of persistent, physical representation. What we will focus on is the role played by design artifacts in supporting communication.

In a sense, even the design activities of a single individual can be classified as a communications activity. For example, note-taking can be viewed as an act of communicating with oneself over time. Schön [13] characterizes design practice as a protracted "conversation with the situation," in which designers embody their ideas in some representational medium, reflect on them, and then modify them. Similarly, Thimbley et al. [15] suggest that work by an individual is a special case of cooperative work—reflexive cooperative work—in which various concrete artifacts support individuals in collaborating with themselves over time. Whether or not one finds the notion of reflexive communication palatable, physical artifacts clearly play a role in both sorts of activity.

2.1.2 Design Artifacts

I use the term *design artifact* to mean any of the physical or informational entities collected or constructed during the design process. Examples of design artifacts include videos of users, snapshots of usage contexts, transcripts of user interviews, scenarios, prototypes, marketing studies, datasets produced by user tests, progress reports, professional publications, and formal documents such as engineering requirements specifications and marketing requirements documents. Design artifacts are produced for a variety of reasons. They may be created as a way of capturing information, or as a way of disseminating information, or simply as a side-effect of a process that is occurring. Regardless of the explicit reason for their creation, many design artifacts play a role in catalyzing communication among the various audiences involved in the design process.

2.1.3 Audiences

There are different audiences for a design that are associated with one or more stages in the design's lifecycle. The actual audiences for a design will vary depending on the nature of the product being designed and the organization within which the design takes place. The different audiences are important because they require different design artifacts, or at least require the same artifact to be used in different ways. For expository purposes, I'll talk about three audiences: the design team itself; the intended end users; and the organization within which the design activity takes place.

The Design Team Many people are involved in the design of new technologies. They are likely to include technologists, graphic designers, psychologists, and industrial designers. In spite of being grouped as one audience, the differences in working methods, evaluation criteria, skills, and inclinations that arise from training in different disciplines make this an extremely diverse audience. If the members of the team have not worked together before, the gaps between team members may be as large as those between the design team and other audiences. And, in participatory design (see Chapters 4 and 6) users may also be full-fledged members of the design team, thus increasing its diversity. For expository purposes, I will refer to members of the design team as *designers*, regardless of their background.

The Users These are the intended users of the final product. They are typically expert in some domain of activity relevant to the product being designed, but are not versed in the technology which will be manifested in the design. For users to provide useful feedback, they must be given a concrete understanding of the nature of the product to be designed.

The Organization An oft-neglected audience for the design is the organization within which it is created and produced. Yet organizations play a fundamental role in shaping the nature of the design process (e.g., [4, 5]). Design processes will differ radically depending on whether they are being carried out by a group in a large, product development organization, an in-house development group, or a design consultancy on contract to a client.

This chapter discusses product development in the context of large, product development organizations. Such organizations are characterized by internal competition for resources as research projects and product investigations struggle to make it onto the product track. Thus, a design team must be prepared to defend the validity of its design throughout the design process, and, if successful, must be able to communicate the rationale behind the design when it is time to implement it. Like the design team, this audience is quite heterogeneous: It includes executives, managers, potential implementors, and designers not on the design team.

2.1.4 The Early Stages of the Design Lifecycle

Like the audiences for a design, the lifecycle of a design depends on what is being designed and the organizational context. Because my concern is the design of new product concepts in product development organizations, I will speak of a design lifecycle with three stages—exploration, refinement, and transition. Other more complex models may be advanced, but these three stages will suffice for our purposes. Another caveat is that the use of the word *stage* is primarily a linguistic convenience. These stages aren't cleanly separated; they are likely to have considerable overlap, with the focus shifting gradually from one to another.

Exploration The exploratory stage of design is where the requirements for the product are gathered and the basic product concept is defined. All designs—except those that are incremental improvements of existing products—go through an exploratory phase. However, depending on the organization and circumstances, the exploratory phase may be done by a marketing group, by a manager or executive, or by a design team. In my remarks I will assume that the exploratory stage is pursued by the design team.

The exploratory stage of design is characterized by confusion and unease within the design team. Nothing is settled. Although the design team has a set of constraints, many are often no more than accidents of circumstance. Typically, the design team will have a set of new technologies to which it has access, some indications of appropriate directions or application areas which may have been provided by upper management or distilled from the corporate zeitgeist, and probably some sort of deadline for formulating a design proposal. The problems to be solved—Who is it for? What will it do? What needs will it address? What practices will it support?—remain to be defined. The main goal of this stage of design is to understand the usage domain, define the problems being addressed, and develop a high-level vision of the product being designed.

In addition, some or all of the designers may be new to the team. Thus, the team needs to arrive at a shared understanding of the skills and expertise of fellow team members, and must develop methods for working together effectively. When the team is composed of members from different disciplines, this team-building can be a major undertaking in itself [7].

Refinement The refinement stage is aimed at filling in the details. Having determined what the design will do, the design team must determine how it will accomplish those ends, what criteria it will use to evaluate the design, and how it will determine tradeoffs between conflicting criteria. It is during this stage that the focus shifts to prototypes; these serve as a medium for team collaboration and as a means for eliciting input from users and from other designers within the organization. The refinement stage concludes with the production of a design specification of sufficient detail that it may be transferred to those who implement it.

Transition The transition stage is devoted to getting the design adopted and implemented by the organization. One set of activities may be characterized as design evangelism. Basically, the validity and worth of the design concept must be sold to the large number of people who have some say on whether the design becomes a product. If evangelism is successful, attention shifts to transferring the design. Transfer activities may involve handing off the design to a product development team, recruiting people to implement the design, or arguing for additional resources to be allocated to the design team so that it can undertake the product development effort itself. In general, transition activities are aimed at marketing the design within the organization, although key customers may sometimes be included.

The lifecycle of the design, of course, continues after the transition stage. A host of new activities arise in conjunction with implementing, marketing, and supporting the product. But the first three stages are sufficient for this discussion.

2.1.5 Summary

In this section, I've laid out a simple model of the design process based on the use of artifacts to mediate communication among various audiences. Depending on the stage of design, the goals of the design team, and the audience being addressed, different artifacts may be used to mediate communication (or the same design artifact may be used for different ends). Table 2.1 summarizes a few of the typical, communication-oriented activities at each stage of the design lifecycle.

Table 2.1 Typical Stages and Activities of the Design Lifecycle

Stages of Design	*Typical Activities and Audiences*
Exploration	*Problem setting.* The design team learns about the problems and practices of the users for whom they are designing. *Team-building.* Internally, the team develops a shared understanding of their project and of the skills and expertise of each member.
Refinement	*Collaborative design.* The team develops the details of the design by embodying it in prototypes, which are used to explore design solutions and evaluate their consequences. *User involvement.* To get useful feedback from users, the team must help the users arrive at an understanding of the design.
Transition	*Design evangelism.* Within the organization the design project must be defended so that it can continue to get resources. (Depending on economic conditions, this activity may occur in earlier stages as well.) *Design transfer.* The rationale behind the design must be communicated to those who will implement it, so that crucial features of the design are not lost.

The perspective of design as communication takes on particular importance because communication is difficult. By and large, the participants in the design process don't understand one another. Users, designers, engineers, managers, psychologists, all have different backgrounds, training, experience, and inclinations. Users understand, at least tacitly, their own needs and daily experience, but they understand little about the proposed design. Designers understand the proposed design, but little about users' experience. The organization, having little exposure to either the design or the users, understands neither. Somehow, these gaps must be bridged.

For the design process to have the best chance of success, the design team must create a shared understanding among the participants in design process. In my view, this involves the creation of design artifacts that are accessible and comprehensible to all. In the remainder of the chapter, we will discuss stories and prototypes, two types of design artifacts that play a crucial role in facilitating such a shared understanding.

2.2 STORIES AS DESIGN TOOLS

In this section, I consider some of the ways in which stories are used to catalyze communication in design, and the properties that make them effective.

First, note that stories differ from scenarios. Stories are concrete accounts of particular people and events, in particular situations; scenarios are often more abstract—they are scripts of events that may leave out details of history, motivation, and personality. The stories I'll be talking about are true stories in the sense that the people, events, and situations to which they refer are real. In contrast, the reality of scenarios is more tenuous; they rarely refer to particular events. Stories are personal: The protagonist, and often the audience, care about the outcome. Scenarios describe events at a greater distance, and there is less chance for identification with a protagonist, if one even exists. Stories are often about atypical situations; they are about events that are exceptional in some way, often events in which the protagonist has triumphed (or foundered) in the face of great odds. Scenarios are about typical situations; they are intended to capture the normal chain of events, the prototypical situations.

2.2.1 Story Gathering—Beginning the Design Process

In an observation of an architect beginning a new design, Wong [19] describes the following behavior:

> He placed the site plan on the table and rolled out the tracing paper over the plan. In order to become familiar with the site, he started by sketching "bubble diagrams" and making annotations on the tracing paper. He was able to see through the translucent tracing paper to the site plan underneath. . . . The design built progressively with each new layer of tracing paper, amorphous forms transformed into partitions of space.

I like this description because it feels like such an easy, gradual, enjoyable way to begin. Roll the tracing paper over the site plan, and start sketching. Pity the poor interaction designer whose domain is less tangible. Rather than an easily mapped site, the domain is a set of tasks situated in an environment that is as much cultural and social as it is physical. Beginning does not seem so easy.

Yet, in part, the appearance of difficulty is deceptive. For me, the analog to the architect's gradual beginning is talking to users and listening to the stories they tell. The stories people tell say a lot about what they do and how they do it. Stories reveal what people like about their work, what they hate about it, what works well, what sorts of things are real problems. As one hears more and more stories, themes gradually emerge, and the designer can begin to get a feel for the structure of the interactions that characterize a particular usage domain.

This is not to say that stories are a direct route to knowledge. Indeed, stories are quite ambiguous; most stories can be interpreted in many ways [12]. However, rather than being a drawback, this property makes stories particularly useful at the beginning of the design process. As the collection of stories grows, the design team can try out different frameworks for making sense of the usage domain. A story that fits one framework in one way, may fit a different framework in a different way. This conceptual ambiguity can help the designer avoid getting prematurely committed to a particular problem definition.

Story gathering is also an excellent way of promoting team building. Team members can sit around and swap stories they've heard, noting similarities and differences and discussing possible interpretations. Stories often require a lot of domain-specific knowledge to be understood, and thus the process of story gathering sensitizes everyone to the usage domain. Talking about stories helps the members of the design team identify things they don't understand, and raises questions and issues to probe for when they next talk with users. In addition, as the members of the design team share and discuss stories, they begin to develop a shared language, a set of common referents that are grounded in the domain of the user. While this by no means guarantees agreement, it does provide a common ground on which constructive argument can occur. Best of all, making up stories is a kind of equalizer. It seems to be something that any member of a design team can participate in, regardless of whether he or she is trained in computer science, psychology, graphic design, or some other discipline.

2.2.2 Story Making—Capturing Design Rationale

As I listen to the stories people tell, I begin to recognize common themes and events, and gradually formulate my own *design stories*. Design stories are a little like scenarios in that they attempt to capture some of the recurring characteristics in stories I've been told, but they are still quite storylike in that they retain their level of detail and are grounded in my personal experience. Design stories often incorporate humorous events, noteworthy quips, and memorable phrases and concepts drawn from users' stories.

Consider this design story, which emerged from a series of interviews on how office workers organized their personal information. It describes one way in which people use piles of paper to organize information:

The Guilt Pile

> You receive something you feel that you ought to read but, because it's not vitally important, you don't want to do it immediately.
>
> Instead, you toss it on a pile of documents, which probably sits on a work surface in a corner of your office. You feel good. Things are under control, and with a minimal investment of time!
>
> Time passes. The pile gets higher and higher. It begins to look like there's literally a mountain of stuff you ought to read. You begin to feel uncomfortable.
>
> Provoked by the pile's height, you sort through it, discarding articles that no longer seem interesting, perhaps selecting one or two to read. The winnowed pile—now of a much more manageable size—is put back in its place. You feel good. Things are under control again.

I like this story because it not only explains how people use piles, but why they use piles. It provides the design rationale behind piles. It is able to do this effectively because stories describe not just actions, but feelings and motivations. This story captured something that struck me when interviewing people about how they organized information in their work environments: Almost everyone was embarrassed at how poorly they managed information. They felt bad because they had lost control over their information, and they felt good at the times when they had managed to sort through everything and organize it, no matter how casually. The desire to feel good and on top of things rather than bad and out of control is one with which most people can empathize. People recognize themselves and their desires in the story.

2.2.3 Involving Users—Storytelling

Stories are a natural way of beginning dialog with users. Consider the following story:

> An office building has an intelligent energy management system that conserves energy on weekends by turning off unneeded lights after an hour has elapsed. An employee, accompanied by his six-year-old daughter, has stopped by to finish up some work. Suddenly, the lights go out.
>
> Daughter: Who turned off the lights?
> Father: (matter-of-factly) The computer turned off the lights.
> Daughter: (pause) Did you turn off the lights?
> Father: No, I told you, the computer turned off the lights.
>
> (Someone manually turns the lights back on)
>
> Daughter: Make the computer turn off the lights again.
> Father: (with irony) It will in a few minutes.

As I tell this story, I use my voice to dramatize it. The little girl is incredulous, she doesn't initially believe the computer turned out the lights. Dad, on the other hand, has experienced this before: His first statement is matter-of-fact; his final statement has an undertone of irony.

The story works on a number of levels. Quite obviously, it illustrates that systems that try to be intelligent can be annoying and perplexing if they're not intelligent enough. The story also raises some deeper issues. As the child indicates, people want to understand why things change, and people want to feel like they are in control. One wonders what kind of mental model she has formed of this capricious, out-of-control computer. And, as the father's responses indicate, people also become accustomed, or at least resigned, to the inconveniences foisted on them by technology.

This story elicits a number of responses from users. People generally laugh at the last line of dialog. The story captures a sense of frustration with technology that many people share. Often those who hear this story will recount their own stories of stupid intelligent technology, or technology that has failed them in some other way. Others will step forward to defend the technology, and argue that the problem is not technology, but badly designed technology; and so on. The important bit here is not the particular conclusion that is reached, if any, but rather that people have been engaged, drawn into discussion of ideas about which—before the story—they would have had nothing to say.

This is, in fact, a good metric for stories. I judge the goodness of a story by telling it to other people, and seeing how much they nod or laugh as they listen. When they hear a good story, listeners say, "Oh yeah, something like that happened to me . . ." and tell me their own version of that story. People who believe they have nothing to say about how technology shapes their lives, or who bridle at possibly exposing their ignorance of technology, are quite happy to tell stories that—to the attentive designer—may be far more revealing than a cautiously ventured generality.

2.2.4 Transferring Design Knowledge

The collection and generation of stories happens most during the exploratory stage of design, and serves as a useful precursor to more formal analyses. However, stories are useful even after the initial fuzzy knowledge has been codified into problem definitions, design principles, lists of user needs, information flow diagrams, and other more formal design artifacts. Once the early stage of design is done, stories become important as mechanisms for communicating with the organization.

One role stories play is in assisting in communicating with high-level management. Depending on the nature of the organization, and the economic conditions under which it is operating, design teams may need to defend the validity of their design in an effort to maintain their funding, or to make the case for moving the design from a product investigation or research track, to a product development track. In both cases, many of the higher-level managers involved in the decision will have neither the time nor the inclination to understand the details of a design. What they need is to quickly understand the gist of the design, why it makes sense, why people will want to buy it. Stories excel at encapsulating this kind of information.

This is not to say that stories are the only source of information considered in making a product decision—certainly not. But stories play more of a role than most people would expect. Consider Norman's [9] description of executive decision making based on his wide experience as a design consultant:

> I remember just such a meeting of senior executives at a major American company, decision makers inundated with statistics and facts. And then one of the highly placed decision makers spoke up: "You know, my daughter came home the other day and said . . . ," and the story poured out. "Hmm," another executive said, "that makes sense, but you know, the other day . . ." and out came a story. A few stories, some discussion of the stories, and the decision.

Stories also support design transfer, by capturing both action and motivation, both the what and the why of the design. For example, the guilt pile story captures a high-level view of the design rationale behind piles: It illustrates how piles are used, and the motivation for using them in that way. When describing the design for an electronic analog of piles [8], it is much easier to convince listeners of the design's value by telling them the guilt pile story, than by just describing piles as self-revealing containers that support casual organization and lightweight browsing. The response to the latter is often, "well, folders could be used to do most of that." Somehow, when the guilt pile story is told, listeners don't respond that a "guilt folder" would work as well. The guilt pile story enables them to relate the design to their personal experience, and they realize that the height and volume of the pile plays an important role in inciting action.

Stories are particularly useful for communicating within the organization for two reasons. First, stories are extremely memorable. People will remember the guilt pile story long after they have forgotten the more formal principles behind piles. Second, stories have an informality that is well-suited to the lack of certainty that characterizes much design-related knowledge. Virtually any kind of information uncovered during the exploratory or refinement stage of design will have uncertainty associated with it: It is likely that it will be true only of certain individuals, in certain situations, under certain circumstances. Presentation of such information as *design principles*, or *findings*, will often elicit arguments about validity and generality from the skeptical. In contrast, stories seem to sidetrack the debates about methodology. People understand that stories are not accurate, that they are likely to bend the truth for rhetorical ends, and so the discussion tends to be of the issues raised by the stories, rather than their obvious shortcomings.

2.2.5 Beyond Stories

As we've just noted, stories are not particularly accurate. Stories are like pearls, layers of gloss accreted around an irritating grain of reality. They exaggerate both the travails and prowess of the teller. Thus, it would be quite unwise to rely on stories as the only source of information.

Fortunately, stories are not the only tool in the designer's repertoire. Stories are well complemented by techniques that provide a direct look at more ordinary aspects of tasks and situations. Techniques such as observations, interviews, ethnographic studies, laboratory studies, and the inclusion of users on the design team can provide different information, which, combined with stories, can yield a more comprehensive picture of the situation. And once a good understanding of the situation has been gained, more structured approaches such as task analysis, scenario generation, and prototyping become much easier.

2.3 PROTOTYPES AS COMMUNICATIONS MEDIA

Stories are used most during the exploratory and transition stages of design; prototypes come into play in the refinement stage. After the design team has made sense of the usage domain by identifying the needs and problems of the users, the focus of the design process shifts to the product being designed. Here prototypes, as concrete representations of the product to be designed, assume a central role.

There are many kinds of prototypes. They range from crude and noninteractive, to realistic simulations that cannot, at a glance, be distinguished from the final product. A prototype may be no more than a rough pencil sketch. It may be a mockup of a device made from foam core or cardboard, intended only to mimic the form of the final product. It may be a simple slideshow of images on a computer screen, accompanied, perhaps, by narration. It may be a videotape that shows the simulated behavior of a proposed product. It may be simulated in a software prototyping environment that supports some of the interaction that will characterize the product. Or it may be a partially implemented version of the product that has most of the properties and behaviors of the real thing.

A number of different prototypes will usually be created during the design process, often for different purposes. It is important to emphasize that even prototypes that are crude and support no interactivity at all are essential. Crude, noninteractive prototypes allow designers to quickly capture rough concepts early in the design. Prototypes with a more polished appearance may be used to help communicate about the gist of the design. Prototypes that support interactivity may be used to elicit feedback from users.

Because of the range of forms that prototypes can take on, I will discuss them in terms of the roles they play in the design process. I will distinguish between vision prototypes, which are used in the exploratory stage of design to capture a high-level picture of the design, and working prototypes, which are used to represent details of the design and to explore solutions to design problems.

2.3.1 Embodying the Vision

A central activity of the exploratory stage of design is the construction of a vision prototype. A vision prototype is usually some sort of concrete representation with an embedded story or scenario that shows actions at a very high level. The purpose of the vision prototype is to communicate what the gist of the design is, how it helps people with things they care about, how it fits into the flow of activities that characterize a user's day. In a sense, the vision prototype is yet another round of storytelling, but with the story focused on the product to be designed. The usual audience for a vision prototype is the organization.

The method we favor is to produce a videotape [17], or a partially interactive computer demonstration, featuring line drawings of users in their environment, drawings of the intended product, and a soundtrack [18]. Typically, drawings are made by hand and then scanned into the computer, where small amounts of interactivity and animation are added, along with a soundtrack. The result is something that seems realistic but cannot be mistaken for something that is real. On the one hand, it must be convincing in the sense that the audience comes away believing it is a realistic depiction of how and why people may use the product. On the other hand, it should be apparent that what is being shown is a product concept, not a product that will soon be ready to ship. Such a misperception can lead to unfortunate pressures on the design team, as well as to irritation on the part of members of the organization who may feel that they have been deceived.

As already noted, the exploratory stage of the design process is complicated by the necessity of the design team developing a smooth working relationship. In this respect, the construction of the vision prototype is a good follow-up to the collection and generation of stories. Because the creation of the vision prototype involves crafting a story or scenario about the product to be designed, everyone can contribute. The process of doing this forces the design team to arrive at a shared understanding of the problems they want to tackle, and the types of solutions they hope to offer. The vision prototype is particularly appropriate because it focuses the design team on the high-level issues about the product being designed and the needs it meets. Details of how the design does things, what it looks like, and other sources of potential discord are deferred until the refinement stage of the design process.

2.3.2 Reaching beyond the Design Community

In some cases, highly polished vision prototypes may be produced (e.g., [3, 16]). This tends to occur if the prototype is going to be shown publicly or to the organization's senior management. For example, as design researcher Michael Schrage comments, "many engineers conceal provocative prototypes from senior management until they have been appropriately polished" [14]. The concern, of course, is that the prototype may be rejected if it has rough edges.

Highly polished prototypes have drawbacks and benefits. On the one hand, the more polished a prototype is, the more likely it is to be used simply as a vehicle for persuasion and public relations. The danger here is that significant energy may be diverted from design to polishing and production. As Schrage notes, "at many large organizations, demonstrating a prototype to senior management assumes all the logistical trappings and investments of a Broadway musical" [14]. A second drawback is that due to the relative expense of producing a polished prototype, and the concern about adverse publicity, there may be internal pressures to avoid pursuing realistic design issues such as what happens when something goes wrong (e.g., [16]). On the other hand, prototypes that are publicly shown can stimulate public discussion about the appropriateness and value of particular technologies.

One of the best-known examples of a highly polished vision prototype is Apple Computer's *Knowledge Navigator* videotape [3]. This five-minute video depicts a computer of the future with capacities such as voice recognition, integrated telecommunications, video conferencing, and a humanlike agent that carries out tasks for the user. The video shows a college professor using the Knowledge Navigator to prepare a lecture at the last minute, retrieving research papers, running a simulation, and contacting a colleague who agrees to show up at the class (over video) to answer questions. (It is worth noting that the Knowledge Navigator is presented as a story: The protagonist's character flaw [procrastination] involves him in a last-minute race to pull together a lecture, with technology coming to the rescue and his nagging mother providing a humorous counterpoint.)

The Knowledge Navigator provoked great debate in the interface design community. For example, a year after its release, a panel at a professional conference conducted a rousing debate on various social issues raised by the prototype [10]. Concerns ranged from the appropriateness of portraying computer programs as humanlike, to how such technology might impact the training of graduate students (in the story, the agent carried out many tasks that would normally have been done by a professor's research assistant). The Knowledge Navigator provoked popular interest as well: At the same conference, librarians from two universities reported that it was the most frequently borrowed tape in their video collections [2]. As a way of stimulating thought and discussion about the consequences of new technologies, the Knowledge Navigator was an unqualified success.

2.3.3 The Working Prototype as a Design Medium

Working prototypes are generally distinct from vision prototypes. Working prototypes emphasize the form, interactivity, and visual appearance of the product itself, not how the product fits with the user's activities. The working prototype's purpose is to embody the current state of the design, and to serve as a medium for interaction among designers and reflection by individual designers. As various authors have noted (e.g., [6, 13]), designers proceed by representing a design idea in some medium, reflecting on the representation, and then modifying it. Thus, designers may, in an iterative manner, explore the consequences of various design decisions. A second purpose of the working prototype is to elicit feedback from those not on the design team—either users or other designers in the organization—thus providing another means of driving the design process.

To be most effective as a medium for interaction, working prototypes should have two properties: accessibility and roughness.

Accessibility First, the prototype should be accessible. Any member of the design team—ideally, anyone who has something to contribute to the design whether on the team or not—should be able to modify it. In traditional design disciplines, such as architecture and graphic design, this accessibility is a given: All members of the discipline are trained in the basic tools and techniques of the trade. In technology design, accessibility is not a given because of the interdisciplinary nature of the process.

In computer-based prototyping, prototyping environments such as HyperCard and MacroMind Director come the closest to being fully accessible. They permit members of an interdisciplinary design team to interact on a first-class basis: The graphic designer can directly change the graphics; the interaction designer can adjust dialogs and feedback; the computer scientist can add in functionality and access to realistic data. Unfortunately, there are limitations to the types of interaction that can be implemented in these environments. Environments with enough power to support implementation of any kind of desired interaction are usually accessible primarily to programmers; if interaction and visual designers have to have their ideas implemented by programmers, the ability to quickly and iteratively explore multiple design paths is lost.

An alternative is the creation of physical mockups. This is particularly viable in the early stages of design where the goal is to embody very general ideas very quickly. It is also ideal for participatory design situations, in which ordinary users play an integral role in producing the design (Chapters 4 and 6). Objects such as small computers can be mocked up with foam core and cardboard, and software interfaces can be simulated with stacks of screen drawings, note cards, and stick-on notes. For example, mockups may be taken into the users' environment and used as a prop with which the users can, in a sense, perform. Something as simple as a picture of a screen pasted on a piece of foam core (to represent an electronic newspaper on a small computer), can raise interesting issues. For example, the user may enact reading the electronic newspaper at the breakfast table and discover that there is no way of supporting the device at a desirable reading angle, or become concerned about the perils of spilling orange juice into an electronic device.

Physical mockups have a variety of uses in the design process. For example, Muller et al. (Chapter 6) and Wirfs-Brock (Chapter 13) describe the use of index cards to elicit a task analysis from users, and to design an object model, respectively. Both note that physicality of the cards—the ability for anyone to write on them, turn them over, or rearrange them—seems to play an important role in their utility. Similarly, as Kyng points out (Chapter 4), if a drawing that has been taped to the wall comes unstuck and falls off when a user is pointing to it, it is an unimportant matter; but if a computer-based prototype crashes as a user is interacting with it, the event feels very different: It is likely to evoke fervent apologies from the user, and may inhibit the user's future interactions with the prototype.

Roughness A second useful property of working prototypes is that they should be rough. One definition of roughness is that the conventions of the prototyping medium are relaxed. For example, rough architectural sketches will often discard scale and continuity, focusing solely on the form of building fragments [6]. An alternate definition of roughness is that the prototype shows implicit evidence of the process through which it was created. It is easy to recognize that a drawing with crooked edges and lines that don't entirely meet has been sketched by hand, perhaps because people understand what is easy and what is difficult when drawing.

This sort of roughness is very valuable in working prototypes. First of all, it creates ambiguity. Different designers—or even the same designer at a later time—may resolve the ambiguity differently, thus making roughness a source of ideas [6].

Second, roughness leaves openings for discussion of the design. Salomon [11] and Wong [18] have observed that omitting a feature from a user interface prototype tends to produce more discussion and ideas than if the feature is present. For example, omitting a text label on a button, or simply leaving out a control mechanism for invoking some type of functionality, can elicit a wide range of alternatives that would be lost if a default label or control mechanism were provided. And Salomon [11] describes an example from the design of an information system, where providing too much detail too early in the design (a button on the screen that had a 3-D look) seemed to shift discussions from the desired focus on basic functionality to a debate about whether buttons should have a 3-D appearance. Similarly, art directors have told me that one trick of the trade is to prepare a preliminary layout on the computer, and then to put tracing paper over the computer-generated layout and trace the design by hand, giving it that hand-done, this-ain't-final-yet look. Otherwise, they say, when the preliminary computer-generated design is presented, clients are liable to react angrily because the design looks final and they didn't get to provide any input (and this occurs even though they have been told that the design is preliminary).

It also seems likely that roughness decreases the level of commitment to the design. With a rough working prototype designers are less likely to feel like they have ego invested in the prototype, and more open to considering changes. If someone criticizes an idea, it's easy for the designer to discount its seriousness ("Oh, I just threw that in as a place holder"). Users, too, are likely to give feedback more readily because they're criticizing something that is obviously rough. A rough prototype has built-in deniability.

Regardless of the reasons roughness is useful, there is some evidence that beginning the refinement stage of design with a rough prototype leads to more satisfactory results. In a study of graphic designers, working either on paper or the computer, those who produced rough early sketches on paper (rather than neat drawings on the screen) were more likely to be satisfied with the final design [1].

It is interesting to note that stories seem to have analogs of these properties of roughness. Stories are ambiguous. The same story can be taken to mean many different things. Stories are full of gaps, which different listeners may fill in differently. Stories, also, do not demand commitment: Like a rough drawing that is criticized and backed off from, any individual story can be discounted as an exceptional case.

2.4 SUMMARY

Although design is often characterized as a process of creating a product, it is also very much a social process in which communication plays a critical role. Designers must communicate both with users and with the organization of which they are part. The designers must also communicate with one another, no mean task when the team is composed of members from different disciplines.

Material and informational artifacts collected and generated during the design process play a key role in mediating and catalyzing this communication. In particular, I've described some of the ways stories and prototypes address some of the messier issues that arise in design practice:

- *Problem setting.* Collecting stories is a valuable method for the initial exploration of usage domains. Story collection and storymaking are useful precursors to more formal analyses.
- *Team-building.* Both stories and prototypes serve as mechanisms for catalyzing interaction within the team. The processes of collecting stories, making stories, and constructing vision prototypes is one that all team members can participate in. Such activities are a good way of generating team cohesion, and the shared language and understanding that is its foundation.
- *User involvement.* Both stories and prototypes provide a means for involving users in the design process. People who would balk at giving feedback about a design idea are often perfectly content to tell stories. Similarly prototypes can be used to elicit comments and reactions, or even as props for role playing.
- *Collaborative design.* Prototypes serve as a medium through which the design team can interact, collectively advancing the design. The most effective prototyping environments seem to be accessible, and to support roughness. Accessibility is important for supporting true collaborative activity, and roughness seems to increase the generation of design alternatives and to lower the resistance to critiques.

- *Design evangelism and transfer.* Designs must be defended and—if the defense is successful—passed on to other people in the organization. Both stories and prototypes can be effective tools for quickly and memorably communicating underlying design rationale.

Just as we can produce better products by adapting them to the needs and practices of users, so we can also make the design process more effective by acknowledging the social nature of design, and developing a better understanding of how concrete artifacts support communication in design.

ACKNOWLEDGMENTS

Much of my thinking about roughness and its role in design has been influenced by the prototyping techniques developed by Laurie Vertelney and Yin Yin Wong, and by discussions with Yin Yin Wong, S. Joy Mountford, Gitta Salomon, and Stephanie Houde, all of the Apple Advanced Technology Human Interface Group. This chapter has benefited from comments by John Carroll, Jonathan Grudin, Morton Kyng, and Don Norman.

REFERENCES

[1] Black, A. (1990). Visible planning on paper and on screen: The impact of working medium on decision-making by novice graphic designers. *Behavior and Information Technology*, *9*(4), 283–296.

[2] Brower, E. (1988). Knowledge navigator draws fire. *MacWeek*, December 6, p. 3.

[3] Dubberly, H. & Mitch, D. (1987). *The Knowledge Navigator*. Apple Computer, videotape.

[4] Grudin, J. (1991a). Systematic sources of suboptimal interface design in large product development organizations. *Human-Computer Interaction*, *6*, 147–196.

[5] Grudin, J. (1991b). Interactive systems: Bridging the gaps between developers and users. *IEEE Computer*, *24*. New York: ACM Press, pp. 59–69.

[6] Herbert, D. M. (1993). *Architectural Study Drawings*. New York: Van Nostrand Reinhold.

[7] Kim, S. (1990). Interdisciplinary collaboration. In B. Laurel (ed.), *The Art of Human-Computer Interface Design*. Reading, MA: Addison-Wesley.

[8] Mander, R., Salomon, G. & Wong, Y. Y. (1992). A "pile" metaphor for supporting casual organization of information. *Human Factors in Computing Systems: CHI '92 Conference Proceedings*. New York: ACM Press, pp. 627–634.

[9] Norman, D. A. (1993). *Things That Make Us Smart: Defending Human Attributes in the Age of the Machine.* Reading, MA: Addison-Wesley.

[10] O'Conner, R. J. (1988). Apple's view of the future is troubling. *San José Mercury News*, Sunday, November 27, p. 1F.

[11] Salomon, G. (1990). How the look affects the feel: Visual design and the creation of an information kiosk. In *Proceedings of the Human Factors Society 34th Annual Meeting,* Orlando, FL, October 8–12. Santa Monica, CA: Human Factors Society, pp. 277–281.

[12] Schank, R. C. (1990). *Tell Me a Story: A New Look at Real and Artificial Memory.* New York: Charles Scribner's Sons.

[13] Schön, D. A. (1987). *Educating the Reflective Practitioner.* San Francisco: Jossey-Bass.

[14] Schrage, M. (1993). The culture of prototyping. *Design Management Journal,* Winter, pp. 55–65.

[15] Thimbley, H., Anderson, S. & Witten, I. H. (1990). Reflexive CSCW: Supporting long-term personal work. *Interacting with Computers, 2*(3), 330–336.

[16] Tognazinni, B. (1994). The "Starfire" video prototype project: A case history. *Human Factors in Computing Systems: CHI '94 Conference Proceedings.* Reading, MA: Addison-Wesley, pp. 99–105.

[17] Vertelney, L. (1989). Using video to prototype user interfaces. *SIGCHI Bulletin, 21*(2), New York: ACM Press, pp. 57–61.

[18] Wong, Y. Y. (1992). Rough and ready prototypes: Lessons from graphic design. *Human Factors in Computing Systems: CHI '92 Conference, Posters and Short Talks.* New York: ACM Press, pp. 83–84.

[19] Wong, Y. Y. (1993). Layer tool: Support for progressive design. *Human Factors in Computing Systems: CHI '92 Conference, Adjunct Proceedings.* New York: ACM Press, pp. 127–128.

CHAPTER 3

Scenarios in Discount Usability Engineering

Jakob Nielsen
SunSoft
2550 Garcia Avenue, MS MTV 21-225
Mountain View, CA 94043-1100
USA

3.1 INTRODUCTION

Usability engineering is the systematic approach to improving the usability of user interfaces by applying a set of proven methods throughout the system development lifecycle [15]. A key element of this development philosophy is the observation that user interfaces do not become good merely because the developers wish for it or have the best of intentions. In contrast, it is necessary to employ a variety of usability methods for each step of the lifecycle, from the very first product concept to the postdeployment stage where the product is studied in the field in order to gain knowledge for the next release.

Even though it sounds appealing to be systematic and to rely on proven engineering methods, experience shows that realistic development projects do not have the time, resources, or personnel to do everything that is normally recommended to improve usability. Thus, there is a need for *discount* usability engineering—that is, methods that are cheap, fast, and easy to use but still achieve most of the intended effect. In most projects, if the only available choice was that between nothing and perfection, nothing would win, but discount usability engineering offers a third alternative that can be chosen to achieve substantial improvements in usability while staying within budget and schedule [11, 12, 15, 16, 18].

For use in discount usability engineering, scenarios have the advantage of limiting the usability engineer to looking at a few (hopefully characteristic and/or important) examples of interaction as opposed to the general case where considerably more data and variety have to be considered. Of course, no usability activities can ever be completely general and consider all possible cases and variations in user and task characteristics, but normally one would try to accommodate the main expected sources of variability. Being as general as possible has the advantage of increasing the probability that the resulting conclusions are valid in all important cases. Unfortunately, the likely downside is that too much generality leads to too few conclusions because the usability specialist gets bogged down in handling the complexity resulting from the interplay of the multiple variables. My preferred alternative is to focus on a smaller and more manageable scenario and then be aware of the need to interpret the results with care. One way of assessing the likely scope of scenario-based results is to study a few scenarios that have been chosen to span the expected range of uses and then conduct a sensitivity analysis on the outcomes. If two very different scenarios lead you to basically the same conclusions with respect to the interface, then those conclusions will very likely hold under many additional circumstances.

My definition of the term *scenario* [13] is an encapsulated (that is, self-contained, portable) description of

- an individual *user*
- interacting with a specific set of computer *facilities*
- to achieve a specific *outcome*
- under specified *circumstances*
- over a certain *time interval* (this in contrast to simple static collections of screens and menus; the scenario explicitly includes a time dimension of what happens when).

For example, together with Jan Maurits Faber, I recently investigated user interfaces to various advanced telephone services, including three-way calling. In our studies, we focused on setting up the three-way call and we did not study what happened after the conversation started. Thus, we were able to simulate the other two users with digitized speech on the computer (they always say the same thing when they answer the phone) and run our tests with a single user. In essence, we viewed the other two users as components of the total system with which this individual interacts, which is why the scenario could be seen as the experience of an individual user.

Within the discount framework, I have a bias in favor of single-user scenarios as they are often the cheapest. On the other hand, there are obviously some user interfaces that depend so much on the interaction between multiple users that it would be hard to analyze them solely from a single user's perspective. A study of three-way calling should be seen from a multiuser perspective if one is interested in the group dynamics of negotiations or problem solving mediated through a telecommunications medium; another example could be the use of a shared electronic whiteboard as a conversational prop [2]. In cases like these I would expand the scope of the scenario to include the experience of all the users.

I will discuss seven applications of scenarios in discount usability engineering:

- Diary scenarios as cheap ways of gathering preliminary field data
- Support for feature brainstorming to envision new directions for computers
- Presentation and contrast of user interface ideas as part of the parallel design method
- Allowing heuristic evaluation of highly domain-specific interfaces by usability specialists without domain expertise
- Scenarios as a simplified prototyping technique for user testing
- Scenarios as a unifying background for a set of tasks in user testing
- Stereotypes for data analysis in exploratory studies

This list has been sorted according to the approximate stage of the usability engineering lifecycle in which the various kinds of scenarios are used. The discussion of the scenarios in the following deviates slightly from this sequence since my example of the last of the scenario uses (exploratory data analysis) is related to the electronic door project used as the example of feature brainstorming and is therefore discussed in the context of that project.

3.2 DIARY SCENARIOS AS DISCOUNT FIELD STUDIES

One of the first stages of the usability engineering lifecycle is a field study of how users currently behave with respect to the tasks of interest to the project. One discount approach to such studies is to build diary scenarios that list those activities and situations a user encounters during a day that are expected to be relevant for the project. Note that the diary is not supposed to be a complete description of *everything* that happened that day since a complete diary would be very expensive to construct. Some important aspects of the user's day will be left out of the diary, so this discount method should be supplemented with alternative usability methods like direct observation for important projects. The diaries can either be written by users themselves (the cheapest approach), or they can be written by an observer. Figure 3.1 shows a single entry from a diary scenario I wrote as part of a long-term project to assess the needs of personal computing in the generation of systems that will follow the object-oriented operating systems currently under development. One of the expected characteristics of such systems is the need to handle extremely large amounts of information leading to the potential to use information retrieval techniques and attributes of the user's personal interaction history as important aspects of the primary user interface.

The example in Figure 3.1 can be used to derive several lessons, including the following: People may remember information in terms of the time when they accessed it (in this example, the year 1989), but they may not remember all details correctly (here, the conference was

---

8:50am: Received an e-mail message from a colleague in Palo Alto (actually sent the night before, but I happened to not have logged in until now) who urgently needed a reference to one of my papers which she seemed to remember having seen as a demo at the Hypertext'89 conference. Note how she uses me as her personal retrieval system! Her description of the system (including the keywords "netnews," "similarity," and "Hypertext'89" (and of course my name) was more than sufficient to immediately allow me to realize that she wanted my paper "A similarity-based hypertext browser for reading the UNIX network news." I went to my filing cabinet and opened the correct drawer (where I keep reprints of all my hypertext papers), and found the relevant folder and picked out a reprint. I then e-mailed her the reference. She indicated that she needed the paper urgently, so I also found the file with the paper to e-mail it to her: This file was in my directory called "papers" under the subdirectory "archived papers" (for papers that have already been published). I scanned an alphabetical list of files in this subdirectory until I came upon the file "HyperNews similarity browser." Note that HyperNews was the name of the system and was very salient to me when I named the file back in 1989. Also note that this system was in fact never demoed at the Hypertext'89 conference, even though it was a paper published in the *Hypermedia* journal in 1989.

Figure 3.1. Sample entry from a diary scenario. The diary was written to focus on personal information retrieval in the day of a scientist.

remembered instead of the journal). Also, the information that seemed most salient as a classification term several years ago (here, the application name HyperNews) may not be used during subsequent retrieval attempts. Furthermore, people tend to interact and use each other as personal databases, so retrieval systems might be networked to agents representing close colleagues, friends, and family in case the information is not found on the user's personal system.

There is an obvious danger in relying on personal diaries, especially if they are collected from user interface scientists and others who are not necessarily representative of the general set of intended users: Not only may people describe actions or situations in ways that misstate or miss important aspects, but people willing to take the time to keep a diary are likely to act differently from those users who are not willing or able to participate in the study. Even so, diary scenarios are a fast and cheap way to get some preliminary data before more elaborate field studies are staged. Also, there is some value to collecting information about the habits of advanced users as they may provide hints for ways computers could support more average users and augment their skill.

Diary scenarios differ from a-day-in-the-life scenarios [5, 27] by describing real observations rather than envisionments. Also, they focus on the experience of particular individuals while abstracting away most of the details of that individual's work (since it would otherwise be too burdensome to write the diary). Diaries have also been used for field studies of program development [9] by asking professional programmers to keep track of daily events in their projects as a way to study larger issues than those typically addressed by laboratory studies where student programmers debug 50-line programs. A more structured version of the diary method is to provide participants with preprinted diary log sheets listing various activities of interest to the study. Participants are then asked to make a note in the log every 15 or 30 minutes and check the activities they have been performing since the last note [24]. This structured approach is "quite effortful" [24] and can be used only for a fairly short duration of about one or two weeks. Typically, the log sheets are supplemented with debriefing sessions at the end of each day or each week where the participants are interviewed in more depth about the activities recorded in the diaries.

3.3 SCENARIOS IN FEATURE BRAINSTORMS

As part of the *beyond being there* project [3, 6], I have been researching ways of managing an electronic presence that can represent a person, a project, a company, or some other entity to the outside world. The project is called the *electronic door* because the computer facilities that were investigated can be seen as a parallel to the way a physical door represents the occupant of an office to people passing by in the corridor. Many people post items of interest on their doors, such as their name, title, or department; office hours or an indication that they are on vacation and when they will return; as well as more or less whimsical posters, pictures, and cartoons that represent their interests.

As can be seen from this brief description, the electronic door is a futuristic computer system that will probably be significantly different from most currently used computer systems.[1] It is impossible to gather sufficient information about such a system by studies of current systems (though some field studies will be useful), and it is completely infeasible to implement an adequate spectrum of running systems to gain experience from the actual use of electronic doors. We therefore decided to use a scenario-building exercise to clarify our thoughts about the electronic door and its potential features and capabilities. Nine researchers participated in a series of five brainstorming sessions, each lasting between one and two hours. In order to approach the development of the scenarios systematically, we used the method described by Tognazzini [26], where scenarios are gradually built by constructing lists of

- Intended users of the system
- User dichotomies (endpoints of various dimensions on which users differ)
- User experience (the various types of background users can be expected to have)
- Users' goals in performing their tasks
- Sources of information accessed by users when performing the task
- Information generated by the users
- Methods employed by the users while performing the task

[1]Actually, at the time of this writing (1994), many users have started constructing *home pages* on the World Wide Web that seem to satisfy some of the needs we identified in the electronic door project. At the time of the project (1992), the World Wide Web and Mosaic had not yet reached their current level of prominence on the Internet [20] and the home page phenomenon was not studied in the project. It is an interesting exercise to compare the project scenarios for future electronic doors with the actual home pages observed two years later: Even though many of the more advanced features are not (yet) seen in practice, the growth of the World Wide Web happened faster than we had expected.

- User needs
- Possible usage scenarios

Some examples from the various lists are reproduced in Figure 3.2 (the full list contained 212 entries). Each of the list elements was effectively a *microscenario* constructed with very low overhead (just writing down a few words on a whiteboard or an overhead foil) and discussed for a few minutes only to envision some specific aspect of electronic doors. These microscenarios made sense to the brainstorm participants in the context of the original sessions since each gave rise to the next, but some of the original richness was lost upon considering the lists in later sessions where most of the context had been lost. The advantage of the method is that it allows for the exploration of a large number of different microscenarios in a short amount of time, with the corresponding disadvantage that each individual scenario is fleshed out only in minimum detail.

Note that the microscenarios may not make sense to people who did not participate in the meetings. For example, one entry under possible users is "Fans of Don Norman." Norman is a cognitive scientist who is famous for his critiques of bad user interface designs and has a wide following on the Internet. (Every month there will be postings asking "What is the title of Norman's new book?" or some such question.) Since our design team was dominated by user interface specialists and cognitive scientists, we happened to think of Norman when we needed an example of a celebrity whose doings people might be interested in keeping track of. In the world at large, a film star would definitely have been a better example.

From the list of possible usage scenarios, we finally picked three scenarios to develop further. The first scenario concerned the use of electronic doors in a family, including both members of a nuclear family and members of their extended family, such as grandparents. The second scenario was business-oriented and concerned interactions between a company and its clients wanting information about one of its products. The third scenario was referred to as the *ultrafuture scenario* and followed a day in the life of a person in a potential future world where everybody and everything would have electronic doors.

Each detailed scenario was basically a list of situations and system features to react to those situations. For example, the business-oriented scenario started out with assuming that a person at one of Bellcore's client companies (MaryX) had heard that Bellcore was supplying a great hypertext product capable of handling large amounts of text and telephone company documents. In order to find out more infor-

Who are the people who might want to use electronic doors:

- Computer science research scientists
- Employees of distributed companies (or even nondistributed companies)
- Historical people
- Composite entities, clubs, joint pseudonyms
- Programs, robots, AIs, Answer Garden
- New people in an organization
- Support people (benefits people, hotline staff)
- Computer dating/personals
- Service advertising which doors to connect to
- Nonindividuals, companies/organizations looking at each other
- Political campaigns
- Fans of Don Norman (wanting to read whatever books he checks out of the library)

Dimensions along which different classes of users might differ:

- Zero-time to maintain my door versus "my door is my life," so I will spend endless time maintaining it
- Lots to express versus nothing to say
- Users at fixed location/workstation versus people on the go
- Telling the truth versus lies/half-truths
- Fully automated versus completely manual door construction

Existing technologies and concepts users know that have similar attributes:

- Answering machines in movie theaters giving times for shows
- Real doors with things on them
- Bulletin boards
- Business cards
- Clothing selection
- Birth, wedding, death announcements
- Tombstones, epitaphs
- Autobiographies
- Censorship (of information posted on doors)
- Security, privacy, skepticism

Why would people want to use electronic doors?

- Make friends
- Influence people
- Keep in touch with friends

Figure 3.2. Examples of microscenarios built as part of a brainstorm on possible uses of the electronic door. The notes are basically shown as they were written on the whiteboard during the scenario sessions, meaning that they are sometimes very brief.

- Find out facts without bothering people
- Let others find out about you
- Barrier to prevent people from bothering you
- Create a persona
- Get others' opinions/experience (e.g., movie reviews, recommendations)
- Post and find out reactions/opinions to external events/things
- Surrogate for self on job

Where would users get the information they would post on the electronic door?

- Scanned images
- Photos from digitizing camera
- Net articles
- Previously written papers
- Demons watching your computer activities
- Infrared detectors
- Smart badges that transmit information about where the user is

Figure 3.2. *(Continued)*

mation about this product, she connected to Bellcore's corporate electronic door, which allowed her to find the electronic door for the specific product. From this door, MaryX could get further information about the product, and a demo, and connect to the electronic door of various Bellcore employees with further expertise. The first Bellcore person she tried to contact was on vacation, but since the electronic door of that person had a message saying so as well as a reference to the electronic door of another person who could handle urgent business, MaryX succeeded in getting the information she needed. The full scenario had several other details, including a discussion of social issues related to some aspects of the envisioned use of the electronic door. For example, we hypothesized that one reason MaryX started by connecting to the electronic door was that she wanted to check out the product without the commitment implicit in asking somebody to come out and show it to her.

Developing these scenarios was a worthwhile exercise, resulting in an increased understanding of the concept of an electronic door. At the same time, the participants in the brainstorming sessions felt that the systematic list-building method did not fit very well with our project and its very undefined nature. Certainly, some good came of trying to be systematic. For example, when listing possible users, we had to consider whether a historic person like Napoleon could have an electronic door (the answer was yes). Having included historic persons on the list of users again led to a user dichotomy between living and dead users, which again led to a discussion of the general issues involved in having electronic doors for dead people who might want to leave an electronic epitaph.

Mostly, though, our feeling was that the list-building format was better suited for the development of scenarios for more constrained types of systems. In our case, there were no real answers, and we constantly felt the urge to develop slightly larger *miniscenarios* for each item added to a list as a microscenario (for example, *how* a dead person's electronic door would look and why people might want to build it). Thus, it may be the case that scenario building for highly unconstrained development projects should start with the detailed specification of a few specific scenarios to clarify the product concept before more detailed lists are constructed.

In any case, scenario building did seem to be a valid method to brainstorm about desired features and possible uses of a new product that had yet to be defined. After the sessions we had a much better idea of the possible uses of electronic doors and possible paths for the project. Unfortunately, it did not seem that the scenarios helped us decide between these possibilities.

The scenario-building exercise utilized the fact that the human imagination is the cheapest multimedia prototyping system around. Just a few words serve to call up reasonably vivid pictures and imagined interfaces. Of course, reliance on human imagination as a prototyping tool leaves the system even more underspecified than more traditional prototyping, so the different participants in a scenario-building session may have somewhat different understandings of the system that is being discussed. These differences emerge over time as more detail is added and more examples are discussed.

3.3.1 Field Study of Prototype Design

Given the vagueness of the scenarios, it was decided to implement a limited version of the electronic door called an *electronic business card* to serve as a vertical prototype.[2] A full-featured electronic door would presumably be some kind of highly interactive hypermedia system allowing users to connect to remote servers in real time and navigate their information spaces through a graphical user interface that would

[2]Vertical prototypes have fully working functionality and can thus be used for real but are limited in only supporting a small part of the features in the full system.

be difficult to implement and could only be tested if all users had access to the same platform. In contrast, the electronic business card was envisioned as a more modest version that was accessed through electronic mail (instead of through a real-time dynamic interface) and might initially be text-only (thus making it accessible worldwide without any special equipment). The eventual use of electronic business cards is expected to come with the widespread use of personal digital assistants (PDAs). Assuming that all participants in a meeting bring a PDA and that these PDAs can connect to each other through some kind of wireless network (e.g., infrared beaming), it will be possible for the PDAs to exchange electronic business cards for their owners. Upon leaving the meeting, each participant will thus have a complete list of electronic business cards for all other participants stored in his or her PDA.

Many considerations lead to the conclusion that the information exchanged between the PDAs will not be the complete set of information available for a given participant. Bandwidth and storage limitations might limit each record to a few kilobytes, even though many people will have many megabytes of information available about themselves (when video starts being used as a data medium, most people will have gigabytes of information available for distribution). Also, to avoid information overload most people will not want to have the complete set of available information stored for each person they have ever met, even if it were technologically feasible. Therefore, the electronic business card will be a hypertext link to remote servers (called *electronic business card servers*), which can provide more information over the net upon request. Typical information that may be retrieved from an electronic business card server could be a description of the owner's personal and professional interests, including a publication list in the case of scientists, digitized photos, video, and sound clips, and electronic documents of various sorts (for example, paper reprints for scientists, price lists for salespeople, and policy statements and speeches for politicians).

The electronic business card that was actually implemented was limited to working through standard electronic mail. The advantage of this approach is that it was easily accessible to anybody who had e-mail access and that it was reasonably easy to implement. Also, pointers to the electronic business card could be given simply as an e-mail address that could be printed on paper documents such as letterhead and articles in conference proceedings.

As can be seen from Table 3.1, the author's electronic business card server had been accessed by 556 users over twelve months. In contrast to expectations, most users only used the electronic business card a few times and did not return for further information. Of course, it is pos-

Table 3.1 Usage Statics for Jakob Nielsen's Electronic Business Card for the Period March 22, 1993 to March 20, 1994

Domain	*Users*	*Commands*	*Commands per Users*
.ar (Argentina)	1	1	1.00
.at (Austria)	1	5	5.00
.au (Australia)	13	69	5.31
.be (Belgium)	5	45	9.00
.ch (Switzerland)	2	2	1.00
.cl (Chile)	1	1	1.00
.de (Germany)	32	116	3.62
.dk (Denmark)	6	34	5.67
.fi (Finland)	13	63	4.85
.fr (France)	6	29	4.83
.gr (Greece)	1	1	1.00
.hk (Hong Kong)	1	1	1.00
.ie (Ireland)	4	25	6.25
.il (Israel)	1	1	1.00
.it (Italy)	7	26	3.71
.jp (Japan)	13	57	4.38
.kr (Korea)	1	1	1.00
.mx (Mexico)	1	20	20.00
.nl (Netherlands)	20	91	4.55
.no (Norway)	6	24	4.00
.nz (New Zealand)	1	43	43.00
.pl (Poland)	2	83	41.50
.se (Sweden)	14	146	10.43
.sg (Singapore)	1	2	2.00
.su (Russia)	2	2	1.00
.tw (Taiwan)	2	3	1.50
.uk (United Kingdom)	53	271	5.11
.za (South Africa)	1	1	1.00
Non-US/Canada total	**213**	**1,165**	**5.47**
.ca (Canada)	19	61	3.21
.com (Commercial)	188	483	2.57

Table 3.1 *(Continued)*

Domain	*Users*	*Commands*	*Commands per Users*
.edu (Universities)	97	288	2.97
.gov (Government)	9	52	5.78
.mil (Military)	3	4	1.33
.net (Network providers)	12	27	2.25
.org (Organizations)	8	18	2.25
.us (other USA)	1	1	1.00
US/Canadian total	**337**	**934**	**2.77**
BITNET users	5	23	4.60
Userids without domain	1	1	1.00
Grand Total	**556**	**2,123**	**3.82**

Note: Furthermore, 60 commands were received from anonymous users. While the server was in operation, updated versions of this table could be retrieved by sending it e-mail with the line **get user_stats_by_domain.txt**. This reference was itself an example of the use of the electronic business card to support dead hypertext links.

sible that some users may want to return to the server after an extended period of time not captured by the small window represented by the statistics in Table 3.1. The table shows that users outside North America accessed the service considerably more than did users within North America. This result may indicate that people who are further away from a given locus of information have larger needs for rapid, electronically disseminated information, but the tendency is too weak for any real conclusions. However, given the many studies showing that most electronic communication occurs between people who are geographically proximate [1, 8], the contrasting results in Table 3.1 at least lend some support to the beyond-being-there idea.

A closer look at the actual commands issued by the various users indicates that the overwhelming use of the electronic business card server came from cases where specific instructions had been given for accessing a specific piece of information (similar to the footnote to Table 3.1). In other words, the use of the electronic business card server as a hypertext system with half-dead links [20] was much more pronounced than its use as a primitive electronic door, which people contacted to learn more about its owner. This latter result does not necessarily mean that the electronic door idea is doomed, since the failure of the electronic business card to serve as an electronic door may be a function of its primitive, e-mail-oriented interface. Also, the system did see *some* use that followed the patterns expected from our electronic door scenarios.

The electronic business card project served as a reality check on the electronic door scenarios and provided valuable field data about people's actual use of the kind of facilities we are discussing. It confirmed the feasibility of implementing some of the features and provided data showing that some features were more frequently used than others. Thus, even a simple real system can supplement envisioning exercises and help keep them on track as researchers explore future advanced computer capabilities.

As an aside regarding electronic business cards, I learned after having completed the project that a somewhat similar concept is described in the science fiction novel *Snow Crash* [25]. Of course, since verbal fiction is unconstrained by mere implementation details, the version described in the novel has many interesting and advanced features. In effect, reading a science fiction book can serve as a kind of (entertaining) scenario of future use of a system.

3.3.2 Scenarios as Stereotypes for Data Analysis

In the electronic door example, the collected data from the users were analyzed according to a few stereotyped scenarios of system usage. For this particular application, it was deemed unacceptable to increase the users' overhead by sending them questionnaires asking them to explain how and why they used the system. Doing so would quickly have caused people to stop using the system. Instead, usage logs were collected automatically by the system. Eyeballing these logs made it apparent that the system was being used in ways that were slightly different from the main usage as envisioned before the start of the study. Instead of a formal data analysis with previously defined hypotheses, the data were analyzed by a kind of pattern matching, where a human analyst built up a model of stereotypical uses in the form of miniscenarios. For example, one stereotype scenario was a user who had read instructions about how to get a specific file and wanted to get only that one information object, and another stereotype scenario was a user browsing the information base to see what was available. Matching the actual log data to these stereotypes was fairly easy and made it possible to gain a rough understanding of the data in a short amount of time. To some extent, stereotype scenarios are similar to use cases [7] in describing possible sequences of actions, but since the stereotype scenarios are intended to capture user behavior rather than system behavior, they are by necessity less well defined, and many different series of user actions could match the same stereotype scenario.

A key element is that the stereotype scenarios emerged as part of the data analysis they were intended to help. As more user observations became available, the stereotype scenarios crystallized and could then be used to match additional data. Some stereotype scenarios were carried over from the initial design brainstorms (summarized in Figure 3.2) though most of these scenarios turned out not to be well represented in the data. Given that a field trial shows new usage patterns (which will very frequently be the case), it will not be sufficient to simply reuse the scenarios that were developed as part of the envisioning part of the project.

The fact that many of the original envisioning scenarios were not found in the data might lead to two different kinds of conclusions, and one would need to rely on general user interface experience and insights to determine which one was most likely to be true. One possibility is that many of the original scenarios were simply not realistic and that users would not want to behave in the ways the designers envisioned. Another possible explanation is that the vertical prototype implementation was too limited in the range of user activities for which it offered support and that more complex user scenarios would be observed only with more complex software. My personal guess is actually a little of both: More advanced software (like Mosaic and the World Wide Web pages in common use today) does indeed lead to more of the predicted usage scenarios, but there are also cases where the design meetings got carried away and generated scenarios that are unlikely to be seen in real use.

3.4 SCENARIOS IN PARALLEL DESIGN

Parallel design [15, 22] is a usability engineering method intended to supplement iterative design in its initial stages. It involves having multiple designers develop initial sketches of a user interface design based on a given functional specification. The goal of parallel design is to explore the design space and to be able to build the first complete interface design on the best aspects of several ideas without the constraints inherent in iterating from a previous design.

Each of the resulting designs from a parallel design project can obviously be described in detail with the use of traditional specification languages, whether formal or as informal as a set of annotated screen mockups. However, we have found usage scenarios to be a particularly effective way of quickly communicating a set of alternative designs to a group (for further discussion). A rough understanding of the designs can be achieved in as little as ten minutes per design by having each designer give a presentation stating what would happen as a hypothetical user progressed through a typical interaction scenario using the interface.

In communicating parallel designs, one can use the same scenario for all designs to make it easier to contrast them, or one can use different scenarios that highlight the particular strengths of each design. The choice between these two options will depend on the available time, since it is easier for the individual designers to use scenarios that match their own design style.

3.5 SCENARIOS IN HEURISTIC EVALUATION

Heuristic evaluation [17, 21] is a highly informal usability inspection method, where a set of evaluators (preferably usability specialists [14]) inspect a user interface in order to generate a list of the usability problems in the interface. In contract to other, more systematic usability inspection methods like cognitive walkthroughs [23, 28], heuristic evaluation does not depend on previously defined user tasks, since it is based on checking the various interface elements against the evaluators' usability expertise and a small set of generally applicable heuristics (such as, "be consistent"). Even so, it would be very difficult for a usability specialist to perform a heuristic evaluation of a highly domain-dependent user interface if the usability specialist had no understanding of the meaning of the information contained in the various dialog elements.

We have successfully used the heuristic evaluation method for the evaluation of a highly domain-dependent user interface for a telephone company application. The system will be referred to here as the Integrating System (see [17, 18] for more detail). It is intended to be used by highly trained telephone company technicians and the interface is full of cryptic abbreviations and concepts that are basically meaningless to others. The evaluations were made possible by supplying the evaluators with a usage scenario that had been developed on the basis of a task analysis of the users, resulting in a step-by-step description of the handling of a typical task. At each step, the scenario described what information a real user would extract from the current screen, what inferences the user would make, and what operation the user would perform next. Following these detailed instructions, the evaluators were able to use the system even though they did not truly understand what they were doing or why they were doing it. The result of the heuristic evaluation was a list of forty core usability problems in the part of the interface covered by the scenario as well as four additional problems that were found when some evaluators deviated from the scenario. As could certainly be expected, later user testing revealed additional problems, including some that would never have been found by a heuristic evaluator without any domain knowledge. However, the heuristic evaluation could still be deemed a success, since the usage scenario allowed the usability specialists to evaluate many basic interaction principles and find many usability problems.

Heuristic evaluation was originally not scenario-based. On the contrary, to some extent it is one of the method's strengths that each evaluator approaches the interface differently. When a usage scenario is given, it will constrain the ways the evaluators analyze the interface, and some usability problems will be overlooked. Scenarios have many good aspects, but users always find new ways of using things that would not be covered by the scenarios, so there are some reasons to support a nonscenario inspection of an interface. Heuristic evaluation finds many usability problems not found by user testing, and one reason for this is that it is not tied to a predefined task or use of the system.

Even so, there are also times when it is advantageous to use a scenario for a heuristic evaluation. The example mentioned in my abstract was one such case, where the evaluation could not have been done without a scenario. The integrating system was an interface to a highly specialized task with screens filled with obscure codes (that were second nature to the technicians using the system). We could have done a standard heuristic evaluation and contemplated the nature of these codes, but in order to assess the higher levels of the dialog, the evaluators needed to know what the system was *doing* with the codes, and we deemed a scenario the most efficient way of achieving that goal. Another approach would have been to teach the codes and the related properties of the telephone system, but that would probably have taken several months instead of the two hours needed to teach the scenario and thus would not have been in the spirit of discount usability engineering.

3.6 SCENARIOS AS A PROTOTYPING TECHNIQUE

Scenarios can be used as a prototyping technique. All user interface prototypes work by reducing the complexity of the full system in some way, either by eliminating functionality or by eliminating coverage of some parts of the interface. Prototype scenarios eliminate both kinds of complexity by offering a simulation of a single user path through the system. In other words, a scenario is a user interface prototype that can be used to do exactly one thing. As such, they are very cheap to build and are a perfect method for use as part of a discount usability engineering approach [11, 12, 19].

A prototype scenario may be as simple as a textual description of the steps a user would take to achieve the single goal supported by the scenario. This is the kind of scenario produced by the electronic door brainstorm sessions discussed above, though a scenario would need a detailed description of the user interface at each user step to truly count as a prototype. Text-only prototypes rely on the reader's imagination to fill in details of screen design and so forth and only allow an evaluation of the higher-level design issues.

A prototype scenario can also be a set of screen mockups that exist either on paper or as screens displayed by a simple slide-show computer program [10]. Such scenarios can be used for heuristic evaluation [13] and also for some simple user testing. The use of this kind of prototype scenario for user testing is somewhat different than the *scenario machine* described by Carroll and Kay [4]. The scenario machine (often a fully functional interface modified for instructional purposes) blocks the user from performing any actions that are not part of a prespecified scenario in the hope that a novice user will learn faster by being prevented from garden pathing and from spending less time to recover from errors. In a prototype scenario, users will also be unable to complete actions that are not part of the predetermined small action set, but the user is still encouraged to consider all possible actions at each step through the scenario: Instead of just showing the next screen, no matter what the user did (as done by the most extreme version of the scenario machine), the experimenter in a scenario user test will discuss each screen with the user and let the user choose freely what the next action *ought* to be according to that user. Very likely, that next action will not be implemented, and the experimenter will then explain that to the user and encourage further exploration. In this way, a user test of a scenario can collect at least some information about alternative user strategies that do not match the path intended by the designers, even though that path will be the only one to be tested in its entirety.

Common for this form of scenario is that it tries to give as good an impression as possible of the way the user interface will be, even though the interface does not exist yet. See Figure 3.3 for an example of a single screen from one such scenario of the use of a nonexisting graphical user interface for information access. The full scenario contained several such screens and was designed by an iterative design approach, where three early versions were tested with users and modified according to the usability problems discovered. The version in Figure 3.3 is thus the

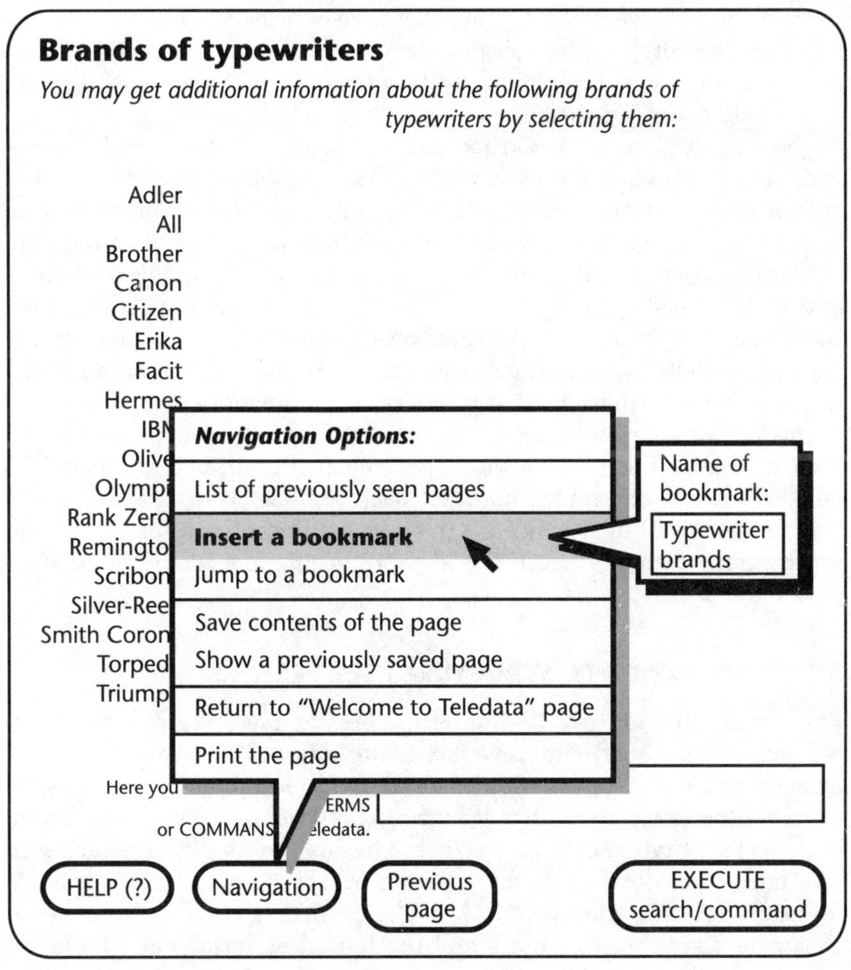

Figure 3.3. Example of a screen from a scenario developed to prototype on-line information access using a graphical user interface. The scenario is that the user wants to buy a typewriter. Here, the user has found the listing of the (many) manufacturers of typewriters and may want to return to it later. Therefore the user inserts a bookmark at this screen [10].

fourth version of the scenario. It was possible to produce four versions of the interface in a very short amount of time because the use of scenarios made the prototyping trivial (just draw new screens in a graphics editor—or even easier, modify earlier drawings) and the user testing quick (since only a single interaction stream had to be tested).

Several lessons were learned during the tests of the scenario represented in Figure 3.3. For example, the users had been asked to use the system as if they were interested in buying a typewriter and they often wanted to return to the screen listing all the typewriters. As a result of this observation, the system design was modified to include a bookmark option for users to mark locations in the information space to make them easier to return to. Another observation was that users easily became overwhelmed by the amount of information and wanted a way to filter the information base to show only information of interest to them (for example, only typewriters costing less than a certain amount). Such a filtering mechanism would have been difficult to implement in a general system and might have set back the user testing schedule by several months, but it was easy to try out different options in the scenario where various filtering needs and mechanisms could be presupposed and precomputed.

3.7 SCENARIOS TO STRUCTURE USER TESTING

Even in traditional user testing of a more complete system, a form of scenario can be used to improve the test situation. To prevent a user test from being a set of irrelevant and unrelated isolated tasks, it is possible to relate the tasks through a scenario. This form of scenario is a rough outline of a situation in which users might find themselves together with a rationale for why they might want to perform the tasks they are asked to do. By relating the tasks to a larger context, the scenario makes it easier for the users to understand the task descriptions and makes it possible for the user to reuse objects from previous test tasks. Also, having a scenario in mind allows the usability specialist planning the test to construct a coherent and realistic set of test tasks.

For example, we recently performed a series of user tests with alternative user interfaces to a personal communication service. A personal communication service would assign a single telephone number to an individual and then forward calls to that number to different physical telephones, depending on various instructions given by the user. For example, calls could be forwarded to the user's home, car phone, and office phone at different times of day, except that no calls would be forwarded at night unless the caller knew a special password. The system does not exist in the real world, so we do not know for sure how people are going to use it. To come up with a reasonable set of test tasks, we relied on a scenario centered around a person working in an office on a project with people from another office, and who is going on vacation.

3.8 CONCLUSIONS

In earlier work [13], I suggested that scenarios could be classified along three dimensions, purpose, medium of expression, and source of inspiration, giving rise to the taxonomy described in the following and summarized in Table 3.2.

The first dimension of the taxonomy is the purpose of the scenario. The experienced usability professional will want to choose very different kinds of scenarios to achieve different goals. Scenarios can be used as a communication tool, as a thinking or design tool for the scenario developer him- or herself, and they can be used as an artifact in testing (which again can have multiple goals: to test the actual interface design or to test and compare various HCI theories).

The second dimension is the medium of expression and implementation chosen for the scenario. The three main media types are textual

Table 3.2 The Three Dimensions of the Taxonomy of Scenarios Proposed in this Chapter

- **Purpose**
  - Communicate user interface issues to an audience
    * managers, colleagues
    * users
  - Structure thinking and provide background for refinements
  - Testing
    * interfaces
    * HCI theories
- **Medium of expression and implementation**
  - Textual description
  - Storyboards (screen designs on paper, video, etc.)
  - Running system on an actual computer
- **Source of inspiration**
  - Empirical observations
  - Designers' ideas and analysis

descriptions (leaving the visualization of the scenario to the human imagination), storyboards (leaving the dynamic transitions and behavior to the viewer's imagination), and finally, running systems on actual computer equipment (or whatever implementation platform is intended for the final system). As the scenario progresses along the media type dimension, it is typically necessary to invest more work, but the result will be more precisely specified. Precise specifications are normally an advantage but they can also be a disadvantage early in the design process where one does not want to unduly limit one's imagination.

The final dimension of the taxonomy is the source of inspiration for the elements of the scenario. The two main types of inspiration are empirical observations and the designers' ideas, meaning that scenarios can be built to reflect either the world as it is now or the world as it may become.

Using the taxonomy in Table 3.2 to classify the five types of scenario discussed above gives the following result:

- Diary scenarios: Structure thinking, textual descriptions, empirical observations
- Scenarios in feature brainstorms: Structure thinking, textual description, designers' ideas and analysis
- Scenarios in parallel design: Communicate user interface issues to an audience (colleagues), storyboards, designers' ideas and analysis
- Scenarios in heuristic evaluation: Testing (interfaces), textual description combined with a running system, empirical observations
- Scenarios as a prototyping technique: Testing (interface), any of the three media, designers' ideas and analysis
- Scenarios to structure user testing: Testing (interface), textual description, empirical observation (if derived from field studies or task analysis), or designers' ideas and analysis
- Scenarios as stereotypes to analyze exploratory data: Structure thinking, textual data, empirical observation

The kinds of scenarios discussed here are all tools for use at various stages of the usability engineering lifecycle [15]. By focusing on a single use of an interface, scenarios enable us to understand and communicate the interface better and thus make our work easier and cheaper.

ACKNOWLEDGMENTS

The electronic door brainstorm project was in collaboration with members of the Bellcore *beyond being there* research project: Steve Abney,

David Ackley, Laurence Brothers, George Furnas, Will Hill, Jim Hollan, Joel Remde, Scott Stornetta, and Jeff Zacks. The parallel design project was in collaboration with Heather Desurvire (NYNEX), Bob Durr (Bell Atlantic), Jim Kondziela (NYNEX), Adam Marx (U S WEST), Janet Davidson (Pacific Bell), Randy Kerr (Microsoft), Dan Rosenberg (Oracle), Gitta Salomon (IDEO Product Development), Rolf Molich (Kommunedata), and Tom Stewart (System Concepts Ltd.). The heuristic evaluation of a highly domain-dependent user interface was in collaboration with Gay Norwood from Bellcore's Operations Technology area. The study of personal communication services was in collaboration with Marco Bergman from Delft University of Technology. In all cases, the way these projects have been interpreted in this chapter is solely the responsibility of Jakob Nielsen and does not necessarily represent the positions of the collaborators in the underlying projects.

REFERENCES

[1] Bikson, T. K. & Eveland, J. D. (1990). The interplay of work group structures and computer support. In J. Galegher, R Kraut. & C. Egido (eds.), *Intellectual Teamwork: Social and Technological Foundations of Cooperative Work.* Hillsdale, NJ: Lawrence Erlbaum, pp.245–290.

[2] Brinck, T. & Gomez, L. M. (1992). A collaborative medium for the support of conversational props. In *Proceedings of ACM CSCW'92 Conference on Computer-Supported Cooperative Work,* Toronto, November 1–4, pp. 171–178.

[3] Brothers, L., Hollan, J., Nielsen, J., Stornetta, S., Abney, S., Furnas, G. & Littman, M. (1992). Supporting informal communication via ephemeral interest groups. In *Proceedings of ACM CSCW'92 Conference on Computer-Supported Cooperative Work,* Toronto, November 1–4, pp. 84–90.

[4] Carroll, J. M. & Kay, D. S. (1985). Prompting, feedback and error correction in the design of a scenario machine. In *Proceedings of ACM CHI'85 Conference,* San Francisco, CA, April 14–18, pp. 149–153. Also in the *International Journal of Man-Machine Studies, 28,* 1 (1988): 11–27.

[5] Erickson, T. (1995). Notes on design practice: Stories and prototypes as catalysts for communication. *Chapter 2 in the present book.*

[6] Hollan, J. & Stornetta, S. (1992). Beyond being there. In *Proceedings of ACM CHI'92 Conference,* Monterey, CA, May 3–7, pp. 119–125.

[7] Jacobson, I. (1995). The use-case construct in object-oriented software engineering. *Chapter 12 in the present book.*

[8] Kraut, R. E., Egido, C. & Galegher, J. (1990). Patterns of contact and communication in scientific research collaboration. In J. Galegher, R. Kraut & C. Egido (eds.), *Intellectual Teamwork: Social and Technological Foundations of Cooperative Work.* Hillsdale, NJ: Lawrence Erlbaum, pp.149–171.

[9] Naur, P. (1983). Program development studies based on diaries. In T. R. G. Green, S. J. Payne & G. C. van der Veer (eds.), *The Psychology of Computer Use*. London: Academic Press, pp. 159–170.

[10] Nielsen, J. (1987). Using scenarios to develop user friendly videotex systems. In *Proceedings of NordDATA'87 Joint Scandinavian Computer Conference,* Trondheim, Norway, June 15–18, pp. 133–138.

[11] Nielsen, J. (1989). Usability engineering at a discount. In G. Salvendy, & M. J. Smith (eds.), *Designing and Using Human-Computer Interfaces and Knowledge Based Systems*. Amsterdam: Elsevier Science, pp. 394–401.

[12] Nielsen, J. (1990a). Big paybacks from "discount" usability engineering. *IEEE Software, 7*, 3 (May): 107–108.

[13] Nielsen, J. (1990b). Paper versus computer implementations as mockup scenarios for heuristic evaluation. In *Proceedings of IFIP INTERACT'90 Third International Conference on Human-Computer Interaction,* Cambridge, U.K., August 27–31, pp. 315–320.

[14] Nielsen, J. (1992). Finding usability problems through heuristic evaluation. In *Proceedings of ACM CHI'92 Conference,* Monterey, CA, May 3–7, pp. 373–380.

[15] Nielsen, J. (1993a). *Usability Engineering*. Boston: Academic Press. Paperback edition, 1994.

[16] Nielsen, J. (1993b). Is usability engineering really worth it? *IEEE Software, 10*, 6 (November): 90–92.

[17] Nielsen, J. (1994a). Heuristic evaluation. In J. Nielsen, & R. L. Mack (eds.), *Usability Inspection Methods*. New York: Wiley, pp. 25–62.

[18] Nielsen, J. (1994b). Guerrilla HCI: Using discount usability engineering to penetrate the intimidation barrier. In R. G. Bias & D. J. Mayhew (eds.), *Cost-Justifying Usability*. Boston: Academic Press, pp. 245–272.

[19] Nielsen, J. (1994c). Why GUI panic is good panic. *ACM Interactions Magazine, 1*, 2 (April): 55–58.

[20] Nielsen, J. (1995). *Multimedia and Hypertext: The Internet and Beyond.* Boston: Academic Press.

[21] Nielsen, J. & Molich, R. (1990). Heuristic evaluation of user interfaces. In *Proceedings of ACM CHI'90,* Seattle, WA, April 1–5, pp. 249–256.

[22] Nielsen, J., Desurvire, H., Kerr, R., Rosenberg, D., Salomon, G., Molich, R. & Stewart, T. (1993). Comparative design review: An exercise in parallel design. In *Proceedings of ACM INTERCHI'93 Conference,* Amsterdam, April 24–29, pp. 414–417.

[23] Polson, P., Lewis, C., Rieman, J. & Wharton, C. (1992). Cognitive walkthroughs: A method for theory-based evaluation of user interfaces. *International Journal of Man-Machine Studies*, *36*, 741–773.

[24] Rieman, J. (1993). The diary study: A workplace-oriented research tool to guide laboratory efforts. In *Proceedings of ACM INTERCHI'93 Conference,* Amsterdam, April 24–29, pp. 321–326.

[25] Stephenson, N. (1992). *Snow Crash.* New York: Bantram Spectra.

[26] Tognazzini, B. (1992). *Tog on Interface.* Reading, MA: Addison-Wesley.

[27] Vertelney, L. (1989). Using video to prototype user interfaces. *ACM SIGCHI Bulletin, 21,* 2 (October): 57–61.

[28] Wharton, C., Rieman, J., Lewis, C. & Polson, P. (1994). The cognitive walkthrough method: A practitioner's guide. In J. Nielsen & R. L. Mack (eds.), *Usability Inspection Methods.* New York: Wiley, pp. 105–140.

CHAPTER 4

Creating Contexts for Design

Morten Kyng
Department of Computer Science
Aarhus University
Building 540, Ny Munkegade
DK-8000 Aarhus C, Denmark

4.1 COMPUTERS IN CONTEXT

How to make computer systems and applications fit the work they are to support is a question that has received growing attention over the last decade. In most of the work trying to answer this question, users have a prominent position. In the U.S. literature this is reflected in the term *user-centered design* [18] from the mid-eighties, and the more recent *participatory design* ([17, 19] and Chapter 6 of this volume). These terms also illustrate a development in the understanding of how to approach an answer. User-centered design indicates a focus on the users, but also that this focus can be achieved by the developers, that the critical issue is the user centeredness of activities carried out by the developers. Participatory design explicitly acknowledges that the end users should play an active role in the design process themselves.

But why? Why not leave it to the experts? Well, that *is* what we are advocating. The point is that the end-users are the experts on what constitutes good computer support in *their* context of work.

As a first illustration, consider the following example from the European Esprit project EuroCoOp.[1] This is a project developing a number of

[1]For more information about the EuroCoOp project, see [8].

CSCW tools, including a work group planning and coordination tool. As a response to a suggestion from a user, a *cut & paste* facility has been added to the coordination tool, allowing a user to copy parts of a plan for a specific month and paste it into the plans being developed for the following months. Although this facility had worked fine when tested by the developers, it failed in the user workshop. The reason was that the developers testing it had done so in the capacity of *group leader*, which implied that they had privileges to change all attributes of the plan being copied/pasted. At the user workshop, however, it turned out that in most cases the user doing the copy/paste was a secretary who did not have the privileges needed to make the necessary changes to the plan after the paste—since changes could be done only by the *task responsible*.

As the example illustrates, designers may overlook crucial, obvious-after-the-fact issues due to lack of fit between their laboratory setting and the work situation of the users. A first important step toward bridging the gap is to get the users themselves into the design process; but it is not enough. As long as the users don't experience what it would be like to work with a system under development, their contributions will mainly be based on prejudice, that is, on prejudgment.

In the above-mentioned EuroCoOp project, one of the tools being developed was a distributed hypermedia. When the hypermedia-idea was first introduced to the end users, the reaction was "well, this is probably a nice concept, but we can't use it—all our archives, and our related work, are based on keywords and keyword search." It was only as the project developed, and they were allowed to jointly evolve their understanding of hypermedia and of working with hypermedia, that they were able to see how their work might be supported by hypermedia, to see where hypermedia could be beneficial and where it should not be used.

It is thus important to create a worklike context for exercising an emerging design—one that doesn't force mediation through description upon the users, but allows them to be and *act* as end users, to simulate use of the merging design, and in this way draw on their tacit, nonexplicit knowledge in the process. But even then, when the users are active in the design loop, great care has to be taken in creating effective contexts for the design work. Just as artificial lab settings create problems, artificially delimited work settings and tasks may do so, as illustrated in the following.

Another example is taken from a project developing prototypes to explore possibilities for computer support at the technical department of a municipal office [2]. The session in question involved the use of a prototype containing different types of maps, mainly organized hierarchically, and textual information about buildings that were also represented at the lower levels of the map hierarchies. The previous paper-based system had required the office workers to go via a textual database to find the code for the detailed building information, and then to use this code as the key to the actual information. The new concept, supported by the prototype, was hierarchical, map-based search.

During the session, where an architect from the technical department was using the prototype to do some work in his office, it turned out that going down through the map hierarchy to find a specific building and the associated information was indeed considered efficient. Now, let us for a moment imagine that a closed set of evaluation tasks had been specified in advance by the designers. They might then have described a set of tasks corresponding to the number of different types of information contained in the prototype, and left it at that. If this had been the case, then the conclusion would have been as just indicated—that the proposed method of finding detailed information worked effectively. However, this conclusion would have been wrong. What turned out later in the session was that the hierarchical search was indeed considered effective, but only the first time. That is, if the employee wanted to find the detailed map of a specific building, a map that the employee had worked with recently, the expectation was that this should be faster and more direct than going down through the hierarchy. This expectation was easily accommodated once the problem had been noted.[2]

4.2 COOPERATIVE DESIGN

Inspired by examples such as the ones described above, we have, over the last decades, developed a number of design techniques under the label of *Cooperative Design* [6, 12]. Basic to this work is a view of design as a cooperative activity involving different groups of people with important, but different competencies. Since neither professional designers nor end users can fully understand each others' practices or meanings, we must actively bring these experiences closer together,

---

[2]One could also argue that even if a set of predefined evaluation tasks *included* refinding a previously used map, the result could still have been wrong: The architect in a lab setting doing the test cases might simply be satisfied that the second time a map must be found, he or she can do it a bit quicker, because now it is known exactly where on the screen the specific building will show up on the overview map. This might happen if the lab setting doesn't give sufficient clues as reminder of the work context, but leaves a focus on the prototype.

with the aim of jointly creating both new computer applications and a design process that makes sense to all those involved. Where traditional system development methods treat specific work tasks as formalizable data processing done by individuals, communicating via data channels, our approach sees groups interacting in a multitude of ways within complex organizational contexts. Where traditional methods treat descriptions of these work tasks as the primary input from the work context to the design process, our approach is based on the belief that the complex texture of workplace life should be handled primarily through action-based techniques. Such tools and techniques must encourage users to bring their knowledge and skill to bear on design, without forcing on them mediation through explicit description. In order to support this kind of creative end-user participation in the design processes themselves, we have developed techniques based on mockups, prototypes, and scenarios. The aim is to envision and simulate future use situations in order to allow end users to *experience* what it would be like to work with the system under development and thereby to draw on their tacit, nonexplicit knowledge and experience. This knowledge and experience is not brought into play when the user reads a description or watches a demonstration by a designer. It does not exist inside the heads of the users, but unfolds in the context of work, in the use relation, when the users are confronted with the work at hand.

4.3 SPECIFIC INQUIRIES: GROUNDING DESIGN WORK

At the heart of our approach to design is an insistence on the specific as the primary source of new insight. When involved in in-house projects, like the development of a new archive system for a specific trade school, this is probably not so surprising. But we consider the specific equally important when developing new technology and work organization for general-purpose newspaper production or new off-the-shelf hypertext products. Also in such cases our main source of new ideas is working with possible changes at specific, existing (i.e., nonfictional) workplaces [13].

The main arguments for grounding design work in specific situations have already been hinted at earlier. First, concreteness is needed to allow the users to exercise their expertise. Their skill is not in evaluating abstract specifications, but in working in specific contexts. And in order for them to contribute to the design process with this expertise, we need to create specific, worklike contexts, scenarios. Second, we need to ground these scenarios in existing situations at real workplaces. This grounding of scenarios serves two important purposes. The first is to support real-world references. This implies, for instance, that when breakdowns of simulated future work occur, due to an underspecified scenario, we are usually able to discuss modifications of the scenario by referring to the reality behind the scenario, such as the three or four situations encountered during analysis that were the major inspiration.

The second main argument for grounding our design contexts in situations from existing workplaces is that in this way we avoid the blindness created by designers choosing test cases without the application area, the reality, to which these cases belong fighting back. To reiterate: In an artificial lab setting it is unlikely that the problems with permissions in relation to the cut & paste facility discussed earlier will surface, even if users are involved. The designers will not know that there is a difference in roles and permissions between the lab and the work setting, and the users will not find out that the difference matters.

This concludes my introductory discussion of cooperative design. In the next section I present the design process from one of our recent projects: the different cooperative techniques, their relationships, and the design artifacts employed. This creates some concrete reference points for the main section of the chapter: a presentation and discussion of our design artifacts with a focus on the creation of concrete worklike contexts for cooperative design activities. This chapter concludes with a discussion of some implications for roles in cooperative design.

4.4 A COOPERATIVE DESIGN PROCESS: THE EUROCOOP/GREAT BELT CASE

The EuroCoOp project concerns the development of four generic, interrelated CSCW applications/systems including a coordination tool and a hypermedia. The four systems were developed by four loosely coordinated groups, where the one developing the hypermedia was from the University of Aarhus (UA). The UA group was the only one with previous experience from cooperative design. Thus the University of Aarhus was also responsible for organizing the cooperation between the design teams and the end users, including the work on creating the design context. All four teams had decided to cooperate with the company Great Belt Link Ltd. (GBL). This is a Danish state-owned company responsible for the building of a bridge/tunnel between Zealand and Funen, a project that involves the world's largest suspension bridge.

Figure 4.1 outlines the main types of design activities with a focus on the cooperation between end users and professional designers; see [6] for more details about the techniques referred to in Figure 4.1. In between the outlined main activities, designers and implementors were working on technical development activities and documentation. The

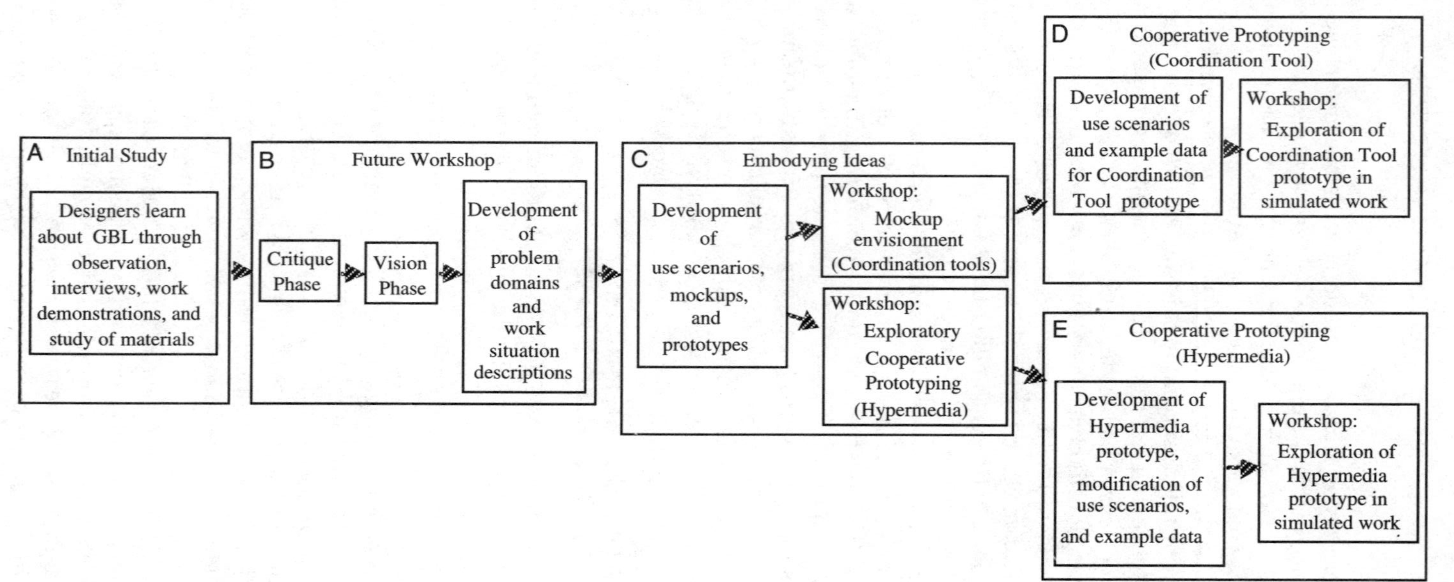

Figure 4.1. Cooperative design activities.

designers also had several informal contacts with the end users at GBL. The design activities spread over a two-year period, and approximately 10 developers and 20 users were involved. The prototypes developed are currently being turned into general products by some of the industrial partners in the project.

4.4.1 Sequence and Preunderstanding

With respect to Figure 4.1, it should be noted that it represents a post hoc account made in order to support presentation and discussion—the sequentiality of the real project was obviously more blurred. However, the sequence in which we *began* the activities is accurately reflected. But the designers' understanding of the work of the users didn't stop developing when the Future Workshop began, and in this sense the study (Figure 4.1A) continued. In other situations more direct iteration was involved, as when the work situation descriptions used in preparing the workshops on embodying ideas (Figure 4.1C) were revised for use in later workshops (Figure 4.1D and E). Such revisions usually imply revisiting the workplace. Another aspect of this sequence is that it reflects the primary direction of influence: Use scenarios, for example, are developed on the basis of work situation descriptions and in general build on the understanding developed in the initial study. However, the emerging understanding of possibilities for support, that is, the forerunner of explicit use scenarios, is also important in shaping the work situations through directing focus to specific aspects at the expense of others.

Similarly, the preunderstanding of possibilities for support plays an important role in shaping the initial study. Finally, the most direct coupling is between use scenarios on the one hand and mockups and prototypes on the other. Major changes to one of these usually imply, or rather inspire, changes to the other. And if one of the two is developed too far without paying attention to the other, the project is at risk.

Moving from initial study (Figure 4.1A) toward simulation of future work (Figure 4.1C, D, and E) calls for a creation of a narrower focus on specific areas and specific situations. This may be facilitated in different ways. In the EuroCoOp project we used Future Workshops (Figure 4.1B) in order to generate the specific problem domains forming the basis for subsequent design activities. Other possibilities include metaphorical design [10]. The design artifacts resulting from these activities are, for example, work situation descriptions. At the same time, ideas for use scenarios and computer support begin to take form. The work situation descriptions are then used in developing these ideas, on the one hand, into use scenarios that sketch possible future uses of computer support, and on the other, into concrete mockups and prototypes with example data to be used in simulating such future use (Figure 4.1C).

4.4.2 Contextual Design Artifacts

In order to do cooperative design as described above, and particularly to create the future worklike situations, we develop a number of contextual design artifacts. In the following I illustrate and discuss these artifacts, using the EuroCoOp project outlined in Figure 4.1 as an example. Listed in approximately the sequence in which we began working with them in that project, these design artifacts are:

- Reminders of initial study: key insights, summaries, etc. (Figure 4.1A).
- Work situation descriptions and work situation overviews (Figure 4.1B).
- Use scenarios (Figure 4.1C, D, and E).
- Mockups and prototypes with example data (Figure 4.1C, D, and E).

In addition to these cooperative design artifacts we use two other types of scenarios:

- Exploration/requirement scenarios.
- Explanation scenarios.

In the following I present and discuss these artifacts with a focus on the creation of concrete worklike context.

Reminders of Initial Study: Key Insights and Summaries These are descriptions created during the initial study of the work of the end users. They function as pointers to particular, important situations, and they summarize the way that work in the organization in question is interpreted by the design team. Often the reminders are parts of a proper analysis report, with organizational diagrams, appendixes with copies of forms, letters, minutes, and so forth, but their value is not directly related to the degree to which they minutely describe the work. Their primary function is to support the members of the design team, both professional designers and participating end users, in evolving their understanding of the work of the end users, not in the abstract, but in the field of tension between the technical intentions of the professional designers and the organizational or work-oriented needs of the end users. Often this tension results in a very focused understanding

The GBL organization is characterized by extensive use of computers to support different aspects of work. The computer systems are used in two different ways in the organization. On the one hand, a few large systems are used to support vertical information flow between different organizational levels and registration of data about the bridge (mainly drawings and quality documentation) and the building process (mainly plans and economy data) in large databases. On the other hand, PCs and off-the-shelf software are used by individuals for text processing, calculations, and the like. The computer systems do not, however, support horizontal information flow (except for e-mail), sharing of materials, and planning/monitoring of activities in daily work. The horizontal information flow and sharing of materials are currently accomplished by circulating multiple hard copies of documents among the personnel who need access to the documents. Each person maintains personal archives of relevant materials. In the planning and monitoring of daily work activities, three kinds of manual systems are maintained: a meeting calendar for the next week is distributed in each section, in Prefabrication so-called Action lists and Completed lists are maintained to keep track of the status of ongoing cases, in Progress Monitoring a set of standard request forms are used every month to request comments from the supervisors on the monthly progress report.

Figure 4.2. Initial study summary.

that, to the participants, summarizes key insights of the analysis. In the EuroCoOp project described above such insight was summarized in Figure 4.2.[3]

On one hand, the description in Figure 4.2 is a straightforward summary of the situation regarding computer use at GBL. To those involved in the project, however, it summarized an important shift in focus from the so-called vertical systems to the need for horizontal support. To better understand this, let's look at the situation at the beginning of the project. At this point in time, the first version of the vertical systems was almost in place. These were mainly developed by contract, and thus represented a huge investment both in money and, as it turned out, in time. They were considered to address the most important needs of the organization and to be very advanced, as opposed to the off-the-

[3]Since the original text produced during the project created some ambiguity for readers of drafts of this chapter, the text in Figure 4.2 has been modified slightly. The original text read: "The GBL organization is characterized by extensive use of computers to support different aspects of work. The computer systems are used at two levels in the organization. On the one hand, a few large systems are used to support vertical information flow in the organization. . . ."

shelf software, and thus more interesting. These and other factors had resulted in a situation where the *computer-support-focus* of the organization was on the vertical systems. Consequently, these systems, and the related work, consumed a lot of effort in the initial study—the implicit assumption being that the next logical step would be to improve upon these systems, or at least cater to supplementary *vertical needs*. The realization of the comprehensive need for improved *horizontal* support was a rather slow process.

Work Situation Descriptions and Work Situation Overviews These are descriptions of relevant, existing situations within the users' workplace. Here the word relevant indicates that users find that these situations are important parts of their work and that currently they constitute a bottleneck, are error prone, or for other reasons need to be changed. With respect to the designers the relevance criterion indicates that the kind of technology they are considering may potentially support the work in question. Work situations are first encountered through in-depth studies of the workplace of the users. Later, in a focus activity, specific work situations are selected and descriptions elaborated (Figure 4.1B). A brief example of a work situation overview from the EuroCoOp project is given in Figure 4.3.

The work situation overviews and work situation descriptions are to be understood on the basis of the insight generated in the initial study. Thus, on the one hand, the Archiving work situation overview is

---

Beside the registration in the Journal system, the regular correspondence, such as letters and faxes, is copied and archived. Photocopies are made for a journal archive and for each of the persons who are on the distribution list for the type of document being treated. In addition, the original letters are stored in a main archive sorted by date. In the journal archive the copies of letters are sorted by category number and then by date. But since most of the correspondence is with the contractor, ESG (and ESG is one category), the journal archive boils down to a copy of the main archive. In conjunction with the central archiving, a number of the individual sections such as the Prefabrication Supervision stores copies of letters in local archives. The special correspondence such as Quality documentation, drawings, and plan revisions are entered into the Quality Control system, KIS, the Drawing Management System (DMS), and the time planning system, Artemis, respectively, and this correspondence is archived by the responsible departments.

Figure 4.3. Archiving (work situation overview).

'just' a description of that, of archiving at GBL. On the other hand, the reasons for selecting archiving, for delimiting it, and for describing it the way it is done in Figure 4.3, are tied to the understanding generated in the initial study, and pointed to as in the initial study summary in Figure 4.2. In the GBL case there were hundreds of different work situations that could have been selected. Indeed, the original vertical focus of the initial study made the situation in Figure 4.3 almost invisible, at the expense of work situations related to vertical information needs. But once the understanding of the horizontal needs surfaced in the design team, work situations like the ones covered by Figure 4.3 became visible almost everywhere—literally, when we subsequently visited the user organization, GBL, but also in the ongoing discussions of past experiences.

Around work situation overviews, such as Figure 4.3, problems and bottlenecks are discussed and formulated. In relation to archiving at GBL these included: redundant archiving, handling different types of materials, and refinding materials.

The text in Figure 4.4 was actually written down rather late in the process. It was done in order to keep a record of the reasoning in the design group, one that could be used to convey this reasoning to outsiders. For the design group itself—the professional designers and the participating end users—the reasoning was so much a part of the ongoing activities that a written record wasn't needed. Every now and then, during the discussions of problems and bottlenecks that we wanted to address, someone would refer to a version of refinding as described in Figure 4.4.

The second major use of work situation descriptions and overviews, and the related problems and bottlenecks, is in the process of developing use scenarios and mockups. In fact, the description in Figure 4.4 indicates that the designers making the description had some kind of hypermedia system in mind. Such bias is unavoidable; the technical background of designers will always shape the way they view possibilities for support, but once this bias is realized, explicit measures can be taken to broaden the technical scope, if this is considered important.

The work situation descriptions and overviews function primarily as reminders, that is, they record and support understanding in the design group and, in doing so, they play a role in the continued development of that understanding. They are, however, not intended to be so detailed as to be a self-contained, independent source for developing, for example, use scenarios.

For the users of these design artifacts—the end users and the professional designers—adding detail would not be an improvement, since

---

The possibilities for refinding materials naturally depends on what archive is in question: In refinding correspondence one can search by date and category in the paper-based archives; in the Journal system one can also search by keywords; the refinding of drawings in DMS can be done by search on names and numbers; all the materials archived locally can be refound by the key according to which they are archived. In general, provided one has (parts of) the proper key, refinding is easy. Very often, though, this is not the case.

A typical task for a Supervisor has the form of a case, denoted an "action," such as assessment of a Quality Control form, handling of a nonconformance report, handling of a change-request, etc. These are all mostly initiated by a letter from ESG (the contractor). The information needed is of the form:

- Any similar cases from the past?
- Previous correspondence concerning this issue?
- Pictures of this or similar parts of the bridge?
- Notes concerning this issue?
- Videos concerning the applied procedure?
- Drawings of the part of the bridge in question?
- Any correspondence from GBL or CCL to ESG concerning this issue?

In these cases, the refinding of materials is not easy. First, the proper key to the proper archive is seldom present. Second, if the keys are present, it is rather cumbersome to find the material in (many) different archives in different locations.

Figure 4.4. Refinding (work situation overview).

they have the background from the initial study. For design artifact users without this background, adding enough detail is not possible. Professional designers have to themselves participate in at least parts of the initial study, and end users need work experience from the organization in question, or a similar one. Without such personal access to the reality behind the design artifacts it is not possible to go beyond the understanding already reflected in the artifacts. They become a confinement, and eventually may contribute to the kind of development process where stated requirements are met, but with a mediocre system and to the dissatisfaction of the users.

Use Scenarios, Mockups, and Prototypes with Example Data Based on work situation descriptions and overviews a number of use scenarios are developed in parallel with the design of the computer support itself in terms of mockups and prototypes. A brief example of a use scenario from the EuroCoOp project is given in Figure 4.5. The scenario covers the work situation overview of Figure 4.3.

Use scenarios indicate how computer support and (or) changes in work organization may improve upon work situations. Where work situation descriptions and overviews are about existing situations, use scenarios describe future possibilities. As illustrated in Figure 4.5 these scenarios presuppose certain qualities of the computer support, and in this sense they also give some indication of requirements and thus re-

---

The hypermedia services should be available to all GBL personnel in the WAN subject to suitable access restrictions. Due to performance requirements, separate link servers for each LAN are needed, but it should be possible to link across LANs.

A Journal system is an integrated part of the hypermedia. The secretaries currently responsible for registering correspondence become responsible for entering letters, faxes, change requests, and nonconformance reports into the hypermedia network. As a supplement and partly a substitute for registering keywords, they establish initial sets of public links between new and existing materials in the hypermedia. When, for example, an incoming letter is a response to a letter already stored in the network, a "Refer-to"- link is established between them.

Instead of having secretaries photocopy incoming materials for manual distribution and filing in several local archives, the entry of material into the hypermedia (e.g., by scanning) should imply automatic notifications to personnel subscribing to that type of material. This procedure requires less photocopying, but probably more printers for enabling people to get hard copies quickly. Photocopies of certain materials may be made for a few persons who have to print anyway.

Other personnel can immediately inspect materials in the system. They can follow links made during "journalization," add links to existing materials, and annotate materials, thus sharing their reactions with others.

For instance, when a supervisor gets the responsibility for carrying out an action, he or she may want to find all earlier correspondence and notes regarding this matter. Assuming existing materials were entered and interlinked during earlier work on the case, the relevant materials could be accessed directly by following links. Semiautomatic gathering of materials from the hypermedia is supported by browsers of nodes and links with certain characteristics. Specifying a linearization of subsets of nodes for making printouts should also be supported.

Figure 4.5. Archiving (use scenario).

semble the use cases of Jacobson (Chapter 12). But our use scenarios are not fixed requirements; rather, they represent hypotheses to be evaluated through workshops—and further revised and developed. Our use scenarios don't make sense in themselves. Concepts like *"Refer-to"-links, public links, automatic notification*, and *subscribing* in Figure 4.5 are understood through the mockups or prototypes realizing them. Thus, we don't develop our use scenarios *before* our mockups and prototypes, but concurrent with them.

While use scenarios presuppose certain qualities of the computer support, they don't describe interfaces or prescribe sequences of operations. Interfaces are mainly presented through the mockups and prototypes themselves, and the sequences unfold in the workshops when the prototypes are actually used (Figure 4.1C, D, and E). Thus the main function of the use scenarios is really that they set the stage for how end users in these workshops use mockups and prototypes. The scenarios are understood based on the workplace of which they are a part—and they draw on the understanding that end users and professional designers have developed so far. Some aspects of this understanding are reflected in the above-mentioned work situation descriptions. Other, equally important aspects, concern the end-users' understanding of new technical possibilities. Thus, in the example in Figure 4.5 it is crucial that the end users, for whom the scenario is setting the stage for simulation of future work, have acquired a working understanding of hypermedia. If not, concepts like *link-server*, *public links*, and *follow links*, as well as *automatic notification* and *subscribing*, don't make sense.

Such understanding is most effectively developed through working with hypermedia prototypes in envisionment workshops (Figure 4.1C), where we introduce the use of scenarios, which in turn presupposes this understanding of hypermedia. Thus, what happens is that the first time the end users are confronted with use scenarios, such as the one in Figure 4.5, and begin working with a prototype, they have only a partial understanding, which is then developed through the different cooperative design workshops.

In these workshops the users are confronted with mockups and prototypes. They simulate work, and through this process they experience possibilities and limitations of the current design. When a breakdown occurs, the specific actions that led to it form the basis for discussions of the situation and how to remedy it. Other elements in such discussions are the mockup/prototype itself and the existing understanding of the space possibilities and limitations among users and designers.

Figure 4.6 shows part of our first hypermedia prototype from the

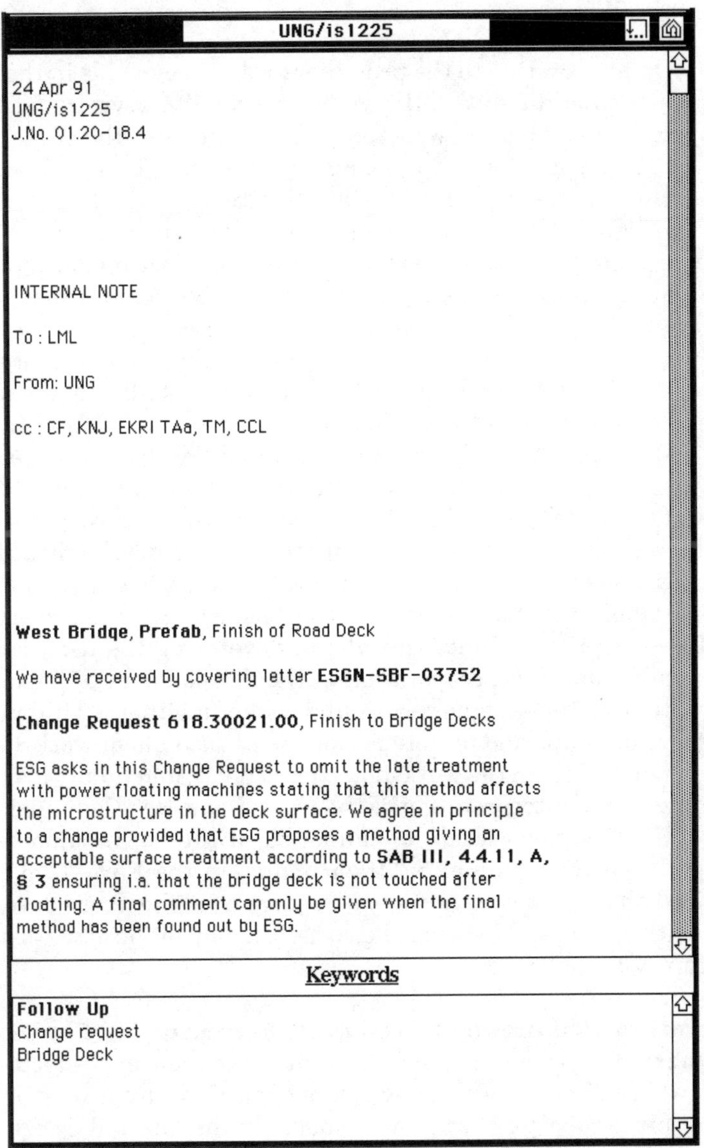

UNG/is1225

24 Apr 91
UNG/is1225
J.No. 01.20-18.4

INTERNAL NOTE

To : LML

From: UNG

cc : CF, KNJ, EKRI TAa, TM, CCL

West Bridge, Prefab, Finish of Road Deck

We have received by covering letter **ESGN-SBF-03752**

Change Request 618.30021.00, Finish to Bridge Decks

ESG asks in this Change Request to omit the late treatment with power floating machines stating that this method affects the microstructure in the deck surface. We agree in principle to a change provided that ESG proposes a method giving an acceptable surface treatment according to **SAB III, 4.4.11, A, § 3** ensuring i.a. that the bridge deck is not touched after floating. A final comment can only be given when the final method has been found out by ESG.

Keywords

Follow Up
Change request
Bridge Deck

Note: The bold chunks of the text represent anchors with attached links. The Keywords field is used to add keywords as in the current Journal system. In addition, keywords can also be anchors for linking. The buttons in the top-right corner are used to return to the last visited node or the startup node for the system.

Figure 4.6. The appearance of an internal note letter in the hypermedia prototype.

EuroCoOp project. Due to the prominent role of keywords in the established work procedures at GBL we incorporated a keyword feature in the hypermedia. This allowed the end users to use the prototype to compare their usual way of working with new and different possibilities—including the ones illustrated in Figure 4.5 and other scenarios.

What happens at the workshops starts from the scenarios and the mockups or prototypes, but how the workshops develop depends more on the participating end users, their work, and the organization in which they are embedded. In this sense the use scenarios are *open ended.* They are interpreted by the participants mainly through reference to the work of the users, and changed as the understanding of the participants develops through the workshops.

It is therefore crucial that end users and developers cooperate in developing the use scenarios. User participation in making them is needed to provide knowledge of the demands that the work places on computer support. And user participation in the development of use scenarios also provides the users with valuable understanding of technical possibilities. Participation of designers is needed in order to provide the necessary technical insight in developing the use scenarios. But equally important, cooperation in the development of the use scenarios provides the designers with understanding that is vital in order to prepare mockups and prototypes for the envisionment workshops, in order to participate in the workshops themselves, and finally in order to cooperate in the interpretation of the workshops. Reading the descriptions of the situations/scenarios cannot substitute for the understanding developed through making them. Thus, in the EuroCoOp project described above end users and key designers from the teams developing coordination tools and hypermedia cooperated in all the activities listed in Figure 4.1.

Exploration/Requirement Scenarios: Scenarios for Professional Designers The scenarios discussed so far have been open ended, and of a kind where, for example, sequences of operations are usually left out, that is, left to the users at the workshops. In the internal design work, which involves only the professional designers, we use a different kind: exploration/requirement scenarios. These are rather abstract in the sense that they don't depend on explicit references to specific situations or even specific workplaces. They are also much more detailed than work situation descriptions and use scenarios. The reason is that these exploration/requirement scenarios are intended to supply the use-details needed for discussing whether current technical capabilities meet the requirements of the scenario. They are thus intended to be closed, not to need external references to specific organizations to be useful. On the other hand, the major point in formulating these as scenarios, is that this makes it relatively straightforward to maintain a connection between the work situations and use scenarios that inspired the requirement scenario and that scenario itself, and in this way keep the design on track and prevent the development of technical solutions to irrelevant problems. Thus one of our aims in using this scenario form for requirements is to keep a trace of the design rationale, a pointer to the situations that inspired the requirements, and in this way constitute some of the reasons for the requirement. See MacLean & McKerlie and Rossen & Carroll (Chapters 8 and 10) for related discussions of design rationale. Figure 4.7 presents an example of such a requirement scenario from the EuroCoOp project. It was written by Kaj Grønbæk as a contribution to the design of the locking mechanism in an object-oriented database used to store hypermedia documents.

At the time when the scenario was written, we had been working on low-level mechanisms for support of cooperation based on sharing of material. We had developed a set of concepts and realized these in our

---

U1 and U2 have started a session on the same hypertext H1. U1 has opened the text component C1 with read lock, and U2 has opened it with a write lock. They both set the immediate update preference on C1. U2 is making changes to C1, but hasn't committed any changes, hence U1's view of C1 has not been updated for a while. U1 attempts to create a public link from some region of C1 to a region of text component C2, and when trying to commit the addition of the link U1 receives the message: "U2 is currently having a write lock on C1! Do you want to request a temporary linking access to C1? OK, CANCEL." U1 says OK. U2 receives the message: "Are you willing to commit your changes and let U1 create a link with C1 as an endpoint? OK, NO." U2 answers OK, and performs a save. U1's view of C1 is immediately updated with U2's changes. This implies that U1's selection of a region for the new link is canceled, because this selection may not be correct after U2's changes to C1. U1 makes a new selection for link creation, creates the link, commits the link creation, this commit turns over the write lock to U2 again, and U2's view is immediately updated.

Comment: This scenario is inspired by Randy's comment. I think this scenario raises some new questions about locks. U2 maintains a "reservation" of the write lock on C1 while U1 temporarily accesses the anchors list with a write lock. Can we implement that on top of the current OODB lock mechanisms?

Figure 4.7. Simultaneous linking with a mix of read/write locks (requirements scenario).

prototype, including one called *cooperative transactions*. This was a type of transaction that allowed several people to work on and share changes to hypermedia documents without committing these changes to the database. The situations behind the scenario described in Figure 4.7 had originally been thought of as belonging to this *cooperative transaction category*, but we were now exploring alternatives. By drawing on our understanding of work at GBL as a source of inspiration and subsequently as a yardstick—together with the usual technical criteria, such as simplicity and effectiveness—we developed scenarios such as the one in Figure 4.7, and through these achieved effective guidance in the design space. Compared with the use scenarios, requirement scenarios are more closed. Where use scenarios set the stage for future activities at a workshop, requirement scenarios take their point of departure in a known situation. They are intended to adequately reflect situations that we want our software to support, and then to function as discussion tools in the process of understanding and developing the concepts of the software design, not primarily of the work situation. However, the basis for understanding and using such scenarios is the technical understanding of the software being developed *and* some insight into the work situations and user organization that originally inspired the scenario.

Explanation Scenarios The last type of design artifacts that we consider are explanation scenarios. These explain new possibilities for support using terms related to work situation descriptions and use scenarios. Like exploration/requirement scenarios they are more abstract and more detailed than use scenarios. They are produced later in the design process than use scenarios, typically when the audience, the end users and the professional designers, have acquired a good understanding of possibilities for support as well as of concrete solutions—often as a follow-up on requirement scenarios. The explanation scenarios record some of the hypothesizing involved in developing specific aspects of a system/tool, and thus preserve the hypothesis for later inclusion in one or more use scenarios and workshops.

In the explanation scenario of Figure 4.8 we could obviously have used names from the GBL setting to make the scenario more concrete. However, the sequence of events is hypothesized, and in order not to mislead the reader into believing that we are actually giving an account of events that transpired at GBL we use the abstract terms of Figure 4.8. The point is that we can't just check the validity of a scenario like the one in Figure 4.8 by means of analysis or discussion—the only feasible path is via a workshop simulating future work using the computer support described.

The larger issue of cooperation support has led to the design of special notification mechanisms to support cooperation awareness in the hypermedia system. An example of the use of notifications in a GBL setting is the following: The supervisor S1 has asked another supervisor S2 to help him with some information on a Change Request that S1 is responsible for handling. S1 and S2 have each started a session on the hyperdocument CR. S2 has started writing an internal note IN, which is linked to some of the existing nodes in CR. S2 has obtained a write lock on the IN hypermedia component. S1 has opened IN with read access and set a preference in the editor asking to receive immediate updates when IN is changed by other users. Setting this preference makes the hypermedia automatically subscribe to notifications on all changes to IN. The hypermedia editor that handles IN will then make an update of the editor's contents from the most recent version of IN represented in the OODB whenever it receives a change notification. This way S1 will always have the most updated version of S2's internal note IN in a window on the screen. This kind of immediate update is particularly useful when the deadline for handling the Change Request is only a few days away. A different use of basically the same notification mechanism is provided by setting a preference in the editor that directs a log of changes to a console.

Figure 4.8. Cooperation awareness (explanation scenario).

Design Artifact Summary To support understanding of the artifacts and their use as described above, a summary is presented in Table 4.1. Like all such summaries it is a bit simplistic.

4.4.3 Concrete Implications

This ends the presentation of design artifacts for the creation of concrete, worklike contexts for design. The focus in this presentation has been on the artifacts used by the design group—the end users and professional designers, including analysts and implementors. The importance of concrete examples, however, extends beyond the design group, and I briefly present a few examples of this in the following. Finally I discuss some implications for roles in design.

As already mentioned, descriptions of problems and bottlenecks, like the one in Figure 4.4, are useful in presentations, for example, at external reviews. At another level there is the question of *teaching* cooperative design, to students of computer science and similar disciplines, to practitioners of design, and to end users. Also in such situations we apply an approach based on concrete cases, which we introduce

Table 4.1 Design Artifact Summary

Design Artifact:	*Description:*	*Produced in or as a Result of:*	*Produced by (typically):*	*Used in:*	*Used by (primarily):*
Reminders of initial study	summarize the way current work in the organization is interpreted by the design team	initial study (Fig. 4.1A)	designers	focus activities, e.g., Future Workshops (Fig. 4.1B)	designers and end users
Work situation descriptions and work situation overviews	describe relevant, *existing* situations, within the users' workplace	focus activities, e.g., Future Workshops (Fig. 4.1B)	designers	development of use scenarios and mockup/prototypes (Fig. 4.1C, D, E)	designers and end users
Use scenarios	indicate how computer support and (or) changes in work organization in the future may improve upon work situations, and set the stage for simulation at workshops	embodying ideas and workshop preparations, (Fig. 4.1C, D, E)	designers and end users	workshops (Fig. 4.1C,D, E)	end users
Mockups and prototypes with example data	artifacts supporting hands-on experience through simulation of future work in the user organization	embodying ideas and workshop preparations (Fig. 4.1C, D, E)	designers and end users	workshops (Fig. 4.1C, D, E)	end users
Exploration/ requirement scenarios	detailed scenarios supplying the use-details needed for discussing whether current technical capabilities meet the requirements of the scenario	explorations of capabilities of existing software designs	designers	discussions of capabilities of existing software designs	designers
Explanation scenarios	explain/hypothesize about new possibilities for support with the current prototypes using terms related to work situation descriptions and use scenarios	work on prototype design	designers	development of use scenarios and proto-types (Fig. 4.1E)	designers and end users

and discuss based on material such as the descriptions in this chapter. And there is the question of how to promote this way of working, not only with design projects, but in general as an approach to changing organizations, partially through the use of technology. Concrete examples play a prominent role in most of our writings, since understanding the importance of paying attention to the specific situation is basic in our approach and—as experience shows—difficult to grasp.

In a new attempt to create pedagogical material presenting the steps involving work situation descriptions and use scenarios above, we are currently working on a new approach for organizations that considers introducing computer support in the CSCW area. This approach supports investigations carried out by people in the organization itself. The material presents the concepts of work situation description and use scenario together with those of work and technology checklists and a number of so-called technology scenarios. The latter illustrate concrete uses of a spectrum of CSCW systems in order to provide some initial understanding of technical possibilities and limitations, whereas the checklists are intended to help structure the initial steps in analyzing work situations and developing use scenarios for the organization in question. The presentations are done through a combination of concrete examples and descriptions of elements of techniques.

From Proxy to Facilitator Finally we consider the implications for roles in design projects using the artifacts and techniques discussed above. The emphasis on concrete situations and the experience generated through hands-on simulation of future work imply that it is necessary to involve both end users and designers in the preparations, in the conduct of workshops, and in the interpretation of workshop results. Thus the role of user proxy—suggested by Hughes, Randall, and Shapiro [9]—is not available. Marketing people, HCI specialists, ethnographers, or user managers cannot make the user-contributions in design mainly because they don't have the knowledge needed to go beyond the insights established prior to the activity where they are supposed to act as proxy. Neither can HCI- or evaluation-specialists act as designer proxies during envisionment workshops. Often they lack the insight into the design needed to cooperate on changes together with the users, and, even more important, they cannot convey the relevant aspects of workshops to the designers after the fact. But that doesn't mean that this kind of cooperative design leaves no room for others besides end users and hard-core designers. Design as described above, doing initial analysis, developing work situation descriptions and use scenarios, preparing mockups for specific envisionment, and conducting workshops requires specific skills that are difficult and time-consuming to develop. Often designers, and obviously end users, lack such skills. Thus, cooperative design definitely needs facilitators, people skilled in working with the different kinds of design representations and in involving both users and designers in the cooperative activities; people who can convince designers, end users, and managers of the benefits of working cooperatively; in particular, people who can organize the workshops where mockups and prototypes of new design are tried out by end users in worklike settings.

ACKNOWLEDGMENTS

Thanks to Jack Carroll for suggesting that this chapter be written, and to Jack, Olav Bertelsen, Susanne Bødker, Tom Ericksson, John Karat, Mike Robinson, and Mary Beth Rossen for insightful and stimulating comments on earlier drafts.

REFERENCES

[1] Bødker, S., Ehn, P., Kammersgaard, J., Kyng, M. & Sundblad, Y. (1987). A Utopian experience. In G. Bjerknes, P. Ehn & M. Kyng (eds.): *Computers and Democracy—A Scandinavian Challenge.* Aldershot U.K.: Avebury, Gower Publishing Company Ltd.

[2] Bødker, S. & Grønbæk, K. (1991). Cooperative prototyping: Users and designers in mutual activity. *International Journal of Man-Machine Studies, 34,* Special Issue on CSCW.

[3] Ehn, P. (1989). *Work-Oriented Design of Computer Artifacts.* Hillsdale, NJ: Lawrence Erlbaum.

[4] Ehn, P. & Kyng, M. (1987). The collective resource approach to system design. In G. Bjerknes, P. Ehn & M. Kyng (eds.), *Computers and Democracy—A Scandinavian Challenge.* Aldershot, U.K.: Avebury, pp. 17–57.

[5] Ehn, P. & Kyng, M. (1991). Cardboard computers: Mocking-it-up or hands-on the future. In J. Greenbaum & M. Kyng (eds.), *Design at Work: Cooperative Design of Computer Systems.* Hillsdale, NJ: Lawrence Erlbaum.

[6] Greenbaum, J. & Kyng, M. (eds.). (1991). *Design at Work: Cooperative Design of Computer Systems.* Hillsdale, NJ: Lawrence Erlbaum.

[7] Grudin, J. (1991). Systematic sources of suboptimal interface design in large product development organizations. *Human-Computer Interaction, 6*(2), 147–196.

[8] Grønbæk, K., Kyng, M. & Mogensen, P. (1993). CSCW challenges in large-scale technical projects—A case study. In *Proceedings of CSCW '92,* November 1992. (Also in CACM, June 1993.)

[9] Hughes, J. A., Randall, D. & Shapiro, D. (1993). From ethnographic record to system design. *Computer Supported Cooperative Work, 1*(3).

[10] Kensing & Madsen (1991). Generating visions: Future workshops and metaphorical design. In J. Greenbaum & M. Kyng (eds.), *Design at Work: Cooperative Design of Computer Systems*. Hillsdale, NJ: Lawrence Erlbaum.

[11] Kyng, M. (1988). Designing for a dollar a day. *Office: Technology and People, 4*, 157–170.

[12] Kyng, M. (1991). Designing for cooperation—Cooperating in design. *Communications of the ACM, 34*(12), 64–73.

[13] Kyng, M. (1994). Scandinavian design: Users in product development. In B. Adelson, S. Dumais & J. Olson (eds.), *Celebrating Interdependence, Conference Proceedings CHI '94.* Boston: ACM Press, pp. 3–9.

[14] Kyng, M. in cooperation with Greenbaum, J. (1991). Cooperative design: Bringing together the practices of users and designers. In H.-E. Nissen, H. K. Klein & R. Hirschheim (eds.), *The Information Systems Research Arena of the 90's.* Amsterdam: North-Holland.

[15] Kyng, M. & Mathiassen, L. (1982). Systems development and trade union activities. In N. Bjørn-Andersen (ed.), *Information Society, for Richer, for Poorer.* Amsterdam: North-Holland.

[16] Kyng, M. & Mogensen, P. (1992). EuroCoOp workpackage WP1 task T1.3: Evaluation of EuroCoOp prototypes re work at A/S Storebæltsforbindelsen (Great Belt Link Ltd.). ECO-AU-92-13. Aarhus, Denmark: Computer Science Department, University of Aarhus.

[17] Muller, M. (1991). Participatory design in Britain and North America: Responding to the "Scandinavian Challenge." In S. P. Robertson, G. M. Olson & J. S. Olson (eds.), *Reaching through Technology, CHI '91 Conference Proceedings,* New Orleans, April 28–May 2. New York: ACM Press, pp. 389–392.

[18] Norman, D. A. & Draper, S. W. (eds.). (1986). *User Centered System Design—New Perspectives on Human Computer Interaction.* Hillsdale, NJ: Lawrence Erlbaum.

[19] Schuler, D. & Namioka, A. (eds.). (1993). *Participatory Design: Principles and Practices.* Hillsdale, NJ: Lawrence Erlbaum.

CHAPTER 5

Scenario Use in the Design of a Speech Recognition System

John Karat
IBM Watson Research Center
Box 704
Yorktown Heights, NY 10598
USA

5.1 INTRODUCTION

Although there is a growing literature within the domain of human-computer interaction, we are still missing an organized understanding of design that can be applied to the development of computer systems. Recommendations for good design practice are being assembled from reflections on the wide range of activities in current use, but the advice is often considered either too general to indicate what should be done for a specific project or too specific to apply to the current context.

It is interesting to look at the evolution of work done within the human-computer interaction community in developing techniques to support the design of computer systems. The field moved from being primarily involved with empirical studies of user interface components to a broad consideration of techniques to support design and development. Rather than viewing this as a situation in disarray, it seems important to acknowledge that understanding and supporting design is an activity that draws on multiple perspectives. A question appropriate to trying to decide what to do in a particular situation is "Is there something shared by all of these techniques that can assist in understanding design?"

Consider the ongoing attempt within the International Standards Organization (ISO) to document recommended practices for ergonomic design of human-system interaction. Contained in a standard that is intended to cover all aspects of working with computer systems in office environments (ISO 9241) are principles of dialog design and a definition of usability. The principles contained in Part 10 of the standard [9] direct designers to develop systems that

- are suitable for the task
- are self-descriptive
- provide for user control
- conform to user expectations
- are error tolerant
- can be customized
- support user learning

On one hand we cannot argue with the merit of such design guidelines. On the other we have difficulty knowing what use to make of such advice in actual design. No process for how to satisfy the guidelines such as "making a system suitable to a task" is provided (or even recommended) within the standard. The claim is that the way they are applied will depend on characteristics of the user, task, and environment. Part 11 of ISO 9241 [9] goes on to define usability as

> the effectiveness, efficiency, and satisfaction with which specified users achieve specified goals in particular environments.

Is this a step forward from the advice to "know users and their tasks" that can guide design in any domain? Does stressing the importance of context help designers know what to do, or make them throw up their hands in despair because no one knows how to deal with the issue?

Without entering into a long discussion of the merits of providing high-level design guidance in the form of a standard (see [1, 4] for a more complete discussion of the development and implications of ISO 9241), I would like to suggest that we should consider the principles sound, and focus our attention on developing our understanding of what activities will support designing systems with desirable usability characteristics.

Practitioners engaged in software design are providing reports of case studies, which will prove useful in developing distinctions and abstractions important for design. However, such reports are still relatively rare in the literature, and it is not yet clear that we know what constitutes a good case study (one which illustrates important aspects of an effective design process) for human-computer interaction design. Design of complex systems is not a well-structured problem (one with clearly defined goals), and success or failure of any given project can be attributed to a variety of technical and social factors. If we think it is important to report everything, we are overwhelmed. If we select a narrow range of activities to report, we will miss important information.

There is an unfortunate tendency to view the various techniques being reported as being in competition rather than as different approaches to providing insights into what might make a particular design good. As someone who has had a chance to practice a number of approaches to design over the years, I now tend to see something very much in common to any approach that brings about increased understanding of users and their work—that a component of any such technique is a description of someone trying to do something. Techniques may differ in the characteristics they bring forward, or in the methods for representing users and work, but they must contain some component that considers users, tasks, and environment if they are going to help inform design.

This is particularly true when considering other chapters within this book. The use of scenarios that I will describe here has much in common with the techniques described by other authors. For example, the techniques described by Nielsen in Chapter 3 (collecting field data, brainstorming, and heuristic evaluations) were all a part of the design effort described here. The kind of analysis described by Jacobson (Chapter 12)—though not the specific procedure for carrying it out—seems similar in nature to the use of scenarios described here. This is also true of the chapters by Rosson and Carroll and by Kyng (Chapters 10 and 4)—in each case it seems that scenarios contribute to an understanding of what to build and how to build it. I will not argue here that any one of the approaches presented in this book is right or wrong—experiments to compare the efficiency of such techniques are too resource intensive to be practical. I will focus on illustrating how a flexible (not narrowly defined) notion of scenarios was broadly useful in design of a complex system.

5.2 SCENARIOS AS A COMMON THREAD

If usability is a function of user, task, and environment characteristics, and principles of good dialog design are also dependent on these same characteristics, it seems likely that techniques to support design should also consider these elements. This would seem to be suggesting that techniques for dealing with the problem space would be very complex, and actually I think that they are. In general we have addressed such problems by reducing their complexity through simplifying assumptions (e.g., treat all users as model information processors or ignore the social context of the workplace). But rather than trying to reduce the complexity of the design task by eliminating (or taking as constant) much of the problem space, I think we can capitalize on human reasoning even if we don't really understand it. A way to do this is to express the problem in an easy-to-understand representation, and equip the designers with problem-solving tools they all understand. I suggest that natural language text descriptions of system use offer just such a technique.

That narrative descriptions of use of a system (scenarios) are valuable in design is widely accepted, but we know little about the details of what constitutes good scenarios and how they should be used in a complex development process. What should the content of the narratives be? When and how ought they be used to guide design? In this chapter I will have a little to say about the varied ways such narratives were used in the course of developing one system. What I hope to provide is a glimpse at the use of scenarios in the very complex activity of system design.

To help in discussing the varied use of scenarios I will use a simple definition of a scenario here: A scenario is a narrative that describes someone trying to do something in some environment. As such it is a description of a context, which contains information about users, tasks, and environment. This leaves unspecified how much information and at what level of granularity a narrative needs to contain each of these components. My experience is that this varies with the use being made of the scenario and the technique being used to analyze it.

Human-computer interaction researchers have offered a variety of techniques to software designers to support gathering information about users and their tasks—cognitive modeling, participatory design, anthropomorphic analysis, usability testing—the list of practices and their advocates is quite large. They all include (explicitly or implicitly) some use of scenarios. For example, when performing a GOMS analysis [11], one tends to utilize a very detailed description of some task, a very generic description of the user (a model human-information processor), and a limited description of the environment (e.g., descriptions of general work contexts are not used in practice).

The use of scenarios that I will focus on here is their role in facilitating communication in a variety of design activities. I will broadly refer to activities in which scenarios are used to focus discussion on usability issues as use-centered scenario discussions. I believe that it is through discussion of these scenarios that designers gain an understanding of the goals of the design. This clarification of goals helps designers structure the design problem, which facilitates the problem-solving task [12].

5.3 A CASE STUDY

Let me begin by briefly sketching the motivation behind the project that I will describe. Like many projects, it was technology driven (looking for a useful way to employ a specific technology) rather than problem driven (developed in response to a specific requirement). Research on speech recognition had reached a point where providing this capability to users of personal computers now seemed feasible (moderate cost and real-time response). We were given a general goal of developing a product using a technology rather than a well-defined set of user requirements. Because both the design (the identification of what the system would do and how it would look) and development (the implementation of these ideas in code and hardware) were done by the same team in a continuous process, I will not draw a sharp distinction between these two activities.

I will illustrate the varied use of scenarios in this by offering some of the details of my involvement in the development of a speech recognition product. The system we designed and developed provides speech-to-text (dictation) capabilities and also speech command capabilities for any application running on the platform. The system provides speaker-specific recognition of isolated words or phrases (words spoken with a brief pause between them). The project was of medium size (about 20 people) and duration (about 18 months). I would suggest that the system has good usability characteristics but also has some limitations. Like any general-purpose system, I think that there are contexts in which it will be considered usable, and those in which it will be considered less so. But I do suggest that it was a successful project (it met schedule and cost objectives, and passed some usability tests) and that use-centered scenario discussions had a role in its success. The project developed a product (hardware and software package) from initial conception to shipment in 18 months. It is too early in the product's life to comment on its success in the marketplace, though it did receive awards at a major industry trade show and has received favorable reviews in the trade press.

My intention here is to provide some illustrations of how I think scenarios were used in some parts of this project, not to completely chronicle the product design and development. I will not try to present a detailed description of the system, the issues in speech recognition technology, or all of the design decisions that were involved in developing this product, but it is important to provide the reader with some of the design context. For each section I will attempt to provide a brief description of some of the issues we were attempting to address through scenario discussions.

I do not mean to suggest that there was an explicit strategy to use scenarios throughout the project. Use of scenarios is a technique that seems to naturally occur in design of computer systems (at least in some situations). As such, I am not introducing the technique as much as I am discovering its use. I will provide example descriptions of scenarios we used. The scenarios were sometimes brought to the meeting as detailed descriptions of specific activities (like "change font size to 18"). Sometimes the detail was developed through discussion in response to questions or general statements that served to describe a general use context.

5.3.1 Basic Direction Setting

A brief characterization of the use of scenarios in this project is as follows. During the early stages of design (before we had committed to a vision of what we were building and for whom), we used scenarios to discuss the basic directions in the design of the system. Initially, we argued about whether the scenario was *correct* or not (whether people would want to use such a system to do such a task and why) more than we discussed details such has how things would appear on the screen. Once this high-level vision began to take shape, we used scenarios to sketch out (actually draw by hand) interface and component ideas and in developing an early user guide. We began to explore *what-if* scenarios to question what information might be needed under different circumstances to use the system. Discussions contributed both to what information should be placed on the screen (e.g., what command had been recognized, whether the microphone was on or not), and what components of the system might need to be developed (e.g., a component to allow creation of macros).

Soon after a decision had been made to assemble a group to develop a product, several people began meeting to create a vision of what the system might do and how it might look. This might be considered a form of Envisionment Workshop (Chapter 4, this volume), but we did not have a clear set of procedures to distinguish this as any special kind of design meeting. Discussions around use-oriented scenarios formed a substantial part of these meetings. We discussed what someone might want to say to their system in different situations. Development of a shared understanding of what sorts of activities the system might support was facilitated through elaborations of stories about imagined interactions. We put forward suggestions about how we might process commands or provide for dictation in place of typing as input.

Goals in Selecting Scenarios

- Gain some understanding of what kind of system we might want to build.
- Develop a shared understanding of the technology capabilities and limitations.

Example Scenario

- Imagine taking away the keyboard and mouse from your current workstation and describe doing everything through voice commands.
- What will happen if the system misrecognizes a command?

The earliest discussions focused on the capabilities of the base technology (the speed and accuracy of the recognition engine, the cost of the hardware necessary for a system, an analysis of competitive systems, the expected delivery date of the unspecified product). Our scenario discussions had led to an agreement that our system would provide supplemental input for the system, and not try to completely replace existing mouse and keyboard techniques. Given what we knew of the limitations of the speech technology, we found it difficult to imagine speech-only input as a goal. From these discussions, and others that took place among product management, a general product direction arose. It was decided that we would design and develop a speech-driven command navigation facility for IBM PS/2–compatible hardware.

There were several considerations that led to this initial decision (which was later to be significantly changed). The recognition engine could provide acceptable speaker-independent accuracy for small vocabularies (in the range of a few hundred words), and we felt that this was an important feature. Also, there was a commercially available system for competitive hardware that we were confident we could make significant improvements on. The existence of another product stood in for extensive market research and requirements-gathering activity as justification of our initial direction.

5.3.2 The Initial Scenarios

Once the basic direction for the project had been established, we began to discuss the components of the system. Questions were raised with great frequency, and explored only briefly before discussion moved to another topic. Would the system replace or augment other input devices? What would happen if you were using multiple devices simultaneously? Would the vocabulary remain constant or would it change with context? How would you make additions or changes to it? How would the user know what the system thought it heard? Would additional facilities for correction be needed?

While descriptions of system use were brought informally into these discussions, they were not explicitly recorded and did not become a formal part of the design until a few weeks had passed. At this point there was a request to develop a few scenarios that we might use to help focus the design discussions (this request came from the project manager). Though we were all developing a feeling for interacting with the system (and indeed some members of the team had begun developing code to reflect the design-in-progress), it remained difficult to see how all of the possible design decisions that we were making or deferring would combine in actual use.

Several scenario-based efforts began in parallel. In one case, a member of the team explored the possibilities of a continuous speech recognition interface for a scheduling application (we initially had the possibility of also working with a different recognition engine that allowed continuous rather than isolated speech). I developed a scenario based on use of a text editor, and in a series of meetings facilitated a discussion that moved from a description of what was logically necessary for a small task (changing the font of a document) to a description of a shared vision of a specific design.

Goals in Selecting Scenarios

- Explore typical use of speech commands to issue editor commands.
- Track vocabulary contents to check for typical size of active vocabulary.

Example Scenario

Overall Task	Open System Editor, find file **REPORT.TXT**, Change font to Times 16, save changes, and exit the editor.
Voice Scenario Steps	"system_editor" "open" "open" "file" "find" "r" "e" "p" "open" "font" "times" "16" "ok" "save" "close"

A series of scenarios similar to the one above were developed, and a number of meetings were held in which we walked through simulated executions of such scenarios. These discussions were sometimes focused on consideration of the users (e.g., How do they know what to say? Does this seem easier than doing the same thing with a mouse? What happens if a command is incorrectly recognized?) and sometimes on considerations of the underlying technology (e.g., How quickly will we be able to change the active vocabulary? What commands should always be active? How big would the vocabulary be if we place all submenu items in it and allow people to skip commands?).

At some of the design meetings we attempted to maintain a narrow focus, but often the discussion flowed freely and opportunistically between different perspectives. This seems to be a common aspect of early design discussions [7]. Our experience does not suggest any particular guidelines for structuring such discussions other than to suggest that they not dwell overly long on any one perspective, and that they be encouraged to favor breadth of considerations over depth of discussion on a single aspect of the design.

5.3.3 The User Guide

Partly overlapping the introduction of the basic use scenarios was an effort to begin developing a user's guide to the system. Developing user documentation early in design is generally regarded as desirable, though it seems to be rarely done unless the documentation developers are well integrated with the design team. In this case our intention was not to develop the final, complete documentation for the product, but rather to develop some ideas for quick reference material. As such, we hoped that the material would be very compact (only a few pages), and would contain all the information necessary to get someone started using the system. The outline for this material was created by developing a set of questions that users might need to answer (some of which arose during the discussions of the initial scenarios), and then providing answers to those questions. Our use of questions to motivate this discussion is similar to that described by Robertson (Chapter 11, this volume). This guide (eventually sixteen pages in length) contained many scenarios about the use of the system in different situations.

Goals in Selecting Scenarios

- List questions that cover what a typical user has to know in order to use the system.
- Provide a prototype of a quick reference guide.

Example Scenarios

- What is speech manager?
- How do I know what I can say?
- What if my word is not correctly recognized?

Figure 5.1 shows a typical page from the initial user guide that we developed. While this guide was passed on to the developers of the actual product documentation, very little of it was used. Still this work was not considered as wasted effort, but rather just one of those first drafts that we should not be afraid to throw away (Brooks, Mythical Man Month). While the user guide quickly fell out of touch with the rapidly developing prototype of the system, it proved to be the most complete *functional specification* for the system for about six months when an official product specification was developed. It also provided us with a guide to use in our early system testing with users. The topics in the guide were those that we tried to cover in the testing, and we watched for how well users could discover how to work with the system.

5.3.4 Scenarios in Early Testing with Users

When the code was developed so that we had initial working versions of the system (often referred to as early prototypes), we used the use scenarios, along with additional tasks, to form the basis for our early user tests. We did not ask users to carry out the step-by-step procedures, which we had defined as the right way to carry out a task, but simply asked them to reach the goal that was the objective of the scenario. This provided us with a chance to revise or validate many of the design decisions that had developed around the discussion of the scenarios.

If things go wrong: What if the wrong action occurs?

What happens if Speech Manager does the wrong thing with what you said?

Sometimes Speech Manager will listen to what you said and decide that it matches the word in the Active Vocabulary that you intended, but that the wrong action occurs. For Speech Manager this is not really an error . . . the action is only incorrect to you the user who intended for something different to occur. This happens when the word you said can be interpreted as having different actions appropriate to it in different situations. What you have to do is to understand what action did occur and how to tell Speech Manager what the correct action should be.

To see and change the actions associated with words, you use the Voice Action Editor, which you can access by saying:

Voice_Action_Editor

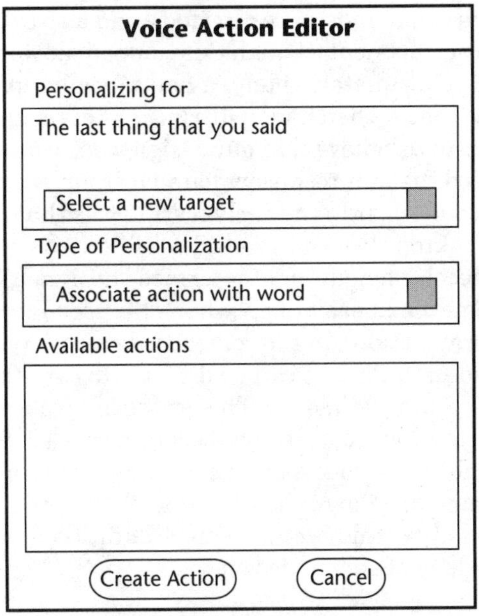

Figure 5.1. Early draft of the user's guide.

Goals in Selecting Scenarios

- Provide input on using speech to control applications in a window to use the system.
- Provide coverage of interaction including keyboard and mouse.

Example Scenarios

- Change the font in document **TEXT.TST** to Times Roman, and change the font size to 18 point.
- Move the text editor window to the upper-left-hand portion of the display.
- Change the background color of the icon for the communications folder to red.

In our case the testing provided a great deal of useful information. The basic recognition worked well, but people had a difficult time figuring out what they could say at any given point. While we had developed a component of the system to answer the "What can I say" questions, this component was itself difficult to use. Testing information led us to include a form of focus highlighting to the system (to more clearly indicate the component to which speech commands were directed), and also to the redesign of the What Can I Say component (though this component would remain more difficult to design adequately than we had initially imagined). Actually, the difficulties that we had had in discussing this component in design meetings led us all to believe that our design work was not done, and we were not surprised that our test users found it troublesome.

The second thing that became clear in the early testing was that the capability of navigating the desktop with voice would be of limited value to users of such a system. Speech navigation of interfaces designed for other input techniques is sometimes easy (e.g., when the user knows the name of the command for an action), but is sometimes clumsy (e.g., without natural language understanding it can be difficult to carry out actions such as repositioning desktop windows). Though we felt we could deliver such a system at a very low cost, it was becoming clear that there would be little demand for it without a more general speech input capability. A decision was made to change the direction of the product to include full dictation capability, and we developed additional scenarios to explore the implications of such a decision.

5.3.5 Potential Customer Input (Project Redirection)

Later in the project we went outside of the design team to present scenarios describing use of the system to potential customers. Reactions that they had to these scenarios (presented through video clips) were largely given to us in the form of scenarios themselves (descriptions of how they imagined such a system would be used in a particular environment). We used these scenarios as input to a redirection of the product to include full dictation capabilities.

In reaction to our concern about the overall direction of the project, we undertook an effort to explore implications of the introduction of speech recognition technology with communities that we felt would be likely users of this technology. While we might have carried out this study in ways more consistent with participatory design practice, time and resource limitations encouraged use of other techniques. We organized a focus session. Participants included representatives of the media, insurance, and health industries (schedule and resource constraints directed us to use marketing representatives rather than actual professionals in these industries—a tradeoff that we accepted as reasonable in the given circumstances). Slightly over half of the participants had some experience with speech recognition systems (ranging from quite a bit to some familiarity). The participants were asked to consider their customers' point of view of each of the issues raised for discussion in the session.

The session began with introductions and a discussion of the general document production requirements in the various fields represented. Following this, the session was divided into segments in which brief informational video clips and demonstrations were shown to stimulate discussion on the topics on which we hoped to obtain information. In total there were five clips of about 2 minutes each followed by 10- to 15-minute discussion sessions. The clips presented demonstrations of isolated speech dictation, application integration, error correction, homophone recognition, and enrollment. Additionally, microphones were passed around for hands-on experience. Only limited technical information about speech recognition was presented.

There was a general goal in this procedure of extracting scenarios from the participants to bring this information into the design process. We did this through a sort of *scenario exchange* in which we presented and collected use-centered scenarios. The comments of the participants on the themes we explored are summarized below.

Goals in Selecting Scenarios

- Explore current text creation practices.
- Explore expectations about computer speech recognition.
- Explore impact of known technology limitations.

Example Scenarios Presented

- Describe your current text creation activities.
- We presented a simulation of speech recognition in a medical examination.
- We presented a simulation to demonstrate error correction.

Current Practices Before presenting speech recognition scenarios through the video clips, we asked participants to describe current practices for text creation. Participants described applications ranging from the creation of radiology reports and patient medical records, to magazine and newspaper creation, to executive memorandums and speeches, to insurance customer correspondence. These applications use a variety of techniques, including dictation (onto tape or into digital systems), handwriting followed by transcription, and immediate entry into copy flow systems or word processors. In some cases, the producers of the text (e.g., doctors and executives) are not currently entering their own text into electronic form. In other cases (e.g., newspaper and magazine writers) the creators enter their own text and it passes into a process in which others work on it.

Example Scenario Collected

- The doctor will dictate his or her report onto a tape, give it to the secretary for typing, proofread it, return it for corrections, and then send it out. This process can take a week for nonurgent reports.

Design Implication

- In providing dictation using speech recognition, we might include a function to allow someone other than the creator of the text to do proofreading and correction.

In general, the scenarios described by the participants gave us a mixture of stories to bring back to the design team. There were existing practices, which were found to be lacking (e.g., hands were not always free to enter necessary text; transcription from taped dictation to text was often lengthy).

Problems with Current Practices Participants were asked if there were problems with current practices and tools. The consensus was that the word processing revolution has not solved the problem of creating text. Physicians and executives are very impatient, and have low tolerance for using a keyboard. The perception is that it takes a long time to learn how to use a wordprocessing package effectively. Processes that separate the creation of the initial text from entry of the text for processing also were seen as having problems. When a word processing pool is used, changes and revisions sometimes take a long time. Additionally, creating documents in time-critical situations takes too long.

Use of keyboard was mentioned by several participants as a major (and increasing) problem because of RSI (repetitive stress injury). Estimates of incidents range from 100 out of 800 editors, to about 0.6 percent of personnel involved in heavy text entry (about 2 percent was seen as a reasonable estimate). The costs associated with RSI were seen as substantial.

A number of other problems with keyboard entry were briefly mentioned. To use a keyboard you have to sit at the computer, you can't walk around the office, and you can't create text while on the road. In doctor-patient situations, a keyboard creates a barrier between the doctor and the patient.

Another communication technology, voice mail, has the problem that unlike e-mail, it cannot be forwarded to another site, and cannot be easily scanned by a person or a computer.

Example Scenario Collected

- Most editors working on the newspaper enter a lot of text; when they have an injury, even though they can be in the office it becomes very difficult for them to do their job.

Design Implication

- An audience was identified that might serve as a willing test group for early systems.

Talking to a Computer We then asked participants to think about entering text by talking to a computer. There was wide agreement that talking to a computer is a good idea, if it can overcome some of the problems with current practices.

The perceived benefits were: faster and easier than using a keyboard; the ability to walk around the room while dictating; the ability to create text while on the road, either by using a hand-held device or by phoning in.

However, there were some areas of concern, including disturbing others (side noise) and being overheard (lack of privacy). Executives can close their doors, but if you work in an open area or bullpen that is not possible.

When asked to think about ways in which they would like to see speech-to-text work, participants quickly developed ideas. A quick survey of applications that participants mentioned as being desirable included production of meeting minutes, speech transcripts, and TV show transcripts, as well as reports of medical studies, surveys, and focus groups.

Example Scenario Collected

- Project staff could set up a system in a meeting room and have it produce a transcription of the meeting discussion.

Design Implication

- Actually this scenario is outside of the technical capabilities, in that it relies on speaker-independent continuous recognition. Ways to manage user expectations of the system were discussed in design meetings.

Presenting Isolated Speech Recognition The remainder of the session was focused on presenting samples of speech recognition systems and encouraging participants to respond. First, we presented a video clip, which demonstrated dictation with isolated speech recognition (the clip also mentioned that after years of research, accuracy and cost were now acceptable for application). We asked participants for reactions to the clip. Following the discussion of this clip, we presented additional clips and asked questions on a number of topics.

Isolated speech recognition involves speaking with pauses between words (resulting in an entry rate of 60 to 100 words per minute compared to a normal speech rate of 150 to 200 wpm). Additionally, current technology requires the speaker to also speak required punctuation (such as *period*, *comma*, and so on). The talking speed was seen as a problem: a big inhibitor to acceptance of the system. However, some participants felt one would get used to it. It was seen as taking too much time (especially for executives); and people felt they would lose their train of thought while dictating. Some participants were worried that using the system would change the way they talk to people. One participant expected to write a document out by hand before dictating in this way.

Having to dictate punctuation and formatting information was seen as a problem; some participants felt that the computer should put this in automatically when they paused, or that they should be able to click somewhere to start a new line or a new paragraph.

One participant pointed out that people who don't use e-mail today are probably using voice mail, and they probably wouldn't like to switch because of the need to talk slowly.

Example Scenario Collected

- Executives will not want to take the time to learn to talk this way and will often forget to use the punctuation.

Design Implication

- We discussed solutions (e.g., connecting in a parser to provide generation of punctuation) but did not find a satisfactory one.

Using a Microphone We presented the participants with samples of a number of different kinds of microphones, including various hand-held, clip-on, head-set, and table-stand products (developing our own microphone was not a part of the project, but including one with the product was planned). In general, participants felt that finding a suitable microphone would not be a problem.

Participants expressed several desirable features for microphones: easy to put on and remove, doesn't mess up the hair, doesn't clutter the desktop, allows movement around a room, and operates hands-free. Of the microphones shown, participants preferred the ear-mounted telephone mike. Several participants liked the lapel mike, but others expressed a concern about ease of attaching to clothing without lapels. One participant expressed a preference for an integrated telephone handset (one is already on everyone's desk). None felt that the headsets or hand-held mikes would be acceptable for their applications. All were interested in wireless microphones, so they could walk around the room and think, or shuffle papers, while dictating.

Microphone selection depends somewhat on how long or how intensively you use the system: Someone who now sits at a keyboard for hours at a time may not mind being tethered, but a doctor would need something that is very easy to put on and take off. Someone who does only occasional dictation may prefer to use a telephone handset, but this has to be the one on the existing desk telephone. Finally, it would be desirable if a person could use the same mike at a workstation and also on the road, so it should be compact and portable.

Example Scenario Collected

- I would like to be able to walk around while I dictate.

Design Implication

- Make mobility a factor in microphone selection.

Recognition Accuracy—Error Correction We presented a video clip, which demonstrated the general error dialog that we had developed, and asked people for ideas about error correction. Because people never speak the same word exactly the same, speech recognition systems make errors. The current recognition accuracy, above 95 percent correct, was not felt to be an obstacle for using the system. The worst example shown, of 93 percent accuracy, was considered unacceptable. It was, however, considered acceptable for initial use, provided that it could be improved by training the system.

The process for correcting the errors was not seen as problematic, since it is like correcting typos made by the typing pool. One participant felt more tolerant toward errors made by the system. Also, it was seen as a benefit that the system never forgets what it learns, while there may be turnover among typists. Subjects did comment that it seemed to take an unacceptably long time to correct some errors (when the word was being added to the vocabulary). Another comment was that the proofreading process might be facilitated if words that the system found questionable could be highlighted in some fashion. Playback was seen as an important function.

People don't have a consistent measure for accuracy—no one seemed able to consistently relate *errors per page*, *percent accuracy*, and *percent errors*. For example, after people agreed that the sample shown with 7 percent errors was unacceptable, one participant still referred to *super performance* as being "a 90 percent OK rating or something." When asked what they thought the error rate was in the clip with 93 percent accuracy, they guessed that it was about 80 percent.

Example Scenario Collected

- I won't mind errors so much if they are easy to find and correct.

Design Implication

- Acceptable error rate is more than just the percent correct. It is a function of ease of correction and other factors. Since we did not have much control over the recognition accuracy, we focused efforts on correction mechanisms.

Decoding Delay Some of the clips that we showed were constructed to present speech recognition as immediate. We presented a clip that demonstrated more accurately the anticipated delay between speaking and the appearance of the recognized word on the display and asked for reactions. While recognition of speech input is done in real time, there is a delay (up to a few seconds) before the recognized word is displayed. The decoding delay was initially seen by some as disturbing, but others did not think it was a problem (participants could see the delay on the video clips presented, but did not have hands-on experience). Participants felt that as users gained confidence with the system, they would probably not rely on the screen while dictating.

Since you can't see an error when it is made, participants felt it would be helpful to have some indication of low-confidence words.

Example Scenario Collected

- If I am creating text while I am dictating, I like to be able to review what I have dictated.

Design Implication

- Monitoring dictated text will be distracting. We realized we were going to be requiring new user behavior (i.e., not to watch the screen all the time), and focused on informing users about the limitation.

There are some interesting points about the design discussions that followed on this topic. First, there was some indication that the process of dictating text through speech recognition would lead to different *monitoring* behavior (how much you look at the display) than typing text. The delay actually makes it difficult to watch the display and maintain concentration on what you are saying, and consequently people quickly stop trying to do it. Rather than word-by-word monitoring for errors, there is reliance on a proofreading pass of larger chunks of a dictated document. Awareness of this type of behavior led us to include error correction mechanisms to support it. For example, with delayed review of dictated text people can forget what they said (misrecognized words can be quite different than the word spoken). To accommodate correction we provided the ability to play back any word (or set of words) in the text.

Second, we had long thought that providing information about the confidence of the recognition might be useful, and took the group comment that they would like to see it as an incentive to provide this information. However, while the scenario describing the value of such a function seemed reasonable in our discussions ("To support proofreading, we could highlight words that fell below a certain value in recognition confidence"), we never were able to provide a useful design that involved confidence level. In real use, there was not a sufficiently strong relationship between recognition errors and the value of the confidence score produced by the recognition algorithm. Proofreading was not facilitated by such highlighting.

Having to Enroll Enrollment is the process of providing a speaker-specific (and possibly environment-specific) speech sample from which a model is developed and used in recognition. We did not present a demonstration of the enrollment process currently designed, but discussed general aspects of the process (its length, purpose, etc.) and asked for comments.

An impact of changing from a small vocabulary command recognition system to a large vocabulary system was that we would have to require speaker-specific information to reach acceptable recognition accuracy. We asked people how long an enrollment would be acceptable. The answer was that something in the 15-to-30-minute range would be acceptable, with executives requiring a brief (15 minutes) process. The group did not seem to feel that segmenting the enrollment into multiple sessions would be a major benefit: Doing it once up front was seen as most desirable. In general, the willingness to train also was said to depend on how much you would use the system. Two hours of enrollment was seen as a problem for most applications. Making the enrollment process more fun was not seen as a way to help. One participant who knew the enrollment application felt it was a well-designed application.

People expect the system to improve continually during use. When given the choice between speaker independence, which would work fine for some people but not for others, and a system where you have to train, most said that some training up front was probably good. The participants suggested that enrollment would also be valuable in training the user in the right speaking style. The participants believed that an enrollment process should be capable of recognition. It would be ideal if the system could tell you when you were making too many errors and would ask you to read a few more sentences.

Having to enroll more than once (for different environments or for different microphones) was not seen as acceptable in any situation.

Example Scenario Collected

- I should be able to train the system with no more than a half hour of speech.

Design Implication

- This motivated some action to explore shorter training sessions, but in the end we decided to leave the session length at about two hours. We did make a number of changes to the enrollment process to improve the nature of the session (e.g., made the text that users read informative and interesting).

Price Sensitivity Participants were asked how much the technology should cost. The participants uniformly felt that $100 or $250 was no problem, but $500 and $1,000 were seen as a problem for most people. When there are many workstations in a department, price is very important. On the other hand, for executive use, $2,500 per workstation was seen as acceptable.

RSI situations seemed to provide for a different price sensitivity. The potential cost of RSI to employers has been put at $375 a week for life for a totally disabled employee. Clearly, technology that can eliminate or reduce the incidence of RSI could be justified against this rather large cost.

5.3.6 Later Involvement

We decided to go forward by including the large vocabulary dictation. With the general outline of the components discussed and agreed to within the design group, work focused on developing a working system within the agreed-to (funded) time frame. Prototype versions of the system were available to the design group, and we passed into a stage where real use of the system (in a sense, real scenarios rather than artificial ones) were used to comment on and direct any changes in the design. Through various releases of test versions of the system, users of the system passed comments about its use through a formal comment tracking mechanism. Comments such as "When I tried to do *X* (generally a goal) I tried *Y* (a procedure) and *Z* happened (an unexpected or undesired result)" became input for meetings to address such issues.

Issues raised at such meetings were dealt with in a number of ways. The scenario description could lead to a design change. The likelihood of this happening decreased as the project went along, reflecting some stabilization of the design and also resistance to major changes to it. The scenario could suggest ways (through documentation of one form or another) of accommodating the users' expectations. For example, screen layouts and wording were changed, information was provided in the user guide or help text, or default actions might be changed. The comment could also be dismissed from consideration (e.g., because it dealt with a known bug or because it called for a function not planned for in this release of the product).

Such meetings were tightly focused and productive (in the sense that many scenarios were considered and specific activities for addressing them were determined). Hundreds of such comments were considered and addressed over several months of the project in which groups outside of the design team were evaluating early versions of the system.

There was also considerable use of various scenarios in the development of documentation (on-line and paper), which was included with the product. Descriptions of how to do various tasks that had been a part of earlier discussions (generated by people both inside and outside of the development process), as well as answers to questions that seemed to be "what users might need to know" guided the development of large parts of the documentation package. Figure 5.2 shows a sample page from the user's guide [8], and demonstrates how scenarios made their way into task-related information.

5.4 DISCUSSION

As I mentioned above, I did not introduce the use of scenarios in this project, but I did encourage making discussions of them an explicit part of some design meetings and throughout the design and development activities. They were used to focus discussions, elicit requirements from potential users of the technology, and to report requirements back to the design team. They had impact on the final design in a pervasive way (the process was filled with scenarios), and the design of the documentation for the product made considerable explicit use of use-centered scenarios in determining what to describe and how to describe it.

The design of any system that impacts human work is a complex task involving many activities. While the picture that I have provided of the design and development of a speech recognition component for personal computers might seem very complicated, it is actually a major simplification of what actually took place during the 18 months of the project. What I wanted to focus on here was some of the roles scenarios played in this project. In doing this I am acting more to report on the use of narratives than to offer a recommendation on how to correctly use them.

What sort of guidance might we offer based on this and similar experiences? For the purpose of this project, it seems important that we did not try to overly constrain our notion of what a scenario was. The use-centered discussions that took place early in the project allowed the

Dictating and Editing Your Work

1 Say "Stop dictation" before you begin to correct words that Voice Manager does not recognize correctly.

2 Say "Microphone off" to turn off the microphone until you need it.

3 When you have the mouse pointer pointing to the word, or words, you want, click mouse button 2 once to get the Correct Word pop-up menu.

4 Listen to the automatic playback of what you dictated.

5 If you see the correct alternative word in the Correct Word pop-up menu, select it.

When you encounter a word that Voice Manager does not recognize correctly, move your mouse pointer to the word and click mouse button 2 one to highlight the word and access the Correct Word pop-up menu. You can choose among some alternative words listed in the pop-up menu, or you can choose other correction options.

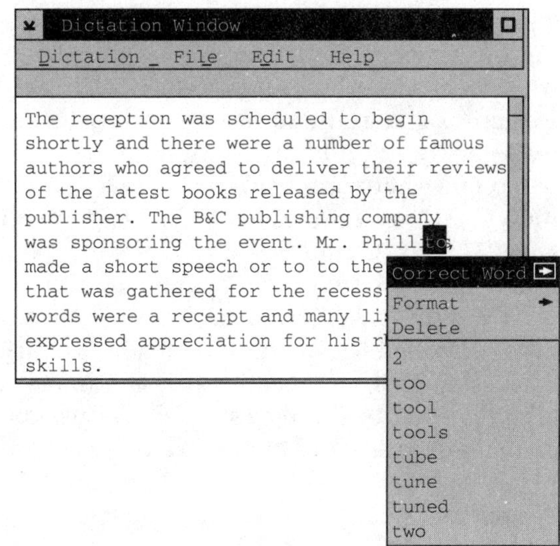

Figure 5.2. Sample page from the user's guide.

design team to variously consider the users, the specific task being undertaken, and the general environment in which the tasks fit.

Would a more rigorously developed science of scenarios have helped in this or other projects? I am not so sure. I can draw some parallels to the development of GOMS as a detailed technique for doing another pervasive activity (task analysis) within design. There are detailed descriptions, which provide guidance on exactly how to do such an analysis [5, 11], but questions remain about whether this represents progress for actual design. With regard to GOMS, the guidelines have identified how to decompose and analyze some tasks, but such guidance has not affected a broad spectrum of task analysis activities. Similarly, while we might develop useful specifications about how to work with scenarios in certain domains, it may be that these guidelines would either need to be very general or would apply only to narrow domains.

Design of the system was a group activity—while much work was by individuals (rather than in meetings), coordinated action and a sense of partnership were critical factors. While scenarios were useful in developing teamwork, they did not guarantee it. Guidelines for a complex activity such as design can provide a partial picture of how to achieve successful results. For example, there are good guidelines for conducting meetings [6], but using them without a deeper understanding of what meetings are about in a work setting will lessen their usefulness. Design in general, and use of scenarios in design in particular, is at least partly art, and attaining high skill in use of scenarios in design will require both practical guidelines of the sort offered in this book and individual understanding of the design process achieved with experience. Argyris [2] and Schön [13] provide valuable discussions of reflection on practice that seem to apply to design in general.

I have been involved in design projects and meetings where the discussion has become unproductive for various reasons (see [3] for a discussion of design meetings). Sometimes teams lose track of the goal of the project, and become stuck on discussions that are at either too low or too high a level of detail. We have argued that scenarios can help bring such discussions back in line [10]. But it is not clear how much specificity is called for in such advice. Use-centered scenarios would seem important to the design of any system, but how much attention should be given to the various components of such scenarios (users, tasks, and environments) would seem to necessarily depend on the context. I have tried to show that scenarios (broadly defined) can be useful in designing usable systems. I believe that reflecting on their use will provide additional distinctions in how and when to use them, but expect that such distinctions will rely heavily on experience for their own usability and will not be contained in a walk-up-and-use cookbook.

REFERENCES

[1] Abernethy, C. (1993). Expanding jurisdictions and other facets of human-machine interface IT standards. *Standard View, 1*, 9–21.

[2] Argyris, C. (1982). *Reasoning, Learning, and Action.* San Francisco: Jossey-Bass.

[3] Bennett, J. & Karat, J. (1994). Facilitating effective HCI design meetings. In B. Adelson, S. Dumais & J. Olson (eds.), *CHI '94 Conference Proceedings: ACM Conference on Human Factors in Computing Systems*. New York: ACM Press, pp. 198–204.

[4] Brown, L. (1993). Human-computer interaction and standardization. *Standard View, 1*, 3–8.

[5] Card, S. K., Moran, T. P. & Newell, A. (1983). *The Psychology of Human Computer Interaction*. Hillsdale, NJ: Lawrence Erlbaum.

[6] Doyle, M. & Straus, D. (1976). *How to Make Meetings Work*. New York: Berkeley Publishing.

[7] Guindon, R. (1990). Designing the design process: Exploiting opportunistic thoughts. *Human Computer Interaction, 5*, 305–344.

[8] International Business Machines Corporation. (1993). IBM Personal Dictation System User's Guide Version 1.0.

[9] International Standards Organization. (1994). Ergonomic requirements for office work with visual display terminals (VDTs)—Part 11: Measuring usability.

[10] Karat, J. & Bennett, J. (1991). Using scenarios in design meetings—A case study example. In J. Karat (ed.), *Taking Software Design Seriously: Practical Techniques for Human-Computer Interaction Design*. Boston: Academic Press.

[11] Kieras, D. E. (1988). Towards a practical GOMS model methodology for user interface design. In M. Helander (ed.), *Handbook of Human-Computer Interaction*. Amsterdam: Elsevier.

[12] Newell, A. & Simon, H. A. (1972). *Human Problem Solving*. Englewood Cliffs, NJ: Prentice Hall.

[13] Schön, D. (1987). Educating the reflective practitioner. San Francisco: Jossey-Bass.

CHAPTER 6

Bifocal Tools for Scenarios and Representations in Participatory Activities with Users

Michael J. Muller,*§ Leslie G. Tudor, Daniel M. Wildman,*** Ellen A. White,*** Robert W. Root,*** Tom Dayton,*** Rebecca Carr,**** Barbara Diekmann,* and Elizabeth Dykstra-Erickson*†**

* *U S WEST Technologies, 4001 Discovery Drive, Boulder, CO 80303 USA*

** *AT&T Bell Laboratories, 200 Laurel Avenue, Middletown, NJ 07748 USA*

*** *Bellcore, 444 Hoes Lane, Piscataway, NJ 08854 USA*

**** *U S WEST Communications, 1801 California, Denver, CO 80202 USA*

[§]Correspondence: Michael J. Muller, U S WEST Technologies, 4001 Discovery Drive, Boulder, CO 80303 USA, +1-303-541-6564 (voice), +1-303-541-6003 or -8182 (fax), michael@uswest.com or muller.chi@xerox.com.

[†]Now at Apple Computer.

6.1 INTRODUCTION

This book offers diverse applications of scenarios in the analysis, design, and assessment of systems to support human work, including computer systems. In this chapter, we consider two methods through which scenarios can be used to support the activities of teams that are composed of heterogeneous stakeholders—software professionals and others who have a stake in the outcome of an analysis, design, or assessment project (see also Chapter 4, this volume).

For our purposes, scenarios may be thought of as informal narratives, collaboratively constructed by a team, that describe human work processes; some of these work processes involve a computer. An important aspect of our approach to scenarios is that they include more than a simple description of work flow. In our scenarios we attempt to address, where appropriate, human goals and motivations, design alternatives, and other questions that extend and deepen our understanding of the problems that the team is trying to solve and the human issues that gave rise to, or are affected by, those problems.

The two methods described in this chapter can provide a bifocal view, using two different granularities of perspective:

- The CARD[1] technique offers a macroscopic or "big picture" approach, which considers the user's goals, motivations, and overall task flow—the *what* and *why* questions.
- The PICTIVE[2] technique offers a microscopic or detailed design approach, which considers the microstructure of what the user does, and what he or she uses to do it—the *how* and (in some cases) the *when* questions.

We also critique our macroscopic/microscopic distinction. We show that our mapping of this distinction to specific techniques, while based in sound practice, is by no means absolute or required.

Other chapters in this book share our concern for working with users and with software professionals. We hope that the reader will consider the methods in this chapter as specific tools, which can be added to his or her toolbox (e.g., [21]) of methods for collaborating with users and other stakeholders in work and computer systems.

---

[1]CARD stands for Collaborative Analysis of Requirements and Design [46].
[2]PICTIVE stands for Plastic Interface for Collaborative Technology Initiatives through Video Exploration [25, 26].

The structure of this chapter is shaped by several interrelated concerns:

- *Representations.* Our methods depend crucially upon representations,[3] as well as upon scenarios. The low-tech physical representations that we use provide a concrete common language through which diverse stakeholders can articulate their views, clarify their disagreements, and work toward consensus. The embodiment of ideas in paper-and-pencil artifacts appears to have been key in making these techniques into effective communication experiences for the participants. We therefore spend some time on representations, showing how they support scenario work.
- *Group Process.* Our methods depend upon the social processes involved in using them. A set of working materials can be used by people in many ways—from egalitarian, collaborative approaches to arbitrary and even exploitive manipulations. We therefore provide relatively specific process information about using the low-tech representations in democratic ways.
- *Methodological Rigor.* Finally, we are mindful of recent constructive critiques, which state that many techniques in HCI are underspecified, at least in contrast with other practices in software engineering. We therefore provide relatively formal descriptions of our practices with the hope that the reader may be able both to carry out these techniques in his or her own setting, and that he or she may be able to integrate these techniques into local software development processes.

We begin by situating our work within the broader domain of participatory design. We then describe our methods in relatively formal terms, followed by a discussion of how they have been used to support scenario work at various phases within the lifecycle.

6.2 PARTICIPATORY DESIGN

6.2.1 Scandinavian Origins

Our practice of participatory design originates from the Scandinavian workplace democracy movement and its applications in theory and

---

[3]The representation associated with each method will be described in detail in that method's "object model."

method of software design (e.g., [2]).[4] More specifically, we see our practices as direct outgrowths and adaptations of the low-tech prototyping tradition of the UTOPIA and "scripts for action" projects [4, 5, 12].

One of the goals of these efforts is to facilitate the direct involvement of users in the design of systems that will influence their worklives. This is fundamentally a democratic goal, whether the justification is provided in the historical language of Marx (e.g., [11]) or of Jefferson (e.g., [24]): That is, people who are affected by decisions should have an effective voice in decision making. They can thus become self-advocates for the quality of their worklives, and for the supports required by them to do their work. We have argued elsewhere that the goal of democracy converges easily with other business goals, such as product quality and stakeholder commitment [35]. Participatory practices can make a contribution to improving the quality of our shared work as well as the quality of our work products.

6.2.2 Locating Our Practices within Participatory Design

Participatory design practices span the entire software development lifecycle, and range from work-centered analyses to prototyping and testing collaboratively with users [34]. Many of the relatively concrete and direct techniques from participatory work can be mapped directly onto more abstract tools and practices that are used within communities of software professionals [21]. The techniques that we describe in this paper can fit into these frameworks in several ways:

- *Analysis.* Users can manipulate low-tech representations of the people, objects, and tasks in their work domain to construct scenarios about how they do their work in the present, and about how they would like to do their work in the future (in this volume, see Chapters 2 and 4). Other participants can manipulate the representations to ask queries, propose alternatives, and so on.

---

[4]This work has been developed in volumes edited by Bodker [3], Greenbaum and Kyng [18], Muller, Kuhn, and Meskill [30], and Schuler and Namioka [44]. Important reviews of this tradition include Clement and van den Besselaar [8] and Floyd, Mehl, Reisin, Schmidt, and Wolf [14]. Surveys of participatory practices appeared in Kensing and Munk-Madsen [21] and Muller, White, and Wildman [34].

- *Design.* The team can create and rearrange low-tech representations to develop alternative scenarios for how work processes might be revised, extended, and so on. These scenarios can become the motivating basis for designs. Participants can explore possible applications of new technologies (in this volume, see again Chapters 2 and 4). The team can also identify problem points and foci for subsequent prototyping or testing.
- *Assessment.* The team can explore scenarios of how a particular design would impact real or imagined work processes. This can be done relatively early in the software lifecycle, before the design has been implemented in software (in this volume, see Chapters 3 and 4; see also [43, 47]).

6.2.3 The Shifting Focus of the Participatory Activity: Process-Oriented and Product-Oriented Approaches

The movement that we sketched above, from analysis through design to assessment, often involves a shift in the conceptual locus of the work—even if the same people participate throughout. Early analysis activities take place, for the most part, on the users' turf. That is to say, the most important referent for participatory *analysis* is the users' work process. These analyses are usually best done in the users' real work context.

Design work is often more strongly influenced by implementation platforms and other technology concerns. While this activity should probably be done at the users' work site, the focus often narrows to a concern with how specific tasks can be carried out with specific materials (computer or otherwise). The use of low-tech representations may help the team members maintain a partial focus on the users' work process, and thus remember that the design should be constrained by *both* the limits set by the target implementation environment *and* the work process that is to be supported.

Finally, assessment activities represent in some ways the narrowest focus. The goal of the activity is to determine whether a particular design artifact meets the users' needs. Initial testing of software products is often done on the developers' turf, in a software organization office or a human factors laboratory. The use of low-tech representations may help the team to resituate the assessment in the users' work context. The plasticity of low-tech representations—that is, the ease with which participants can change them—may help the team break out of unsuccessful designs, and use the assessment activity as an opportunity for redesign.

This movement of attention from the users' work process to the domain of the software professional is a critical attribute of participatory work. It is a major determinant of how scenarios can be constructed—of whose language is used to tell stories. An excessively work-focused vocabulary may not translate well into the domain of software engineering. An excessively abstract, software-focused vocabulary may be impenetrable to users and to other stakeholders who are not software professionals.

We attempted to capture this dimension with the question *who participates in what with whom?* [34]. That is, do the software professionals participate in the users' world? Do the users participate in the software professionals' world? Or do they meet somewhere in the middle? Kensing and Munk-Madsen [21] explored a similar distinction with their characterization of practices along a *concrete-abstract* dimension. In more theoretical terms, Floyd [13] articulated two paradigms for software engineering: *process-oriented* approaches, which were based in the users' work process; and *product-oriented* approaches, which were focused on the software artifact. Similar theoretical distinctions were offered by Carter [6], Checkland [7], and Thoresen [45].

6.2.4 Problematizing the Familiar

The use of simple, low-tech representations helps the team to develop a common language for their discussions. This artificial language makes reference to the participants' home languages (we are using *home* in the sense of the language that is comfortable for each participant to use). For example, we might use a picture of an office colleague as a design object in discussion of a CSCW system (e.g., [31]). The picture is not the person—but neither is the set of parameters that have been instantiated to represent that person in a database of workplace collaborators.

The picture is obviously *different* from each participant's home language. Its differentness lifts the object out of a language space that might be owned by one participant, and moves it into a shared language space that is owned by no one (or everyone). Its differentness also tends to transform all of the attributes of the concept, so that they become open for discussion and reflection: Because the low-tech objects don't have any inherent functionality, we must discuss what we know about them, what others know about them, what a system could know about them, and so on. The attributes of the objects are thus taken away from the domain of unexamined, tacit knowledge, and are moved into the focus of the group's reflection and attention. They are thus *problematized*—transformed from assumptions (that may be assumed differently by different participants) into open questions.

In Chapter 10, Rosson and Carroll used a different approach to the problem of examining assumptions. Their Scenario Browser provides explicit text-based representations of both a scenario and a structured set of comments and interpretations of the scenario. However, Chapters 9 and 11, for example, are concerned with more formal representations (models) of aspects of scenarios—although it is not clear whether this is for the purpose of problematization.

This problematizing has another, perhaps paradoxical advantage: It puts *everyone* at a partial disadvantage. No one is in his or her home domain, and everyone can relate to everyone else's discomfort. The team must then find process assumptions that they can hold in common to deal with this situation of unfamiliar objects. We have often used the metaphor of *games* to provide a familiar social process through which diverse stakeholders can work together with complex concepts that have become problematized through being represented as unfamiliar, low-tech objects. Games work in this context because they are reasonably familiar to all participants. If we understand him correctly, Erickson uses the metaphor of *stories* for similar purposes (Chapter 2, this volume).

6.3 PARTICIPATORY METHODS FOR TELECOMMUNICATIONS WORK

In our work with telephone company users (employees and customers), we became dissatisfied with computer-based and/or formal usability techniques, such as specification languages, dataflow diagrams, computer-based prototyping environments, and so on. Our users are often not computer professionals. These techniques can have an unintended adverse impact upon such users: They may become disenfranchised in design activities in comparison with their collaborators who are computer literate. The software professionals tend to be regarded as the owners and operators of the techniques. The users are often incapable of making a concrete expression of their ideas without having to negotiate with and through the software professionals. By contrast, the software professionals are always capable of using the technique to make a concrete expression of their own ideas.

Thus, many of the available approaches may contain implicit politics that work against the interests of our users, and against the capture of the users' expertise in products designed through these environments.[5] This led us to explore low-tech approaches, with considerable initial success [25, 26, 46].

6.3.1 The Need for *Bifocal* Methods

However, much of participatory work is concerned directly with the process of design. This had led—in our own early PICTIVE practice [26] and in that of others—to complaints that it was too easy to dive into the details. There was insufficient support for big-picture or work-level analysis, representation, and design. We began to look for ways of developing both a macroscopic and a microscopic focus.

Rosson and Carroll (Chapter 10) have also pursued this theme. Their Scenario Browser takes on a second problem that we have encountered: That is, nearly all participatory activities focus their representations on specific *designed artifacts*, rather than on the people using those artifacts. While it is not difficult to discuss the goals or motivations of the users during a session, there is little or no provision for recording those assumptions of the user's state in design artifacts or session records *that are accessible to the user*. This lack of representation of the user's changing internal state can allow participants to make assumptions about what the user is trying to do, and—crucially—to *allow those assumptions to go unexamined*. Using the language of the preceding section, we think that the user's goals and motivations should be problematized along with the rest of the design problem. This is probably best done at the macroscopic level.

Unlike most work in this area, Rosson and Carroll provide for hypertext annotations of textual scenario descriptions, which explicitly represent assumptions about the users' goals.[6] For reasons of ease of manipulation by users and other stakeholders, we have chosen to use low-tech cardlike artifacts for representing *both* components of the work *and* events in the user's internal life. The intent of our efforts and those of Rosson and Carroll, we think, is similar. We suspect that our methods differ because of the somewhat different user populations, the diversity of stakeholders in our work, and our experiences in developing materials

---

[5]For further discussions of the politics of technological artifacts, see Winner's essay, "Do Artifacts Have Politics?" [49], and Friedman and Nissenbaum's analysis of bias in computer systems [16]; see also Nisonen [38], Weisman [48].

[6]Chapters 9 and 11 employ a more formal approach that makes it difficult for users who are not software professionals to participate directly in the discussion of their own internal states.

that are not owned by any participant. This is to say, in our context with telecommunications employees and customers, a workstation capable of hypertext might be considered to be owned by software professionals. Therefore, we have resorted to two sets of low-tech objects.

It may be possible for a single method to represent both macroscopic and microscopic levels of a design. In fact, in a few cases, we have used the same technique for both aspects (see below). However, for most visual interfaces—and some auditory ones—we have found it useful to make a clear separation between

- one analytical domain that considers overall task flow and user cognitions, and
- a second analytical domain that is concerned with detailed design within the context given by the high-level analysis.

We have used CARD and PICTIVE, respectively, for these two bifocal levels of our work. We now prepare to describe them.

6.3.2 How Should a Method Be Described?

With a few exceptions,[7] published descriptions of participatory methods have tended to be broad and allusory, rather than well-specified. This is consistent with the theoretical position that methods are evolving, socially constructed practices (e.g., [13, 15]). However, it makes claims of methodological efficacy difficult to assess: What exactly was done? Can the reader repeat the method? How would the reader know if an author's claim to have followed a particular method was credible?

More specifically, Olson and Moran [40] and Hix, Hartson, and Nielsen [20] noted that it is difficult to integrate usability-oriented methods into software lifecycle practices, unless those methods are specified in language that is accessible to other users of lifecycle models (i.e., software engineers). Hefley et al. [19] argued for the importance of making such an integration possible. Olson and Moran suggested that the following four attributes might constitute a usable description of a method:

- A statement of the problem that the method addresses.
- A device (a tool, technique, model, and/or representation).

[7]See, e.g., Dray [9], Kyng and Greenbaum [22], Monk, Wright, and Davenport [23], Muller, Wildman, and White [35], Noro and Imada [39], and perhaps Palshaugen [42].

- A procedure for using the device.
- A result (how is the outcome of the method to be used?).

In general, we find the Olson and Moran description model a useful critique of our work. We restate their attributes in our own language, collapsing two of them into a single item, and adding one new item of our own:

- An object model (What materials do the participants work with?) [the equivalent, we think, of Olson and Moran's *device*].
- A process model (What do the participants do? How do they work together?) [Olson and Moran's *procedure*].
- A participation model (Who participates, and why?).
- A statement of how the method fits into the lifecycle (What problem is to be solved? What information must be available before we can use this method? What information will the method produce? What can be done with this new information?) [Olson and Moran's *problem statement* and *result*].

We are beginning to believe that the process model and the participation model are reasonably consistent across methods. We will therefore present them in general terms. We will then describe each method in the more specific terms of its object model and its place in the lifecycle.

Process Model The process model (Figure 6.1) involves mutual preparation, education, and validation across diverse perspectives, with designs emerging as the participants communicate about and combine their diverse expertise. Key attributes of the communication process are concreteness, clarity, and consensus.[8] As with any small group exercise, the facilitator must take care to sense the mood of the meeting, as well as any individual difficulties that may arise. Because of the focus on bringing *everyone's* expertise to bear on the design problem, the facilitator typically engages in a great deal of checking-in behavior, intended to keep all members of the group engaged and contributing. This approach tends to focus the group's attention on meeting the needs of all of its members.

Our participatory design sessions have a default agenda of four items, which is subject to change for the immediate or individual needs

---

[8]It may be useful to make explicit reference to models of small group democratic processes (e.g., [17]).

Process Model

1. **Stakeholder/Participant Introductions**
   videotape if desired
   - Names
   - Personal and organizational stakes
   - Anticipated contributions and expertise
2. **Minitutorials,** if needed
   videotape if desired
3. **Work together**
   videotape if desired
   - Mutual preparation
   - Mutual education
   - Mutual validation
   - Emergent ideas
   - Checking in
   - Consensus decision making
4. **Review and/or Walkthrough**
   videotape if at all possible

Figure 6.1. Process model for our participatory methods.

of specific projects or products. Ideally, all of these stages of the design meeting are videotaped, for use in recovering design rationale. If this is not possible, then at least the fourth stage—the closing walkthrough—should be videotaped, for use as one representation of the design.[9]

1. **Stakeholder introductions.** Sessions typically begin with an introduction of all of the members of the group, explicitly including their personal or organizational stakes in the outcome of the project or product, as well as the expertise that they bring.

---

[9]The videotaped design and scenario record may be useful after the product cycle is completed, similar to the work reported by Carey and Rusli (Chapter 7, this volume).

2. **Mutual education.** If appropriate, one or more members of the group may then present brief tutorial introductions to their domains. For example, technologists may provide a proposed scenario of work in the new, target implementation environment [29], or technical writers may introduce the other participants to the documentary style of manuals for the family of products into which the current design will move. In one project, each design session began with a demonstration of changes made to the implementation as a result of the previous design session [32].
3. **Brainstorming the design.** Participants then work with the low-tech materials to discuss design alternatives. In many cases, this part of the work is led by the users' scenarios of how their work flow or task flow proceeds. In other cases, an analyst or technologist might provide an imagined scenario of usage for discussion and critique by the team. A crucial aspect of these discussions is that the ideas be developed and explicated in concrete terms, usually using the low-tech materials to represent, for example, task flows or the detailed layout, dynamics, and behavior of the interface. Other typical small group facilitation techniques may also be used (e.g., boarding issues, graphical facilitation, etc.—see [1]).
4. **Closing walkthrough.** The last 10 to 20 minutes of the session are reserved for a summary walkthrough of the design. This works analogously to the reading of the minutes at the conclusion of a group meeting. It also helps the group to reflect on its achievements, building collective competence for future meetings. A videotaped record of this section of the meeting can serve as a relatively brief design description, sometimes referred to as the "video minutes of the meeting" or, more grandly, as a "multimedia design document."

Participation Model The participation model (Figure 6.2) is based on the notion that anyone whose worklife is affected by the product or service is a stakeholder in that product or service. Stakeholders are candidates to participate in decisions that will have impact upon their worklives. The group of stakeholders for a product or project often includes several of the following: users, developers, human factors workers, technical writers, trainers, marketers, systems analysts, and systems engineers. In general, the active participation by these stakeholders is motivated by three convergent arguments:

- Capture of diverse expertise for quality products or services.
- Commitments of all of the parties who may have influence upon the success of the product or service.

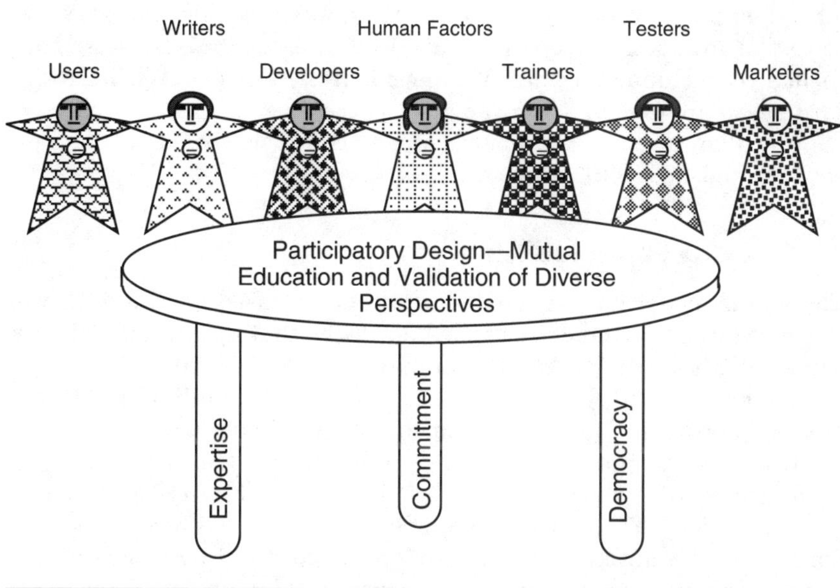

Figure 6.2. Participation model.

- Democratic participation by people whose worklives will be affected by the product or service.

With this common basis in processes and participation, we now describe the object model and the place in the lifecycle for each method in greater detail.

6.4 CARD

The CARD technique combines some of the elements of simple storyboard prototyping with some of the dynamic, participatory attributes of games for design [12, 35]. Each screen image or task component is represented as a playing card. Participants describe and critique the task at the macroscopic level by playing and manipulating the cards—and by creating new ones.

Wirfs-Brock (Chapter 13) makes a different use of cards to represent a different type of scenario. In her work, cards are developed to represent the interrelations of software modules (and, potentially, entities outside of the software system). These can be used to explore scenarios focusing on the responsibilities of one entity to one another. Elsewhere, we have attempted to develop a similar scenario-based representation in a technique called Interface Theater [35]. However, our theatrical technique remains experimental, whereas Wirfs-Brock's card-based approach has proven quite successful.

For quantitative assessments of CARD in use, see Tudor, Muller, Dayton, and Root [46].

6.4.1 CARD Object Model

The object model for the CARD technique is based on the notion of playing cards. We make use of the knowledge that most people have of games as a general category of human play, and of card games as a particular case [35]. We also make use of people's familiarity with the physical manipulation of card-shaped, card-sized artifacts.

One version of our work with this technique involves formatted and preprinted cards, whose images were developed for specific projects or work situations. These images become representations of specific components of the design, and the surfaces onto which they are placed become design representations. The sequential laying out of cards into work flows becomes a representation of work scenarios (e.g., [28, 46]).

In some cases, each card maps directly onto a screen in a software system. In other cases, each card represents an event in the work flow—including both human-computer interaction events and noncomputer events. The latter category can include, for example, the use of paper records, or specific events in a relatively structured telephone conversation with a customer. For example, Figure 6.3 shows a set of cards that we have used in teaching the technique. In this example, the cards are used to describe a simple computer dial-up grocery-shopping scenario [35]. The scenario in Figure 6.3 records one way to use the system components to place a simple grocery order.

Color is often used to help participants understand the organization of card types in an object (or event) class hierarchy. This is an example of how the CARD physical vocabulary can serve as a bridge between the (perhaps implicit) vocabulary of the workplace and the formal vocabulary of software engineering. For example, in a visual system, report-generation screens might be printed on blue cards, while data-entry screens might be printed on pink cards, and so on. In more complex examples, all input events might be printed on yellow cards, with one shade of yellow for voice input and a second shade of yellow for keypad input (e.g., [33]). Similarly, output events might be printed on

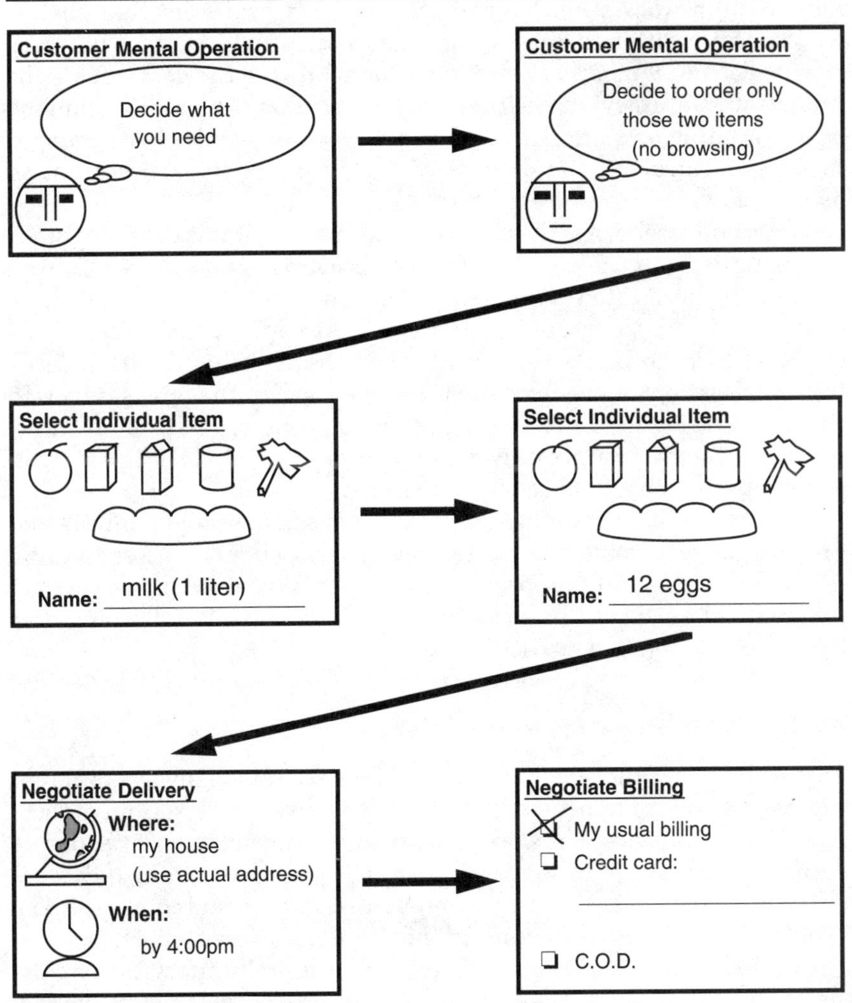

Figure 6.3. Simple CARD example.

green cards, with one shade of green for voice output, and a second shade of green for nonspeech audio.

A major strength of the CARD technique is that cards can be developed to represent the assumed cognitive or motivational state of the user(s). The participants can agree, for example, on the user's goal during a certain work scenario, and can explicitly represent that goal as well as the position in the work sequence at which the user develops that goal. Subsequent user strategies for achieving the goal can also be represented, at relevant positions in the work flow. The user's changing understanding and priorities can be represented explicitly as changes in goals and strategies, and can be added to the scenario representation as needed.

A second strength of the CARD technique is that it is easy for participants to develop their own cards. Blank cards are provided, as well as partially formatted cards (e.g., "keypad input—other" and "voice output—other"), to encourage participants to add to the class hierarchy. If the group meets repeatedly, then the new, handwritten cards from one session can be formally printed for use in the next session. In this way, the facilitator can keep faith with the group by directly incorporating the group's growth in understanding and collective competence into the materials used by the group.

The preceding examples clearly involve considerable analysis and preparation work before the CARD session. In circumstances that did not permit this sort of preparatory work, we have used blank cards of different colors. These sessions involved a great deal of drawing onto the blank cards by all participants.

6.4.2 CARD Scenarios in the Lifecycle

Task Analysis Different applications of the technique involve different representation approaches. If the problem involves describing, documenting, or innovating a work flow, then it is useful to print separate cards for each event in the work flow. These events can include data entry, data lookup, access to noncomputer resources, and conversational events (each with its own subclass hierarchy, if necessary).

In this case, the analyst often completes a preliminary task analysis in order to develop an initial set of cards. These need not be perfect, because part of the point of an ongoing series of CARD sessions for task analysis is collaborative elaboration of the set of CARD materials. That is, the analyst updates the set of materials from one session to the next, including new insights (from users or others), in part, through extending the card materials into new instances and even new classes. At this level of analysis, there is a need for the following knowledge: preliminary knowledge of the current work processes, a general sense of the work issues to be explored, and some sense of the goal of the analysis. The result usually takes the form of a report. However, our experience has been that the design artifacts—a pasteup record of card sequences—

are of great value in communicating both the quality of the analytic activity and the outcome. These should be preserved, and should be carried to review meetings for inspection by people who were not part of the session.

Design By contrast, if the problem involves designing a work flow or interaction system, then it is useful to develop CARD materials that correspond to the users' perspective of the work process, represented in terms of work objects but also in terms of user interface objects [33]. If possible, these should also correspond to the developers' view of interaction objects—however, this is a secondary goal. The design activity follows a framework or skeleton that is initially provided by walking through the users' work scenarios.[10] Later phases (or subsequent design meetings) may share the initiative between users' work scenarios and analysts', designers', or developers' proposed solutions. Note, however, that these solutions remain abstract (and difficult to appreciate, in terms of their impact on real work) until they too are explored as technology-shaped work scenarios.

In this case, there is a need for prior agreement about the nature of the design problem to be solved, and about the implementation platforms, environments, and other resources to be used in developing solutions. The result should take the form of a detailed work flow with implementation notes—either in written or annotated storyboard form. A videotaped record is valuable to supplement this more formal, denotative design representation.

Assessment Finally, if the problem involves critiquing an existing system, then it is often useful to print each screen (for example) of the system onto a separate card. The participants can then use the cards to lay out scenarios from the work flow, describe its shortcomings, and then revise the flow—for example, by discarding some unnecessary screens, rearranging others, and paper-clipping together screens whose contents or functions are redundant.

In this case, an analyst has usually constructed a preliminary representation of the system. The result of the exercise may take several forms, including: a written report of problems encountered; a physical record of

---

[10]We think that it should be possible to do this for more exploratory cases, such as Karat's example (Chapter 5, this volume) of "Imagine taking away the keyboard and mouse from your current workstation and describe doing everything though voice commands." However, we have not had the opportunity to try this technique on so open-ended a problem.

the users' recommendations for high-level system redesign; and/or a videotaped summary of the users' recommendations. Note that all three of these representations permit annotation by the users, to explain the problems or the design recommendations in their own language.

6.5 PICTIVE

The PICTIVE technique uses everyday office objects to represent the components of computer systems, often at the level of detailed screen design. Participants manipulate these objects to describe their ideas about the design, and about the work and other domains behind the design. For quantitative and qualitative assessments of PICTIVE in use, see Muller [26].

6.5.1 PICTIVE Object Model

The PICTIVE technique uses familiar office materials, optionally supplemented by customized materials. The conventional office materials include colored pens, Post-It notes, highlighters, colored paper, and tape. Large papers represent screens or windows. Smaller papers, or large Post-It notes, represent dialog boxes or menus. Small Post-It notes make good data fields or field labels. Icons are drawn onto paper or acetate. Pens are used to draw more complex graphics. Scissors are used to tailor the interface. Colored acetate represents highlighting of fields or windows. Images drawn or printed onto acetate represent one or more cursor shapes.

In addition to the off-the-shelf office materials described above, we have sometimes used customized materials for certain task domains or development environments. For example, in the design of an experimental asynchronous work coordination system [31], we developed an initial set of preprinted icons, which user participants subsequently modified through hand drawing [26]. In a series of workshops to teach graphical user interface design to experienced developers [37], we preprinted paper interface components that were consistent with the Motif Style Guide [41].

These components can then be combined to form screen designs. Participants can manipulate these components to explain not only the static layout of the screen, but also its dynamics and behaviors. In this way, PICTIVE becomes another support tool for scenario exploration.

As discussed in Section 6.4.1, above, it is important that the PICTIVE materials be changeable and extensible by the participants. If the same group meets over multiple sessions, then the facilitators should attempt to transform newly developed materials from one session into standard preprinted materials for the next.

In a convergent development, Young has used similar materials to develop videotaped scenarios of the dynamics of a human-computer interaction using stop-action animation techniques [50].

6.5.2 PICTIVE Scenarios in the Lifecycle

Analysis If the problem to be solved involves an understanding of how people use a current document or computer interface, then the system can be mocked up using PICTIVE materials. Users can then walk through this mockup while narrating and explaining their work scenarios. Using PICTIVE materials in this sort of analysis is helpful, because people can both (a) annotate the materials directly, and (b) rearrange or replace materials to explain how the work could be done differently.[11] This reduces the social distance between the users and the task analysis record.

In this case, as with CARD, the analyst often completes a preliminary task analysis in order to develop an initial set of PICTIVE materials. Unlike task analysis with CARD, however, these materials usually need to be quite accurate, showing the details of the design of the system under analysis. At this level of analysis, there is a need for the following knowledge: preliminary knowledge of the current work processes, a general sense of the work issues to be explored, and some sense of the goal of the analysis. As with CARD, the result usually takes the form of a report, often supplemented with the physical record of the user-modified PICTIVE components.

Design The strongest case for PICTIVE has been in detailed design of visual interfaces, based on user-enacted scenarios. This is well documented in Muller [25, 26]. As stated above, PICTIVE materials may be generic office supplies for many applications—especially character-based interfaces. It is often helpful to customize the materials for particular development environments (e.g., [32, 37]), or for particular application domains [29]. As with CARD, PICTIVE provides an opportunity to elaborate and refine application-specific materials from one

[11]In one informal study, we "annotated" a working system by applying Post-It notes directly to the screen of a workstation, and capturing the session on videotape (Moyer and Muller, unpublished).

session to another. This helps the team to see and appreciate its achievements, and to develop mutual commitment and collective competence.

One particularly strong way to use PICTIVE is in a prototyping cycle. In the exploration of the TelePICTIVE experimental groupware application, we met once every two or three weeks to review the current state of the software implementation [32]. We then used PICTIVE to extend the prototype's design through collaborative scenario development. The paper and video records of these sessions became the input to the next several weeks' software prototyping efforts. Using PICTIVE, rather than the software system itself, made it easier for all of the participants to express their ideas directly. In a more truncated fashion, we used a similar software-to-PICTIVE approach to design a facilities allocation application [29].

As with CARD, there is a need for prior agreement about the nature of the design problem to be solved, and about the implementation platforms, environments, and other resources to be used in developing solutions. The result should take the form of one or more detailed designs with implementation notes—either in written or annotated design drawing form. A videotaped record is valuable to supplement this more formal, denotative design representation.

Assessment Finally, paper-and-pencil mockups have been used for preimplementation assessments of designs for several years (e.g., [36] and Chapter 3 in this volume; [43, 47]). These approaches generally use a form of instructed scenario in which the users are asked to execute the analyst's selected scenario using the system. In some cases, users are asked to work through their own scenarios (Chapter 3, this volume). We have tended not to use PICTIVE in this manner—that is, as a form of usability testing. Instead, we have usually relied on software prototypes for this purpose. However, as noted in the preceding "Design" subsection, we have often used PICTIVE in an iterative design setting, in which several different media were involved (software prototype and PICTIVE).

If PICTIVE were to be used for assessments, then it would probably correspond in its lifecycle position to usability assessments, and particularly to usability testing. Prerequisite knowledge would include the following (in addition to the completed design, implemented in PICTIVE materials): detailed knowledge of who the users are and of what their relevant tasks are. Task scenarios would usually be constructed in advance. The result would be a report, perhaps supplemented with annotated PICTIVE objects and video records, of the users' simulated usage of the design.

6.6 BIFOCAL SCENARIOS

As we noted earlier, we have found a need for bifocal representations to support scenarios at different levels of detail and of intent. We now explore several examples that used the CARD and PICTIVE techniques in different ways.

6.6.1 Task Analysis of Directory Assistance Operators

In an analysis of the work of directory assistance telephone operators, we began with CARD materials to understand the overall flow of the work. One category of cards that turned out to be crucial was called "operator mental work." Initially, the analyst thought that this was a minor part of the job. Instead, through collaborative scenario development, the team identified a number of high-frequency types of transformation, interpretation, and expert knowledge that operators perform or use routinely.

A subset of the class hierarchy of events and activities in the operators' work flow, represented as cards, is shown in Figure 6.4. Note that most classes of events or activities include a card that is deliberately underspecified: This encourages participants to design new class instances (e.g., new examples of mental operations or knowledge work) or even new classes of events or activities.

A portion of a representative task flow is shown in Figure 6.5. For the conversational cards, each has been hand-annotated to show not only the *class* provided by the analyst, but also some details of conversation provided by the other session participants. Many of the keyboard cards have been hand-annotated to show what was keyed. Thus, this record is both abstract (it is in the language of the class hierarchy) and concrete (annotations are in the language of the workplace).

There were some aspects of the analysis that required more detailed work. For example, it was sometimes necessary to critique the layout of keys on the keyboard, or to discuss possible changes to the keyboard or to the softkeys that were displayed at the bottom of the screen.[12] For these discussions, we moved from the CARD representation of task flow to detailed PICTIVE representations of the screen or the keyboard. At the conclusion of the detailed discussion, we returned to the CARD representation to pursue other task flow issues.

The outcome of our bifocal task analysis was diverse and valuable. Subject-matter expert participants rated the entire process quite highly

---

[12]Examples of these will *not* be shown, to avoid vendor-specific comments.

Class Hierarchy of Task Components Represented in Cards

- *Class:* Customer conversation
    - Customer request
    - Customer clarification
    - Customer conversation (other)
- *Class:* Operator conversation
    - Operator inquiry
    - Operator report to Customer
    - Operator conversation (other)
- *Class:* Operator mental work
    - Information translation
    - Use of local knowledge
    - *Subclass:* Strategy
        - Named search strategy
        - Unnamed search strategy
        - Strategy (other)
    - Operator mental work (other)
- *Class:* Keyboard activities
    - Softkey
    - Key field
    - File trigger key
    - ExpLoc and Page keys
    - Audio key
    - Toll key
    - Keyboard (generic)
- *Class:* Screen activities
    - Key fields
    - Softkeys
    - Screen (listing)
- *Class:* Automated voice events
    - Personal response system
    - Audio response system
- *Class:* Miscellaneous cards
    - Title card - ("The Directory Assistance CARD Game")
    - New ideas card

Figure 6.4. Class hierarchy of events in directory assistance operator task analysis.

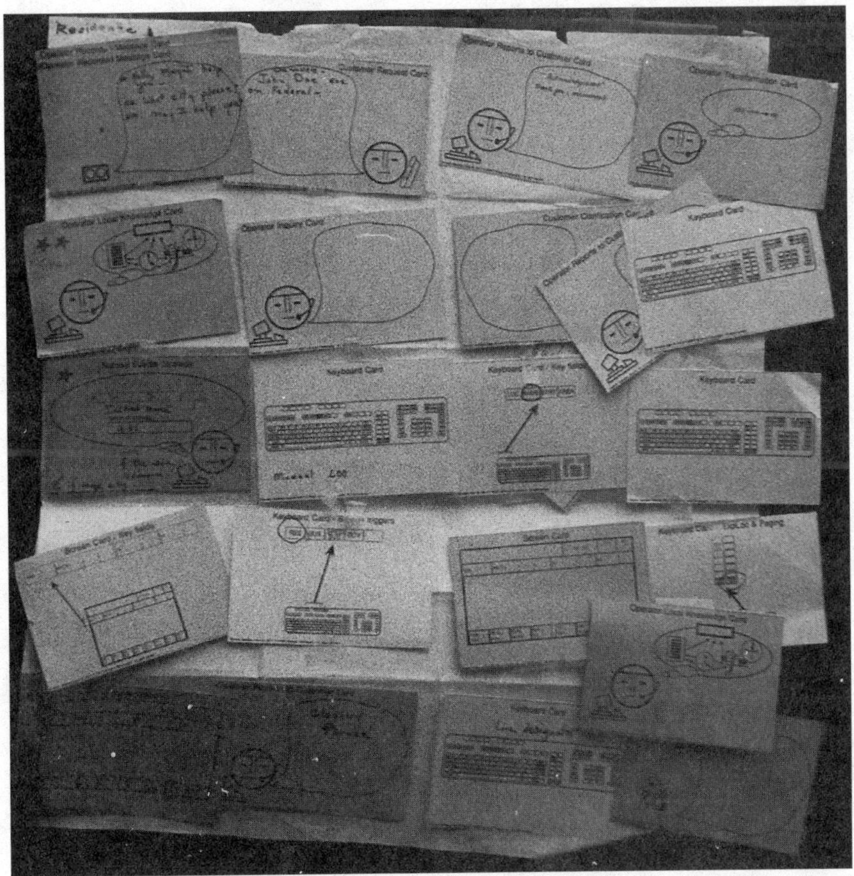

Figure 6.5. Subset of collaboratively developed scenario of directory assistance operator work flow.

(Figure 6.6). We developed a new understanding of operators as knowledge workers, which has been warmly received by operators, union, and management [28]. Our bifocal analysis, coupled with a follow-up quantitative analysis, had direct implications for mediated communications, job aids, training, and customer relations. On the basis of the bifocal analyses alone, we also developed a set of proposals for modified and/or enhanced functionalities that have been presented to the vendor as desirable features.

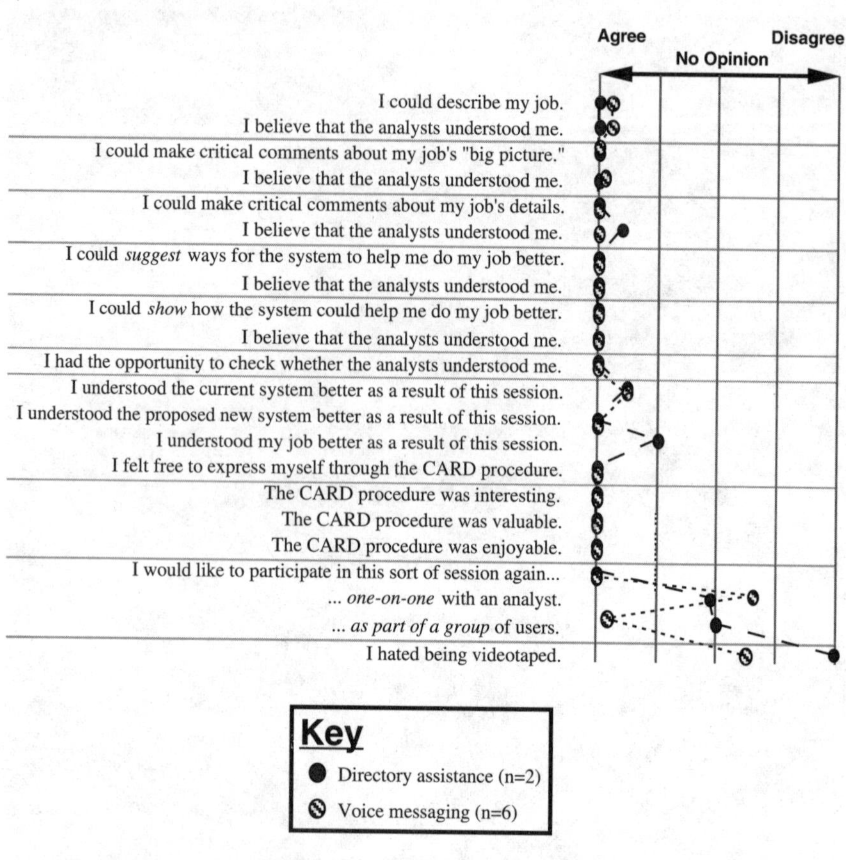

Figure 6.6. Participant assessment of operator task analysis sessions.

6.6.2 Voice Interfaces

A second example of bifocal analyses involves voice interfaces that can be used over the telephone. In general terms, these involve digitized voice output to the caller, and either telephone keypad or voice-recognition input from the caller.

For this domain, some of us have developed a set of generic voice interface cards [33] that are beginning to be used in product design. These cards combine high-level work flow (user goal and strategy, etc.) with detailed design (message wording, keypad input, etc.). While quite successful (see Figure 6.6), the result is somewhat uncomfortable: Users complain that the set of CARD materials is too complex, and that they are uncertain which card to apply when. By contrast, another of us (Tudor, unpublished) has used cards for the work flow design, but has supplemented them with PICTIVE-like Post-It notes for detailed design directly on the cards. Assessments of both of these developments are ongoing.

6.7 CONCLUSION

Together, PICTIVE and CARD provide a set of *bifocals for design*: CARD supports a relatively macroscopic or *distance view* in which to develop scenarios focusing on the work flow, task components, and user's goal, strategies, and motivations. PICTIVE supports a relatively microscopic or *closeup view* in which the components within each task can become the foci of scenarios at almost any extent of detail. The different materials associated with each technique can help the team remember what they are currently doing, and also what they *were* doing before the current subtask. Thus, in our experience, the two distinct object models have the advantage exactly because they are distinct and different.

Finally, we note that each of the authors uses these techniques somewhat differently. While we have attempted to provide specific methodological details and even models, we think it is premature to think of PICTIVE and CARD as if they were conventional *engineering methods with guaranteed outcomes*. Rather, we recognize that each practitioner must select, adapt, and innovate techniques and practices that work well with his or her situation of use and personal attributes [27]. We offer this discussion of PICTIVE and CARD in the spirit of the tools-for-the-toolbox approach to participatory design outlined by Kensing and Munk-Madsen [21].

ACKNOWLEDGMENTS

We thank the following people for contributing to our understanding of PICTIVE and CARD through feedback on their use of the techniques, either with one or more of us, or independently: Rita Bush, Kathleen Cebulka, Peter Clitherow, Susan Davies, Harry Goldberg, Kim Halskov Madsen, Cathy House, Janice Housten, Darren Kall, Connie Kaye, Agnes Lee, David Miller, Nancy Mond, Jakob Nielsen, Robert Root, John Sauer, J. Zach Shoher, John G. Smith, Steve Stein, Courtney Vargo, and Jayson Webb. Jean MacKendree and Thea Turner asked the right, difficult questions. Emilie Young pointed out important connections between PICTIVE and other participatory techniques. Helpful support and encouragement were provided by Annette Adler, Bill Anderson, John Bennett, Pamela Burke, Rita Bush, Kathy Carter, Ed Freeman, Paul Freeman, John Karat, Wendy Kellogg, Sarah Kuhn, Mike Mase, Hal Miller-Jacobs, Jakob Nielsen, Terry Roberts, Aita Salasoo, Jared Spool, John Thomas, Kari Thoresen, Bud Wonsiewicz, and Emilie Young.

REFERENCES

[1] Bennett, J. L. & Karat, J. (1994). Facilitating effective HCI design meetings. In *Proceedings of CHI'94,* Boston (April).

[2] Bjerknes, G., Ehn, P. & Kyng, M. (1987). *Computers and Democracy: A Scandinavian Challenge.* Brookfield, VT: Gower.

[3] Bødker, S. (ed.). (1989). *Proceedings of the 12th IRIS: Information Systems Research Seminar in Scandinavia.* Aarhus, Denmark: University of Aarhus.

[4] Bødker, S. (1991). *Through the Interface: A Human Activity Approach to User Interface Design.* Hillsdale, NJ: Lawrence Erlbaum.

[5] Bødker, S., Ehn, P., Kammarsgaard, J., Kyng, M. & Sundblad, Y. (1987). A UTOPIAN experience: On design of powerful computer-based tools for skilled graphic workers. In G. Bjerknes, P. Ehn & M. Kyng (eds.), *Computers and Democracy: A Scandinavian Challenge.* Brookfield, VT: Gower.

[6] Carter, K. (1989). Two conceptions of designing. In S. Bødker (ed.), *Proceedings of the 12th IRIS: Information Systems Research Seminar in Scandinavia.* Aarhus, Denmark: University of Aarhus, pp. 101–110.

[7] Checkland, P. (1984). Rethinking a systems approach. In R. Tomlinson & I. Kiss (eds.), *Rethinking the Process of Operational Research and Systems Analysis.* Oxford U.K.: Pergamon.

[8] Clement, A. & van den Besselaar, P. (1993). A retrospective look at PD projects. *Communications of the ACM, 36*(6), 29–37 (June).

[9] Dray, S. M. (1992). Understanding and supporting successful group work in software design: Lessons from IDS. Position paper of J. Karat & J. Bennett (cochairs), *Understanding and Supporting Successful Group Work in Software Design.* Workshop at CSCW'92, Toronto, October.

[10] Dray, S., Dayton, T., Mrazek, D., Muckler, F. A. & Rafeld, M. (1993). Making human factors usable. In *Proceedings of HFES'93.* Seattle, WA: Human Factors and Ergonomics Society, pp. 863–866.

[11] Ehn, P. (1988). *Work-Oriented Design of Computer Artifacts.* Stockholm: Arbetslivscentrum.

[12] Ehn, P. & Sjogren, D. (1991). From system descriptions to scripts for action. In J. Greenbaum & M. Kyng (eds.), *Design at Work: Cooperative Design of Computer Systems.* Hillsdale, NJ: Lawrence Erlbaum.

[13] Floyd, C. (1987). Outline of a paradigm change in software engineering. In G. Bjerknes, P. Ehn & M. Kyng (eds.), *Computers and Democracy: A Scandinavian Challenge.* Brookfield, VT: Gower.

[14] Floyd, C., Mehl, W.-M., Reisin, F.-M., Schmidt, G. & Wolf, G. (1989). Out of Scandinavia: Alternative approaches to software design and system development. *Human-Computer Interaction, 4*(4), 253–350.

[15] Floyd, C., Zullighoven, H., Budde, R. & Keil-Slawik, R. (eds.), *Software Development and Reality Construction.* Berlin: Springer-Verlag.

[16] Friedman, B. & Nissenbaum, H. (1993). Discerning bias in computer systems. In *INTERCHI'93 Adjunct Proceedings.* Amsterdam: ACM Press, pp. 141–142.

[17] Gastil, J. (1993). *Democracy in Small Groups: Participation, Decision Making, and Communication.* Philadelphia: New Society.

[18] Greenbaum, J. & Kyng, M. (1991). *Design at Work: Cooperative Design of Computer Systems.* Hillsdale, NJ: Lawrence Erlbaum.

[19] Hefley, W. F., Buie, E. A., Lynch, G. F., Muller, M. J., Hoecker, D. G., Carter, J. & Roth, J. T. (1994). Integrating human factors with software engineering practices. Paper in *Proceedings of Human Factors and Ergonomics Society Annual Meeting.*

[20] Hix, D., Hartson, H. R. & Nielsen, J. (1994). A taxonomic model for developing high impact formative usability evaluation methods. In *CHI'94 Conference Companion.* Workshop at CHI'94. Boston: ACM Press, p. 464.

[21] Kensing, F. & Munk-Madsen, A. (1993). PD: Structure in the toolbox. *Communications of the ACM, 36*(6), 78–85 (June).

[22] Kyng, M. & Greenbaum, J. (1992). Participatory design. *Tutorial at CHI'92.* Monterey, CA: ACM Press.

[23] Monk, A., Wright, P. & Davenport, L. (1992). A cost-effective technique for refining the usability of prototype systems. *Tutorial at CHI'92.* Monterey, CA: ACM Press.

[24] Muller, M. J. (1991a). No mechanization without representation: Who participates in participatory design of large software products? Panelist's remarks in *Reaching through Technology: CHI'91 Conference Proceedings*, p. 391.

[25] Muller, M. J. (1991b). PICTIVE—An exploration in participatory design. In *Reaching through Technology: CHI'91 Conference Proceedings*, pp. 225–231.

[26] Muller, M. J. (1992). Retrospective on a year of participatory design using the PICTIVE technique. Paper in *Striking a Balance: Proceedings of CHI'92.* Monterey, CA: ACM Press, pp. 455–462.

[27] Muller, M. J., Blomberg, J. L., Carter, K., Dykstra, E. A., Greenbaum, J. & Halskov Madsen, K. (1991). Panel: Participatory design in Britain and North America: Responses to the "Scandinavian challenge." In *Reaching through Technology: CHI'91 Conference Proceedings*, pp. 389–392.

[28] Muller, M. J., Carr, R., Eickstaedt, C., Clonts, J., Diekmann, B., Wharton, C., Ashworth, C. A. & Dykstra-Erickson, E. A. (1994). Telephone operators as

knowledge workers: Contrasting "North American" and "Scandinavian" task analytic approaches. Paper at *Human Computer Interface Consortium*, Frasier, CO, February.

[29] Muller, M. J., Kaye, C. & Sauer, J. E., Jr. (1991). Case study of transformation of screen layout and dynamics through participatory design. Poster at *Human Factors Society Annual Meeting*, San Francisco, September.

[30] Muller, M. J., Kuhn, S. & Meskill, J. A. (1992). *PDC'92: Proceedings of the Participatory Design Conference.* Cambridge, MA: Computer Professionals for Social Responsibility.

[31] Muller, M. J., Smith, J. G., Goldberg, H. & Shoher, J. Z. (1991). Privacy, anonymity, and interpersonal competition issues identified during participatory design of project management groupware. *SIGCHI Bulletin, 23*(1), 82–87 (January).

[32] Muller, M. J., Smith, J. G., Miller, D. S., White, E. A. & Wildman, D. M. (1992). Designing a groupware implementation of a manual participatory design process. In *Proceedings of PDC'92.* Cambridge, MA: Computer Professionals for Social Responsibility, pp. 145–153.

[33] Muller, M. J., Webb, J. & Davies, S. (1993). Toward participatory design of community oriented systems and services. *Workshop at Computer Professionals for Social Responsibility Annual Meeting,* October, Seattle, WA: Computer Professionals for Social Responsibility.

[34] Muller, M. J., White, E. A. & Wildman, D. M. (1993). Taxonomy of PD practices: A brief practitioner's guide. *Communications of the ACM, 36*(4), 26–28 (June).

[35] Muller, M. J., Wildman, D. M. & White, E. A. (1994). Participatory design through games and other group exercises. *Tutorial at CHI'94*, April. Boston: ACM Press.

[36] Nielsen, J. (1990). Paper versus computer implementations as mockup scenarios for heuristic evaluation. In *Proceedings of INTERACT'90.* Cambridge, U.K.: Elsevier, pp. 315–320.

[37] Nielsen, J., Bush, R. M., Dayton, J. T., Mond, N. E., Muller, M. J. & Root, R. W. (1992). Teaching experienced developers to design graphical user interfaces. Paper in *Striking a Balance: Proceedings of CHI'92.* Monterey, CA: ACM Press, pp. 557–564.

[38] Nisonen, E. (1994). Women's safety audit guide—An action plan and a grass roots community development tool. *CPSR Newsletter, 12*(3), 7.

[39] Noro, K. & Imada, A. S. (eds.). (1991). *Participatory Ergonomics.* London: Taylor and Francis.

[40] Olson, J. S. & Moran, T. P. (1993). Mapping the method muddle: Guidance in using methods for user interface design. *Technical Report No. 49.* October. Ann Arbor, MI: University of Michigan, Cognitive Science and Machine Intelligence Laboratory.

[41] Open Software Foundation. (1991). *OSF/Motif Style Guide, Revision 1.1.* Englewood Cliffs, NJ: Prentice Hall.

[42] Palshaugen, O. (1986). *Method of Designing a Starting Conference.* Oslo: Work Research Institute.

[43] Rettig, M. (1994). Practical programmer: Prototyping for tiny fingers. *Communications of the ACM, 37*(4), 21–27 (April).

[44] Schuler, D. & Namioka, A. (eds.). (1993) *Participatory Design: Principles and Practices.* Hillsdale, NJ: Lawrence Erlbaum.

[45] Thoresen, K. (1989). Systems development alternative design strategies. In K. Tijdens, M. Jennings, I. Wagner & M. Weggelaar (eds.), *Women, Work, and Computerization: Forming New Alliances.* Amsterdam: North-Holland.

[46] Tudor, L. G., Muller, M. J., Dayton, T. & Root, R. W. (1993). A participatory design technique for high-level task analysis, critique, and redesign: The CARD method. In *Proceedings of the Human Factors and Ergonomics Society 1993 Meeting,* Seattle, WA, October.

[47] Virzi, R. A. (1989). What can you learn from a low-fidelity prototype? In *Proceedings of the Human Factors Society 33rd Annual Meeting,* Denver, CO, pp. 224–228.

[48] Weisman, L. K. (1992). *Discrimination by Design: A Feminist Critique of the Man-Made Environment.* Urbana, IL: University of Illinois.

[49] Winner, L. (1980). Do artifacts have politics? *Daedelus, 109*, 121–136.

[50] Young, E. (1992). Participatory video prototyping. Poster at CHI'92, Monterey, CA, April.

CHAPTER 7

Usage Representations for Reuse of Design Insights: A Case Study of Access to On-Line Books

Tom Carey and Mak Rusli

Department of Computing and Information Science
University of Guelph, Ontario N1G ZW1, Canada

The research described here examines the role of scenario representations as a mechanism for promoting reuse of design insights for human-computer interaction. In contrast to the role of scenarios in many other chapters in this volume, we consider scenarios here as a retrospective technique, to enable other designers to find, absorb, and apply the design insights from a library of cases. This has implications both for learning HCI design and in the wider context of reusing software designs.

In the case study we describe here, the insights gained from a particular design project were generated through an in-depth analysis of usage, in which an abstract, graphical representation was developed to represent how various users chose to employ the system's features. We describe the shortcomings of that abstract representation as an aid to later redesign, and present scenarios as a potential alternative. We have turned to interpretive scenarios as a mechanism for presenting the design insights from this study, and have found them to be an effective way to encapsulate the richness of user behavior in a complex discretionary task.

7.1 INTRODUCTION

In this chapter we consider the use of interpretative scenarios to summarize the insights resulting from a design case study. This contrasts with the other uses of scenarios in this volume, such as envisioning expected use of a system (Chapters 1, 4, 6, 8, 10, 12, 13) or recording a design team's shared understanding of anticipated usage (Chapter 2).

In these other applications, scenarios are a substitute for data on actual usage (which has not yet occurred). When usage data is available, it can be recorded for later reuse in numerous ways. Statistics comparing performance with different systems can demonstrate the effectiveness of particular design choices [5, 6]. Noteworthy incidents, particularly difficulties with certain features, can be illustrated with transcripts of verbal protocols or videotaped records. More extensive quantitative analysis can reveal patterns of use, especially the interactions within sequences of operations. Records from debriefing interviews can provide information about users' subjective reactions to the interactive experience.

Why, then, would we use scenarios to describe usage? All of the media above are restricted in their ability to provide interpretation of users' actions. Precisely because they show the *data* of operational usage directly, they are not as effective at illuminating the *meaning* of user actions. We are particularly interested in discretionary usage, where people exercise considerable choice over how they combine system features to achieve desired goals. For example, given a set of changes to be made in a word processing document, there are typically many different tactics and features that could be employed to achieve the end result. In these cases, understanding usage requires that we understand more than the frequency of use for individual features, or even the patterns of use shown by classes of users. We must understand why the choices of particular features by users emerged as they did, to effectively enhance, extend, or generalize from our designs.

Consider, for example, the case of SuperBook[1] [6], a classic instance of applying HCI principles and iterative design to improve user access to on-line information. Data from a series of studies have been pub-

[1]SuperBook is a trademark of Bellcore.

lished, including statistics for performance on benchmark tasks with different design alternatives. One of the innovations in SuperBook was the integration of an expandable table of contents with a keyword search facility. For a designer facing a different but related design problem, say with a system including an index feature, additional information on how people used the system features would be very useful—indeed, the insights from the SuperBook case are of limited application without knowing more about the tactics employed in discretionary use. When did people use the table of contents without the keyword search facility, when did they use the keyword search without attending to the table of contents structure, and when did they choose to integrate their use of both facilities?

The answers to such questions are not easily generated. They require an intensive analysis of videotapes and a deeper debriefing of study participants than would be needed when tactics are not an issue. The results will be messy: The patterns of use are likely to vary with user, task (such as how much the user knows about the particular information being sought), and context of use (such as whether the search is just starting or has been ongoing with limited success). Some of the meaning of user actions must be inferred by judgment based on developing understanding of individual users: Was a switch in search tactics the result of abandoning an unproductive attempt or the result of gaining knowledge from the last few actions? Based on our experience with similar data, there are likely to be valuable patterns of use, which deep familiarity with the data can reveal.

If we do generate such complex results, how could we communicate them? A tabular form, which matches characteristics to feature choice and search tactic, will not do justice to the messiness of the data [2]. We claim that a few well-constructed scenarios can provide the essential insights. In flavor these will be closer to Tom Erickson's "stories" than to "vision scenarios" (Chapter 2, this volume). But they will be interpretations of observable behaviors rather than envisionings. We call these reconstructions of events **interpretive scenarios**. They can provide a context within which individual transcripts or video clips make sense, in terms of the reasons for user actions.

In Jakob Nielsen's taxonomy (Chapter 3, this volume) their purpose is to communicate issues and to structure designer thinking, their format is textual description, and their inspiration is empirical observation *plus* analysis and interpretation. Our use of these scenarios suggests an additional classifier for the taxonomy: description at the operational, tactical, and/or strategic level. Within Jack Carroll's classification of lifecycle roles for scenarios, our use falls into the "generalization" category, in which design insights are made available for reuse in related design settings (introduction to this volume).

As Erickson relates (Chapter 2, this volume), such an approach to understanding design issues is at odds with our methodological upbringing. Relying on interpretation of user actions takes us off the seemingly firm ground of data into the quicksand of individual analysts' abilities to deconstruct events. But this is always the nature of the war stories by which so much of case knowledge gets disseminated within a community of practice. In our use of such data we are in a growing company of scholars in differing domains who have to make sense out of the complexities of individual patterns of behavior. Kurt Van Lehn points out that in the educational community the focus has shifted from comparing *treatment conditions* to understanding how various changes in pedagogy affect the cognitive and tactical processes of the learner [13]. Lee Shulman makes the same claim for expertise in university instruction, arguing that *case knowledge* is the vehicle for formulating and communicating insights rather than quantitative data analysis [11]. Of course, this reporting of results through interpretation of individual cases has long characterized anthropological methods.

In this chapter we present interpretive scenarios as representations for a particular design case study. We describe first the system and usage being represented. The next section then presents the analysis tools, which we developed to help us understand the diversity of discretionary usage for this particular design. Our interpretation of user actions was thus based on extensive study and incremental development of appropriate representations. We then describe some of the problems encountered by inexperienced designers attempting to apply the insights from these graphical representations to redesign the user interface. Then we discuss scenario representations for the same usage data, and the final section describes the potential for such representations to aid in the process of learning HCI design.

7.2 THE CASE STUDY: ACCESS TO ON-LINE INFORMATION IN BOOKMANAGER

As part of a larger study of usage of BookManager,[2] an IBM program product for access to on-line books, we investigated how people made discretionary use of the features available to support access. Users were information technology professionals solving a set of problems that required them to access on-line technical documentation for an applica-

---

[2]BookManager is a registered trademark of IBM Corporation.

Using the ISQL Guide and Reference manual (ISQ), perform the following task:

It can be tedious to retype queries for minor changes and corrections. The commands store, start, recall, and change can be used to avoid retyping. Use these commands to simplify the execution of the select command below so when information for a new student is required, the entire command does not have to be retyped:

select * from students where studid = 595043

Figure 7.1. Task #4 for BookManager study.

tion development tool. A typical task is listed in Figure 7.1. The on-line information was organized in booklike fashion. The BookManager tool provided a number of features for access to the on-line information. We consider here a part of the study in which the only access aids available were the table of contents, the index, and a keyword search facility.

The original mandate for this part of the larger study was to develop a strategy to improve inefficient usage of the system's features. Some users clearly were able to find the required information more efficiently than others, even taking into account differences in initial knowledge. We were asked to identify from the usage data the most efficient choice of features for various situations, which could then be incorporated into a tactical section of the on-line help facility to complement the existing operational help. We were also asked to consider whether some form of active help could be used to monitor people's actions and suggest to them more efficient tactics for choosing when to use the table of contents, index, or keyword search.

Our work revealed that the designers' conceptions of the product were centered around the task of locating information. What the users experienced was more like **information discernment**, constantly sifting through information to determine both meaning and relevancy. This uncertainty about the appropriateness of information led to much more tentativeness for many users, and invalidated some of the designers' perceptions of the cost and benefit of the system's features. We established that neither active help nor on-line hints for tactics were feasible, because no one set of tactics could be recommended for most users, even when their operations with the system seemed similar. The best improvement strategy was to redesign features to provide better perceptual orientation to effective actions.

A key component of our work was to study in depth several representative users, to define why they chose a specific access feature at particular points in their tasks. Understanding the factors that determined feature choice was critical to making recommendations about effective redesign. For example, the extreme case of apparent inefficiency was one user who chose to ignore most of the aids available and browsed through the on-line documents extensively. This resulted in the longest access times observed. This usage was initially conceived as a lack of familiarity with the variety of features available, to be solved through more training on the benefits of other features. But a closer look revealed that this user was very deliberate in his choice—he experienced marked disorientation in moving around the document with the original feature design, and had made an implicit assessment that the costs of this disorientation outweighed the potential benefits of the various access features. (Subsequent redesign of the tool improved the orientation in later product versions.)

The results generated during this analysis seemed well suited to our ongoing goal of documenting design insights for reuse by others, especially inexperienced designers, as part of their process of learning HCI design. The next section explains the representations we developed as part of our analysis, and then we describe an experiment in which inexperienced designers were asked to use them to inform their own redesign of one aspect of the BookManager interface. Further information about the BookManager studies can be found in [2, 8].

7.3 REPRESENTING AND INTERPRETING FEATURE SELECTION

One of the products of our analysis process was a graphical representation relating feature choice (table of contents, index, or keyword search) to some of the factors that helped determine the choice. This helped us to interpret users' choices in terms of the underlying factors that shaped them. The representations were developed incrementally: The anomalies in our data revealed by one representation were addressed by extending the dimensions of analysis to produce new representation. In each case we were interpreting the contexts of user actions. Jack Carroll refers to this need for interpretive judgment as "the razor's edge between creative intuition and grounded analysis" (introduction to this volume).

A sample task, #4, was previously shown in Figure 7.1. A condensed transcript from the videotape of user "John" on this task is shown in Figure 7.2.

Based on the transcripts, debriefing interviews, and observers' notes from the task sessions, each use of an access feature—keyword search, index, or table of contents—was categorized with the users' state of knowl-

Preliminary	• understands the question • gives a good description of what he needs to do: "let's do it" ...
Scans TOC	• expands TOC horizontally [4_1] • looks at titles and quickly says he likes Chapter 6.0, "Using ISQL Commands to Save Time..." ...
Reading Chapter 6.0	• spends some time reading intro. paragraph • careful reading going on here • questions the use of "Press Enter" in the text as it applies to what he should do at the keyboard • pages down again... continues to read carefully ...
Search for store	• leaves intro. material and wants to search on "store" [4_2] • gets 56 hits and doesn't like that volume much ...
Search for store example	• keyword search on "store" and "example" [4_3] • selects a promising hit and reviews example • pages down and reads text ...
Tries it out	• does a command • stores command • reads feedback • recalls stored command • does a change • start • SUCCESS

Figure 7.2. Condensed transcript of John on task #4.

edge in the information discernment process. For example, for task #4, user "John" begins with very little knowledge about what information is required to solve the task problem, but some knowledge about how the structure of the on-line documents relates to what he needs. These two dimensions of certainty in information discernment are taken from work by Geoffrey Stephenson on usage of statistical database systems [12]. After perusing the table of contents and reading one content item, John has a better idea of what information will address his need, but is not now sure where it might be (it wasn't in chapter 6 as he originally thought). After the first keyword search, he expresses certainty that he needs to see a particular example of the store command.

This progression through varying degrees of knowledge, about what is needed and how to get to it, is shown in the disretionary usage choice graph in Figure 7.3. The step numbers in the graph—4_1, 4_2, 4_3—correspond to feature selections in the transcript of Figure 7.2. The uses of keyword search are indicated by unshaded nodes, the use of table of contents by the light gray shading. The final feature choice, which resulted in finding the required information, is shown with a black border, and the arrows show the general direction of change in certainty about the information required. Note that the final feature choice is not necessarily one with which the user should have begun; its success at the end is in part the product of less successful accesses earlier, which moved the user through the information dimensions. Mapping the use of a feature against the dimensions of certainty helps us see the patterns in individual tactics for information discernment.

Figure 7.4 shows the pattern of feature choice for John across six problem tasks. The figure is called a *discretionary usage choice graph*. John's pattern of usage begins to emerge when we study the graph, especially the way the features cluster. Note the anomaly in his use of table of contents to begin task #4.

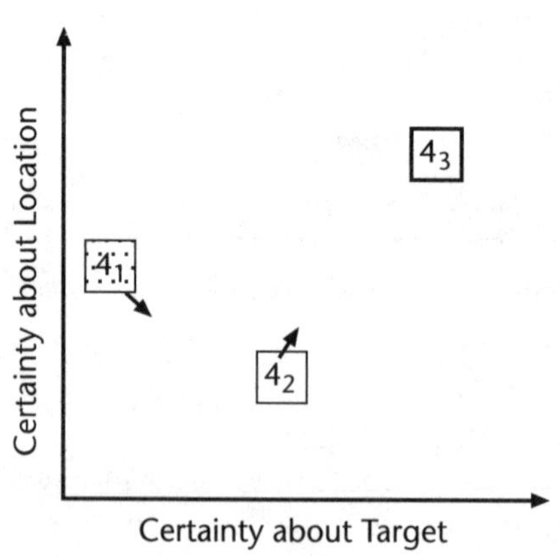

Figure 7.3. Discretionary usage choice graph for John on task #4.

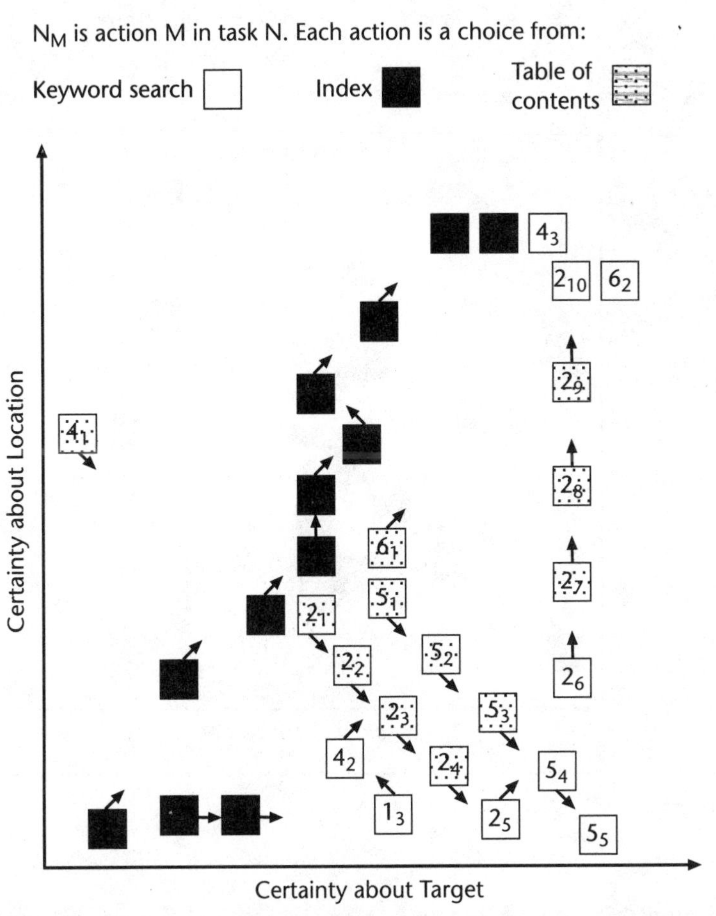

Figure 7.4. Discretionary usage choice graph for John.

Figure 7.5 shows a similar composite graph for another user, "Mary." While the task statement is the same for each user, their experience of information discernment depends on their prior knowledge, their own tactical preferences, and their personal styles. There are a number of differences in the patterns of John and Mary. For example, John tends to move fairly systematically toward increased certainty about what he needs and how to get to it (indicated by the fact that each path tends to move in one direction at a time, without reversals). Al-

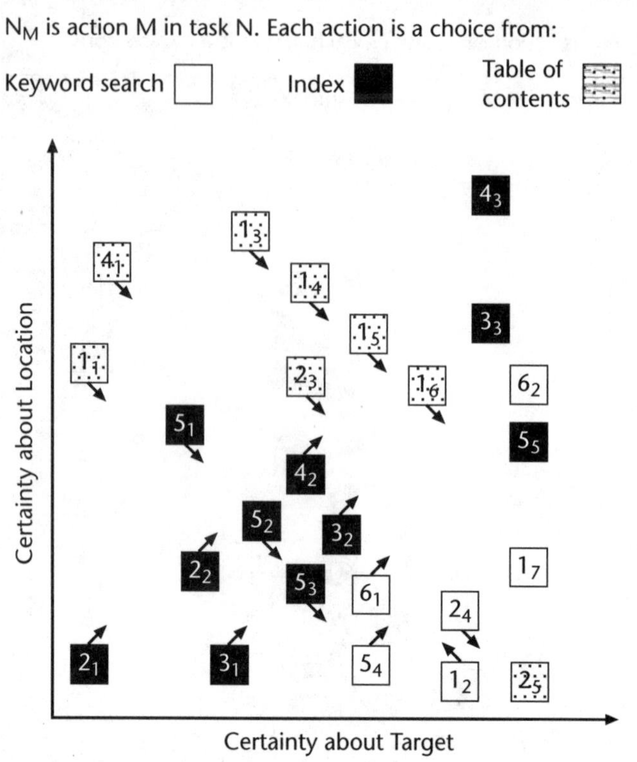

Figure 7.5. Discretionary usage choice graph for Mary.

most all of his final states end up in the top right quadrant, whereas Mary ends up with considerable certainty about what is needed but not always where to expect it to be. Some of Mary's successful accesses were serendipitous; for example, in task#2 she gradually determined exactly what was needed and then scanned the table of contents until she found it in the end (access 5 in task 2).

In the further analysis of the BookManager data, we considered additional dimensions such as the semantic type of the target information (information about a concept, an object, a function or about the task) and the persistence of users with a particular feature. For example, the anomaly noted above for John in the first access for task #4 relates to the type of information being sought: At that point he is thinking of a concept for which he does know the appropriate terms in this system, and he tends to use the table of contents for such conceptual information. On the other hand, the index categorizes information in terms of system objects and functions, so sometimes it is used where one might expect a different feature choice (e.g., Mary's access 5 for task 5). We extended the discretionary choice graphs to include these dimensions, adding shapes for the nodes and indicators of feature use change.

These comments illustrate the richness of discretionary use in this study. Many of the users' frustrations occur when these mappings conflict. For example, the index is the preferred choice when not much is known about either what is needed or how it relates to the document structure, but it is not a good choice if the user's conception of it is not tied to system objects and functions. This suggests that future redesigns of the system could offer some new feature to address these conflicts.

Further information about the interpretation of individual usage patterns can be found in [4].

7.4 APPLYING REPRESENTATIONS FOR REDESIGN

The discretionary usage graph representations were generated to aid analysis of the data from our studies. As part of our larger research agenda to develop aids for learning about HCI, we also wanted to investigate how such coproducts of the development process could be reused in other development projects. To generate some ideas about how these representations might contribute to future design efforts, we conducted some initial testing with six people: two HCI professionals, two senior undergraduate students with some HCI training, and two software engineers with no HCI training.

The testing involved the following steps:

- Subjects were shown a videotape of BookManager's three main features.
- Subjects described how they would employ the features of BookManager to access on-line technical information, and how they would expect other people to use them.
- Subjects were presented with a possible design change to BookManager: They were shown a videotape of SuperBook's use of table of contents to augment keyword search, and asked to describe how changing BookManager to include such a feature would alter usage (their own and others').
- Subjects were then given the graphical representations generated during the analysis, beginning with the transcript and representation for a single user and task.

- Subjects were asked with each representation to reconsider their expectations about the impact of the possible design change to BookManager.

We can summarize the results of this pilot study as follows:

- The subjects with more HCI experience initially showed more awareness of the factors that might lead to different patterns of usage, especially as related to task. On the other hand, they did not show any greater insight into the complexity of their own behavior or the overall phenomena.
- The subjects with more HCI experience were able to make effective use of the representations. Some quotes:

> If I had looked at this, I would have answered the earlier questions differently.
>
> (If the SuperBook alternative had been present) he wouldn't have this dropping in target location. This cluster of repeated operations would have been eliminated.
>
> This user would have been able to get his information faster, which I never thought of before.

- The subjects with less HCI experience were able to pick up important information about how usage would differ across different people:

> He is kind of scrambling to remember where he last saw the words.
>
> He is having some sort of problem about what he needs.

  They were not as successful in applying this information to the redesign exercise, although it is not clear whether this relates to their lack of HCI expertise or more general lack of awareness of design rationale and design methods (which the HCI-experienced subjects were also familiar with).
- All subjects had problems comprehending the representations and several subjects had initial problems understanding how the usage data could contribute to their assessments of the design alternative. The increasing complexity of the representations produced too much visual clutter for some subjects.

We concluded that the representations contained information that could be usefully applied to later design problems, but that the format of presentation needed considerable revision. The most obvious weaknesses stem from the attempt to transport the representations directly from the analysis to later reuse. Much more redesign of the representations could have been done to make them more accessible. For example, subjects experiencing the most difficulty with the representations focused initially on the usage patterns without spending enough time understanding the axes. These should have been isolated in some way to convey one of the key insights about on-line information seeking, instead of seeming to form just a backdrop for the data.

We did not feel that any of our test subjects developed a real insight into information discernment as a task. They were not able to readily identify with the original users' experiences from the abstractions of the representations. Overall, our test subjects had to expend a lot of cognitive effort to decode and apply the representations, and we would have to reduce this substantially before we could expect reuse of the analysis to be effective. In the next section, we consider the use of scenarios as an alternative.

Further information about the testing of the discretionary usage choice graphs can be found in [10].

7.5 THE POTENTIAL FOR SCENARIOS TO COMMUNICATE DESIGN INSIGHTS

We have previously used scenarios in various ways to represent aspects of design cases for reuse. For example, in previous work we found that augmenting design rationales with explicit scenarios of use helped to convey the reasoning behind design decisions [1]. In the prototype system to support our HCI design library, we have further employed scenarios for description of the work context and roles [3].

We consider in this section the use of scenarios to present some of the design insights gained from the BookManager case study. The previous sections presented discretionary usage choice graphs as a data representation. Consider the following composite-usage scenarios as an alternative to those graphical representations.

John is the 38-year-old manager of a database programming group, who occasionally likes to keep his hand in by writing some applications himself.[3] His colleagues view him as thoughtful and reflective, although

---

[3]While the personality aspect may seem frivolous, we suspect it is important in bridging the abstraction gap. It is critical that we not design for users as automata, but as people with feelings, values, and idiosyncrasies. The trick, of course, is to choose what personal facets and quirks to present, not just to personalize the users but to reveal significant aspects of the context. We could not have generated these scenarios without the analysis and the representations, which enabled us to identify the relevant aspects.

they also know he has a wild side as well (which shows up in his attire). When John is looking for information on-line to support this kind of work, he tends to reflect on what he needs and to collect background information before attempting to compose programs. John tends to use the index when he is least sure about the exact nature of what he needs, and uses the table of contents mostly when he has a notion about a specific place where he might find what he wants or when he wants conceptual background. He is more likely to use keyword search when he has a good idea about a command or object he needs but not where to find it. John will stick with an access feature if it is producing useful information for him.

Mary is a 31-year-old software engineer. She is heavily committed to fitness and athletics, and likes to take time off work for travel. When Mary is looking for information on-line, she prefers to go after specific information about functions and objects. She tends to be opportunistic, and doesn't pursue a particular focus long before trying something else. When her efforts to find information are not successful, she will often change both the feature she is using and what she is looking for; when a particular feature seems to be producing useful information, she will, like most users, stay with it. Mary sometimes uses the table of contents for browsing to suggest new ideas (especially when she thinks she may know where to look), but she also tends to scan the index. She wants to get on with the job, and experiences frustration when she can't locate what she needs.

Terry is a 42-year-old, self-confessed hacker (in the best sense of the word). He doesn't usually spend much time on conceptual background, preferring to try something out as soon as it looks promising. Terry doesn't like using keyword search, mostly because he doesn't get information right away (i.e., he has to decide and select again to get anything) and he prefers to scan and pounce. Terry seems to use the index as a last resort, but he says that is because it is a little harder to get to than the table of contents (two more keystrokes). Terry has a lot of confidence in his own ability to "hack and pray."

These scenarios reduce the abstract nature of the data presented, at the cost of presenting more interpretation on top of the data. The interpretive scenarios present a concise composite. For discretionary tasks, this composite level seems necessary to convey the essential insights about why particular activities take place in response to interactive situations.

We also can augment the composites with specific instances of online navigation, to illustrate the typical patterns of individual users and the interplay of local factors in the analysis. The transcript given above for John on task 4 is one such instance, although it would come alive more in a video record. The specific instances convey a sense of *what* happened, the composites provide a context for *why*.

We have presented these scenarios to several groups of designers as well as to researchers. The interpretive scenarios strike a responsive chord with the design audiences;[4] the research audiences find them useful, but want to see the discretionary usage choice graphs as partial validation of the analysis behind the interpretation.

We have found the interpretive scenarios useful in our own design processes. Our design recommendations from the BookManager study make sense only when accompanied by recognition of the richness of the usage phenomena. In considering design alternatives, we are able to conjure up the ghosts of users past—"What would John do in response to this new design?"

There are evident shortcomings of interpretive scenarios as a representation of the data from a usage study. For instance, how do we know that we have enough composites to fully represent user behavior? In the BookManager study, the composites reflected the insights we had generated. While we did an informal walkthrough of other users' transcripts to compare with those we studied in more depth, there are probably other interesting patterns of behavior that we have not presented. Many of these are inaccessible because subjects were working too intensely to provide good verbalizations of their activities. Our sample is inevitably concentrated on subjects who verbalized most fully. Of course, the graphical representations have the same limitation.

As Erickson suggests in his chapter, this uncertainty reflects the unknowns that always characterize design knowledge. As with his design stories, the interpretive scenarios should not be taken as predictors of future events, but as important insights about "certain individuals, in certain situations, under certain circumstances" (Chapter 2, this volume).

7.6 MAKING DESIGN INSIGHTS ACCESSIBLE

To support the process of learning HCI design, we are developing a library of design case studies, which are intended to clarify design issues and design reasoning. We have found existing design rationale methods helpful in this regard [1], but inadequate to support the after-the-fact analysis, which later designers must engage in to reuse the

[4]Inexperienced designers continue to find the variety of user behaviors surprising, and often expect that there will be one *right* pattern of usage.

design insights. Appropriate design representations, like the scenarios presented above, must be developed to capture the salient aspects of the interaction.[5] We describe in this section how the results from the BookManager study and the use of composite scenarios are influencing our efforts to develop the case library.

For highly structured tasks, task decomposition methods like the task diagrams of cognitive task analysis have proven successful [3] We have also used Thomas Green's adaptations of E-R diagrams to help analyze the relation between the envisioned user tasks and the information presented by the system [7]. However, for many HCI designs, such highly structured representations are not sufficient. When users exercise discretion over the process of the task, the HCI designer must anticipate the ways users will choose to carry out their tasks under various design alternatives. As we have seen in the BookManager study, there may be important differences among users, which designers must plan to accommodate.

Understanding data from previous usage studies with related tasks, tactics, and systems can assist designers in discerning the range of likely behaviors that need to be considered. The composite scenarios presented above are a good first step in that direction, because they explicitly distinguish various types of user and patterns of use. The scenarios of individual use, the graphic representations for individual aggregates and the potential use of selected video clips would concretize the fundamental insights about the complexity of behaviors and the factors contributing to individual choices.

Given the promising potential for such representations to convey insights from design, we still have to consider how the appropriate information can be made available to designers. We outline here the ongoing challenge this presents in our current research, to illustrate that the representation issues considered in this chapter are only one component of what we need to support HCI design practice.

Our early work presented HCI design information by linking it to widgets in user interface design toolkits [2]. For more complex design insights, which require an integrated view of design issues at several levels of abstraction, we have experimented with reuse paradigms from software engineering as a mechanism for linking together the various facets of a design problem [3].

---

[5]Such representations would presumably contribute to an ongoing design process as well, by illuminating and even suggesting pertinent design issues. However, our focus for the time being is on representing existing systems and their usage in a way that illustrates the design reasoning and design tradeoffs involved.

But the BookManager study illustrates that for discretionary use of a complex system the reuse of design insights will require a more sophisticated approach. A designer considering the role of table of contents in on-line navigation cannot be presented with a set of guidelines like those we might specify for pull-down menus. Nor can a table of contents be treated as a reusable feature with appropriate documentation about its application in previous cases. Since users exercise a large measure of discretion and diversity in their use of the various on-line navigation aids, designers seeking insight from previous usage must be prepared to invest sufficient time to do justice to the richness of the usage choices. For the BookManager case, preliminary results from our ongoing work suggest that one or two hours will likely be needed for designers to master the complexity of the case, before attempting to apply the results. This suggests that browsing for reusable information will not be a satisfactory tactic for acquiring relevant design insights, because the amount of effort expended to understand a previous design prohibits quick choices about the relevance of particular cases.

At the moment we are rebuilding our library of HCI design insights in a form that will allow it to be used as an aid for case-based learning. That is, designers commit explicit learning time to master the insights from previous usage studies, rather than attempting to find and apply relevant information during development of another interface. In the long run, our aim remains to integrate learning from previous design insight with ongoing development, so that HCI designers have a comprehensive performance support system. However, this will require more extensive knowledge about categorizing design contexts to permit identification of relevant cases and generalization from them to the design problem at hand.

ACKNOWLEDGMENTS

Allan MacLean made helpful suggestions, which, improved this report before the Kittle House workshop. All the workshop participants contributed to the refinement of the ideas, especially Jack Carroll, Bob Mack, and Scott Robertson.

Blair Nonnecke provided numerous insights into the nature of the usage phenomena. Dov Lungu and John Mitterer contributed to the design of the initial study, which was supported by IBM Canada Ltd. and the University Research Incentive Fund of Ontario. This research was supported by the Natural Sciences and Engineering Research Council of Canada. Parts of this chapter were written while the first author was on leave from the Open University (Milton Keynes, U.K.)

and Rank Xerox EuroParc (Cambridge, U.K.), with support from the Science and Engineering Research Council of the United Kingdom.

REFERENCES

[1] Carey, T. T., McKerlie, D., Bubie, W. & Wilson, J. (1991). Communicating human factors expertise through usability design rationales. In *Proceedings HCI'91,* Edinburgh, U.K., August.

[2] Carey, T. T., Nonnecke, R. B., Mitterer, J. & Lungu, D. (1992). Prospects for active help in on-line documentation. In *Proceedings ACM SIGDOC Conference,* Ottawa, October.

[3] Carey, T. T., Ellis, M. & Rusli, M. (1993). Reusing user interface designs: Experiences with a prototype tool and high-level representations. In *Proceedings HCI'93,* Loughborough, U.K., September.

[4] Carey, T. T., Nonnecke, R. B. & Mitterer, J. (1993). Interpreting individual usage differences in access to on-line books. Submitted for publication.

[5] Carroll, J. M. (1990). *The Nürnberg Funnel.* Cambridge, MA: MIT Press.

[6] Egan, D. E., Remde, J. R., Landauer, T. K., Lochbaum, C. C. & Gomez, L. M. (1989). Behaviour evaluation and analysis of a hypertext browser. In K. Bice and C. Lewis (eds.), *Proceedings of CHI'89 Human Factors in Computing Systems Conference.* New York: ACM Press, pp. 205–210.

[7] Green, T. R. G. (1991). Describing information artifacts with cognitive dimensions and structure maps. In *Proceedings of the HCI'91 Conference,* pp. 297–315.

[8] Hendry, D. G. (1994). Breakdowns in writing intentions when deploying printed and electronic form simultaneously. *Behaviour & Information Technology,* in press.

[9] Hendry, D. G., Nonnecke, B., Carey, T. T., Mitterer, J., Sobiesiak, R. & Lungu, D. (1991). How people use softcopy manuals: A case study. In *International Professional Communication Conference: Proceedings, Vol. 2.* Orlando, FL: IEEE Computer Society Press, pp. 221–224.

[10] Rusli, M. (1993). A graphical representation of usage behaviors in information seeking. M.Sc. thesis, University of Guelph, Ontario.

[11] Shulman, L. (1993). Teaching as community property. *Change, 25*(6), 6–13.

[12] Stephenson, G. A. (1988). Knowledge browsing—Front ends to statistical databases, IV. *International Working Conference on Statistical and Scientific Database Management, 2,* 55–65.

[13] Van Lehn, K. (1993). Cascade: A simulation of human learning and its applications. In *Proceedings Artificial Intelligence in Education 93.* Association for the Advancement of Computing in Education, pp. 1–3.

CHAPTER 8

Design Space Analysis and Use Representations

Allan MacLean and Diane McKerlie[1]

Rank Xerox Research Centre
61 Regent Street
Cambridge CB2 1AB
England

8.1 INTRODUCTION

Over the last few years we have been developing a perspective on design, which emphasizes the role and representation of design rationale [1, 2]. We refer to the approach as Design Space Analysis (DSA). One of its key characteristics is that the output of design is conceived of as a design space rather than a single artifact. The approach therefore contrasts with the traditional conception of design, which assumes that the eventual output is simply a specification or artifact. The final artifact, although embodying the designer's decisions, does not normally preserve any of the thinking and reasoning that went into its creation. We use a semiformal notation (called QOC, for Questions, Options, and Criteria) to represent the design space around an artifact being produced. This design space is an explicit representation of alternative design options and reasons for choosing among those options. The main concepts we use for the representation are *Questions,* which highlight key issues in the design, *Options,* which are effectively answers to the

[1]Current Address: CIS Department, University of Guelph, Ontario, Canada, N1G 2W1.

Questions, and *Criteria,* which are the reasons that argue for or against the possible Options.

DSA is a central part of a long-term project in which we are addressing a wide range of issues in the software lifecycle from early design through to maintenance and redesign. An important set of properties we are exploring relate to the support of group processes in design. Explicit documentation of the rationale involved in the design promises to be a useful aid for communication between members of the design team, between designers and users, and between the current design team and future design teams who want to build on or reuse parts of the current design. In addition to the communicative function in group processes, the approach also shows promise for encouraging reflection on the current state of the design, leading to a better understanding and possible improvements. While it is difficult to be very analytic in the heat of the creative phases of designing, design projects are punctuated by reviews, reports, and presentations. These are natural times for standing back and reflecting on the state of the design. DSA seems to be a useful framework to help structure such reflection—for example, justifying design decisions and considering other opportunities for exploration.

Most of our published work to date has focused on the properties of the approach and of the QOC notation, although some of it has begun to look at the way in which it relates to design practice. For example, we have used the QOC notation to describe the discussions of pairs of designers working on a simple design exercise [2, 3]. The main output of this has been to demonstrate the parallels between the QOC concepts, which are the basis of our approach, and the concepts naturally used by designers. Our main conclusions were that, broadly speaking, over 90 percent of a design discussion could be directly related to QOC concepts, but also that there are a number of areas where an approach such as DSA might help to improve the effectiveness of the design process—for example, by encouraging an explicit emphasis on important issues and by helping to organize, structure, and index the progress of the design process. It should be emphasized here that we do not claim QOC to be the only design representation that is necessary—rather, it is typically used in conjunction with other representations, including physical ones such as sketches, notes, and prototypes and conceptual ones such as requirements, lists of attributes, analogies, and scenarios [4, 5].

The aim of the present chapter is to describe in more detail ways in which a QOC representation builds on and relates to other design representations. We do this in the context of describing a twelve-month project in which we explored user interface designs for future educational hypermedia systems. We take the scenario (or more generally, *use representation*) theme of the book as a focus and develop two threads. The first thread describes the generation and evolution of a set of Criteria, which guide the design. In the present case, these Criteria are strongly grounded in a consideration of how the system will be used and they act as a reference to help guide the design process throughout its lifecycle. The second thread considers the relationship between the QOC representation and use-oriented representations such as tasks, scenarios, and storyboards. The main theme of this thread is to illustrate the ways in which a QOC representation provides a mechanism to focus on and abstract from salient features of these other more concrete representations. The QOC representation therefore complements the other representations by summarizing and generalizing their key attributes.

8.2 THE DESIGN PROJECT

8.2.1 Process

The examples used here are drawn from a twelve-month project in which we collaborated with the Open University using QOC to help design hypermedia interfaces for presenting course material (currently textbooks, course notes, and videos). The five-person design team is distributed across two geographical locations, about 60 miles apart. The design activities include individuals working on their own, the use of various forms of electronic communication, and face-to-face meetings of all or part of the project team. Many design-related issues and ideas are informally recorded in personal and group notes and sketches, electronic mail messages, posted letters, and fax documents. From these various artifacts of the design process, one member of the design team has also had responsibility for producing a record of design issues and decisions using the QOC notation. Design spaces around approximately 200 QOC Questions were produced in either hand- or computer-drawn formats. They were used both as independent records of design reasoning, and to organize and index the variety of other design representations used in the project. More details of how QOC was used in this project can be found elsewhere [6, 7].

8.2.2 Aims

The goal of the project was to design a hypermedia interface to accompany Open University course material on Human-Computer Interaction. Some of the key requirements were to balance *guidance* using various pedagogic techniques with *flexibility* to accommodate various learning styles. The hypermedia learning environment was to emphasize the application of theoretical concepts in the real world. This implied support of learning by experience as one of the learning styles. Since the users would have wide and varied experiences, it was important to *minimize complexity* in the interface as well. These key requirements formed the starting point for developing the design Criteria to which we will return in the next section.

8.3 GENERATING AND DEVELOPING THE CRITERIA

We started the design process by considering the key requirements mentioned in Section 8.2.2. We considered what various user interface styles might be appropriate and decided that a next step should be to determine suitable metaphors to guide the design. We also began to develop a more detailed set of Criteria to support the requirements (which are themselves basically high-level Criteria). Initially this was done by brainstorming within the design group. Much of the discussion involved considering user tasks and casting these in terms of Criteria that the design would have to satisfy to support the tasks. For example, more specific concerns in the area of *supporting pedagogic guidance* would be helping the user to *retain, recognize, and recall* the information presented and to support the *comprehension of the content.*

8.3.1 SELECTING A METAPHOR

The decision of which metaphor to pursue was extremely difficult. Figure 8.1 is a QOC diagram, which shows as Options a number of metaphors that were discussed and some of the specific Criteria that were considered relevant in helping to choose among them. It also shows a decision matrix, which summarizes the assessment of the Options against the Criteria. (Much of the QOC in this project was produced using paper and pencil. The figure is taken directly from the original corpus.)

Two of the Options were eventually decided to be worth exploring further (the boxed Options in Figure 8.1). The first was a signposting/map metaphor, which we called "roundabouts" (traffic circles for North Americans), and the second was a metaphor focusing on the manipulation of objects, which we described as "workroom."

The roundabouts idea is based on selecting routes that run through and connect the content material, making use of conventions normally associated with driving through roundabouts. The roundabouts there-

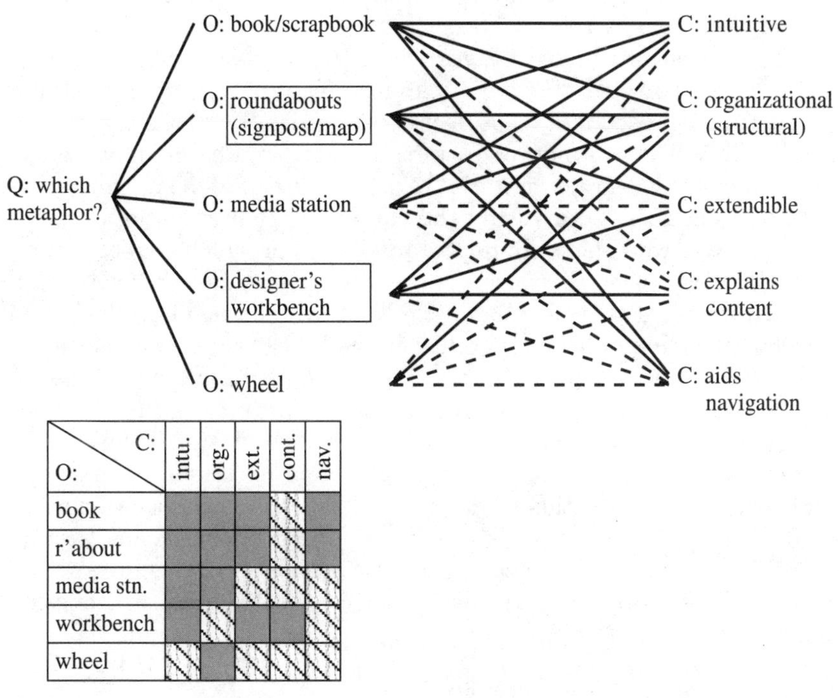

Figure 8.1. QOC diagram supporting the choice of "workroom" and "roundabout" metaphors. Solid lines between Options and Criteria (or solid boxes in the decision matrix) represent positive Assessments (i.e., the Criterion supports that Option) and dashed lines (or shaded boxes) represent negative Assessments.

fore indicate choice points and the possible routes out of them the specific choices that are available. The emphasis is therefore on reflecting the structure and organization of the material and supporting navigation through it in a fairly rigid way.

The workroom metaphor is based on manipulating objects (e.g., file drawers, equipment, etc.) in order to find information and derive feedback from actions and queries. The underlying concept therefore places emphasis on exploration and construction, in much the same way as a do-it-yourselfer might do in pursuing a home improvement project, making use of available materials and constructing something new out of them. However, in the present case, the intent is to allow students to explore available information and manipulate it to help them discover relationships and learn new ideas.

The assessment links in Figure 8.1 of Options against Criteria reflect our positioning of the two metaphors. The roundabouts metaphor is structurally based, able to reflect the *organization* of the course material. The workroom metaphor, in contrast, could be made to reflect the *content* of the course material (e.g., the interface designer's workroom and expertise). Mirroring the content of course material in the metaphor was considered an important way to provide pedagogic guidance. For this reason the workroom metaphor became the favored Option. However, the workroom (unlike the roundabouts) lacks an inherent *structure* and was therefore judged to be weak on its ability to provide *navigational* cues. This became the central challenge for developing the workroom metaphor and we concentrate on it in the examples used in the rest of this chapter. In fact, much of our design effort focused on developing the workroom metaphor, paying particular attention to implications for navigation as more detailed design developed. In other words, Design Space Analysis was used to help explore issues around something that was recognized as a critical area of the design—we did not use it for every detail of the design space (see [2] for more discussion of this point).

8.3.2 Exploring Navigation

Let us now look in more detail at how the Criteria began to evolve. We noted that "navigation" was used as a Criterion in Figure 8.1. At this level of detail it reflects a fairly crude and general kind of task, but the level of description is adequate for gaining an initial understanding of the properties of the different metaphors being considered. However, it is important to note that the weakness identified on the workroom metaphor relative to navigation encouraged us to explore it in more depth to try to improve that solution. The navigation Criterion then became the basis of a Question, which pushes on understanding what is relevant about navigation in rather more detail (Figure 8.2). This helped reveal a number of common devices for supporting navigation, such as maps, signposts, tables of contents, and association between objects. Perhaps more importantly it encouraged us to consider a more detailed set of navigation tasks (represented as the Criteria in Figure 8.2). Since this part of the design space explores navigation in a generic way, its results could potentially be applied to refine interfaces based on either the roundabout or workroom metaphors. An interesting insight made clear

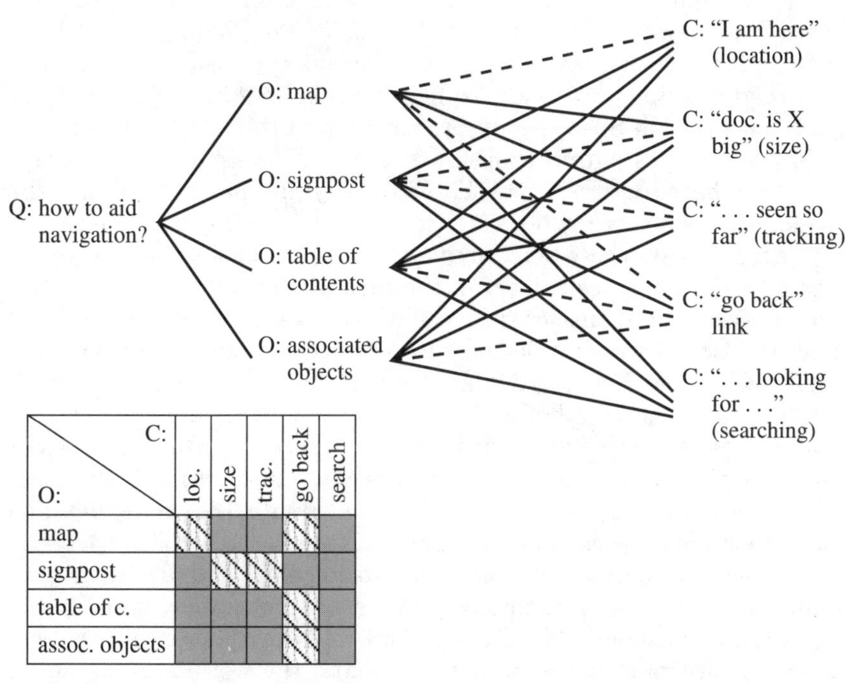

Figure 8.2. QOC diagram showing different navigation properties.

here is that maps and signposts satisfy different Criteria, with the implication that if used together, they could satisfy all Criteria.

8.3.3 Tasks and Criteria

It has already been noted that many of the Criteria we developed were derived from tasks the user would be expected to perform with the system. In this context, a working definition of what we mean by a task is that it reflects a discrete and relevant activity, which the user must be able to perform. That activity is then reflected in the design reasoning by a QOC Criterion. The important point for now is that such tasks characterise a use-situation, which in turn suggests Criteria to be included in the QOC design space. In a comprehensive representation of the design space, the task itself acts as part of the argumentation justifying the presence of the Criteria derived from it (see also [2]).

We should stress, however, the Criteria are not exclusively task based. For example, the Criterion of "intuitive" in Figure 8.1 is at least once removed from a task—it may be a means to a task-based end, but that relationship is not made explicit here. More generally, one of our goals with Design Space Analysis is to support the integration of multiple perspectives within a design space (e.g., system-based Criteria [8]). Task-based Criteria are therefore only one perspective and the reader should not overgeneralize from the examples given here.

In many ways these tasks are very similar to the kinds of tasks that Carroll and colleagues extract in the task artifact approach [8]. However, they use a notion of *basic tasks*, which attempts to define the level of abstraction at which tasks are characterized. We prefer the notion of *relevance,* which tries to articulate the task (or Criterion) at the appropriate level for the kind of design deliberation being undertaken. For example, the Criterion of "navigation" was appropriate for discriminating among possible metaphors in Figure 8.1, but more specific navigation-based Criteria were necessary to evaluate the more detailed navigation aids represented in Figure 8.2.

It should be noted that a metaphor itself can be a kind of use representation as it relies on familiarity with a given domain to assist in the transfer to a new domain. So the roundabout metaphor carries with it use implications of following directions and the workroom metaphor implies assembling things. Metaphors as use representations will not be explored any further here, but more detail can be found in [4].

Keeping track of the evolving Criteria is a useful way to encourage coherence in the design by making sure that Criteria that were important early in the process do not get forgotten later on. The Criteria can be reused and further refined throughout the still-more-detailed design explorations, which occur later in the process. We find that a useful way to support this is to maintain a list of Criteria throughout the design process. Figure 8.3 gives a summary of the relevant Criteria, which were used up to the point just outlined in the process we are describing here. (We will continue to show how the list developed as more detailed design is described in the sections that follow.)

8.4 USE REPRESENTATIONS AND QOC

A QOC network is only one of several design representations. Others include the lists of Criteria, sketches, storyboards, screen shots, usage-scenario descriptions, excerpts from documents that were important parts of the history of the development, and, of course, textual descriptions. Multiple representations such as these are critical for providing

provide pedagogic guidance
- aid retention, recognition, and recall
- aid comprehension of content
- provide organization and structure
- emphasize content (rather than interaction)
- extendible (i.e., in terms of metaphor)

provide flexible learning
- support quick learning
- support quality learning

minimize interface complexity
- intuitive
- aid navigation
  - "I am here" (location)
  - "the document is ... big" (size)
  - "this is what I've seen so far" (tracking)
  - "go back" link
  - "I am looking for..." (searching)

Figure 8.3. Initial Criteria developed in considering suitable metaphors and some of the navigational issues.

adequate descriptions of the intended design. They have different properties, which complement each other. Of particular interest in this chapter are the variety of representations that emphasize use of the system being developed. This section focuses on some of these use representations and explores how they relate to QOC, whether helping to generate QOC elements, evaluate them, or simply provide a complementary representation.

8.4.1 Scenarios

In contrast to the discrete task representation, discussed in the previous section, which is reflected in a single Criterion, a scenario is a richer and more dynamic use representation. It represents the set of actions a user would have to engage in to carry out some activity. These actions may correspond to tasks in the previous section, or, conversely, a scenario may spell out how to carry out a single task in more detail. The precise relationships depend on the level of description required by the design problem being considered (compare with the navigation example in the previous section). The scenario may be represented in one of many ways—for example, as a textual description, as a storyboard, or as a video. Because of the richness of a scenario representation, its relationship to a QOC design space is correspondingly more complex. That said, a pattern we will see in the relationship is that of the QOC providing a way of abstracting from the detail in the scenario and of highlighting the aspects that are salient for the design problem being addressed.

There are two distinct roles for scenarios. One is in supporting the generation of design ideas, the other is in evaluating a proposed design. We will refer to these as *envisioner* and *evaluator* scenarios. This distinction places different constraints on the scenarios. For example, it is important to have systematic scenarios, which are well grounded in the final use of the system for evaluation purposes, but this may be less critical for generative purposes where the scenario may simply serve a role of helping the designer to reason about the design and to help organize ideas coherently. Note that the approach taken by Kyng [9] effectively combines the evaluation and generation components in that it derives scenarios, which describe an existing work situation, and then uses these to help generate a system solution. There is clear value in such an approach for supporting the mapping between the old and new ways of working, but it also implies scenarios that are rather more detailed than some of the ones we consider here. Similarly, developing a systematic set of scenarios is a core part of the approach of Carroll and colleagues [10, 11].

8.4.1.1 Envisioner Scenarios We can illustrate an envisioner scenario being used to drive the design and contribute to the evolving design space from an example in which one of our team members prepared a written account of some of her design ideas. The document included descriptions of cause and effect as a user progressed through an assumed scenario. It also contained sketches of possible icons and sketches of ways of structuring the content information. Entries of designer's insights or *editorial notes* were also present in the descriptions. She sent this material to the other team members well in advance of the next meeting she was able to attend.

The following is a transcription of some text from the document:

> The open drawer can be enlarged . . . and can cover the whole work bench if the user so wishes. Some icons have the same role wherever they appear (I am calling them generic context specific icons): The user clicks on the book and will get "introduction to the topic," for example.
>
> Double-clicking on one of the other (topic specific) icons will

> open (i.e., lead the user into that area of information). So double-clicking on the magnifying glass takes the user into the "Analytical Evaluation" section.
>
> Clicking on "Task Analysis" causes a cascade of the three types of TA to be presented in the form of cascading menus. I am not sure how cascading menus are normally presented (staggered, I think). Anyway what has happened here is this: User selected TA, Macro, and will select Ethics (say) . . . which will open a media window . . . .

The first step in using QOC to explore the ideas in the document was to decompose it into issue, solution, and evaluation components. Representing this information as QOC provided a way of organizing and evaluating the components of the proposed solution. This process of analysis helped the rest of the design team gain a better understanding of the specific design problems being tackled. Because the document described design ideas in terms of a usage envisionment (rather than explicit problems and solutions), the process of developing the design space involved inferring the appropriate Questions. This process is very similar to that followed in [2] for representing design discussions. However, in this case we used the result as a seed to begin further exploration of the design space. It acted as a basis for critiquing and evolving the design solution—we directly used the QOC as a resource to gain further insights into the design problem and to lead us toward a more effective solution.

The analysis showed that the fragments provide a common function: access to information. Figure 8.4 shows the QOC analysis, which revealed that as three Options, they solve the same problem. This is an important insight for overall consistency. The Criteria in Figure 8.4 emphasize our interest in providing support for navigation. For example, *searching,* knowing your *location*, and knowing the *size and scope* of the document expressed our early ideas about the kind of navigation functions that were desirable. These Criteria are reused from those already listed in the Criteria hierarchy in Figure 8.3, but were not called on explicitly in the scenario descriptions.

Within the complete written account of the use scenarios, the above fragments were treated as distinctly separate. However, the QOC extracted from the scenario abstracts away from the details with which the scenario was articulated and characterizes them in terms of classes of solution (generic icons, specific icons, and cascading menus). This is what gave us the insight that all of these were solutions to a single issue of information access. This had not been clear to the designer when she

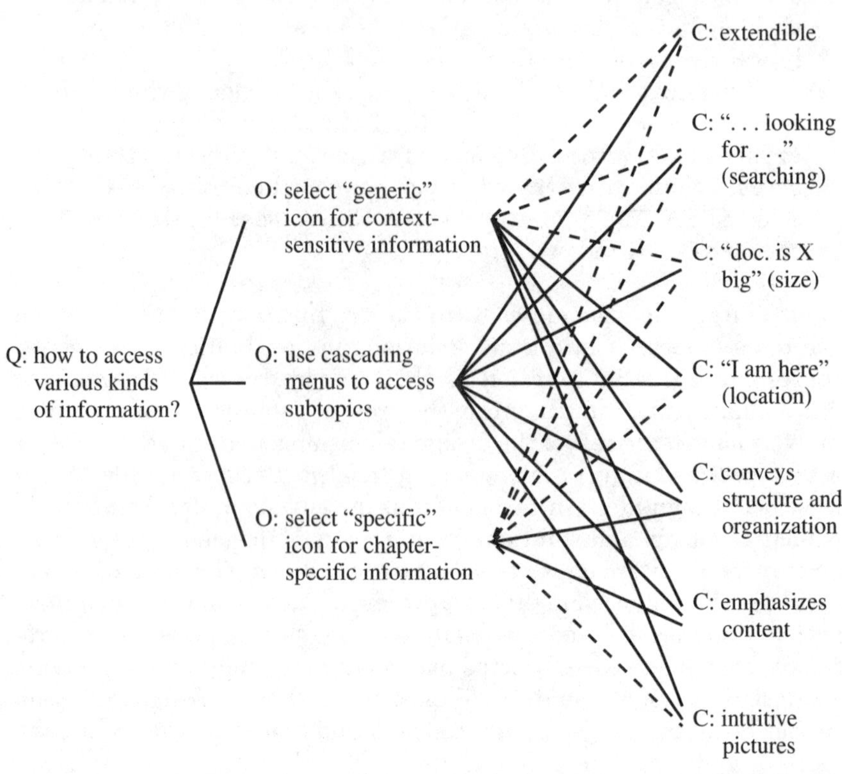

Figure 8.4. QOC diagram showing the analysis surrounding the use representation fragments from the scenario document.

developed the scenario, but is revealed by the form of the resulting QOC. Also, note how the scenarios are described in very concrete terms in the original description (e.g., "so double-clicking on the magnifying glass takes the user into the 'Analytical Evaluation' section"). The description at the detailed level is clearly not complete, but neither are the abstractions drawn out clearly in the scenario articulation. Summarizing via QOC appears to help encourage the abstractions to be drawn out and emphasized.

Another thing to be aware of in this kind of situation is that there may not be a strong commitment to the concrete instantiations used in articulating the scenario, but this is not clear from the descriptions given. For example, the detailed suggestions in this scenario are not necessarily picked up in more detailed exploration of the same issues; however, the more abstract ideas are. We would argue that QOC helps to identify and emphasize the relevant abstractions and helps avoid getting prematurely sidetracked by the detail. This is similar to an example described in [2], where designers are observed revisiting an issue of how many preset cash amounts should be offered by a bank Automated Teller Machine. It was striking that each time it was revisited different possible alternatives were discussed, but there was no feeling that the issues were changing drastically. The essence of the issue seemed to be whether there were many or few amounts available—the precise number could be decided later. However, this was not at all clear from the surface level of the protocol, or from the sketches produced. Since such concrete representations *require* detail to make them real, the designer is forced into providing a place holder whether or not there is yet a commitment to use it as a solution to be used in the final design.

8.4.1.2 Evaluator Scenarios Evaluator scenarios also involve visualizing what it would be like to use the artifact being designed. However, where envisioner scenarios can do their job even if they are relatively vague, open-ended, or even inconsistent, the role of evaluator scenarios is to demonstrate the coherence of the proposed solution relative to its context of use, and so the scenario must be more clearly and carefully grounded in the details of the actual or proposed system. From the QOC perspective, such a representation shows how the set of current design decisions (i.e., preferred Options) fit together within a context of use. If the evaluation is successful, the representation of the steps in the walkthrough acts as a *holistic* justification for the set of Options over which it is applied (i.e., a broader scope than an individual Criterion can typically provide). Alternatively, the walkthrough may point up flaws in a possible solution. MacLean and colleagues [2] describe how in visualizing the steps required to use a new bank ATM, the designers might reach the point where the customer wants to select another service, only to realize that the proposed interface neither displays the services available nor provides a means of reaching them. This highlights two things, both expressible in QOC: It suggests additional Options to resolve the problem, and a new Criterion of ensuring that relevant facilities are accessible. We did not pursue scenario-based evaluation in any depth in the hypermedia interface design project, although informal examples emerged in critiquing design suggestions such as those described in the previous section.

The scenario-based approach described by Carey and Rusli [12] is similar in some respects to this way of using scenarios since both rely on comparing performance with a system to descriptions of its use. However, it differs in that Carey and Rusli [12] emphasize the scenario as a description of how the system is *actually* used, whereas we are placing more emphasis here on describing how the system *should be* or is *expected to be* used.

Although it is convenient to discuss envisioner and evaluator scenarios separately to draw out the distinctions between them, it is perhaps more realistic to regard them as points on a dimension. For example, the developing QOC design space described in this chapter gradually became more detailed as the design progressed and the corresponding use representations also included more detail and were used in ways that gradually included a greater and greater evaluation component. This is similar in some ways to the description provided by Rosson and Carroll [11] for using scenarios to bridge from specification to implementation, which also involves drawing more and more out of the scenario in terms of its implications for system details.

8.4.2 Graphical Representations

The scenarios discussed so far have primarily been represented with textual descriptions (although there were some sketches in the example described in Section 8.4.1.1). However, graphical representations played an important role in the project. Many of these graphics have *use representation* components of the scenario kind (i.e., they all have a broad scope and explicitly address the sequencing of actions for using the proposed solution).

8.4.2.1 Sketch from Design Meeting Figure 8.5 shows an image from a whiteboard sketch produced during a design meeting, which we preserved for our design documentation by using a video frame grabber. It illustrates various components of a workroom interface. The aspect of the design picked up in the QOC diagram in Figure 8.6 focuses on the provision of navigation cues, and in particular cues that help orient the user to the contents of a folder opened from within the filing cabinet. The basic argument is that the use of animation to show selection feedback and the origin of information is preferable to simply producing a list of labels with the contents of the folder. For example, the filing cabinet drawer would slide open in response to a user selection of the drawer; a file in the drawer would float up and reveal its contents on the whiteboard in response to a user selection of the file; and as a video

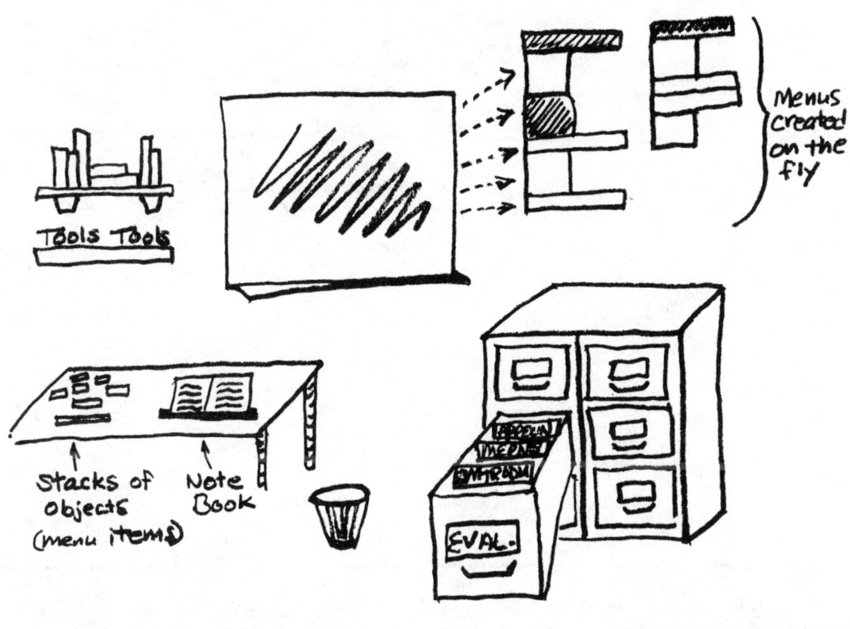

Figure 8.5. Digitized whiteboard sketch describing the workroom design.

played on the whiteboard, it would launch link buttons at appropriate stages in the video. In addition, this solution is claimed to satisfy other Criteria such as engagement. In this case, the sketch is not a screen shot but illustrates a number of components of a proposed interface and also illustrates some of its behavior over time to support the animation.

The sketch in Figure 8.5 describes a further evolution in the workroom design from that described in the above use scenario (Section 8.4.1.1). It suggests the use of animation to cue users about interface responses to various user selections. As the QOC in Figure 8.6 suggests, animation is one Option for addressing the issue of how to provide navigational cues. It is successful because it answers *"where am I?"*—*"how did I get here?"*—and *"where can I get to?"* Because animation is able to show the effect of a user action, it can satisfy more of the Criteria for navigation than the other Option (labels) can. It is also within the spirit of the workroom metaphor (compare with cascading menus, which are foreign to workrooms). Note also that as the ideas for the workroom evolved, QOC analyses were revisited and revised.

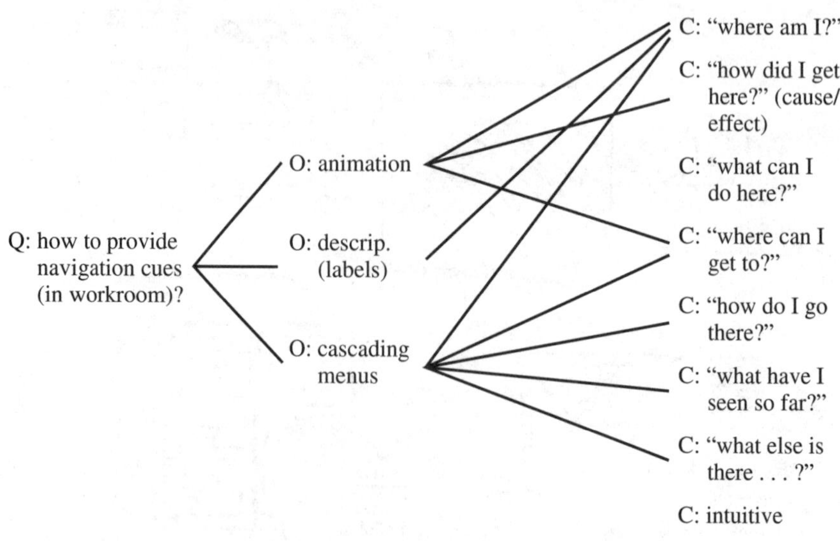

Figure 8.6. QOC diagram showing the analysis behind the workroom design in Figure 8.5—only positive Assessments are shown in assessing Options against Criteria.

Figure 8.6 is really a refinement of the earlier analysis represented by Figure 8.4. A stronger emphasis on navigation support is represented by Figure 8.6, however. For example, the Question in Figure 8.6 is phrased to emphasize the navigation problem. Further, many of the Criteria from Figure 8.4 have been carried over to Figure 8.6, but the navigation Criteria take a new perspective. They reflect a set of "questions to answer for successful navigation" from Fischer & Mandl [13] and McKerlie & Preece [14].

Our list of Criteria was updated at this stage, as shown in Figure 8.7 (additions we have just discussed in italics) to reflect this refinement of navigation Criteria. (Note that some categories have been condensed for brevity here.) Two further general design goals became important in discussions parallel to those presented here. We felt it was important to *provide engagement* for the user to make using the hypermedia fun as well as educational. We also decided that in making use of multiple media we needed to make sure we addressed concerns of *integrating media* appropriately. These two are included in the list, as

provide pedagogic guidance
- aid retention, recognition, and recall
- aid comprehension of content
- provide organization and structure
- emphasize content (rather than interaction)
- extendible (i.e., in terms of metaphor)

provide flexible learning
minimize interface complexity
- intuitive
- aid navigation
  - where am I?
  - how did I get here?
  - what can I do here?
  - where can I get to?
  - how do I go there?
  - what have I seen so far?
  - what else is there to see?
- avoid ambiguity
- familiar
- visible

provide engagement
integrate media

Figure 8.7. Revised and updated list of Criteria.

they are important for motivating some of the examples we use here, although they are not the central concerns we address in this chapter.

8.4.2.2 Storyboard As a different kind of example, Figure 8.8 shows a storyboard, which was produced to explore the design in still more detail. Each picture in the storyboard is a potential screen shot and the use representation is produced by the changes occurring in the transitions between the pictures. The sequence of pictures and short text descriptions captured use scenarios whose functionality and appearance closely resembled the resulting prototype. For example, Figure 8.8 describes the sequence of steps, which demonstrates how users would navigate their way to a particular piece of information. Again, this is a refinement of the previous thinking described above and shows more detail of one specific user selection (of a file drawer). This issue is explored in the corresponding QOC diagram (Figure 8.9): *"how to present*

DEVELOPMENT OF INITIAL OBSERVATION

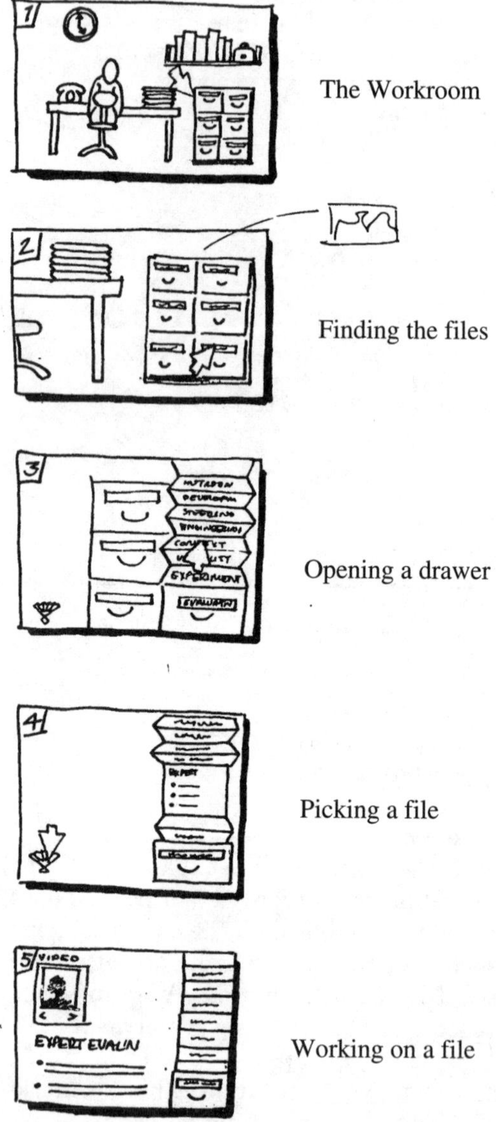

Figure 8.8. A storyboard describing a refinement of the file cabinet functionality.

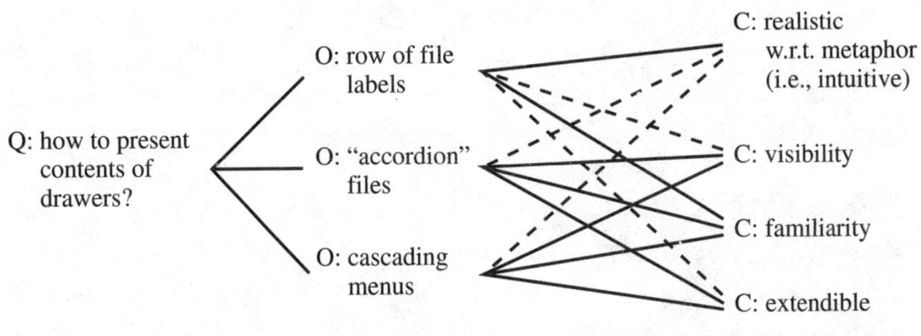

Figure 8.9. QOC diagram showing the analysis of the file cabinet design in Figure 8.8.

the contents of the drawers?" In this case the Options considered in the QOC are the *row of labels* (similar to one of the Options in the previous example), *cascading menus* (from the example described in section 8.4.1.1), and *accordion files*. The accordion files are a solution derived from consideration of the tradeoff between sticking strictly to the metaphor (and producing a solution that would be poor on legibility of the result) or breaking away from the metaphor back to the computer domain (cascading menus). Figure 8.9 describes the benefits of accordion files as: *visibility* (writing can be large enough), *familiarity* (in terms of metaphor or pop-up-style menus), and *extendible* (any number of files can be accommodated).

8.4.2.3 Screen Prototypes Finally, prototypes were built to envision design ideas as well as to demonstrate functionality and usability. The prototypes were often presented to support scenarios that represented a typical use session. Figure 8.10 is a screen shot from one of these prototypes showing the level of detail used to represent the design idea. Many of the ideas presented earlier are incorporated into this design.

8.4.3 The Criterion List

A major thread in this chapter is the development of an increasingly refined set of Criteria, which start from the requirements of supporting both guided and exploratory learning and encouraging the grounding of concepts in practical application. As the emerging designs were described at increasing levels of detail, the appropriate characterization

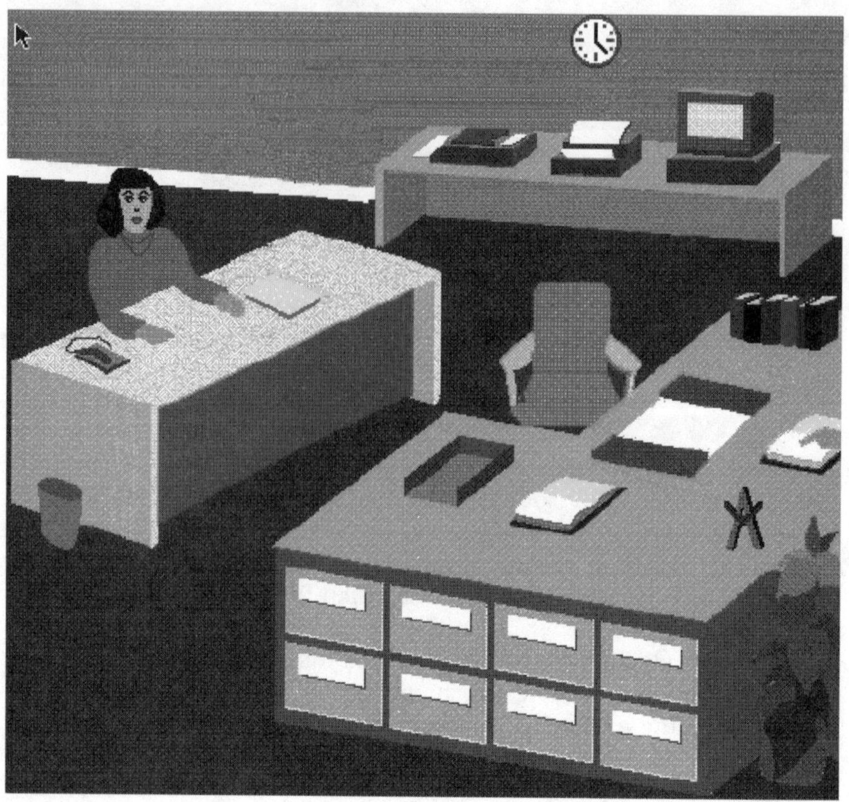

Figure 8.10. Screen shot from a version of the workroom prototype.

of the Criteria also becomes more detailed, in part reflecting the increasing emphasis on navigation, which emerged as a Criterion to be tracked to try to improve the weaknesses of the workroom metaphor.

The final list of Criteria developed throughout this process is given in Figure 8.11. It is represented as a hierarchical list, in which the level of Criteria in the hierarchy is roughly correlated with the level of detail in the design to which it is applied. This is similar to the notion of Bridging and General Criteria introduced in [2] and the Criterion trees described by Shum [15]. However, in this case we illustrate the development of the Criteria alongside the progress of the design rather than as a more retrospectively produced structure in our earlier work.

provide pedagogic guidance
- aid retention, recognition, and recall
- aid comprehension of content
- provide direction
- provide organization and structure
- emphasize content (rather than interaction)
- extendible (i.e., in terms of metaphor)

provide flexible learning
- user control
- support various learning styles
- learn by experience
- learn by example
- support quick learning
- support quality learning

minimize interface complexity
- intuitive
- aid navigation
  - where am I?
  - how did I get here?
  - what can I do here?
  - where can I get to?
  - how do I go there?
  - what have I seen so far?
  - what else is there to see?
- avoid ambiguity
- familiar
- visible
- minimal actions

provide engagement
- create interest
  - animation
- show application to real world

integrate media
- variety
- appropriate media for content
- redundancy

Figure 8.11. Complete list of Criteria, which evolved as the part of the design described here progressed. Initial requirements and other high-level design goals are shown in bold.

8.5 DISCUSSION

The basic philosophy behind the Design Space Analysis approach emphasizes maintaining a focus on the design space and the reasons for making choices within it [2]. The QOC notation provides a way of representing the space, and the main focus in its creation is the gathering, organization, and development of design information [5]. As such, there is no intrinsic emphasis on usability issues *per se*. Nevertheless, one of our aims is to encourage usability to be emphasized without making it the *only* focus to which attention should be given (e.g., [8]). To this end it is important to demonstrate the ways in which use representations and QOC design space representations can inform and complement one another.

Complementarity is especially important. The QOC representation is not supposed to be a standalone representation. Rather, it summarizes the structure of a design space in ways that linear text, diagrams of possible solutions, or even prototypes cannot. The terse wording within the various elements in a QOC diagram is seldom comprehensible on its own. It generally requires further detail or familiarity with the content to be fully understood. The value of the notation is to show alternative design possibilities, how they relate to each other, and what determines their suitability, in a form that allows these relationships to be examined simultaneously. Compare this with representations such as scenarios of the type discussed in this chapter. These show more clearly how the components of possible solutions fit together in a context of use, but do not highlight the differences between possible solutions, much less any reasons for these differences. A similar argument applies to the role that sketches and other kinds of graphical representations play. For example, not only does the sketch in Figure 8.6 represent the issues that were drawn out in the QOC diagrams, it also represents a rich set of other kinds of design information, which sets it in context and indeed that may even represent specific design commitments (but remember the caveat mentioned earlier about concrete design suggestions sometimes being place holders for more abstract entities). In general, if we consider the relationship between QOC and these other forms of design representation, QOC represents local optionality; use representations (or at least scenarios) represent coherence across time in terms of the use of the system; and many graphic representations emphasize coherence across space in terms of how various possible components of the design fit together.

In contrast to some of the approaches in this book, which aim to produce systematic use representations as a major input to design [9, 11, 16, 17], our approach gives use representations a rather less central role and relies on QOC representations to coordinate much of the design content. When tasks are viewed as Criteria, our approach relies on the designer to provide the argumentation to justify the extent to which the task under consideration is satisfied by the possible Options identified. The relatively informal scenarios we cite illustrate an acknowledgment that designers generally find it easier to work in concrete than abstract terms. In many ways, these are closer to the kinds of things that Erickson [18] cites as *design artifacts*. However, QOC also provides a mechanism to help produce abstractions from the scenarios, for example, by encouraging the generation of Questions to encompass several possible solutions. That is not to say we do not believe in more formal or systematic approaches—quite the reverse. For example, in the European Esprit–funded Amodeus project we are exploring ways in which various approaches to user and system modeling can benefit design, and the role that Design Space Analysis can play in helping to achieve these goals (e.g., see [19]). Similarly, other chapters in this volume provide us with insights that promise more effective use of systematic use representations (e.g., [20]). Nevertheless, we would not want to subscribe to a view of design that focuses *only* on well-defined systematic representations. Rather, our goal is to work with a representation to which designers can relate their partially defined and fluid ideas, which emerge from design discussion, but at the same time to which more systematic principles and perspectives can also be related.

In summary, there are a variety of ways in which we have found use representations to be of value within the Design Space Analysis framework. Conversely, we have found the framework useful to help us draw out distinctions in the content and design roles of the different use representations we employed in the project described here.

ACKNOWLEDGMENTS

The authors would like to acknowledge the contribution of the other members of the hypermedia interface design team: Rob Griffiths, Sally Grisedale, Richard Jacques, Blair Nonnecke, and Jenny Preece. Thanks also to Jack Carroll and Richard Young for comments on an earlier version of this chapter, and to the Kittle House workshop attendees for much stimulating discussion.

REFERENCES

[1] MacLean, A., Young, R. & Moran, T. (1989). Design rationale: The argument behind the artifact. In *Proceedings of CHI'89,* Austin, TX, May. New York: ACM Press, pp. 247--252.

[2] MacLean, A., Young, R., Bellotti, V. & Moran, T. (1991). Questions, options, and criteria: Elements of design space analysis. *Human-Computer Interaction, 6* (3&4). Special Issue on Design Rationale: John M. Carroll and Thomas P. Moran (eds.), pp. 201–250.

[3] MacLean, A., Bellotti, V. & Young, R. M. (1990). What rationale is there in design? In *Proceedings of the INTERACT '90 Conference on Human-Computer Interaction.* Amsterdam: North-Holland, pp. 207–212.

[4] MacLean, A., Bellotti, V., Young, R. & Moran, T. (1991). Reaching through analogy: A design rationale perspective on roles of analogy. In *Proceedings of CHI '91 Conference on Human Factors in Computer Systems.* New York: ACM Press, pp. 167–172.

[5] MacLean, A., Bellotti, V. & Shum, S. (1993). Developing the design space with design space analysis. In P. Byerley, P. Barnard, & J. May (eds.), *Usability and Integrated Services: Design Issues and Methods.* Amsterdam: North-Holland.

[6] McKerlie, D. & MacLean, A. (1993). QOC in action: Using design rationale to support design. In *Video Program, INTERCHI'93: Human Factors in Computing Systems, CHI'93 and INTERACT'93,* Amsterdam, April 24–29. (Available in ACM SIGGRAPH Video Review Series.)

[7] McKerlie, D. & MacLean, A. (1994). Reasoning with design rationale: Practical experience with design space analysis. *Design Studies, 15,* 214–226.

[8] Bellotti, V. (1993). Integrating theoreticians' and practitioners' perspectives with design rationale. In *Proceedings of INTERCHI'93: Human Factors in Computing Systems, CHI'93 and INTERACT'93,* Amsterdam, April 24–29. New York: ACM Press.

[9] Kyng, M. (1995). Creating contexts for design. *Chapter 4 in this volume.*

[10] Carroll, J. M. & Rosson, M. B. (1992). Getting around the task-artifact cycle: How to make claims and design by scenario. *ACM Transactions on Information Systems, 10,* 181–212.

[11] Rosson, M. B. & Carroll, J. M. (1995). Narrowing the specification–implementation gap in scenario-based design. *Chapter 10 in this volume.*

[12] Carey, T. & Rusli, M. (1995). Usage representations for reuse of design insights: A case study of access to on-line books. *Chapter 7 in this volume.*

[13] Fischer, P. M. & Mandl, H. (1990). Toward a psychophysics of hypermedia. In D. Jonassen & H. Mandl (eds.), *Designing Hypermedia for Learning,* pp. ix–xxv.

[14] McKerlie, D. & Preece, J. (1992). The hype and the media: Issues concerned with designing hypermedia. *Journal of Microcomputer Applications.* London: Academic Press.

[15] Shum, S. (1991). Cognitive dimensions of design rationale. In D. Diaper & N. V. Hammond (eds.), *People and Computers VI.* Cambridge, U. K.: Cambridge University Press, pp. 331–344.

[16] Muller, M. J., Tudor, L. G., Wildman, D. M., White, E. A., Root, R. W., Dayton, T., Carr, R., Diekmann, B. & Dykstra-Erickson, E. (1995). Bifocal tools for scenarios and representations in participatory activities with users. *Chapter 6 in this volume.*

[17] Jacobson, I. (1995). The use–case construct in object-oriented software engineering. *Chapter 12 in this volume.*

[18] Erickson, T. (1995). Notes on design practice: Stories and prototypes as catalysts for communication. *Chapter 2 in this volume.*

[19] MacLean, A., Young, R., Bellotti, V. & Moran, T. (1991). Design space analysis: Bridging from theory to practice via design rationale. In *Proceedings of Esprit Conference 1991,* Brussels, November 25–29. Dordrecht, Netherlands: Kluwer Academic, pp. 720–730.

[20] Johnson, P., Johnson, H. & Wilson, S. (1995). Rapid prototyping of user interfaces driven by task models. *Chapter 9 in this volume.*

CHAPTER 9

Rapid Prototyping of User Interfaces Driven by Task Models

Peter Johnson, Hilary Johnson, and Stephanie Wilson

HCI Laboratory
Department of Computer Science
Queen Mary and Westfield College
University of London
Mile End Road, London, E1 4NS
England

9.1 INTRODUCTION

In the fictional country of Erewhon, Samuel Butler [1] presents many scenarios of life and work in a society in which people serve the needs of machines rather than machines serving the needs of people. In his novel Butler warned of the dangers of isolating the design and development of technology from people and society, and from any considerations of the effects of technology on people's lives. While in Erewhon the technology was that of steam engines and mechanical devices, the serious consequences of focusing design solely on machines rather than on people's needs, and how those needs might be best served by the design and development of machines, were clearly envisioned. People became the servants of machines. The task of looking after the machines became the prime focus of work, with little consideration for subsequent effects on the quality of the work experience or indeed the quality of the end product. The design and development of technology to improve the quality of work and the quality of the products of work require us to pay close attention to the nature of the work, and to be explicit about how any technology that we design might affect people and their work. The mistake is to believe that computer system designers are only responsible for the software and hardware that they produce. System design must include taking responsibility for the total system, comprising people, software, and hardware. Understanding how the software and hardware will affect people in terms of how they could use it, what tasks it will and will not be good for, what changes it will require from users, and how it might improve, impair, or otherwise change work, are all issues that must be addressed in design and are fundamentally the responsibility of the system designer. Taking seriously the concerns of people who use or are otherwise affected by a computer system will require changes to the practices and methods of system design. Understanding users and their tasks is a central concern of the system designer. Scenarios provide explicit user and task information, which can better equip the designer to accommodate the rich perspective of the people and work for which he or she is designing computer systems.

In developing the technology of computer systems it is often necessary to focus upon properties of the technology. However, in developing systems that are intended to be used by people in the varied contexts of their work, private, social, and leisure activities, the focus of design must be on the suitability of the designed artifact to support and complement human activity. Developing technology that serves the needs of people, rather than vice versa, requires a revised conception of computer system design. The activities of design must still allow systems to be well engineered such that they are reliable, efficient, and easily maintained; however, over and above this, the people who will use and be affected by the design in the context of its usage must be sharply in focus in the design process. Scenarios that include rich information about users and their tasks can bring such a focus to the design. Scenarios are snapshots of human activity from which the designer can gain understanding about users and tasks, and through which users can see how any design is likely to affect them and their work. Users and designers need to be able to communicate with each other to understand the domain, users, and tasks and the possible design-induced changes that may come about.

To address this concern requires more than just an awareness of the dangers. New ways of approaching design are required that make artifact usage the focus of the design rather than a consequence of it. Changing the design viewpoint from the artifact in isolation to the artifact in its context of usage also requires supporting changes to design practice. The design team needs ways of communicating with users, ways of understanding users' activities, knowledge about how to relate properties of designs to properties of usage, and tools to allow the usage of the artifact to be explicit and visible throughout the evolution of the design. In addition, the users need to be able to understand the design as it evolves and to directly contribute to artifactual design and prospective usage. Scenarios depicting how tasks are, or might be, carried out by particular individuals or specific classes of people using current and envisioned technology can bring about a change in design practice. Changes in design practice will result in the development of systems that improve the quality and efficiency of work and of the lives of the users. This chapter provides an insight into scenario-based design by allowing designers and users to describe existing tasks, to change existing activities, and to envision new activities in terms of tasks. Scenario-based design also allows designers and users to develop artifacts to support activities from documented scenarios describing existing, changed, and new tasks, and to consider the relations between the artifact and its usage at all stages of design.

Rather than attempting to provide a universally accepted definition of the term *scenario*, we feel it is more important in this chapter to clarify how we use the term, and the role we see scenarios playing in our approach to participatory design. We use the term scenario in two different but related ways, both very much related to the drama context in which scenes and scenarios are well established. In the first conceptualization, scenarios are used to characterize an episode or a sequence of activities, or even units of dialog that might be observed by an onlooker, much like one would in a story, play, or film. The second usage is of a scenario as depicting a synopsis or account of a proposed course of action (in our case, a proposed design). The two different conceptualizations directly relate to two necessary activities in system design: requirements gathering and prototyping.

In the first conceptualization, scenarios are used to describe courses of action and help to identify user and task requirements. Our approach to task analysis, known as Task Knowledge Structures (TKS), directly supports the process of identifying what people currently do in their work within a given domain. A scenario in this context describes human activity which includes detail about who is carrying out the activity, what the activity is (including its purpose), the context in which the activity is carried out, and the way (including the methods and tools) that the activity is undertaken. A fundamental aspect of a scenario is how the scenario describes the users and the tasks. This information is gathered using many different techniques, including observation and listening to what people do and say in the context of their work. The designer must gain understanding about the users and their work, preferably from direct contact and communication between the designers and users. During this process of information gathering, scenarios will be used by both designers and users at any point in time. Therefore, one important role of a scenario is to capture this rich and complex nature of tasks and allow designers to understand what characterizes the nature of the work in the domain and how people carry out that work.

The second role of scenarios is in depicting a synopsis or account of a proposed course of action, and this relates directly to another area of system design, prototyping, where our approach supports user participation in design through the use of scenarios. Here the scenarios are used as episodes or sequences of task activities carried out by users, which are used as testbeds for the prototyped design, depicting changes to the current work tasks and showing how it is envisioned that the design might be used. This use of task scenarios is supported by a rapid prototyping environment we have developed, known as ADEPT (Advanced Design Environment for Prototyping with Task models). The ADEPT toolset can be used as the design environment to express task models. These task models provide the basis for design decisions taken by both users and designers. The design ideas generated from considering the requirements give rise to prospective design solutions, which, through running a series of scenarios of their proposed usage, allow the user to comment on the quality and usability of the prototypes. The manner in which we have conceived of using scenarios, task analysis, and rapid prototyping will be made clearer in the design study outlined later in this chapter.

While it is important to outline how we use scenarios, we also feel compelled to dispel any confusion about what a task is. In our view, a task includes those activities that are carried out to achieve a given purpose. Often in human-computer interaction a task is considered to be something as trivial as, for example, deleting a word on a word processor. This is far too simplistic an action for us to consider as a task. Instead, we would consider a task in the domain of office work to be an activity such as managing the stationery supply, or scheduling departmental meetings. It is not just the granularity of activity that is at fault here: It is the belief that a user interface designer somehow knows what a task is. A task is a meaningful, purposeful activity in which the meaning and purpose are fixed by the personal, social, organizational, and domain context. In other words, the people and their work determine what is or is not a task. We have yet to come across any office worker who would view deleting a word (or even a whole page of text) as a task. In a domain different from office work, air traffic control, an example of the tasks and contexts of concern might be those of an air traffic controller working in a busy operations room at a civil airport, in conjunction with other air traffic control officers. In our example, the air traffic controller might be covering the takeoff and landing sector of the northwest runway of an airport. The tasks in this instance would include moving planes to takeoff position, managing queues of planes waiting to take off, moving planes to terminals, bringing planes into land, and managing queues of planes waiting to land. These tasks would involve communication with other air traffic controllers managing different sectors of air and ground space; communicating with air crew on the various flights entering, within, and leaving the sector; and also reading and entering data from radar, flight records and strips, and direct observations from the tower. All these activities are taking place in an organization where high safety and throughput are the major objectives. These complexities of real work incorporating concurrent tasks are not reducible to simple linear sequences of actions such as issuing a command to change altitude, or marking a flight strip.

This chapter will describe an example of complex activities that have been the subject of design studies. Through this example we will demonstrate the use of methods and tools, which we have developed to support scenario-based design from the perspective of the users and their tasks. The methods and tools can be separated into two distinct categories. The first category includes the methods and tools employed by us to allow designers and users to communicate with each other in order to gain a better understanding of the organization, domain, activities, tasks, people, and the existing technology. Design never occurs in a vacuum; designs are intended to improve qualitatively and quantitatively the situation into which the designed artifact is placed. For this reason it is important to understand this situation prior to any commitment to a design. The methods and tools in this first category relate to the early stages of participatory design and are exemplified in the following X-ray example as "getting to know the domain, people, and tasks," "developing the task scenarios," and, finally, "summarizing the tasks in terms of Task Knowledge Structures."

The second category of methods and tools allows designers to communicate their design ideas and solutions to users and those otherwise affected by the design. In the X-ray example this second category of methods and tools is exemplified in the section, "developing a design using the ADEPT tools." While these two categories of methods and tools have different foci they are not in any way independent of each other or segmented into a sequential design process. Designers need to be able to understand the context for their designs and the people who use and are affected by their designs. In addition, the users need to be able to understand the design ideas and how they might affect their work. Consequently, both designers and users can fully participate in the design and the development of the artifact. The following design study is used to illustrate how design can occur using these methods and tools, engaging both users and designers in the problem domain and the designed solution. The analysis and design work that is described here occurred as part of the development of the ADEPT tools. Consequently, the only users of the ADEPT tools at this stage were the designers, and much of the interaction with the radiographers was interspersed with development of the tools themselves. However, further studies in a different domain (airborne systems) are now underway in which the users of the ADEPT tools are not the designers.

9.2 THE X-RAY DESIGN STUDY

The starting point for this study is the X-ray theater of a busy London hospital. The hospital has recognized that the X-ray theater plays an important and critical part in the diagnosis and care of patients. A recognized improvement would be to achieve greater throughput, with less errors and repeat X-rays required, while allowing greater attention to be given to patient care during the X-ray process. A solution to this perceived problem is thought to be providing the radiographers with better equipment and support for their work. It is at this stage that a group of computer systems designers are called in. The designers and hospital staff are keen to work together. The designers recognize that the hospital X-ray theater is a busy place where they will not be able to interrupt the work of the radiographers.

9.2.1 Getting to Know the Domain, People and Tasks

A first step in scenario-based design is to gather information or data about the domain, people, and tasks. The designers are familiar with various data collection, analysis, and modeling techniques, for instance, Knowledge Analysis of Tasks (KAT; [2]), which will allow them to understand the domain and activities of the radiographers. At an early stage of the project the designers meet with personnel at the hospital including radiographers and hospital managers. From the meeting the designers learn that there are many different kinds of X-ray theater in the hospital ranging from the busy, varied, and unpredictable work of the casualty department to the more predictable work of the out-patient department. From these meetings the hospital staff and the designers were able to agree upon the range of X-ray work in the hospital and to identify particular X-ray theaters to study in further detail. Subsequently, members of the design team are taken around each of the X-ray theaters in the hospital and the various tasks associated with taking an X-ray are demonstrated. In doing this the designers meet the clerical staff responsible for the patient records and discover that X-rays also involve a nontrivial amount of office work. The radiographers also explain to the designers that they are responsible for patient safety and comfort while the patient is with them. Therefore, much of their effort is geared toward making the patient comfortable while putting the patient in an appropriate position to take clear X-rays of the appropriate part of the patient's anatomy. The radiographers show the designers how they take X-rays of different body parts and the different equipment used. This provides the designers with more information about the variety of X-ray activities. The radiographers explain the technical aspects of taking X-rays, which include determining correct voltage and the ampere settings required to take pictures of different body parts according to the size and form of the patient's anatomy. The radiographers show the designers how they take the photograph and how they develop it. The designers discover that the radiographers inspect and assess the usefulness of the pictures and record the details of the X-ray on the photograph itself to enable medical and clerical staff to identify the photograph. From these various discussions, observations, and demonstrations, the designers and radiographers agree upon a series of descriptions of the various activities of taking X-rays. This involves a number of iterations and further elaboration of the radiographers' tasks. The radiographers supplement and modify the descriptions until they are satisfied with them.

The descriptions form the basis of task scenarios and consequently the resultant task scenarios have the advantage of being evolved through participation between the radiographers and designers. Various data collection techniques from an available array [3, 4] have been employed including interviews, demonstrations and observations of real-life performances, enactments of activities that included the designers themselves going through the radiographers' tasks, and so on. The results are an accumulated understanding of the work and tasks of radiography in this hospital. In addition to this, the designers and radiographers have established a strong communication relationship that will be of benefit throughout the design process.

9.2.2 Developing the Task Scenarios

The designers have gained an intimate knowledge of radiography and established a common ground for communication with the radiographers. The designers and radiographers produce a series of informal, textual, pictorial, and diagrammatic scenarios of exemplar tasks. An extract from one of the textual scenarios of an X-ray task written in conjunction with one of the radiographers is shown in Figure 9.1. The extract in the figure was taken in the accident and emergency X-ray theater and is one radiographer's summary of some of the different activities and responsibilities, and their respective contexts. The scenario, while being quite detailed, is general in nature. Such general scenarios are necessary to provide a detailed overview of the different tasks. However, it is also necessary to generate specific details from actual tasks. The overview scenario is supplemented with particular task scenarios. Together, these provide a fuller account of the work of radiography.

In addition to describing the tasks associated with the work of radiographers, the results of the initial interaction between designers

---

There are many uses of X-rays from diagnosis to treatment and this example involves an accident and emergency unit producing X-rays for diagnosis. This task is done by radiographers and the X-rays are passed to radiologists who do the specialist interpretation. Under normal circumstances only one radiographer will be involved in taking an X-ray.

Taking an X-ray in normal circumstances involves:

- Receiving a request either in paper form from hospital casualty doctor, ward doctor, GP, outpatient dept., etc., or computerized from wards within the hospital (examples of these are provided to the designer).
- Previous X-rays may accompany this.
- On the basis of this information decide which X-ray room to use, which camera to use, which position to put the patient in (standing, on a fixed bed, seated), deciding the area of the body to focus on, deciding where to put the film cassette (under the limb, under the bed, etc.), deciding whether to use a contrast grid or not, and deciding the film type and size to use.
- Collecting the patient, positioning him or her, using extra-protection aprons or foam positioning pads, and comforting the patient while giving him or her information about what is happening and instructions of what he or she must do.

Figure 9.1. An extract from a radiographer's task scenario.

- Preparing the camera, which involves unlocking it, moving it in various planes, locking it, turning it on, and focusing it.
- The radiographer then rechecks the patient's position.
- The radiographer then leaves the patient and moves behind a protective screen (see photograph taken of hospital X-ray theater) to set the controls for taking the X-ray.
- Setting up the control panel involves deciding the "mA," the "kV," and the time. These choices can be made from memory, by using a wall chart, or by using presets in one of the machines. A number of other settings can be made (e.g., choice of tubes, choice of focus of the beam).
- When the settings have been made the X-ray can be taken (there is visual and auditory feedback when this happens).
- The X-ray plate is removed.
- The X-ray is name stamped.
- The film is placed in a machine to be developed and while waiting the film cassette is reloaded using one of four machines (according to film type and size).
- The developed X-ray is date stamped, examined on a lightbox, marked with a pen with extra information for the radiologist (e.g., left and right, standing, etc.), the X-ray is given a colored label according to how many other X-rays the patient has had at this hospital.
- The radiographers then do some preliminary interpretation to decide if the X-ray that they have taken will provide the radiologist with the information he or she needs.
- They may reject an X-ray if, for example, it is too dark and overexposed. If they reject an X-ray they must complete a "reject analysis" and state what type of X-ray it was, which room was used, the size of film, and the cause of its rejection (e.g., patient moved, overexposure, etc.).
- They may decide to take another X-ray if they reject one. They may also take others if, for example, a fracture is longer than thought and continues beyond the edge of the X-ray.
- Taking further X-rays may involve the resetting of the machine (often manually). Also X-rays are often taken in pairs at right angles to each other.
- When the radiographer is satisfied with the X-rays the patient is then returned, often with his or her X-rays.
- The X-ray is then "logged," registering that the request has been completed. In the case where the request came in as a paper form then all the details must be entered on the computer. In this case the paper request forms may be passed on to entry clerks. If the request was received via the computer then the patient's reference number is used by the radiographers to record that an X-ray has been taken.

Figure 9.1. *(Continued)*

and users also produces a scenario, which includes descriptions of the environment and existing technologies used to support these activities. The textual scenario in Figure 9.2 is an extract from this and is accompanied with photographs of the equipment and the situations in which it is used. This description was actually produced by the designer but it could have been produced by the radiographers. It has been produced as a result of observation of the equipment in use, and explanations and demonstrations by the radiographers of their equipment usage. The problems and criticisms of the current equipment are direct comments made by the radiographers and relate to observations made by the designers. The particular criticisms, such as the lack of any correspondence between the spatial layout of the "presets" and the picture of the human body, were agreed between the users and designers and become one of the foci of the redesign. The various techniques of observation and interview used to obtain this information are included in the TKS methodology.

The information provided in the extracts of scenarios shown in Figures 9.1 and 9.2 begins to provide a record of the activity and context for the radiographers' work and the associated tasks of taking X-rays. The form of the scenario is nontechnical from the designer's perspective and as such allows the radiographers to develop and amend the scenario as they choose.

Radiographers categorize X-rays in terms of body parts. Request forms that come to the radiographers name the body part for which an X-ray is needed. From the choice of the body part there follows knowledge of the standard exposure, the standard views (i.e., the positions of the camera and patient), required film size, etc.

At present there are two X-ray rooms with different control panels. The older room uses manual settings and a wall chart with lists of body parts together with their appropriate exposure settings The newer room uses presets built into the control panel display. The presets come in lines and the lines appear next to a drawing of a body. This drawing of a body does not do anything. It looks as if the lines of presets should correspond to the general area of the body at certain heights—for example, the first line might be skull, jaw, neck, etc. Some of the presets do seem to roughly correspond to the general area of the body at the corresponding height but many do not and are random. Consequently, the spatial layout and the categorization of presets are inconsistent and do not make much sense to the users (they often have to flip through all the lines to find the body part that they are seeking).

Figure 9.2. An extract of a scenario featuring radiographers' current equipment.

The importance of the scenarios is not overstated. They are readily modifiable and are not taken as being a complete view of radiography.

The amount of information gleaned from the many observations, meetings, and demonstrations that have occurred is vast. Only some of this is captured in the fragments of task scenarios in Figures 9.1 and 9.2. Other information is captured in the photographs and video and audio recordings of the radiographers at work. Even this does not constitute a complete detailing of the work of radiographers; much more information will have been absorbed by the designers through their interaction with the radiographers themselves than is contained in the recordings and scenario descriptions. However, these scenarios and other recordings serve as effective aide-memoires for preserving, and later retrieving and interpreting, this absorbed information.

The main aim of the design exercise is to improve the quality and efficiency of the radiographers' work as a result of the extensive data collection exercise. Refining this massed information into a problem space from which design ideas are generated continues the process of participatory design, with both designers and radiographers involved in refinement and design.

9.2.3 Summarizing the Tasks in Terms of Task Knowledge Structures (TKS)

As part of the refinement process, more detailed scenarios of the radiographers' tasks are produced from analyzing and studying their work further. This is done following the task-modeling framework provided by Task Knowledge Structures [5]. A Task Knowledge Structure is a summary representation of a person's task knowledge, or more usually with multiple tasks and many people there will be individual TKSs and also generic TKSs to represent common or generic knowledge across different tasks and people. This information guides the designers and users in making decisions about what knowledge possessed by the user will affect his or her interaction with the system and how a design solution might require the user to acquire more knowledge, or, conversely, to no longer require certain knowledge. Also, such information about users' task knowledge will help to identify what should be supported, what will cause problems and errors to occur, and so on. The TKS is constructed by a member of the design team, who can either be an HCI specialist or, alternatively, a system designer. As yet, we have no experience of users directly constructing their own TKS representations. However, we feel that this could be feasible, if deemed desirable. We have purposely kept the psychological underpinnings to TKS separate from its application by nonpsychologists, non-HCI specialists, and possibly even users; therefore, it is possible for any member of the design team to represent task knowledge in TKS format. The theoretical underpinnings to TKS inform the associated data collection, analysis, and generification methodology, which dictates what information is to be collected and how this might be achieved. However, the theoretical underpinnings do not impinge on the use of TKS by users or members of the design team who do not necessarily have to be interested in, concerned with, or understand the reasoning behind, for instance, why components of task knowledge are delineated in the manner in which they are in the modeling framework.

Although in our case study the designer constructs the TKS, it is essential for the resulting TKS to be communicated to and validated by users. In addition, users can, if they so wish, make changes to the TKS and review the design consequences. Task Knowledge Structures are outlined in detail in [5] and [6], and consequently only a very brief outline of the approach will be given here. TKS is one of many different approaches to task analysis. The role of task analysis in system design has generally been one of evaluation, whether of a prototype or fully implemented system. TKS is distinct from other task analysis approaches in that it directly addresses the problem of identifying user and task requirements by providing a supporting methodology for users and designers to follow. These requirements can then be used for evaluation purposes. The focus of TKS is on work tasks while the focus of most other forms of task analysis in HCI such as GOMS [7], TAG [8], and UAN [9] relates to the minute detail of how a user interacts with a computer at the command and input/output level. We would refer readers to Johnson and Johnson [5] for a review of the differences between TKS and other task analysis methods in HCI.

The task analysis approach described here is more comprehensive with respect to analyzing tasks and relating this analysis to rapid prototyping than others in this book. It provides methods and techniques that can be employed to gain summary overviews of the nature of the tasks and the work. For example, it can be contrasted with *story collecting* (described elsewhere in this book), in that initial interviews with people involved in the work will often result in stylized stories about that work. This information will often be the basis from which more detailed analyses will subsequently follow. Similarly, the method of task analysis includes techniques, which involve the workers in creating drawings and diagrams of how they see the various activities being related to each other, as in the methods of PICTIVE, also described in Chapter 6 of this volume. By allowing the people who do the work to create their own diagrams, the analyst is in fact letting the workers themselves analyze the processes of their work. Since much of the nature of human action is often not readily verbalizable by the people who perform the work (there are good psychological theories about the nature of human skill, which explain why this is to be expected; see, for example, [10] and [11]), it is important that any analysis of human activity must involve systematic observation of the activities actually being performed while the work is in progress. This can involve methods of participative observation with the analyst accepted into the workplace, or it can involve less intrusive methods of observation, such as using video. The techniques used in our method of task analysis include both participation by the analyst/designer in the work activity, direct observation of the work activity, and remote observations. This is similar to the methods used in ethnographic studies, some of which are described elsewhere in this volume. On some occasions it is necessary to investigate in greater detail some aspects of work; this can involve the setting up of quasi-experiments to investigate specific aspects of a task. Techniques are provided in our method for such forms of investigation. In all cases, it is necessary to evaluate and validate the designers'/analysts' understanding of the task with the users. Again, techniques for this are included in our method. It should be realized that no analysis of tasks will ever be complete. It is not possible to analyze all instances of a task or all tasks, and it may not be necessary to understand the very low-level detail of some aspect of human behavior. However, that does not imply that a task analysis cannot be validated and evaluated and that its degree of completeness cannot be made explicit. The designer/analyst must declare which tasks have been analyzed, involving which people, and in what settings. Thus the analysis can have a known completeness and can be validated and evaluated in that context.

The methodology supporting Task Knowledge Structures is known as Knowledge Analysis of Tasks (KAT). There are three distinct stages involved in this methodology; first, data collection, via a number of different data-gathering and knowledge-acquisition techniques; second, data analysis, which involves identifying generic or common aspects of tasks across users; and, finally, construction of the task model (i.e., TKS). The TKS is then a composite picture, or representation, of the task knowledge a typical user might have or would bring to bear on his or her performance of the task. Throughout all of these stages the designer can consult and collaborate with the user in the process of refining, changing, and validating the resulting models. Alternatively, the user can take a more active role in constructing and validating a task model as a result of a task analysis being conducted.

Task Knowledge Structures provide a framework for describing the tasks in terms of goals, subgoals, procedures, objects, and actions. The process of refining the previously gained informal and ad hoc information into task models in terms of Task Knowledge Structures, via the abovementioned methodology, provides the designers and radiographers with the opportunity to clarify misunderstandings, identify areas of the radiographers' activity that remain unknown, and to jointly develop a task-oriented model from which subsequent design decisions can be made. The Task Knowledge Structures approach assumes that human activity associated with tasks is nonrandom and follows a structured pattern determined by the organization, domain, task, and the person's experience. It further assumes that people develop task knowledge from these structured patterns. Task Knowledge Structures is a framework for modeling this knowledge. The resultant models are structural in that they reflect the organization of knowledge about the relationships between objects and actions in the domain and the contexts of the various tasks. They also allow common properties and differences between instances of tasks to be identified. A Task Knowledge Structure model contains declarative knowledge about the organization, domain, context of the task, problem-solving and planning knowledge about the relations between conflicting and complementary goals of a task, and procedural knowledge of how task activities are carried out.

An example extract of a TKS model for the radiographers' task of taking an X-ray has been constructed and is shown in Figure 9.3.

The task goals and subgoals are shown in Figure 9.3 with the lower part of the figure providing a structured textual description of the objects and their properties in the task. The goal structure is described in terms of the dependencies between goals. For example, taking an X-ray involves satisfying a number of goals including caring for the patient, taking a useful X-ray, and maintaining a medical record of the X-ray. Each of these goals is satisfied through various activities. Caring for the patient, for example, includes protecting him or her from harmful X-rays; taking a useful X-ray includes choosing the correct position and selecting the correct settings; maintaining the patient's medical record includes the radiographer adding details about what X-ray was taken. In an ongoing episode of activity, these different goals will be fulfilled simultaneously. Consequently, the goals are undertaken simultaneously, rather than consecutively. Each goal can lead to a number of subgoals, which contribute to the achievement of a higher-level goal. These lower-level goals (subgoals) are related to other goals at the same level and to higher and lower levels of a goal structure. For example, the goal of taking the X-ray shot includes lower-level goals of positioning

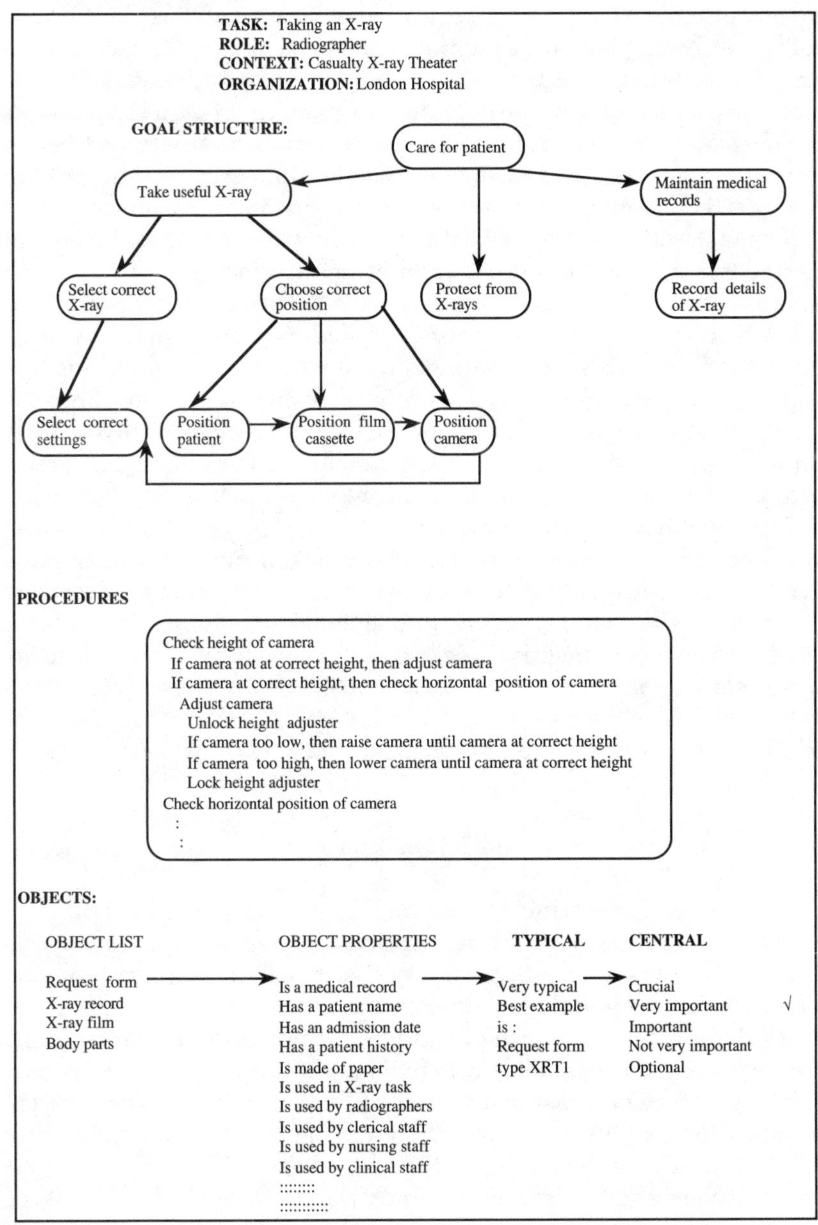

TASK: Taking an X-ray
ROLE: Radiographer
CONTEXT: Casualty X-ray Theater
ORGANIZATION: London Hospital
GOAL STRUCTURE:
Care for patient
Take useful X-ray
Maintain medical records
Select correct X-ray
Choose correct position
Protect from X-rays
Record details of X-ray
Select correct settings
Position patient
Position film cassette
Position camera
PROCEDURES
Check height of camera
If camera not at correct height, then adjust camera
If camera at correct height, then check horizontal position of camera
Adjust camera
Unlock height adjuster
If camera too low, then raise camera until camera at correct height
If camera too high, then lower camera until camera at correct height
Lock height adjuster
Check horizontal position of camera
OBJECTS:
OBJECT LIST
OBJECT PROPERTIES
TYPICAL
CENTRAL
Request form
X-ray record
X-ray film
Body parts
Is a medical record
Has a patient name
Has an admission date
Has a patient history
Is made of paper
Is used in X-ray task
Is used by radiographers
Is used by clerical staff
Is used by nursing staff
Is used by clinical staff
Very typical
Best example is :
Request form type XRT1
Crucial
Very important √
Important
Not very important
Optional

Figure 9.3. An example TKS of "taking an X-ray."

the patient and the film cassette, positioning the camera and setting the controls, and so forth. In this particular case, all of these lower-level goals must be carried out, and, importantly, they are carried out in a particular order, so that the patient and film are positioned before the camera is positioned (this ensures that the camera is not in the patient's or radiographer's way). Additionally, the camera is positioned before the controls are set, thus ensuring that the radiographer and patient are protected before any contact with the control panel is made.

The task model is further detailed to describe the procedures that are undertaken. At the lowest level of description of a task are the combinations of actions that are performed. These actions are organized into activities, which are termed *procedures*. For example, the actions associated with positioning the camera include unlocking the height adjustment, raising or lowering the camera, and relocking the height adjuster. These are carried out in sequence and possibly in iteration with adjusting the horizontal alignment of the camera. The procedural combination of actions in the context of task goals provides a description of how a task is executed.

A final and important part of the TKS task model is the description of the objects within the domain used in the task. These objects are referred to in the goal, procedure, and action descriptions. Examples of objects in the X-ray task include request forms, X-ray records, X-ray control panel, body parts, and X-ray films. Each of these objects will have a number of properties that comprise its description. These will include the task context (i.e., which tasks and parts of tasks it is related to), the "is a" and "has a" relations, which describe what the object is an instance of and its component parts. In addition, objects have further described properties, which depict their form and function in particular task contexts.

In addition to describing these task properties, the TKS approach to modeling tasks includes the description of typical and central aspects of a task. A central task feature is any object, action, procedure, or goal that can lead to task failure. For example, central objects for taking X-rays include patient and camera as well as film and developer, while other objects, such as request form and medical record, are less central. A typical feature of a task is the best exemplar of some object, action, procedure, or goal. For example, there will be typical settings of millivolts and milliamps for taking an X-ray of an arm of a 10-year-old male of normal body weight and height. Similarly, there will be a typical type of X-ray request form that is used. Centrality and typicality are not all-or-none properties, there are degrees of each. Thus any object, action, procedure, or goal in a particular task will be more or less central to the task and more or less typical of an instance of that task. These additional properties of tasks are important in helping the designers and users to interpret, categorize, and prioritize the many examples of tasks that occur, and have important implications for usability.

9.2.4 Developing a Design Using the ADEPT Tools

Producing TKS descriptions of tasks is a further refinement of the informal information about the radiographers and the activities of taking X-rays. To help the designers and radiographers refine their collective knowledge about the tasks, a series of modeling tools have been developed as part of an Advanced Design Environment for Prototyping with Task models—ADEPT [12, 13, 14]. These modeling tools provide editors, browsers, and libraries, which ease the process of organizing the vast amount of information about the task. The tools also allow easy modification of the models. This is important since a main purpose of producing the task models is to check and add to the designers' understanding of the task domain. The ADEPT task-modeling tool is based on the TKS approach.

The shift to computer representation of the tasks of radiographers does not remove the informality of the models or the cooperation between designers and radiographers. The power of the computer representation in ADEPT is the ease with which it can be stored, modified, and, most importantly, form the basis for developing design ideas from the perspective of the radiographers' tasks. The further development of the task models using ADEPT is described first.

The process of producing the computer version of the task models commences when the radiographers and designers have constructed and agreed on the pencil-and-paper versions. However, this does not mean that further changes to the models are not allowed; indeed, part of the reason for transforming the models to computer versions is to allow easier modification, since at this stage it becomes difficult to change, modify, and preserve paper-based models. The shift from paper to computer-based representations may come earlier or later depending upon how easily the designers and users feel that the different media of representation can allow them to develop their joint understanding of the tasks and the design problems. In the radiography example, the designer produced the computer version and was able to do this in a relatively short time (two or three hours) from the pencil-and-paper version. Clearly the work of the analysis has gone on beforehand and the designer is easily able to construct a computer version. The direct use of the ADEPT tools by end users and nondesigners is currently under investigation.

During the radiographer's and designer's development of the task models it will become apparent that there will be many task models produced. There will be one task model for each task and there also could be an overview model, which shows how the different tasks are related. In addition, there will be generalized and specific versions of each task showing generalized and specific task views respectively. As well as describing the general and specific versions of the tasks there will be iteration in the development of these models so the designer and the radiographer will build up a library of the various general and specific task models during this process. The development of these models is informal, cooperative, and iterative.

In Figure 9.4 the designers and radiographers have started to further describe the task of taking an X-ray and are using the task model editor to describe the various subgoals of the task. It can be seen that the editor allows them to rename, delete, or replace an existing entry, add a procedure or a subgoal to the task model, and expand or contract the model in depth. The designer, in consultation with the radiographer, has added a new subgoal and this leads to a further selection of the structural relation of the new subgoal. It is then possible to describe whether this subgoal is to be carried out in sequence, parallel, or interleaved. In addition, it is also possible for the designer and radiographer to define whether or not a subgoal is optional (choice on the editor menu) or disabled (i.e., not possible under particular conditions). Figure 9.4 also shows that beneath the goal structure of the task model editor are two scrollable text windows. In the leftmost of these two windows the radiographer and designer have begun to construct a list of the domain objects that are used in, affect, or are affected by the task. The list includes objects such as request form, patient name, and so on. Each of these items entered into the domain object component of the task model can be selected. The object information provides descriptions of the domain and the way in which the task and organization context affect those objects.

Figure 9.5 shows a further stage in the development of the task models associated with radiography. The screen portrays the task model editor again but this time showing how objects can be edited and their properties changed. The objects are domain objects that are affected by or used in the particular task defined by the currently displayed task model. The same object(s) can be used in many different tasks and in multiple parts of a task. Many of the properties of objects are determined by the task context in which they occur. The task domain object model therefore contains task-specific as well as task-independent properties of the objects. Objects can be added, deleted, or renamed. Upon

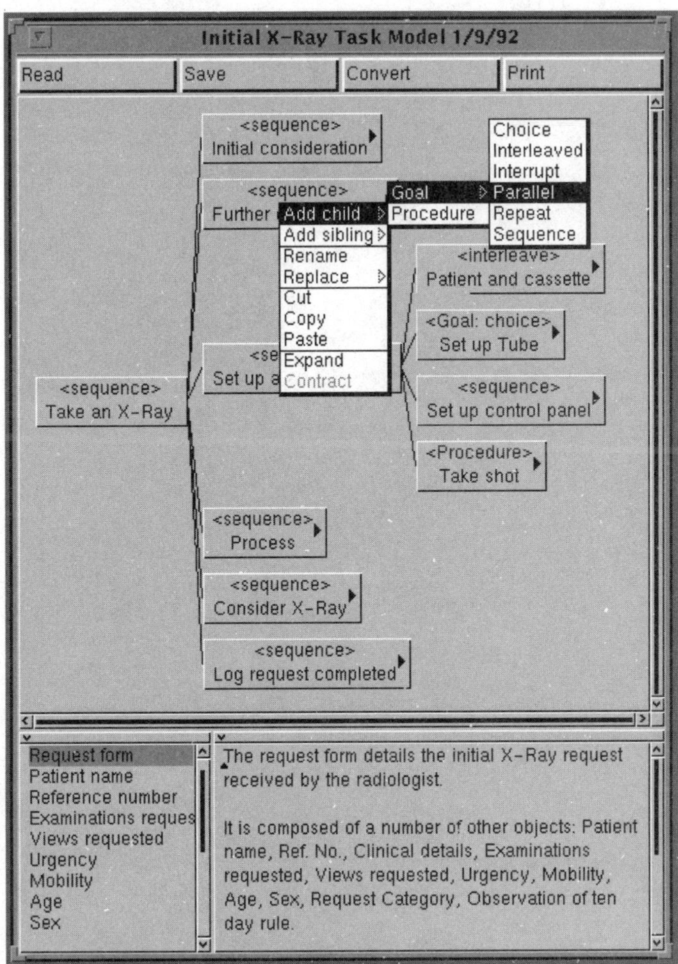

Figure 9.4. Editing a task model with the ADEPT tools.

selection of an object, information about its properties and components can be entered, viewed, and edited. This detailed object information is displayed in the adjacent text window. The object's properties can include its composition and parts hierarchies, the defining features of the object, any possible values and references to other objects, as well as the typicality and centrality estimates of the object. The objects are one

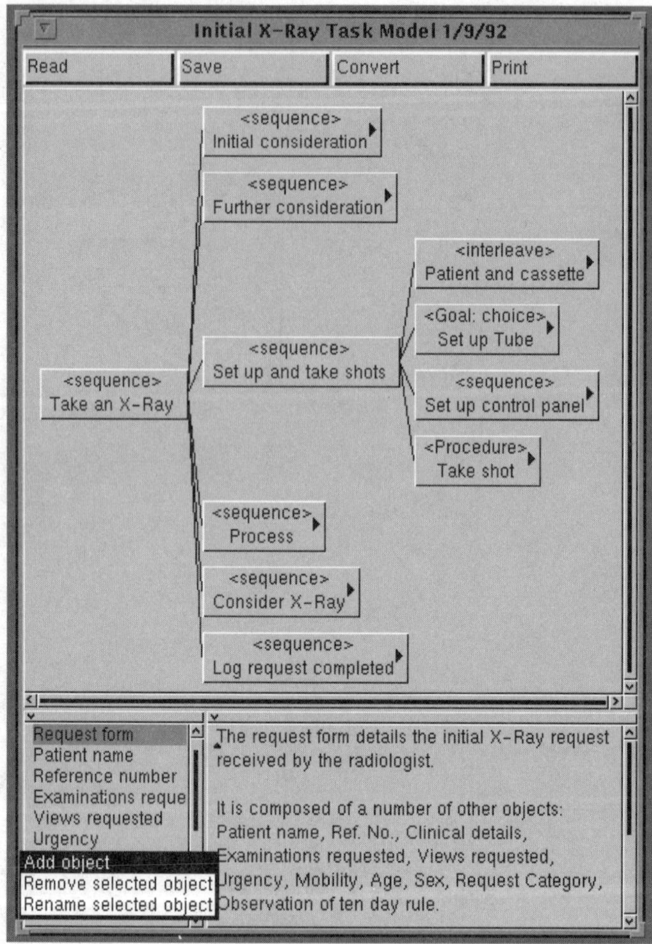

Figure 9.5. Editing the object properties of the task model using ADEPT.

feature by which relations between tasks and parts of tasks can be identified. For example, the medical record is one object that is used in many other tasks both within the work of radiographers and in other spheres of health care, and even within radiography is used by many different roles within the hospital organization, for example, radiographers, clerical staff, clinicians, and consultants.

In Figure 9.6 the task model is now shown with further detail added

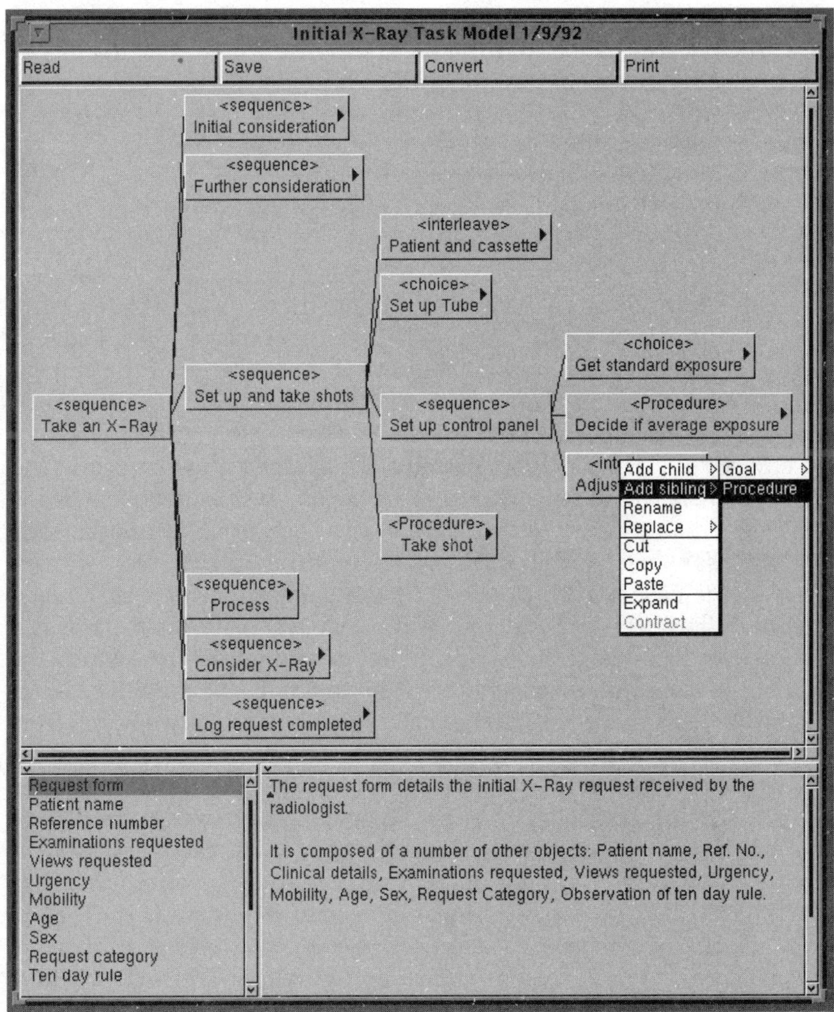

Figure 9.6. Further detailing of the actions associated with "taking a shot."

of the "take shot's" subgoal expanded to show how the activity of taking an X-ray photograph is reliant on other dependent activities taking place. This is shown in the model by notational symbols indicating interleaving, parallel, and sequential activities. The model describes taking a shot as being a sequence of activities that first involves positioning the patient and the cassette, followed by setting up the X-ray camera tube, then setting the values of the exposure time and strength of the X-ray at the control panel, and finally taking the X-ray shot itself. The display also indicates that taking the X-ray shot is further decomposed into a procedural set of actions. Clicking with the mouse on this node of the task model would display the description of that procedure.

The task modeling activity proceeds by developing the detail of the various tasks of the radiographers to produce a series of task models represented in the task model library of the ADEPT toolset.

As well as providing a description of the task, the ADEPT environment also allows details of the radiographers themselves to be recorded. These details are recorded in a simplistic form of user model. The *user model* [15] records information about the characteristics of the current and/or potential users of any system. It provides a profile of users in terms of their skills. It also records other information such as age, sex, and familiarity with computer systems. This information is recorded to provide a background for any design proposals. It is aimed at allowing the designers and users to be aware of the population of likely users. The form of the user model in this version of the ADEPT tools (Figure 9.7) is a rule-base, which provides design suggestions related to user properties. The designers can add to the design rules in the rule-base if they choose. The design rules are in fact design guidelines, which the designer or user can choose to accept or reject. If the guideline is accepted then an appropriate design choice is automatically derived from the rule. If the guideline is rejected, the designer is free to make his or her own design choice.

At this point the designers and radiographers agree that it would be appropriate to begin to develop some design ideas and see how they fit into the activities of radiography. One design suggestion that has emerged is to have an image of the human body displayed on the control panel, which could be used to select settings for the X-ray. An extract of a design scenario that arose is shown in Figure 9.8. This extract illustrates how the designer describes the emergent design idea of a "body widget" and its associated forms of interaction. The design is expressed in terms of how it would be used and how it would relate to the task of taking an X-ray in detail. This is relatively easy for the designer to do at this stage because of the detailed understanding that has been acquired about the activities of radiography.

The radiographers are able to understand and contribute to the design discussions because the focus is on activities, tasks, and objects associated with taking X-rays. The textual version of the design scenario provides a convenient and rough form of communication of the

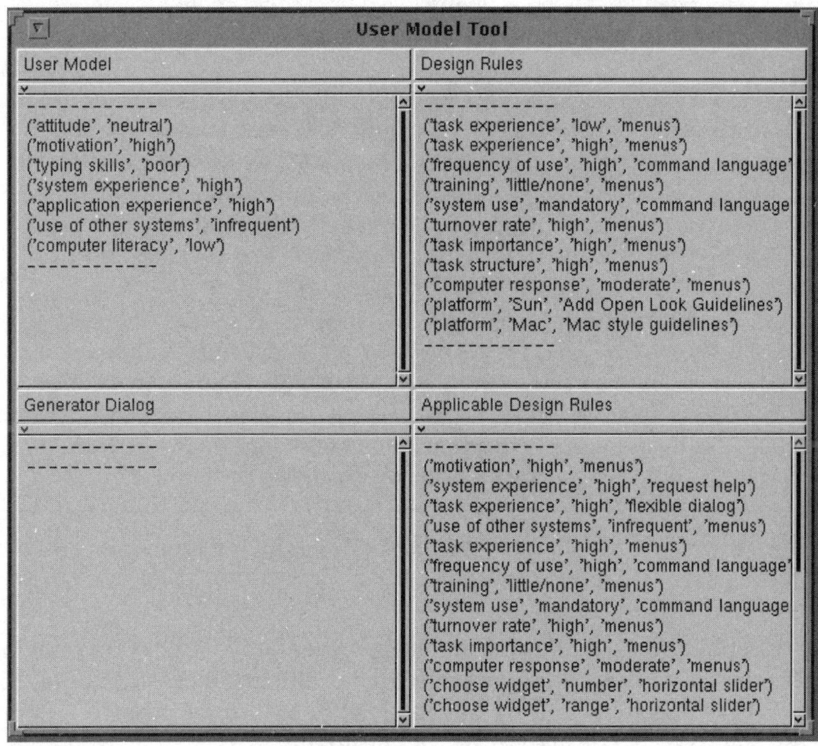

Figure 9.7. The user model constructed using ADEPT.

design ideas between the designers and radiographers. However, at some stage the radiographers require a more concrete view of how these design ideas might impact their work and what it might mean to interact with a body widget (a clear case of designer jargon creeping into the scenario). Consequently, as the design ideas progress, the designers and radiographers return to the ADEPT tools and begin to transform the task model they have constructed into a design. This is approached from the perspective of the task model itself. The tasks are redesigned and developed to provide a model of the proposed changes to the activities and radiographers' tasks.

The designer begins to create a new version of the task model, which is called the "design task model." Together the designer and the

An image representing the body (in medical terms) could improve on this situation. The image might represent more than one view of the body (front, side, back).

It might allow radiographers to click on the relevant body part and zoom in and out as necessary. An alternative is to have buttons at the side corresponding to the body parts but there may be too many body parts to do this.

On selecting a body part the data on standard exposure settings could be provided to the radiographer and the values fed into the control panel. These values could then be adjusted for non standard cases. Text could also be provided about exceptions, acceptable ranges of exposure values, etc.

A further variable in deciding exposure is the body size of the patient, which varies with sex, age, weight, clinical condition, etc. At present in some control panels there are some presets for body size. We might replace these with sliders for more continuous adjustment.

We could also think about whether to reflect these changes in the body image display, that is show the parameterization by expanding the body, etc.

Figure 9.8. The designer's scenario of redesign ideas for the control panel.

radiographer work through their design ideas to see how this might affect the tasks currently performed. The radiographer contributes to the design ideas by making suggestions about which aspects of the tasks he or she would like to see computerized or removed altogether, and also points out to the designer where changes might be unwise. One example of a proposed design change, which originated from the designer, was to make it possible to carry out actions at any time in any order. This is a well motivated and technically feasible design feature of most desktop window-type displays where users are given no constraints over what they might do at any given time. However, the designer had overlooked the fact that in taking X-rays, safety and patient welfare are a major concern, which is realized through the procedures that must be followed. Consequently, incorporating into the design a change from a strict temporal sequencing of actions to a free and unordered set of options would allow any user of the design to break a safety procedure. Thus it was important that the design embedded safety procedures, which either improved or at least kept with current practices.

Developing the design task model includes defining new objects and modifying the properties of objects to enable them to function appropriately in the redesigned tasks. It is clearly impossible for the designer or the radiographers to conceive of all possible tasks in all possible contexts to which the design might be applied. Instead, the design task model is a description of those tasks that the radiographers and designers agree the system *must* be able to support.

The design task model is a high-level specification of what the design will allow the radiographers *to do*. Thus it is the first attempt at meeting the design requirements by saying what the computer system will enable the users to do and how it will affect their work. The designers and radiographers can and should evaluate this stage of the design by comparing it with the scope of the existing task model and the consequences on the work and tasks of the radiographers. In addition, the design should be evaluated against the context of usage in the organizational structure of the wards and hospital.

From the design task model the designers and radiographers can produce an Abstract Interface Model (AIM) using the ADEPT tools (Figure 9.9). The AIM is a model of the interaction aspects of the proposed design. This model details the dialog in which the radiographers would engage to carry out any of the proposed tasks of the design task model. The AIM takes the structure of the tasks as described in the design task model and instantiates that as the structure for the interaction dialog. For example, if in the task model it was decided that for safety reasons the radiographers should always have to set the exposure controls of the X-ray before it was possible to take the X-ray, then the dialog structure of the AIM would maintain this ordering and disable the taking of the X-ray until the settings had been either changed or checked and then confirmed. The AIM model is very similar to the ideas provided in Rosson's *Scenario Browser* and addresses concerns that Jacobsen and Wirfs-Brock each raise regarding modeling the way in which the interaction might be described. Using their terminology, the AIM provides a *use-case* model of the way the various objects of the design will be linked together and used during a particular interaction scenario.

In addition, the AIM details the designed objects with which the radiographers would interact in the course of these dialogs. The relationship between a task, an interaction dialog, and the interaction objects is the focus of this model. The dialog model is defined in terms of the designed tasks. The completeness of the dialog model is an issue of concern for the designer. The dialog model is as complete as the design task model in that it must describe how each task of the design task model would be carried out by the radiographers. This represents the idealized dialog for using the design to carry out each of the defined tasks. The designer and the radiographers are able to walk through the dialogs as if they were interaction scenarios for particular tasks. In this way the designer can involve the radiographer in the further develop-

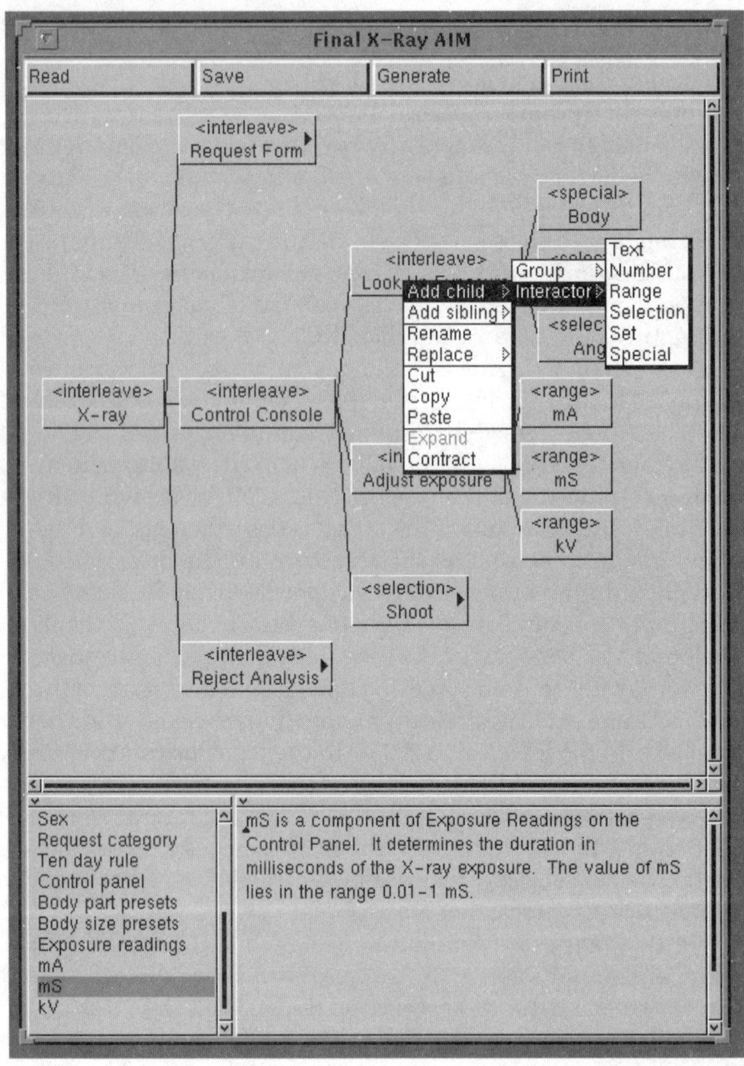

Figure 9.9. Designing the radiography dialog using the ADEPT Abstract Interaction Model.

ment and evaluation of the design at this early stage, identifying inefficient, unnecessary, and incorrect aspects of the design, in addition to noting positive features.

The object component of the AIM provides a complete description of all the objects necessary to support the designed dialogs and to allow the designed tasks to be carried out. This is a textual description of the objects, their properties, and links to other objects, including dialog links. The objects are originally the set of objects defined in the designed task model. However, during the process of developing the design it may be the case that new or changed objects are introduced into the model. In such cases any consequences of introducing or changing objects in the design have to be worked through and appropriate changes made to the dialog component of the AIM.

Having progressed the design as far as they can in terms of the dialog and objects of the abstract interaction model, the radiographers decide that they would like to see a rough version of the design to provide a consideration of the potential usage and usability. This is easily done within the ADEPT tools.

The AIM is developed further to produce a Concrete Interface Model (CIM), which provides a runnable version of an actual interface with which the radiographers and the designer can interact. The method by which the CIM is developed is through refining the design to detail how the interaction described in the AIM is to be realized in an actual computer interface. This includes details of the interaction style to be used and the form of the interaction behaviors of the user and the interface. In this model the designer must define when the user will provide an input or receive an output from the computer in terms of the medium and modality through which that input and output will occur. This level of detail is developed by the designer through further discussions with the radiographers. Together they determine, for example, in which parts of the tasks it is appropriate to use keyboard, mouse, pointing, or other forms of input, and also where they feel graphical, textual, sound, or other forms of output will be required. These design decisions are made jointly and, because of the ADEPT toolset, are easily reversible and changeable.

The ADEPT tools present the results of these design decisions in the form of a runnable model of the interface. At this stage the designer and the radiographer can easily understand the consequences of the design for the users' tasks. Through inspecting and running the CIM the radiographers and designers begin to assess what it will be like to interact with the computer to carry out the designed tasks. The result is a complete system, in the sense that it contains all the physical and behavioral form designed thus far. The designers and radiographers now have a design with which they can interact, undertake further evaluations, and also develop further design changes. The models from which the design was produced are available for inspection on a display separate from the run-time version of the radiography interface.

Further iterations around the design begin to occur immediately as the radiographers decide that changes to the position, ordering, and form of interaction are all needed. These are easily carried out by changing the appropriate models, and within minutes of the redesign being agreed upon a second version of the interface is generated. The process of iterative design continues with little cost being attached to the implementation effort needed to throw away and replace earlier design ideas.

This concludes the design scenario of the X-ray interface. It has demonstrated how methods and tools concerned with modeling task and artifact properties can be used to provide a work- and task-oriented approach to design, which enables greater involvement of users in the design process. In the following section we describe the philosophy behind this approach.

9.3 DISCUSSION

We will now consider the methodological issues underlying scenario-based design and the role of task analysis and the various design models of the ADEPT environment. First, we will consider the general approach to scenario-based design, which we have adopted, and then describe the method involved in using the ADEPT tools in the context of this approach. Our aim has been to bring together the informal and accessible aspects of scenario-based design with a tool-based approach in which we develop more formal representations of the existing (current) tasks and the design of the envisioned task and computer system, which can be used to constrain and feed into the development of a runnable prototype.

9.3.1 Bringing Together Scenario- and Tool-Based Approaches

An approach to design, which puts people and human activity at the fore of the development and deployment of technology, should not only provide a framework for conceptualizing design, but also give rise to processes and tools that support that design approach. Figure 9.10 presents a schematic view of how scenario-based design might be related to tool-based design. The analysis of tasks and the use of scenarios to

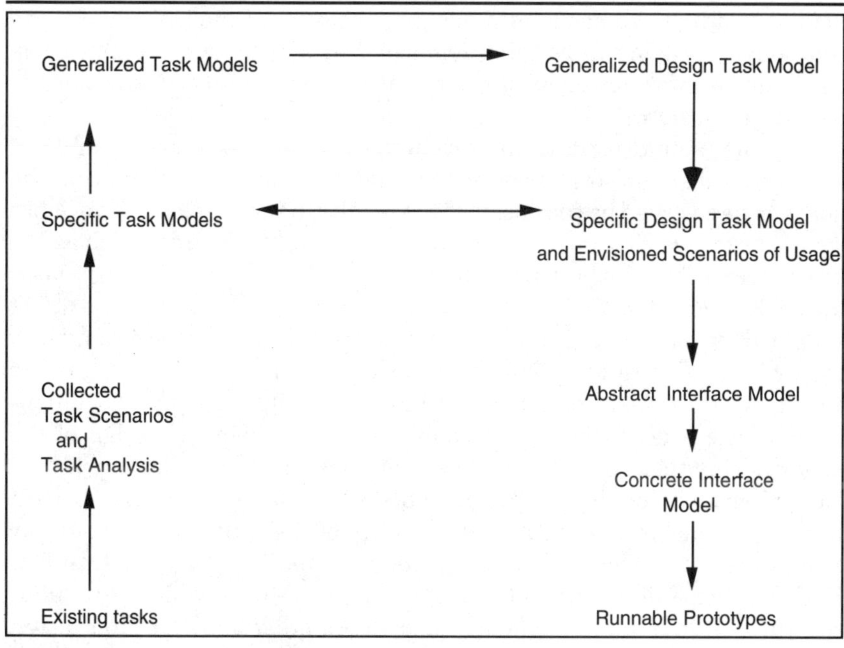

Figure 9.10. A schematic view of the relations between the scenario-based design and tool-based design.

portray snapshots of those tasks are depicted as activities to produce a detailed understanding of the current users and their work tasks. These tasks are described both as specific tasks and also in a more generalized form to allow generalities across different tasks and different users to be identified, while retaining specific task detail to be used to identify exceptions and deviations to the generalized forms. The development of a designed task model can occur in both generalized and specific forms and makes use of scenarios to depict how specific tasks are envisioned in the design. From these designed tasks and scenarios, the design can be progressed, using a tool-based approach such as ADEPT, into abstract interaction models and finally to runnable prototypes. The schematic view in Figure 9.10 shows how task scenarios can be used to influence and constrain design.

We will next consider how the scenario-based approach can be used to relate people and work to the design of artifacts. In the first instance, scenario-based design relates people, tasks, and organizations to artifacts, providing the basis for a design process that makes use of those relations. This generalized view leads to the development of techniques, which allow information arising from users, tasks, and organizations to be used in design.

People (as individuals and groups), tasks (as work, social, and leisure activities), and organizations provide the input to formulating the needs to be satisfied by the design. This results in the development of what we have termed existing *specific* and *generalized* tasks and involves the use of scenarios to collect and communicate information about the user tasks. The *designed task* is an expression of what any proposed artifact should allow particular groups within known organizations to do, and how they will be able to carry out those tasks. Again, scenarios are used to depict how these tasks might be carried out but without any prior commitment to the exact form of the technology or the detailed design of the artifact. This then leads to the design of an artifact (or collection of artifacts) that would enable the designed tasks to be performed. The Abstract Interface Model is a description of the form of the artifact(s) without any commitment to concrete implementation detail. The Abstract Interface Model is then refined into a Concrete Interface Model, which particularizes the design in an implementable form but still allows for alternative, platform-specific versions of the artifact to be created having the same physical and conceptual form. This enables a runnable version of the design to be generated with which the user can interact. The runnable version of the design is based on the tasks and scenarios developed during the analysis and design phases. Throughout the development of the design of the artifact, the framework also provides for a reexpression of the task model that is expected to result from the further detailing of the artifact. Consequently, the design at all times is expressed in terms of the users, whose needs it is expected to serve, and their tasks.

To support this approach to design, our philosophy requires techniques that allow users, tasks, organizations, and designers to participate jointly in the development of the artifact(s). This has caused us to make use of techniques from experimental psychology and anthropology, which include role playing, observations, direct participation, interviews, card sorting, and protocol analysis. Similarly, the philosophy requires designers to ensure that people and organizations can directly understand how the artifacts resulting from design can be used. Consequently, facilitating communication between users and designers is a direct requirement on any method or tools developed to support this design philosophy. A further concern is the evolutionary nature of design. There is an explicit recognition that while users, tasks, and organizations must be strong determinants on the design of an artifact, the artifact will bring about changes to the needs of people and organizations and will give rise to new tasks.

A final feature of the design approach is the need for the development of principles and other forms of design knowledge to support the transitions between the needs and characteristics of users, tasks, and organizations and the properties and functions of artifacts.

In summary, our design philosophy assumes the following:

- Good user interface design comes about through having increased involvement, communication, and participation in design by designers, users, and organizations.
- Increased involvement and communication occurs through greater understanding of users, their tasks, and organizations, and the consequences of usage of the artifacts.
- Design must include a focus on the tasks and activities of the users and organizations.
- It should be possible to ignore and abstract from the detail of implementation issues, that is, not force overcommitment in design.
- The design process requires iteration around the development of all models including those of users, organizations, tasks, and artifacts.
- Design requires the development of principled design knowledge to support the transition between user, organization, and task characteristics on the one hand, and artifact properties and functions on the other.

9.3.2 The ADEPT Design Method

The models and tools of ADEPT have been developed directly in line with the above design philosophy. However, ADEPT is not necessarily the idealized or optimum environment for such an approach to design, but is our first significant attempt at developing tools to support this view of design. Furthermore, ADEPT can be used as part of many different design methodologies, which take seriously the importance of user and task modeling as an input to the design of a computer system and user interface. The aim of the ADEPT models and tools is to make the designer think explicitly about the user group and the tasks or purposes to which any design should be put. The designer is required to explicitly model the nature of the work of the user organization in terms of the roles and tasks that form the substance of that work. The designer is further required to explicitly model how the design will be used as part of that work or how it will be used as part of some envisioned changed work situation. Through using this approach the designer is able to obtain an understanding of the users and their work and the ways that any proposed design options might fit within or change that work context. As part of the process of design it is important that the designers and users are able to communicate about the design and its context of use. To facilitate this communication it is important that the users have a format in which they can describe their tasks and which can be understood by the designers. This communication results in the task models of the ADEPT environment being constructed. Similarly, it is equally important that the designers have a format through which they can relate their design ideas to the users and that enables the users to see how the design relates to their work tasks. Through the use of the ADEPT models, the users and designers are better able to communicate with each other about their relative areas of expertise—namely work and computer technology.

The models and tools of ADEPT have been developed from the above design assumptions of a task-based approach to design, which allows user and designer participation in the design activity. It provides a focus on design issues that affect user tasks and user activity while allowing design considerations resulting from the details of the implementation to be also considered without deflecting the designer away from the important and often overlooked aspects of the context of usage of the design.

The ADEPT method is not a proceduralized method of design that dictates the successive steps in producing a design. Design cannot be proceduralized. Design involves problem solving and the models and tools of ADEPT facilitate identification, definition, and refinement of the problem space and development and evaluation of the design solutions (Figure 9.11).

9.3.3 Requirements Gathering and User and Task Models in ADEPT

The task and user descriptions of ADEPT form an important input to the definition of the design problem space. The task model is a detailed description of the roles and tasks that are currently performed as part of some work activity. The task model details the goal structure and the procedures by which these many and varied goals may be carried out. This model constitutes a description of the existing work context from the perspective of the users' goals and tasks, according to the various roles taken on. The user model is a description of the characteristics of the individual and/or groups of people who commonly perform these defined roles and their associated tasks. As such they can be thought of as components in the definition of the requirements for the design. More correctly,

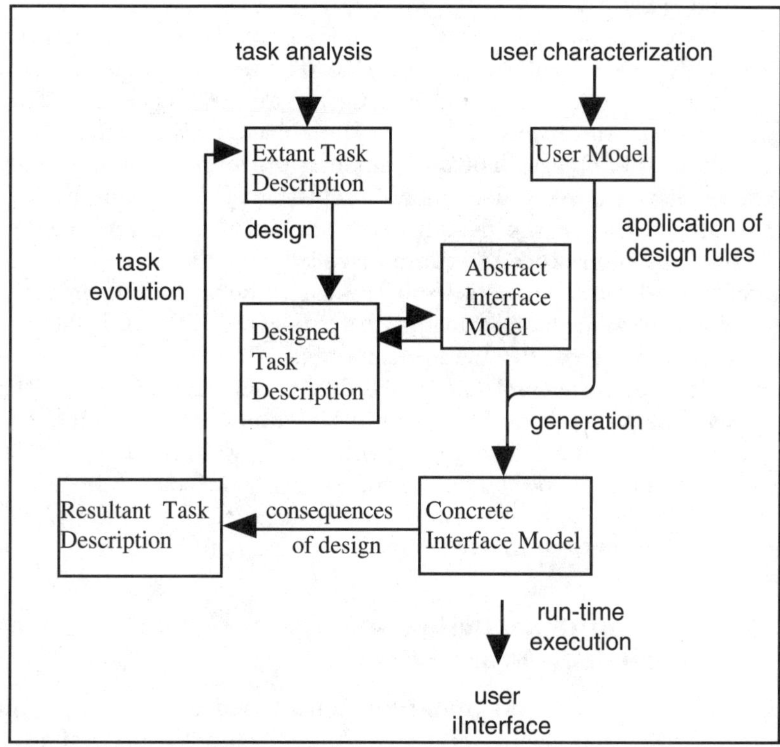

Figure 9.11. The ADEPT design process.

they constitute a definition of the context into which a design would have to be introduced. The form of the description of those requirements is not constrained by ADEPT other than in terms of their content. The content must make explicit the details of the tasks and user characteristics as they are jointly understood by the designers and users.

The techniques used to develop the task and user models include methods from experimental and social psychology, and anthropology. The models are developed first and foremost by the users with the help of the designer/analyst in providing summative descriptions of the information gathered, which the users can check and change. The techniques include participation in the user tasks by the designer/analyst and role playing by the users and designer/analyst. Indirect, nonobtrusive observations are carried out in addition to collecting users' own reports and descriptions of their tasks. For a fuller description of the techniques used, see Johnson [16].

The nature of the task and user models in ADEPT are such that they have different forms of presentation. The task model is presented as a goal and procedural structure diagram and a task domain object list with textual descriptions linking the objects to the actions of the tasks and to other objects. The user model is presented as a list of rules. The descriptive task and user models represent the working material for the progression of the design from which a textual requirements definition may be produced to summarize this information. Where necessary, the relevant extracts from the task and user models can be inserted in the requirements documents to provide direct links between the models and the resultant requirements.

Standard approaches to software design such as SSADM (Structured Systems Analysis and Design Method) and JSD (Jackson System Development) assume that requirements will be written in natural language and will largely be of a functional nature. The focus of the ADEPT approach is to add to these requirements detailed descriptions of the user and task context into which the design must fit.

9.3.4 Decompositional Design—Design Task Model, AIM and CIM

ADEPT does not follow a standard waterfall model for design, which assumes that all requirements can be elicited before the start of design and that high-level design can be completed before any low-level design. However, ADEPT does force the designer to start from users and tasks and to progress this into both high- and low-level design issues. It is difficult to envisage a situation in which the design of a system should be progressed from an artifact to a search for its possible uses. (Note, technology may occasionally progress in this manner, but the development of technology is not the development of artifacts. Ideally, artifact design progresses using available technology or creates a need for the development of new technology.) The ADEPT tools support the designer in constructing a task model of the design. This is a model of the tasks that the designer envisions the user carrying out with the designed artifact. This task model may be an overlapping extension of the existing task model (as in Figure 9.12A), allowing the user group to carry out tasks and attain goals that were not previously part of their responsibility (either because they could not be carried out or because they were carried out by different people or agents). Alternatively, the design task model may be a subset of the existing task model (as in Figure 9.12B). A

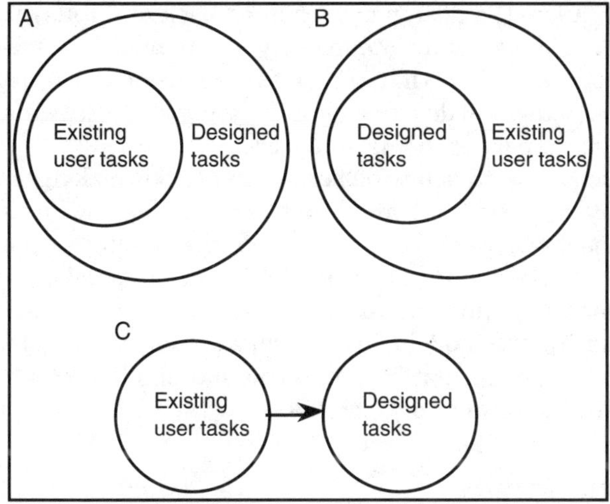

Figure 9.12. Possible relations between existing tasks and design: A shows design extending the range of tasks users can perform, B shows design supporting a subset of existing tasks, and C shows design replicating current tasks with a change of technology.

further option for the design task model is simply as a revision of the existing work by changing the way that the existing tasks are performed (as in Figure 9.12C).

9.3.5 Iteration and Participation in Design

Throughout the design lifecycle the ADEPT models and tools focus on users and tasks, and stress the need for user and designer involvement in a participatory design process. The task and user analyses must be iterative and participative, as must be the development of the task model, user model, design task model, abstract interaction model, and concrete interaction model. The designer and user can view the design in relation to its usage in task contexts. At any stage in the design the user or designer can reflect on the adequacy of the design, in terms of scope, dialog, objects, or the style and form of interaction. For example, it is expected that as designers and users advance the design, users will identify new tasks or ways of performing extant tasks, which were not included in either the extant task model or the design task model. ADEPT will allow the designer to then go back and redevelop the relevant model. This is not an inadequacy of any model or analysis technique: It is a realization that the design environment must allow for iteration at all stages of design and for existing and future task contexts to be modeled as part of the design process.

With such an approach to design, evaluation is no longer a separate activity that is carried out at discrete points. Instead, it is a central feature of the iterative process, which occurs on each occasion a user or a designer reflects upon a given model or set of models. ADEPT supports both formative and summative evaluation. It places great emphasis on evaluating the models directly with the users, and also upon the evaluation of all design decisions in terms of their effects on the usage of the system in the context of work tasks.

9.4 CONCLUSIONS

An aim of our research is ultimately to develop methods and tools to bring about changes to the design process, and, importantly, to the systems that are developed, such that people and human activity will be better served by the technology of computer systems. The focus for our research has been to understand how knowledge of users and their tasks can be derived and incorporated into the design process. Our aim has been to develop an approach to design that places an understanding of people and tasks at the starting point of the design process, rather than solely as phenomena against which artifacts are evaluated.

In the framework for scenario-based design, we identified task, user, and organizational descriptions as constituting important inputs to the design process. The ADEPT tools support particular forms of task and user descriptions, but lack any organizational description. The particular forms of task and user description are highly manipulable but are relatively formal in their appearance. The task model is a combination of a graph diagram of goals and procedures and a textual description of objects, while the user model is a purely rule-based description. The form of the user model leaves much to be desired both in terms of the content of the rules and ability to support user participation in design. The designed task description is an important feature of the design framework and although in ADEPT is not well supported in providing the designer or the user with any form of rationalization or argumentation structure that might be used to support particular reasons for changing or preserving the form of the tasks. In addition, there is little in the way of design principles or design knowledge that either the user or the designer can call upon to support their decision making. The Abstract Interface Model is a clear description of the intended design without forcing the designer to commit to particular design detail over the implementation. However, it is not directly executable or interactive other than in construction; consequently neither the user nor the designer can begin to use the design at this stage. The Concrete Interface Model is interactive and executable. However, it is not easily modified by the user so the designer is likely to have control over making changes to the CIM in ADEPT. Our aim is to make this an operation that the user can also perform so that both designers and users can contribute directly to the development of the detailed, as well as the abstract, form of the design.

It will be clear from the preceding discussion that the ADEPT design tools have evolved from our philosophy yet lag behind our understanding of the problems in carrying out scenario-based design. We are concerned about the lack of design principles, which can be used to guide the designer in developing applications from the perspective of users and their tasks. The development of the ADEPT design tools has enabled us to provide design support for our design philosophy. A principled approach to scenario-based design would involve developing further relations between the philosophy, models, and tools as our understanding increases.

ACKNOWLEDGMENTS

The authors are grateful to James Pycock, who undertook the analysis of the radiographers' tasks. We would like to thank Jack Carroll, Kari Kuutti, and Bob Mack for their helpful comments on an earlier version of this chapter.

The ADEPT Project (Advanced Design Environments for Prototyping with Task models) was a collaboration between Queen Mary and Westfield College, University of London, British Aerospace Plc, British Maritime Technology Ltd and MJC^2. It was led by Queen Mary and Westfield College and funded by the DTI and SERC (Grant No. IED 4/1/1573).

REFERENCES

[1] Butler, S. A. (1883). *Erewhon*. London: Routledge.

[2] Johnson, P. & Johnson, H. (1991). Knowledge analysis of tasks: Analysis and specification for human-computer systems. In A. Downton (ed.), *Engineering the Human-Computer Interface*. London: McGraw-Hill, pp. 119–144.

[3] Johnson, H. & Johnson, P. (1987). The development of task analysis as a design tool: A method for carrying out task analyses. *Deliverable no. 1 to ICL*, March.

[4] Welbank, M. (1983). A review of knowledge acquisition techniques for expert systems. *Martlesham Consultancy Services.*

[5] Johnson, H. & Johnson, P. (1991). Task knowledge structures: Psychological basis and integration into system design. *Acta Psychologica*, *78*, 3–26.

[6] Johnson, P., Johnson H., Waddington, R. & Shouls, A. (1988). Task related knowledge structures: Analysis, modelling and application. In D. M. Jones & R. Winder (eds.), *People and Computers: From Research to Implementation.* Cambridge, U.K.: Cambridge University Press, pp. 35–62.

[7] Card, S. K., Moran, T. P. & Newell, A. (1983). *The Psychology of Human-Computer Interaction.* Hillsdale, NJ: Lawrence Erlbaum.

[8] Payne, S. & Green, T. R. G. (1986). Task-action grammars: A model of the mental representation of task languages. *Human Computer Interaction*, *2*, 93–133.

[9] Hartson, H. R. & Gray, P. D. (1992). Temporal aspects of tasks in the user action notation. *Human Computer Interaction,7*(1), 1–45.

[10] Anderson, J. R. (1981). *Cognitive Skills and Their Acquisition.* Hillsdale, NJ: Lawrence Erlbaum.

[11] Johnson, P. (1982). The functional equivalence of images and movements. *Quarterly Journal of Experimental Psychology*, 34A, 349–365.

[12] Johnson, P., Wilson, S., Markopoulos, P. & Pycock, J. (1993). ADEPT—advanced design environment for prototyping with task models. In *INTERCHI'93 Proceedings of Human Factors in Computing,* Amsterdam. Reading, MA: Addison-Wesley/ACM Press, p. 56.

[13] Wilson, S., Markopoulos, P., Pycock, J. & Johnson, P. (1992). Modelling perspectives in user interface design. In *Proceedings of East-West Conference on Human-Computer Interaction,* pp. 210–216.

[14] Wilson S., Johnson, P., Colgan, L., Kelly, C., Cunningham, J. & Markopoulos, P. (1993). Beyond hacking: A model-based approach to user interface design. In J. L. Alty, D. Diaper & S. Guest (eds.), *People and Computers VIII, Proceedings of HCI'93*, Loughborough. Cambridge, U.K.: Cambridge University Press.

[15] Kelly, C. & Colgan, L. (1992). User modelling and user interface design. In A. Monk, D. Diaper & M. Harrison (eds.), *People and ComputersVII, Proceedings of HCI'92*, York. Cambridge, U.K.: Cambridge University Press, pp. 227–239.

[16] Johnson, P. (1992). *Human-Computer Interaction. Psychology, Task Analysis and Software Engineering.* Maidenhead, U.K.: McGraw-Hill.

CHAPTER 10

Narrowing the Specification-Implementation Gap in Scenario-Based Design

Mary Beth Rosson and John M. Carroll
Department of Computer Science
562 McBryde Hall
Virginia Polytechnic Institute and State University
Blacksburg, VA 24061
USA

In contemporary design practice for applications, user interfaces, and even programming systems, task scenarios provide an organizing framework for a variety of activities: requirements capture and analysis, user-designer communication, system envisionment and development, documentation and training, usability evaluation. For example, a textual narrative or storyboard of a programmer copying a diskette is a representation of the requirements for and envisioned use of an operating system. Scenarios raise the possibility for a flexible and use-oriented design framework that integrates the traditionally separate perspectives of systems and software engineering on the one hand, and human-computer interaction, on the other.

However, scenario-based design methods are not a well-specified technology; currently they are not even a coherent methodology. For example, there is little consensus about the appropriate level or levels at which to couch scenario descriptions: Is it the level of human activity meaningful to the human actors, the level of transactions in the application (e.g., a payroll calculation), the level of input-output transactions, or some combination of all of these perspectives? What are the implications of couching scenario descriptions at various levels? What are the procedures and representations for doing this? How detailed, how complete should a scenario description be? Similar uncertainty exists concerning the role of scenarios in the development lifecycle: Should scenarios be given to software developers as part of a formal specification, or are they best reserved for the more informal exploratory phases of a design project? Regardless of their role, where do scenarios come from? It is more than likely that at the current time no two developers or practitioners of scenario-based methods would render the same answers to these questions.

In this paper we describe the Scenario Browser, a SmallTalk application development tool that integrates the development of task scenarios with the design of object-oriented software implementing these scenarios. The tool supports an iterative process in which designers specify and elaborate basic scenarios of use in parallel with the instantiation and evolution of SmallTalk objects that enact these scenarios. The tool also supports the analysis and documentation of design rationale for each scenario, with respect to both the usability consequences that inhere in task design decisions, and the software quality consequences inhering in the corresponding software design decisions. The work seeks to unify recent scenario-oriented work in object-oriented design methods [14, 20, 33, 37] with scenario-oriented work in the design of human-computer interactions [9, 11]. We argue that if designers interleave development and analysis of an application's task and software models, they will be better able to recognize and address the inevitable interdependencies in the two models, thereby narrowing the gap between specification and implementation.

We first discuss our approach to specifying systems through the elaboration and analysis of task scenarios. We then describe how the Scenario Browser environment integrates this scenario-based approach to system specification with a scenario-based approach to object-oriented design and implementation. For concreteness, our discussion focuses on an example application (a bibliography utility) developed in the Scenario Browser. We close with a general discussion of the role of scenarios in software development.

10.1 SPECIFICATION OF USER TASKS

The first phase of any software development process is a requirements analysis, during which the design team establishes goals concerning the functionality that the system will provide [15]. Requirements are often documented as individual features, specific functions that must be implemented in order to make available the required overall system functionality. This approach entrains the creation of voluminous specification documents couched at the level of individual operations (e.g., [1], Chapters 4 and 6). This tends to create software abstractions at a fairly low level with respect to overall system functionality. It does not support envisionment of a coherent system, that is, as it might ultimately be experienced by users.

We have argued that an important supplement to this function-oriented approach is a use-oriented approach: to specify systems by specifying the user tasks they will support [9].

10.1.1 Scenario Envisionment

We focus on scenarios couched at the level people construe their activities to themselves, the level at which tasks are meaningful to the people who engage in them. We call these task narrative scenarios because they describe specific *instances* of a task; a fully elaborated scenario will include details about the user's goals, expectations, and activities, the system's response, if any, and the user's reactions [11]. For a person building a bibliography, example scenarios might include "adding the Lange and Moher CHI'89 paper"; "updating the volume and pages for Jack's latest CACM article"; "altering citation format from IEEE to ACM"; and so forth.

An initial task specification for "adding the Lange and Moher CHI'89 paper" is displayed in the top portion of Table 10.1. The narrative is fairly brief and contains little detail about the specifications comprising the task. However, even at this very preliminary stage, the scenario describes an envisioned task from the *user's* perspective. As a starting design representation, it seeks to expose and to make explicit hypotheses and observations about how the user thinks about the important objects and relationships constituting the task. For example, a conference paper has components (e.g., authors, a date); the person has conceptualized the reference to the conference paper in terms of its salient content and would like to incorporate this content into a reference nickname.

Note that this initial scenario specification does not include details about the user's interactions with the system. Our approach encourages designers to first address the core tasks of the problem domain, to focus attention on *what* the system will support, and then to turn to *how* it will do this, and develop a user interface for these tasks [18]. From the perspective of usability engineering, we are concerned with enabling an earlier and deeper impact of usage concerns on the software development process. Creating an early usability focus on specify-

Table 10.1 Specification and Elaboration of Bibliography Scenarios

Initial specification of Lange and Moher reference-entry task:

I want to add Beth Lange's paper documenting the copy-edit strategy in OO reuse. I remember that she gave it at CHI'89, and I think it was co-authored with Tom Moher, so I enter that info, but I can't remember where that conference was held or who edited the proceedings. I'd like to give the reference a nickname, but I can't decide between "oo-reuse" and "copyEdit".

Elaborated specification of Lange and Moher reference-entry:

Using the menu from the default browsing screen, I select "Add reference" and then "Conference paper" from the submenu. This brings up a Conference paper form, with "nickname" as the first field, so I figure I should come up with a nickname first. I think about it for a bit, then decide that probably this will be my default reference for the copy-Edit strategy, so I enter "copy-Edit" as my nickname. I then type in the other information, the authors' names and initials, separated by commas, the title, and year just like when I type them in a reference list. I know it is a CHI'89 paper, but I can't remember the editor of the proceedings, or the actual dates of the conference. So I enter the other stuff, the location of the conference, and the publisher and publisher location, the proceedings, and the name and location of the publisher. When I've finished, I press the "OK" button, and the system tells me it has entered a conference paper reference; it also formats the information nicely, and puts question marks into the unfilled spaces. I make a mental note to come back later and try to fill in the missing stuff.

ing appropriate functionality (that is, on usefulness) augments the more typical usability engineering ease-of-learning and ease-of-use concerns.

The bottom portion of Table 10.1 depicts the conference paper addition scenario at a later point in the development of the bibliography utility. Details about how the user enters the reference data have been elaborated, including some characterization of user interface elements (e.g., menus, buttons). At this point in the design we are able to get a more concrete sense of what user actions are required to use the system, and how the system responds to these actions. Note, however, that the high-level task context—what the user is trying to accomplish and how he or she feels as the task unfolds—continues to serve as an integrative framework for the narrative.

An important element of our approach is that designers are always working within a *set* of scenarios. In some cases, different scenarios will be relatively independent. For example, using the bibliography to produce formatted output for a text file appears prima facie to have little in common with using it to create or retrieve a reference item. Other usage situations clearly overlap. Consider a scenario in which the user wants to check the Lange and Moher reference, to verify that it is the one needed for a point being made in a paper. This item-retrieval situation clearly depends on a prior item-entry situation, because the retrieval keywords supplied by the user need to match the previously entered descriptors. Moreover, the two scenarios embody tradeoffs: What may be best from an item-entry perspective (e.g., perhaps providing a default nickname to ease the name-generation burden, allowing incomplete entries to be saved) may not be desirable from the perspective of retrieval (e.g., the default nickname may not be very memorable, the user may be frustrated in trying to find an item via what later turns out to be an empty field). Our method provides no automatic solutions to such potential conflicts. However, it does support the designer in developing and reasoning about design issues such as these in the context of the specific usage situations from which they arise.

Clearly a critical ingredient in scenario envisionment is the development of a comprehensive and coherent set of user tasks. Often these tasks will be identified through analysis of existing work practices [21, 27]. However, in an effort to ensure good coverage, we have also developed a task-analytic framework for scenario generation. Based on our own experiences collecting and analyzing scenarios in various design projects, we have developed a typology of six generic usage situations within which our example scenarios could be classified ([11]; see Table 10.2). Our hope is that these generic situations can be used as a heuristic for recognizing or developing specific scenarios that will be useful in representing a particular design project.

Table 10.2 lists six general usage situations and exemplifies them for the bibliography utility. The first situation captures the concerns of a user who is encountering a system (or perhaps a component of a system) for the first time, and is considering what an appropriate goal might be. In the second, the user has discovered some interesting aspect of a system and taken on the goal of exploring or using that aspect. The "searching for information" category represents a situation in which a user assumes (e.g., from prior experience) that a system supports a particular task but is not sure *where* to find the functionality. In "carrying out procedures" a person is pursuing a goal and simply needs to know what actions to perform; in contrast, "making sense" captures the concerns of a user who has encountered a problem (or even just an interesting system response) and now wishes to better understand *how* the system does what it does. Finally, "reflecting on skills" describes the general situation in which someone pursues the goal of tuning or optimizing his or her own tasks.

Table 10.2 Six General Categories of User Concerns

Orienting to goals:

Using the system for the first time, encountering a browsing screen, exploring the menus, and seeing that it also supports reference entry and formatting; seeing the form for a journal paper and recognizing that it has the same components as I would find in an APA-style citation.

Opportunistic interaction:

Opening the system and just browsing, i.e., scanning the first reference I happen to see, then asking for "next" over and over again; noticing that I can use several different citation formats when setting up a document for printing, and trying them out, just to see what they look like.

Searching for information:

Wondering if there is a special process for collecting together a list of references to be used as the bibliography at the end of a paper; looking for a way to set up citations as footnotes in the body of the paper.

Carrying out procedures:

Adding a reference for the Lange and Moher CHI'89 paper documenting the copy-Edit strategy for reuse in object-oriented programming; finding the reference to use for citing Kevin and Jack's notion of a tutoring environment that then evolves into a tool.

Making sense:

Retrieving Lange and Moher from the nickname spec "copy-edit", even though I gave it the nickname of "copyEdit" originally, and realizing that the system is able to do fuzzy matching; surprised when at some point when I say "Next", I get a reference I have already browsed, then realizing that the system must cycle back to the beginning when it reaches the end of a reference set.

Reflecting on skills:

Realizing that if I fill in one or more components of a template and say "OK", the system first checks to see if this reference exists, and fills in missing fields if so—I can use this technique for retrieving references if I want to; creating a new reference format for the new journal *Interacting with Computers*, by modifying its nearest neighbor.

10.1.2 Scenario Analysis

Although we have found that scenario narratives can often support design reasoning quite effectively, we have also developed a framework for viewing scenarios as sets of causal relations between features of a use situation and consequences for users. For example, the scenario of adding a conference paper to the bibliography involved creating a nickname. Such a feature could have various consequences for a user in this scenario: The user might benefit from being able to make use of personal experience and article content to build a more meaningful citation name. On the other hand, people are often unreliable at designing names, and the user might have difficulties, might even create a quirky nickname that is quickly forgotten, necessitating wasteful search.

We call the set of hypothesized causal relations pertaining to a given feature within a given scenario a *claim*. The nicknaming claim, along with other examples analyzed for the conference paper reference-entry scenario, appears in Table 10.3. We have found that analyzing the usability claims for a few critical or especially complex scenarios significantly strengthens scenario-based design work by focusing design reasoning on the key design tradeoffs associated with particular usage situations [10].

The most important contribution of claims analysis to design is to support design reasoning. Claims document the designer's hypotheses and assumptions about how a system's features may impact usability.

Table 10.3 Example Usability Claims for the Lange and Moher Reference-Entry Scenario

offering a reference nicknaming feature
. . . encourages a conceptual encoding of reference items
. . . *but generating unique, unambiguous, and memorable nicknames may be difficult*

decomposing entries into standard reference components
. . . enables flexible entry and skipping of information
. . . leverages authors' knowledge of bibliographic attributes
. . . *but working at the component level may seem tedious*

accepting partial specification of bibliographic entries
. . . allows flexible entry of reference information when and if it is available
. . . *but users may lose track of, and subsequently have trouble retrieving, incomplete entries*

In our design approach, designers work with these issues as the design evolves, attempting to maintain or enhance positive consequences while mitigating or eliminating negative consequences [8, 10]. As the bibliography design developed, we came back to the conference paper addition scenario, adding an enhancement in which a default unique nickname is offered, to ease the burden of generating nicknames. Of course, such an enhancement has implications of its own, in that it may encourage users to be satisfied and accept the default nickname even when it is not a good match to their personal conception of the item (see Table 10.3). Reasoning about tradeoffs such as these is exactly what a claims analysis is intended to stimulate and facilitate.

Another benefit of developing a claims analysis is that it can be used to elaborate and systematize the relatively informal scenario specification. A given scenario may express a usability consequence, but typically it will not reflect all possible consequences of a feature. Analyzing a feature-consequence relation in a scenario encourages the designer to engage in what-if scenario reasoning, envisioning slight variants of the scenario that may not have been expanded in a narrative but that help to complete the analysis of a feature's consequences. So, for example, in the conference paper scenario, the decision to use **copyEdit** as a nickname may come easily, but what about a future scenario when a second reference documenting this code reuse strategy is added to the bibliography? The full analysis of a feature's possible consequences must often extend beyond the user experience described in the source scenario, and working with a claim structure that assumes multiple positive and negative consequences for any feature encourages the designer to build a more comprehensive analysis of design decisions.

Finally, construction of a claims analysis can help designers keep track of connections *among* scenarios. For example, the same claim might be apparent in more than one scenario, and the designer might want to document this as evidence for the pervasiveness of the claim. Or, a given feature may seem likely to have one consequence in one scenario, and another consequence in a second: The designer might want to link the scenarios so that both are considered in future reasoning about that feature. It might also be that reasoning about a given scenario inspires the design of a feature that has consequences in another scenario, and the designer wants to keep track of the scenario serving as the source of the new feature. Earlier we pointed to some interactions between the item-entry and retrieval scenarios, and argued that it is important to consider some scenarios together when reasoning about a design. For example, the designer would want to minimize the nickname-generation burden as much as possible, but not so much as to interfere with subsequent nickname-based retrieval. A claims analysis can facilitate this conjoint reasoning, in that it allows the designer to record explicitly not only the causal relations in each scenario, but also the ways in which these causal relations interact across scenarios.

10.1.3 Issues for Scenario-Based Specification

We have argued that task scenarios—and their associated usability claims—provide a use-oriented representation for reasoning about design issues and tradeoffs. Clearly, however, these rich contextualized descriptions have costs associated with them. Organizing and maintaining a set of even purely textual scenarios and their usability claims can be a substantial document-management task. Scenarios and rationales may often involve a variety of media, such as storyboards, interactive graphics, and videos [3, 6, 12, 23, 25, 35]. Furthermore, it is typical to find rich dependencies among the various scenarios and their claim rationales, giving these representations a hypertextual character and adding a new level of complexity to the creation and maintenance of the specification documents.

Of course, the tasks of document development and maintenance are not unique to a scenario-based specification. Any requirements analysis will have some document management tasks associated with it. However, because our method hinges on providing enough usage context to reason effectively about concrete task situations, a scenario representation will very likely be more complex than an item-by-item function listing. Moreover, our approach encourages open-ended scenario development; we expect scenario representations to evolve, and perhaps change radically, as the scenarios are developed, elaborated, analyzed, prototyped, and tested with users. In practice, we find it useful to prune some of this design history, but it is important to maintain some background material. Clearly the need for tools to help manage scenario generation and evolution throughout the lifecycle is great.

A more disturbing implication of relying on task scenarios as a design specification is that we may in fact *increase* the gap between specification and implementation. Traditional functional specifications may not be user-centered, but they are easily understood by developers charged with building the specified system—the specification lays out in a well-ordered nonredundant format exactly the features that are expected in the system. In contrast, a use-oriented scenario embeds a system's individual features within an often complex narrative; the narratives are intended to illustrate how individual features affect a user's experience in the context of a specific task, and how the features interact within and across tasks. Prima facie, the job of extracting and implementing a set of features embedded within and distributed across a set of scenarios seems considerably more demanding than that of implementing a list of system functions.

10.2 THE SCENARIO BROWSER ENVIRONMENT

We have addressed the gap between specification and implementation characteristic of a scenario-based approach by recruiting scenarios as a mechanism for integrating the design of user tasks and the software supporting them. We have developed the Scenario Browser, a SmallTalk/V application development environment in which designers use the same scenarios developed to understand user tasks as an organizing framework for developing the corresponding implementation. The tool supports an iterative process in which the specification and elaboration of task scenarios is *interleaved* with the instantiation and evolution of SmallTalk objects that enact these scenarios. Thus the scenario set provides a shared context for reasoning about both specification and implementation.

Application development within the Scenario Browser environment is an iterative process of scenario elaboration and evolution (see Figure 10.1; see also [31]). The process begins by identifying a set of task scenarios. For our bibliography case study, these scenarios involved the addition of different types of references, browsing and retrieving these references, updating them, and formatting references contained in a document; these scenarios are named and described in the tool's Scenario View (see Figure 10.2). As the design work progresses, each scenario is elaborated to include more and more information about the user's concerns, interactions, and reactions in this situation. As the scenarios are elaborated, designers can analyze the expected consequences of particular system features in particular situations, documenting these usability claims in a scenario's Claims View.

As soon as one or more task scenarios have been specified, the designer can begin to develop implementations for the scenarios: Using the tool's Implementation View, each scenario can be modeled as a set of communicating SmallTalk objects (see Figure 10.3). These SmallTalk objects will evolve as the scenarios evolve, with attributes being added or removed, new objects incorporated, existing objects replaced or further decomposed. As the SmallTalk objects (and the SmallTalk abstractions or classes on which they are based) are developed, the designer

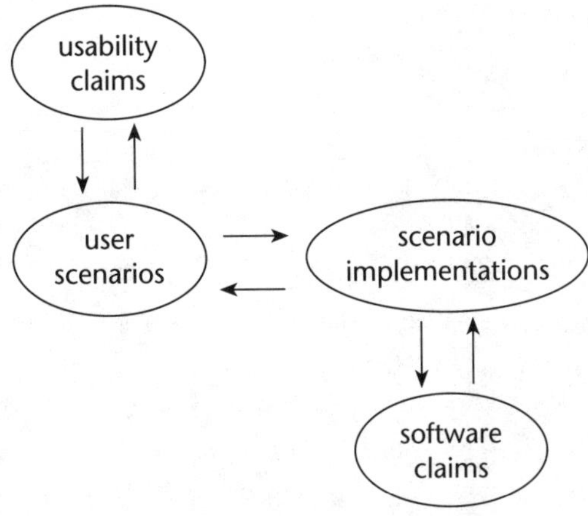

Figure 10.1. Iterative development with the Scenario Browser. Task design and the development of usability rationale take place in parallel with the design of the software and its rationale, enabling continual interaction between task and software design issues.

can note features of the implementation that have implications for the quality of the software design in the context of particular scenarios, documenting them in the scenario's Software Claims View. Throughout, elaboration and modification of the scenario implementations (and the associated rationale) is interleaved with further development of the task scenarios themselves.

In our bibliography case study, we were able to streamline the scenario generation and elaboration process because we had expertise both in the creation and use of bibliographic material and in object-oriented software design. This would not normally be the case, of course, and we assume that users and designers would collaborate in identifying and elaborating task scenarios (see, e.g., [22, 25]). In our case the utility was designed to be used by ourselves and our colleagues. Thus the second author—as a highly experienced writer of technical material—served as the *key user* and the source of domain knowledge; the first author collaborated with him to extract and elaborate the bibliography scenarios, and to develop the corresponding SmallTalk implementation. From the perspective of our design approach, the key aspects of our

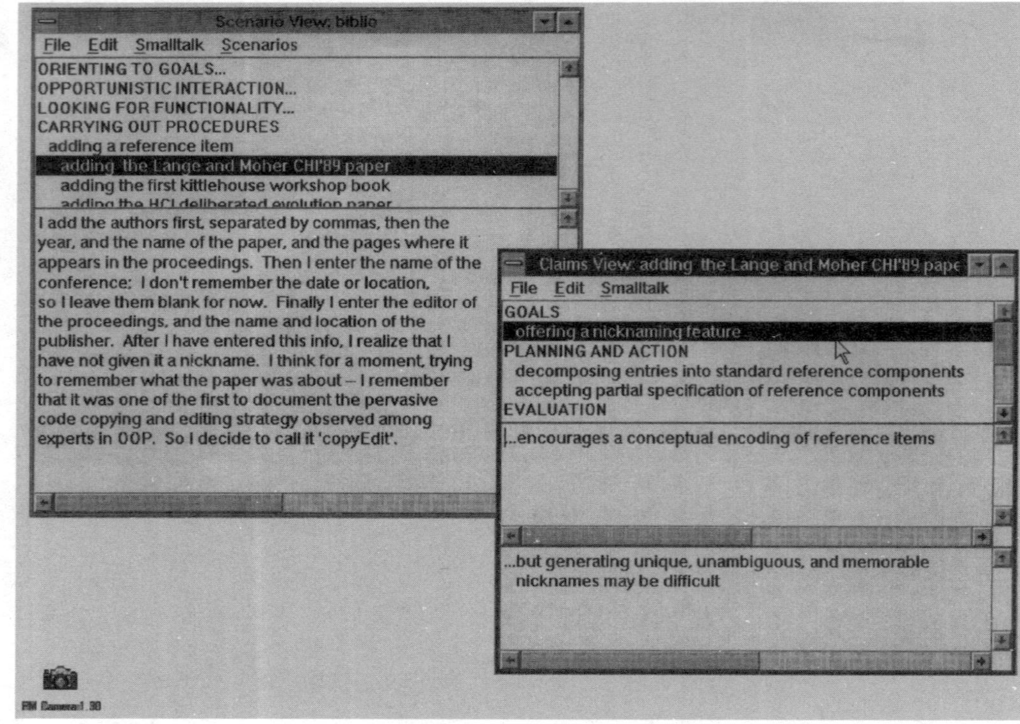

Figure 10.2. Task specification in the Scenario Browser environment: The Scenario View (on the left) allows designers to specify textual versions of core tasks within the TAF user concerns typology; the Claims View serves as a hypertext editor for documenting and linking usability claims associated with the scenario specifications.

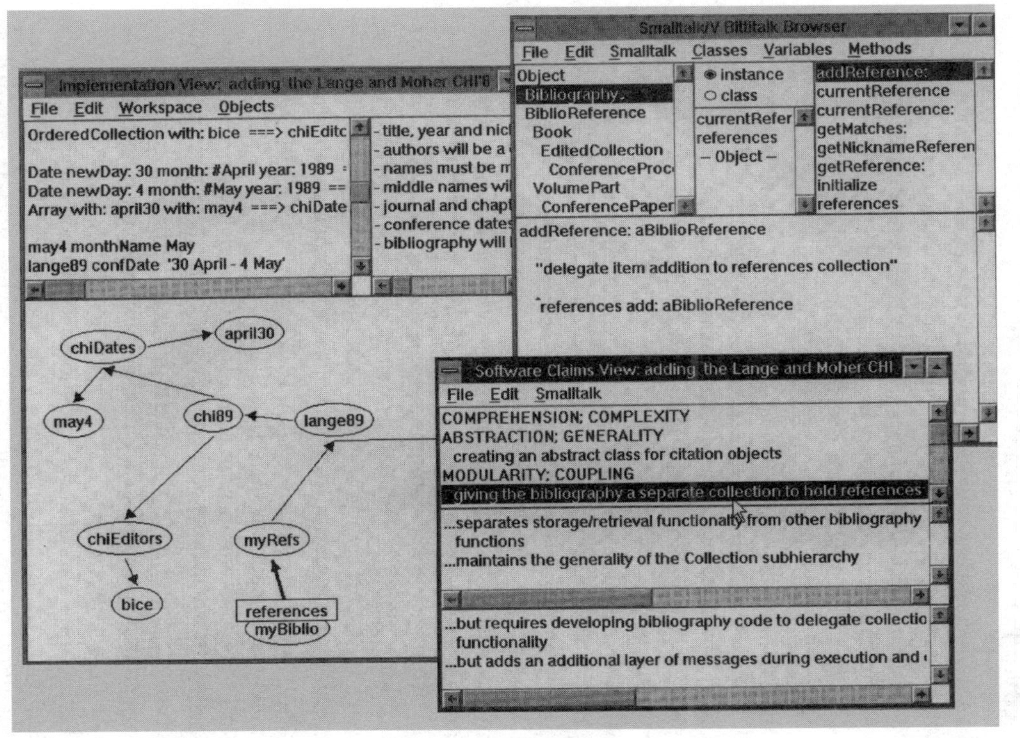

Figure 10.3. Implementing scenarios in the Scenario Browser environment: The Implementation View (on the left) supports the creation and evolution of the SmallTalk instances currently used in the implementation of a scenario; the Bittitalk Browser (upper right) provides scenario-specific access to the SmallTalk class hierarchy; the Software Claims View serves as a hypertext editor for documenting and linking claims associated with the current software design.

scenario discussions were that we always focused on concrete usage situations, and that the process was iterative and proceeded in parallel with development of the SmallTalk code implementing the scenarios.

10.2.1 Specifying the Bibliography Tasks

The bibliography scenarios were developed within the Scenario View (on the left in Figure 10.2). A designer can add a scenario to the list, and use the text editor in the bottom of the window to write and edit its narrative description. The Scenario View includes the typology of usage situations described earlier, as an aid in thinking about possible scenarios as well as to provide a simple organizing framework (each scenario is generated as an example of one of the six generic situations, see Table 10.2). Thus the scenario of adding a conference paper fits into the category "Carrying out Procedures," while browsing the bibliography and discovering a set of references dealing with object-oriented design exemplifies the general "Opportunistic Interaction" situation.

Our design approach concentrates on developing a coherent set of basic tasks first and only then developing an effective user interface to these tasks. One consequence is that most of the early scenario work is directed at the category "Carrying out Procedures," as this situation includes the basic tasks a user can perform with a system. The other situations arise once the system has been elaborated enough to evoke or facilitate particular goals or problem-solving strategies in the user. For example, "Making Sense" scenarios normally describe situations in which the user is trying to understand some unexpected or otherwise attention-grabbing response on the part of the system; envisioning such situations requires that a fairly detailed progression of user actions and system responses has been specified.

Designers may also wish to develop intermediate levels of abstraction to organize their scenarios. For example, there might be many scenario variants involving the creation or modification of references. The designer can express the hierarchical relationship among such variants by creating a generic task in the Scenario View (e.g., "adding a reference item") and then developing specific versions of the task as concrete scenarios. In the bibliography application, we generally used these intermediate scenario abstractions only as headings to organize a set of related scenarios. However, in a few cases, we wrote an *abstract* narrative (e.g., the generic components of adding any type of reference item). The benefit was that we were able to be explicit about those aspects of the generic task that were shared among different specific situations. The cost was that the abstract narrative now became an additional textual description that needed to be maintained as the concrete task specifications evolved.

10.2.2 Rationale for the Bibliography Scenarios

Figure 10.2 depicts work in progress on the conference paper addition scenario. In elaborating this scenario, a designer might choose to work solely with the narrative description, holistically considering the user's goals and expectations, how the system is or is not meeting these expectations, and what the user feels as the task is carried out. However, particularly for critical or complex scenarios, the designer might also wish to consider more analytically the otherwise implicit causal relations articulated in a claims rationale.

On the right in Figure 10.2 is a Claims View of the conference paper scenario. It is used to record and browse the current set of usability claims analyzed for the scenario. The figure displays the nicknaming claim analyzed for the conference paper scenario. The narrative describes a user's efforts to come up with an appropriate nickname, and the claim documents both the positive (middle pane) and negative (bottom pane) consequences of the nicknaming feature. Simply providing for nicknames suggests the strategy of encoding reference items conceptually via an evocative label; however, it also adds a new burden to the user's task, that of generating appropriately evocative, memorable, and unambiguous reference labels.

The Claims View provides a simple heuristic for designers to use in analyzing a scenario's usability claims. It offers three aspects of a user's experience in a task—goals, actions, and evaluation, based on Norman's stage theory of human action [28]—as analytic perspectives to apply in considering a particular scenario. Thus we assume that every scenario has some task goal associated with it (the user either has a goal already or is receptive to having one suggested through interactions with the environment), that it involves some sequence of actions, and that at some point(s) the user will try to evaluate what has happened. Offering a nicknaming feature suggests to users that they can (and perhaps should) encode their reference items conceptually; in this sense the feature is evoking a goal for the user. We have found it useful to consider the experience depicted in a scenario from each of these three perspectives in constructing claims that explain what happened in the scenario.

Using the Claims View, the designer can document design features that may impact the usability of a system; opening this view for a given scenario provides a sort of usability perspective onto that particular task situation. The designer can also browse usability claims collected across all scenarios for a more complete usability analysis; if desired, the scenarios and associated claims can be exported as simple text files to be saved as part of a design project's history, shared with colleagues, or incorporated into other design documents.

Scenarios often share dependencies that can be explicitly documented through claims, and designers use the Claims View to record such relationships. Earlier we described a dependency between reference creation and retrieval mediated by the nicknaming feature. Specifically, we recorded the following claim for the creation scenario:

```
offering a nicknaming feature
. . . encourages a conceptual encoding of reference items
. . . but generating unique, unambiguous, and memorable
      nicknames may be difficult
```

Reasoning from this claim, we elected to provide a default nickname, built from the last name of the first author and the year (e.g., lange89). Later on, when working on a reference-retrieval scenario, we analyzed a related claim:

```
providing an author-year default nickname
. . . suggests a simple scheme for looking up items
. . . but users may not remember author-year for all
      items
. . . but users may not remember whether or not they
      accepted the default scheme or generated their own
      encoding
```

Using the "usability links" option in the Claims View, we created a link between the two nicknaming claims; this menu option produces a list of all other usability claims (indexed by the name of the system feature involved), and selection of any one of these claims establishes a two-way link. In the future, when we were considering changes to the nicknaming feature in the context of either scenario, we could browse the related claim, using the "browse usability links" menu option.

10.2.3 Implementing the Bibliography Scenarios

Once we had specified a bibliography scenario—to any level of detail—we were able to begin work on its implementation, by opening an Implementation View on the currently selected scenario (on the left in Figure 10.3). This view has several components. The workspace in the upper-left can be used to create and send messages to SmallTalk objects. These

SmallTalk objects are *live*; they exemplify the SmallTalk objects that would be created and exercised in the course of using the bibliography application. As in our prior work on the Portia environment for SmallTalk [16], all design work in the Scenario Browser environment is instance-centered: The designer develops new abstractions (classes) and their behaviors (methods) by creating and experimenting with instances of existing classes:[1] The objects used in the scenario's implementation, as well as their connections to one another (an object's state in SmallTalk consists simply of pointers to other objects), are displayed and manipulated graphically in the lower pane. In the upper-right is a text editor used to keep notes on the current implementation plan.

Figure 10.3 displays the Implementation View of the conference paper scenario at an intermediate phase in its development. The conference paper has been modeled as a SmallTalk object; this has involved the design and instantiation of a number of new classes (e.g., to represent the conference paper, author names, dates, etc.). The designer is now working on the addition transaction itself: A bibliography object has been created and given a references collection, and the conference paper is being added to this collection.

Earlier we discussed our *task-first* approach to design, wherein we begin by developing a coherent set of tasks and then subsequently develop a user interface to these tasks. This design approach is very compatible with the *model-first* approach to object-oriented software design [17]. There the goal is to develop a problem domain model, identifying the important problem constructs that should be modeled as software objects, and working out their interrelationships and lines of communication. The work depicted in Figure 10.3 was directed toward building such a problem domain model. Once the problem had been modeled in this way, another layer of design added user interface objects providing access to the underlying problem constructs. The model-first strategy simplifies the initial design exploration (by ignoring details of user interaction). It also tends to increase the software separation between basic application functionality and the user interface, which has a number of desirable benefits from a software engineering perspective [34].

The fact that the objects created in the Implementation View are live SmallTalk instances distinguishes our work from others who advo-

[1]All objects in SmallTalk are instances of classes; a running application consists of instances connected to one another and passing messages among each other. To create an instance a programmer must either instantiate an existing class or create and instantiate a new class. Thus, an important distinction in SmallTalk is between instantiated objects and the classes used to instantiate them.

cate problem domain modeling in object-oriented design (see, e.g., [20, 37]). It reflects an approach to application development in which analysis, design, and implementation are routinely interleaved rather than separable activities in development. We believe that many designers prefer to analyze abstract ideas in a concrete testable fashion [30]. In the Scenario Browser designers carry out their problem analysis by building and testing concrete situations; at the same time they are able to transform these situations as their model of the software becomes more articulated.

The workspace in the upper-left of the Implementation View is used primarily for creating and sending messages to objects. The messages developed for the scenario are implemented as methods in the relevant classes. Designers can implement such messages (e.g., **addReference:**) in a "Bittitalk" browser (in the upper-right of Figure 10.3); this browser is identical to the standard SmallTalk class browser tool, except that it displays only the classes used in the scenario's current implementation [32]. In the figure, the designer has written the piece of code in which the bibliography object delegates the addition of a reference to a collection object containing the reference items.

Note that although designers implement individual scenarios in the Scenario Browser, much of an application's implementation will be shared across two or more scenarios. A good example is the bibliography object (**myBiblio** in the object graph), which was part of every scenario we developed. Designers can exploit the shared needs of different scenarios by using the same SmallTalk instance in more than one scenario—while working on a scenario, the menu choice "Other objects" brings up a submenu listing objects instantiated in other scenarios, and the designer can select an existing object, using it unchanged in the new scenario, or elaborating or modifying its state and behavior as needed. Thus the final design and implementation of a single design abstraction is often accomplished through work with the same instance in a number of different scenarios.

We have already noted that usability claims can be used to capture a more expansive view of a design than that embodied in the scenario narratives. The claims call out specific causal relationships, can link scenarios including similar or complementary relationships, and can refer implicitly to situations not even included within the scenario set. The implementations of the task scenarios have a similar character: When we implemented a bibliography scenario, we almost always developed objects that were more general than the specific situation required—we considered and allowed for variations in object attributes (e.g., names, dates), as well as trying to anticipate and manage exceptions (e.g., missing information, information of the wrong type). This seemed to be a natural consequence of working at the code level, which can be seen as a more symbolic and abstract representation of the scenario. The notepad in the upper-right of the Implementation View served a useful function in this process, providing a convenient spot to record concerns and plans for generalizing from the specific situation reflected in the scenario. However, nothing in the Scenario Browser environment demands this sort of generalization process in the course of developing a given scenario's implementation.

10.2.4 Rationale for the Bibliography Implementation

In developing the Scenario Browser, we extended the task-artifact framework to incorporate software quality claims, specifically relationships between features of a scenario's implementation and consequences for developers (i.e., programmers elaborating or maintaining the application). An example software feature is "modeling the reference collection as a separate component of the bibliography object" (i.e., rather than making the bibliography a kind of collection and inheriting that functionality directly). This modeling decision has a variety of consequences for the developers and maintainers of the classes comprising the bibliography utility. It brings the important benefit of increasing the modularity of the design, separating out the storage and retrieval of reference items from other functionality that a bibliography might have (e.g., assuring reference consistency); it also maintains the generic nature of the SmallTalk Collection subhierarchy. However, it does so at the cost of increasing the number of objects in the design, requiring the designer to develop and maintain code that delegates reference storage and retrieval to the appropriate collection object, and adding another layer of message-passing protocol.

Software claims are like usability claims in that they document design issues, but they do so from the perspective of the software design. Also like usability claims, the software claims are analyzed under the scope of a particular scenario; just as a task scenario provides a concrete context for understanding the implications a design has for its users, so does a scenario implementation offer a concrete context for understanding the implications of the software design for the developers and maintainers of the code. In this our approach contrasts to that of Carey and his colleagues [4, 5] who have been also been exploring the use of scenarios in recording usability design rationale but have focused on the class abstraction as the unit for recording software rationale.

In Figure 10.3, a Software Claims View has been opened on the implementation of the Lange and Moher reference-entry scenario. Like the Claims View, it is seeded with several dimensions to use as a heuristic in reflecting on software design decisions. The dimensions represent some of the software engineering criteria typically used in evaluating object-oriented software (e.g., [24]). The designer has just added the claim documenting the pros and cons of using a separate collection object to hold the bibliography reference items. As in the Claims View, the participating design feature is entered under an appropriate dimension in the upper pane, its positive consequences in the middle pane, and its negative consequences in the bottom pane.

Note that the usability and software claims associated with a given scenario are linked implicitly, in that they are all connected to the same scenario. However, explicit links among software claims from different scenarios can also be created, just as described earlier for usability claims. So, for example, while working on a conference paper editing scenario, we decided that conference papers should be modeled as one reference item (the paper itself) pointing to another item (its associated conference proceedings). We recorded the pros and cons of this decision in our software claims analysis: Modeling the Lange and Moher paper as a conference paper that points to a CHI'89 conference proceedings object allows a clean separation between the behavior specific to a single paper (e.g., management of its title, authors) and that shared among all papers in the volume (e.g., dealing with conference location and date); from the perspective of database design, it allows for shared persistent data, but does so only by making the accuracy of individual entries dependent on the integrity of the shared entry. Later, an analogous decision was made to model a journal paper in the same fashion, with the paper object pointing to a journal issue object. Because the second decision was inspired by analogy to the first case, we created a link between the two claims to record the relationship. Once such a link is established, a designer considering one claim can quickly check to see what other claims might be relevant, and if desired can open a Claims View on one or more related claims so as to more fully analyze or elaborate them.

Designers can also create links between software claims and related usability claims. These relations may be recognized when working on a scenario whose usability issues seem to have implications for the software design or vice versa. So, for example, our software decision to model a conference paper as one reference item pointing to another caused us to consider a task enhancement for the editing scenario. Given the new software model, users would now be able to enter or modify conference proceedings data for all papers in the proceedings simply by editing the reference for one paper. This task view departed considerably from our initial task analysis of reference creation and editing, which was based on experience with flat textual reference strings. It would empower users of the bibliography utility, which is certainly a desirable result. However, it also had its own downsides, in that users might not anticipate this situation, or might be unhappy if typos in one editing episode produced side-effects for existing reference items. This usability claim associated with the enhanced editing scenario was recorded and linked to the software claim that inspired it, making this specific software-task interaction a part of the system's overall design rationale.

10.2.5 Evolving the Bibliography Scenarios

The Scenario Browser environment is intended to support iterative design and redesign of scenarios and their implementations. In the simplest case, the scenarios will develop through accretion—successively more of the problem requirements are discovered, specified, and implemented. For the user scenarios, this will involve adding textual description (and associated claims); for the implementations, new objects and behaviors will be added. As long as the designer has anticipated what objects will be needed, new objects can be implemented and integrated seamlessly into the developing scenario.

However, designers will not always anticipate all of the elements needed in a scenario's implementation, and adding a new object may require changing the underlying structure of an existing object. So, for example, our initial implementation of the conference paper scenario did not model the date and location of the conference itself. At a later point, we realized that some reference formats include this information, and needed to elaborate the conference paper object accordingly. In the standard SmallTalk environment, we would have been forced to destroy the original object, add the new structural information (to the class definition), and then rebuild the object. The Scenario Browser environment includes facilities for adding to (or removing) an existing object's attributes, allowing the designer to add elements to a scenario without disrupting the existing implementation context.

The Scenario Browser also supports cases in which the design develops not merely through accretion but instead needs to be more radically reconceptualized. Designers can *mutate* objects to new implementations without reinitializing the object's state. For example, in the conference paper reference-entry scenario, we implemented the conference paper as a relatively simple object consisting largely of strings and collections of strings (e.g., title, authors, proceedings name, and editors). Later, in the conference paper editing scenario, we reconceptualized the conference paper as described above—a reference item containing information specific to the paper (e.g., title, authors), but also pointing to another type of reference item, a conference proceedings. Using the Scenario Browser facilities, we divided the original conference paper object into two objects—the new conference paper reference and an associated conference proceedings reference.[2]

A key issue in supporting implementation malleability of this sort is the continuing consistency and correctness of the underlying abstractions. Changing the implementation of an object in one scenario may cause another scenario using that object to break. Because the Scenario Browser makes it easy for designers to share objects among scenarios when appropriate, some degree of consistency can be provided automatically: Changing the conference paper implementation in the editing scenario changed it for all other scenarios using that object. Unfortunately, there is no guarantee that these other scenarios will still work as originally implemented. At this point in the development of the Scenario Browser environment, this correctness determination is left to the designer; we merely facilitate it by identifying, and providing browsers onto, all other scenarios making use of a given object. Our working assumption is that designers will know when they have changed an object enough that dependent scenarios should be browsed and retested.

The Scenario Browser also provides a cumulative view of the implementations developed for individual scenarios. Thus, a designer can examine a graph of all the objects in all the scenarios, analyzing it for redundancies or for missed opportunities to make abstractions. Our bibliography application was developed by one designer in a short amount of time, but an application developed by a group of designers over a more extended time period is more likely to develop inconsistencies and redundancies (e.g., two slightly different conference papers objects, one using the built-in Date class, the second representing dates as simple strings). By analyzing the objects in a cumulative graph and the roles that they are playing, a designer can discover objects whose functionality is identical or overlapping, and carry out appropriate

---

[2]The mutation process exploits the SmallTalk "become" operation in which one instance can be substituted for another. We extend this by "unpacking" the original object, holding its current state while the designer indicates the mapping of the old attributes onto those of the new object. As this operation demonstrates, the instance-centered development and evolution supported by the Scenario Browser depends critically on the dynamic features of the SmallTalk language.

modifications (e.g., breaking up one object into two or more others, replacing one object with another, combining one or more objects into a single new object).

The claims associated with particular scenarios or implementations can also be aggregated and examined in concert to better understand the tradeoffs they document at the level of the overall design. A software feature developed in the context of a given scenario, with relevant pros and cons noted, might very well impact other scenarios. A cumulative view can help designers discover and manage these scenario relationships. (Again, this seems most important for large applications developed by multiple designers.) For instance, the decision to hold the bibliography references in a separate collection object was made in the context of a reference creation scenario. But it clearly has implications for any of the scenarios involving manipulation of the reference items, because now this manipulation must be done indirectly through the bibliography object. A designer working later on a reference manipulation scenario can now be primed to consider and address as much as possible the indirection downside of this software modeling decision (perhaps even to the extent of reversing it).

10.3 PROSPECTS FOR SCENARIO-BASED APPLICATION DEVELOPMENT

We have described an approach to application development in which users' tasks and the software that implements them are designed conjointly in an integrated software environment. Scenarios provide a concrete context in which to consider the pros and cons of both task and software features under consideration in the design. The analysis of usability and software claims documents these design tradeoffs as well as their interactions with one another. At the end of the process, the designer has a set of runnable scenarios (plus any variants of these scenarios that figured into design reasoning), as well as the design notes, object graphs, and claim rationale associated with these scenarios.

In our approach designers begin implementing scenarios early in the design process, almost immediately developing an executable prototype of the task scenarios. Of course, a designer might choose to first explore other forms of prototypes—for example, the storyboards, sketches, or other low-tech envisionments described by others in this volume. However, if work on software design is postponed, so are the interactions (both positive and negative) between the task and software models. One of the key proposals of the Scenario Browser work is that these interactions are an important source of design ideas and constraints and thus should be recognized, analyzed, and managed from the start.

A system organized around task scenarios and their implementations might serve a variety of purposes, from system and usability testing to the development of training and documentation materials. In the following sections, we consider the implications of our approach for the design reasoning process and for the integration of usability and software design concerns.

10.3.1 Reasoning from Scenarios

At the center of our design approach is the belief that concrete task scenarios provide an appropriate context for reasoning about design. To some extent, this belief is founded on the general observation that humans excel at reasoning about concrete situations. More specifically though, scenarios offer task designers a rich view of the goals, actions, and experiences of users interacting with the system. As such, they focus design efforts at the right level, on the tasks the system is intended to support. By developing a detailed account of a user's experience in a task, designers become attuned to how the knowledge and goals the user brings to the situation interact with the services offered or implied by the system.

From the perspective of software design, concrete problem episodes facilitate the identification of important problem entities that should be modeled in the solution, as well as the analysis of how these entities cooperate to carry out a task. Of course, there are risks associated with reasoning from specific situations. One can become so engaged by the details of a particular case that attention to the overall coherence of the design is diminished; spurious factors from one case can provoke design decisions felt throughout the design. In developing object-oriented software, one might develop excellent models of individual scenarios, but never recognize or exploit abstractions that emerge across scenarios. We have addressed such concerns to some extent by providing facilities for reflecting on the emerging design (i.e., in the form of claims analysis), and by offering cross-scenario views of the design as it develops. However, the general issue of how best to minimize the risks of using specific situations to reason about design abstractions remains an open research question.

An important boundary condition for scenario-based design reasoning is the quality of the scenario set, and during the course of developing the bibliography we applied various heuristics to develop a good scenario set. One of these was a conscious effort to reuse

SmallTalk objects from one scenario implementation to another. This forced attention to the generality of the design being developed—for example ensuring that the conference paper modeled in the reference creation scenario had the right task and software characteristics to support its subsequent retrieval and formatting. Another heuristic was to consider complex cases early in the design—we deliberately focused first on conference papers because they have a more complex structure than most other references and served as a relatively complete source of requirements for thinking about and manipulating reference entities.

One interesting consequence of working from concrete situations was that it created a natural order among some of the scenarios. For example, all scenarios were dependent on the existence of at least one reference entity, making implementation of a reference-entry scenario a first priority. Furthermore, some of the retrieval scenarios (e.g., opportunistic browsing) depended on the existence of a fairly substantial database of entries, which caused them to be delayed until the database had been filled in with a variety of different references. We did not observe any difficulties stemming from these ordering constraints, but again this seems an open research question.

In the Scenario Browser, software is developed through a process of instantiating and evolving the SmallTalk objects needed by a scenario. This instance-centered style of development had repercussions—both good and bad—on code development. The environment supports the direct manipulation of SmallTalk objects (e.g., connecting two objects in the object graph), and we often found ourselves manipulating objects this way rather than by moving to the browser and writing a piece of code to carry out the manipulation programmatically. Of course, this is exactly what the environment is intended to encourage, with the objective of facilitating rapid experimentation with design ideas. However, it sometimes caused problems when we carried out a manipulation by hand, never wrote the code to do it more generally, and later wondered why the scenario no longer seemed to work.

Another issue that arose in this scenario-based design process was the management of scenario overlap. So, for example, we worked on several reference-entry scenarios (one for every different type of reference), several different retrieval scenarios, and so on. And while each of these scenarios highlighted different aspects of the bibliography tasks, there was still considerable overlap in the functionality they required. In the bibliography implementation, this overlap was reflected through inheritance relationships (e.g., there was an abstract "ReferenceItem" class capturing attributes common to all types of references), or through the direct reuse of individual objects in different scenarios. However, it was less apparent how to manage the overlap in the scenario narratives. We experimented with abstract narratives that captured the shared aspects of overlapping scenarios, but these didn't seem to work very well—when working on an individual scenario, one wants to have the entire narrative available, and not to supplement the unique parts of a specific scenario with common parts abstracted into a separate general description stored elsewhere. It might be possible to develop more elaborate sharing mechanisms (e.g., where the text from the abstract scenario would be automatically *inherited* by its concrete scenarios) that would help to manage overlap among the scenario specifications.

10.3.2 Integrating Usage and Implementation

Our work on the Scenario Browser embodies a new perspective on the gap between task specification and implementation. Rather than rely only on the empirical feedback available through a rapid prototyping process, we propose that tasks and implementation be developed jointly, within an analytic framework that supports recognition and management of their interdependencies. Specifically, we have created a design tool that might integrate use-oriented reasoning with software-oriented reasoning, using scenarios as the unit or context of analysis and design. In this we are integrating two previously independent areas of research and development work: scenario-based design of human-computer interaction, and scenario-based analysis and design in object-oriented software technology.

User tasks and the software designed to support them are interdependent. Tasks set requirements for new systems; as systems are developed, their software and hardware characteristics create constraints or opportunities for the tasks [7]. Many development projects manage this mutual interdependency through tight feedback loops between task specification and implementation, codifying specifications in prototypes early and repeatedly to try out on users [26]. The approach of the Scenario Browser is consistent with rapid prototyping in that it encourages early and continued testing of a design specification. However, it differs from most prototyping approaches in that it interleaves specification and prototyping activities. It also complements the purely empirical feedback of prototyping with the creation of design rationale for user tasks and their implementations.

In the Scenario Browser environment, a designer develops software in the context of specific task needs. So, for example, when we implemented the conference paper reference-entry scenario, we were working directly from an explicit description of a user performing and experiencing this task—thinking about a reference as composed of certain parts (authors, title, etc.), and about the entry task as specifying these parts. This motivated and rationalized the software design implication that these reference components should be easily identifiable and manipulable within the reference item model. This is a common sort of dependency between user tasks and the software supporting them, where some aspect of the user's task structure must be respected or reified in the software model. We believe that a designer's ability to recognize and respond to such dependencies will be facilitated by a concrete scenario context.

The design method embodied in the Scenario Browser environment can be seen as an extension of an emerging family of scenario-based object-oriented design methods [33, 36, 37]. These methods argue that analysis of task scenarios is a useful technique for developing a problem domain model, a fundamental task in object-oriented design. Our work is consistent with these software design methods in that we also have argued that scenarios are the right starting point for constructing a model of cooperating problem objects [31]. But we extend these software-oriented approaches by integrating them with our work on designing user scenarios [9, 11]. Our argument is that the same scenarios that designers use for envisioning and elaborating user tasks can be used for understanding and testing an object-oriented software model (note that there is nothing about a scenario-based specification that demands the development of an object-oriented implementation, although our work on the Scenario Browser certainly exploits the usefulness of scenarios in reasoning about software objects). Furthermore, by closely integrating task scenarios and their implementation, designers will be better able to manage the tradeoffs that will inevitably arise between tasks and the systems that support them.

Most development projects will uncover tradeoffs between usability and implementation concerns, and these tradeoffs represent another important set of task and software dependencies. An example from the bibliography project revolved around the reference-formatting scenarios. The initial scenario described an author citing references in a familiar style, with the added ability to use nicknames. When the implementation began, however, a number of issues arose dealing with how the document was to be parsed (e.g., recognizing a variety of citation forms, distinguishing between citations and other parenthesized material, recognizing and responding appropriately to prior mentions of a reference). These issues were then considered, but in the context of the affected scenarios, so that consequences for usability and for implementation could be considered jointly. The usability and software claims developed at this point documented these concerns, marking the issue as one to be carefully tracked.

Most developers are familiar with the constraints user requirements place on software and vice versa. A less familiar—but perhaps even more important—form of interaction between tasks and software occurs when reasoning about a software model suggests new *opportunities* for user tasks. Users conceptualize their tasks in certain ways and their task requirements will typically reflect this conceptualization. But computerizing a task can significantly change the way it is carried out, enabling or suggesting activities that had been difficult or even impossible to achieve [7, 22].

Decomposing a problem into objects and their responsibilities can change a designer's view of a task; a problem entity that is conceptualized as an *active* agent may be given responsibilities normally carried out by humans or other agents [29]. Thus an object-oriented analysis of a bibliography might suggest that the various reference types should be responsible for their own formatting rules: A conference paper should know how to format itself in IEEE style, in ACM style, and so on. This is in contrast to the noncomputerized version of the task, where formatting rules are stored in the author's head, or in a reference manual of some sort. It is not clear how this new view of the bibliography task will affect a user's experiences, but to the extent that its potential is recognized and explored early in the design process, it is much more likely to be exploited as the design evolves.

In the bibliography project, one case in which the software design did extend the task design came in our decision to model conference papers, book chapters, and journal articles as volume parts connected to their relevant volumes (i.e., the conference proceedings, edited book, or journal issue). Initially we had not modeled the volumes themselves as separate objects—because authors do not normally cite a proceedings or journal issue, these objects did not appear in our task analysis. But as we developed a software model for the conference paper scenarios, we recognized that an individual conference paper should not be responsible for information about its containing volume. This pointed to the need for separate volume objects, which in turn suggested enhancements to the user's tasks (i.e., creating and modifying a volume reference by working on any of the papers it contains). The new task possibility was immediately explored within the context of the affected scenarios. The conclusion was that while the user's problem model would now be more complex (journal articles, book chapters, and conference papers now become *compound* references), the additional power provided by the new model warranted the change. Again, usability and software claims were developed to document our analysis of the tradeoffs; a link between the claims regarding usability and software quality captured the specific interaction of task and software design in this situation.

Our examples have focused on how the Scenario Browser encourages integrative reasoning about task and software design. But implicit in our discussion is another aspect of integration facilitated by this design environment—designer-user communication. This has long been recognized as a problem in development, in that designers tend to think and talk about their design objects, while users think and talk about their tasks [19]. A number of researchers have argued that building object-oriented design models should ease this communication, in that the main elements of the software model will be objects from the problem domain [2, 29]. Applications developed within the Scenario Browser are natural candidates for investigating the contributions of object-oriented designs to designer-user communication: Not only will these designs refer to objects from the user's problem domain, but they will also associate these software objects with concrete task scenarios. Thus if the designer wants to demonstrate a piece of functionality or discuss alternatives with the user (e.g., as in the citation formatting or the compound reference issues), the specific scenarios can serve as a shared context for analysis.

We believe strongly that the usefulness and usability of applications and user interfaces is inherently linked to the underlying problem domain model embodied in the software [13, 29]. It may be possible to paper over slight mismatches between the user's view of a task and the task model inhering in the software (i.e., through a well-engineered user interface), but if system use is to evolve and grow as a user's requirements and skills evolve, it must contain task-relevant abstractions. The most fundamental stage in object-oriented analysis is the enumeration of the problem domain objects, their individual responsibilities, and their collaborations [36, 37]. Our design approach proposes that this enumeration can also play a key role in supporting and extending user tasks.

Our work on the Scenario Browser explores the proposition that scenarios of the *same sort* we have been collecting and constructing to guide envisionment of the external system, the system as directly experienced by the user, can be recruited as an aid in object-oriented analysis, design, and implementation. We have focused on supporting design situations in which the domain model is evolving, situations in which the designer is trying (or at least willing) to get beyond merely producing an accurate model of an extant situation. We want to help designers to evolve a first-pass analysis of the right set of user scenarios, and the right set of objects and behaviors. We want to support a fluid exchange of reasoning between the task level and the implementation level, such that user tasks can inspire software models and software models can extend user tasks.

ACKNOWLEDGMENTS

We would like to thank Morten Kyng and an anonymous reviewer for their valuable comments on an earlier version of this chapter; the workshop participants also contributed a number of useful ideas and perspectives on our work with the Scenario Browser.

REFERENCES

[1] Brooks, F. P. (1975). *The Mythical Man-Month.* Reading, MA: Addison-Wesley.

[2] Bruegge, B., Blythe, J., Jackson, J. & Shufelt, J. (1992). Object-oriented system modeling with OMT. In *Proceedings of OOPLSA '92: Object-Oriented Programming, Systems, and Applications.* New York: ACM Press, pp. 359–376.

[3] Carey, T. & Rusli, M. (1995). Usage representations for reuse of design insights: A case study of access to on-line books. *Chapter 7 in this volume.*

[4] Carey, T. T., McKerlie, D., Bubie, W. & Wilson, J. (1991). Communicating human factors expertise through usability design rationales. In D. Diaper & N. Hammond (eds.), *Computers and People.* Cambridge, MA: Cambridge University Press, pp. 117–130.

[5] Carey, T. T. & Spall, R. (1993). Supporting design rationales in user interface toolkits. In H. R. Hartson & D. Hix (eds.), *Advances in Human-Computer Interaction.* Norwood, NJ: Ablex, pp. 87–109.

[6] Carroll, J. M., Alpert, S. R., Karat, J., Deusen, M. V. & Rosson, M. B. (1994). Raison d'être: Capturing design history and rationale in multimedia narratives. In B. Adelson, S. Dumais & J. Olson (eds.), *Proceedings of CHI'94: Human Factors in Computing Systems.* New York: ACM Press, pp. 192–197.

[7] Carroll, J. M. & Campbell, R. L. (1989). Artifacts as psychological theory: The case of human-computer interaction. *Behavior and Information Technology, 8,* 247–256.

[8] Carroll, J. M. Kellogg, W. A. & Rosson, M. B. (1991). The task-artifact cycle. In J. M. Carroll (ed.), *Designing Interaction: Psychology at the Human-Computer Interface.* New York: Cambridge University Press, pp. 74–102.

[9] Carroll, J. M. & Rosson, M. B. (1990). Human-computer interaction scenarios as a design representation. In *Proceedings of HICSS-23: Hawaii Inter-*

national Conference on System Sciences. Los Alamitos, CA: IEEE Computer Society Press, pp. 555–561.

[10] Carroll, J. M. & Rosson, M. B. (1991). Deliberated evolution: Stalking the View Matcher in design space. *Human-Computer Interaction, 6,* 281–318.

[11] Carroll, J. M. & Rosson, M. B. (1992). Getting around the task-artifact cycle: How to make claims and design by scenario. *ACM Transactions on Information Systems, 10,* 181–212.

[12] Conklin, J. & Begeman, M. L. (1988). gIBIS: A hypertext tool for exploratory policy discussion. *ACM Transactions on Office Information Systems, 6,* 303–331.

[13] Fischer, G. (1992). Domain-oriented design environments. In *Proceedings of KBSE'92: The 7th Annual Knowledge-Based Software Engineering Conference.* Los Alamitos, CA: IEEE Computer Society Press, pp. 204–213.

[14] Gibson, E. (1990). Objects—Born and bred. *Byte,* 245–254.

[15] Gilb, T. (1988). *Principles of Software Engineering Management.* Reading, MA: Addison-Wesley.

[16] Gold, E. & Rosson, M. B. (1991). Portia: An instance-centered environment for SmallTalk. In *Proceedings of OOPSLA'91: Object-Oriented Programming Systems, Languages, and Applications.* New York: ACM Press, pp. 62–74.

[17] Goldberg, A. (1990). Information models, views, and controllers. *Dr. Dobb's Journal, 166,* 54–61.

[18] Göransson, B., Lind, M., Pettersson, E., Sandblad, B. & Schwalbe, P. (1987). The interface is often not the problem. In J. M. Carroll & P. P. Tanner (eds.), *Proceedings of CHI+GI'87: Human Factors in Computing Systems and Graphics Interface.* New York: ACM Press, pp. 133–136.

[19] Greenbaum, J. & Kyng, M. (1991). *Design at Work: Cooperative Design of Computer Systems.* Hillsdale, NJ: Lawrence Erlbaum.

[20] Jacobson, I., Chriserson, M., Jonsson, P. & Overgaard, G. (1992). *Object-Oriented Software Engineering: A Use-Case Driven Approach.* Reading, MA: Addison-Wesley.

[21] Johnson, P., Johnson, H. & Wilson, S. (1995). Rapid prototyping of user interfaces driven by task models. *Chapter 9 in this volume.*

[22] Kyng, M. (1995). Creating contexts for design. *Chapter 4 in this volume.*

[23] MacLean, A. & McKerlie, D. (1995). Design space analysis and use representations. *Chapter 8 in this volume.*

[24] Meyer, B. (1988). *Object-Oriented Software Construction.* New York: Prentice Hall.

[25] Muller, M., Tudor, L. G., Wildman, D. M., White, E. A., Root, R. W., Dayton, T., Carr, R., Diekmann, B. & Dykstra-Erickson, E. (1995). Bifocal tools for scenarios and representations in participatory activities with users. *Chapter 6 in this volume.*

[26] Myers, B. A. & Rosson, M. B. (1992). Survey on user interface programming. In P. Bauersfield, J. Bennett & G. Lynch (eds.), *Proceedings of CHI'92: Human Factors in Computing Systems.* New York: ACM Press, pp. 195–202.

[27] Nardi, B. (1995). Some reflections on scenarios. *Chapter 15 in this volume.*

[28] Norman, D. A. (1986). Cognitive engineering. In D. A. Norman & S. W. Draper (eds.), *User Centered System Design.* Hillsdale, NJ: Lawrence Erlbaum, pp. 31–65.

[29] Rosson, M. B. & Alpert, S. R. (1990). Cognitive consequences of object-oriented design. *Human-Computer Interaction, 5*, 345–379.

[30] Rosson, M. B. & Carroll, J. M. (1993a). Active programming strategies in reuse. In O. M. Nierstrasz (ed.), *Proceedings of ECOOP '93: European Conference on Object-Oriented Programming.* Berlin: Springer-Verlag, pp. 4–18.

[31] Rosson, M. B. & Carroll, J. M. (1993b). Extending the task-artifact framework: Scenario-based design of SmallTalk applications. In H. R. Hartson & D. Hix (eds.), *Advances in Human-Computer Interaction.* Norwood, NJ: Ablex, pp. 31–57.

[32] Rosson, M. B., Carroll, J. M. & Bellamy, R. K. E. (1990). SmallTalk scaffolding: A case study in Minimalist instruction. In J. C. Chew & J. Whiteside (eds.), *Proceedings of CHI'90: Human Factors in Computing Systems.* New York: ACM Press, pp. 423–429.

[33] Rubin, K. S. & Goldberg, A. (1992). Object behavior analysis. *Communications of the ACM, 35*(9), 48–62.

[34] Tanner, P. P. & Buxton, W. (1985). Some issues in future user interface management systems. In G. E. Pfaff (ed.), *User Interface Management Systems.* Berlin: Springer-Verlag, pp. 67–80.

[35] Vertelney, L. (1989). Using video to prototype user interfaces. *SIGCHI Bulletin, 21*(2), 57–61.

[36] Wirfs-Brock, R. (1995). Designing objects and their interactions: A brief look at responsibility-driven design. *Chapter 13 in this volume.*

[37] Wirfs-Brock, R., Wilkerson, B. & Wiener, L. (1990). *Designing Object-Oriented Software.* Englewood Cliffs, NJ: Prentice Hall.

CHAPTER 11

Generating Object-Oriented Design Representations via Scenario Queries

Scott P. Robertson

Applied Research and Multimedia Services
U S WEST Technologies
4001 Discovery Drive
Boulder, CO 80303
USA

11.1 INTRODUCTION

Object-oriented analysis (OOA) and design (OOD) involve development of an application domain model that emphasizes identification of the active entities in the domain (called *objects*), description of their responsibilities and behaviors, and definitions of the ways in which model objects interact [4, 7, 19, 23, 31, 32, 38]. An increasingly popular method for performing OOA and OOD is scenario-based design [6, 19]. Scenario-based design approaches utilize analyses of particular *use cases* [19] and stress object analysis in the context of specific, observed, or described sequences of events in the application domain. Scenarios are narrative descriptions of use cases, and proponents assert that use-case scenarios provide appropriate information for truly user-centered designs.

System design involves complex perceptual and cognitive skills. Studies of system designers [16, 17, 18, 20, 22, 37] and programmers [1, 2, 3, 8, 9, 24, 26, 27, 28, 29, 33, 34] have shown that they manipulate many types of knowledge, both domain-specific knowledge and more abstract knowledge about system structures and language conventions. In OOA and OOD, the ideal is to bring conceptual modeling of the domain into more or less direct correspondence with the ultimate system design. Computer-aided software engineering (CASE) tools to aid knowledge manipulation and concept modeling have been developed, but few benefit from methods or theory from the cognitive sciences.

In this chapter, a method from natural language comprehension research within cognitive science is introduced for use in object-oriented system design. A few methods and tools for moving from natural language descriptions to design of information systems have been developed [25, 30, 36], but methods have not been applied to scenario analysis and object-oriented models. Cognitive scientists interested in comprehension have faced the problem of how people understand narrative and expository information [10, 11, 13, 15, 21, 35]. It is evident that even when a brief text is understood a considerable amount of prior knowledge is involved in building a cognitive representation. Generating an elaborated cognitive representation of a narrative is much like extracting a design from a scenario, thus a method for studying the former process should be useful in the latter. This is especially true for object-oriented designs since they ideally reflect the structure of some real-world problem and, hence, the structure of knowledge representing the real-world problem.

This chapter is organized into four sections. First, the scenario-based approach to object-oriented design is discussed and the analogy between narrative comprehension and scenario-based design is drawn. Next the systematic question-asking method, used to study narrative comprehension, is applied to a short text to show its use in the cognitive science context. In the next section the question-asking method is paired with scenario-based analysis and applied to a system design problem. The final section provides a summary and outlines directions for future development of the question-asking technique.

11.2 SCENARIO-BASED DESIGN

The analysts' ultimate goals in an object-oriented project are to identify a set of classes and objects, specify their interrelations, and define their behaviors and responsibilities in such a way that they support a variety of activities within an application domain. Because object-oriented designs incorporate objects that correspond to real-world objects or natural concepts, some designers and theorists have advocated the use of concrete, user-centered scenarios to guide design [5, 6, 19, and this book].

In a scenario-based approach, narrative descriptions of an episode within the problem domain are obtained. These narratives are then used as sources of information about the objects in the domain and how they interact. The scenario-based approach contrasts with abstract domain analyses that are characteristic of traditional systems-analysis techniques.

The problem that faces analysts and designers who use scenarios is depicted in Figure 11.1. The problem domain consists of a set of objects, which can have many states and interact in many ways. The *problem domain* can be thought of as consisting of a set of objects and associated state transition diagrams that specify how each object might change states and what operations are required to move from one state to the next. Underlying the objects and their behaviors is a *domain semantics,* which can be thought of as the set of rules that govern changes in the states in the problem domain. An analyst seeks to identify the objects, capture the state transitions in their methods, and reflect the domain semantics in the structure of their interactions.

In scenario-based analysis and design, *use cases* are identified in which a subset of the domain objects performs a few of their permissible actions. The process of scenario creation consists of selecting a subset of object behaviors that reflect a meaningful task in the problem domain and that provide important information to the analyst. An analyst makes observations of the scenario, identifies the objects involved, and tries to define methods and interactions that would produce the observed behavior. The analyst is using the scenario to generate an understanding of the domain semantics. This understanding, in turn, is used to draw inferences about the behaviors of the objects. The analyst uses domain knowledge and system design skills to elaborate on the explicit knowledge provided by the scenario, abstract from instance-oriented scenario elements, and draw inferences about the existence and behavior of objects in the problem domain that were not observed in the particular scenario.

Since a single scenario gives partial information, scenario-based analysis involves the observation of a set of scenarios. Each scenario provides more information to update the analyst's understanding of the problem domain and evaluate components of the design concept map that have been generated by inference and abstraction. The use of several scenarios forces an analyst to produce a generalized domain model, but the completeness of this model depends on the analyst's ability to make inferences that elaborate on the domain model.

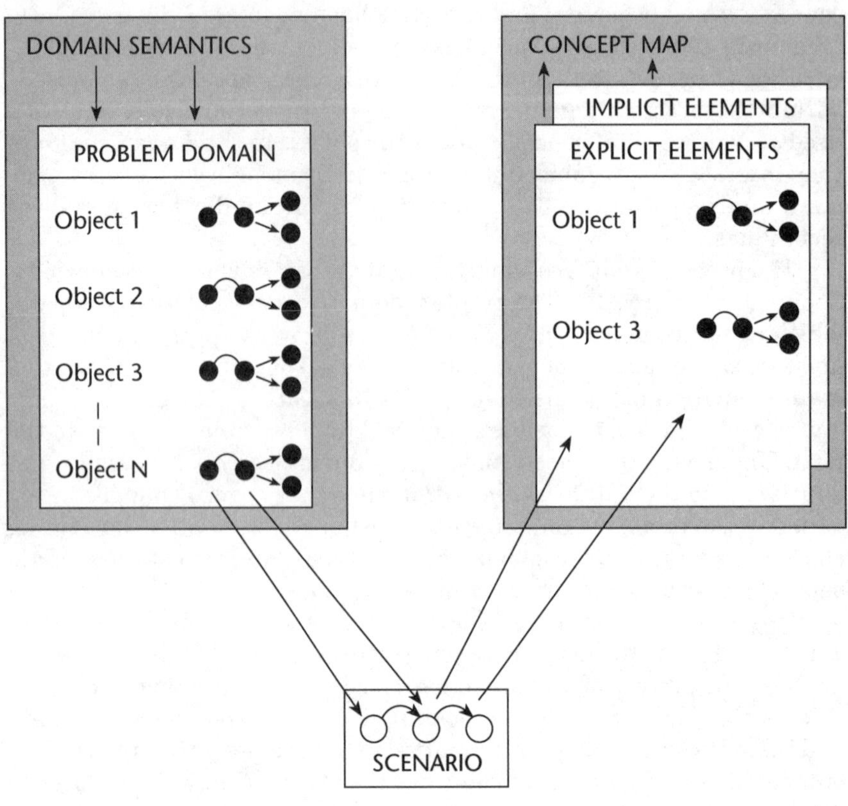

Figure 11.1. Scenario-based design involves building an elaborate concept map of a problem domain by observing a selected set of specific events (often in the form of a text or dialog). Designers use domain knowledge and design skills to generate inferences and abstractions about the problem domain.

The situation facing researchers in the area of human text comprehension is analogous to that facing system analysts and designers, as Figure 11.2 suggests. A narrative text is a summary of some actual or imagined event. Underlying the event are domain semantics that constrain what can happen to the actors and objects. Typically the domain semantics for stories are rules of the relevant physical, social, and psychological environment (they can be real-world rules or special rules for fairy tales, science fiction, and other exceptional tales of various kinds).

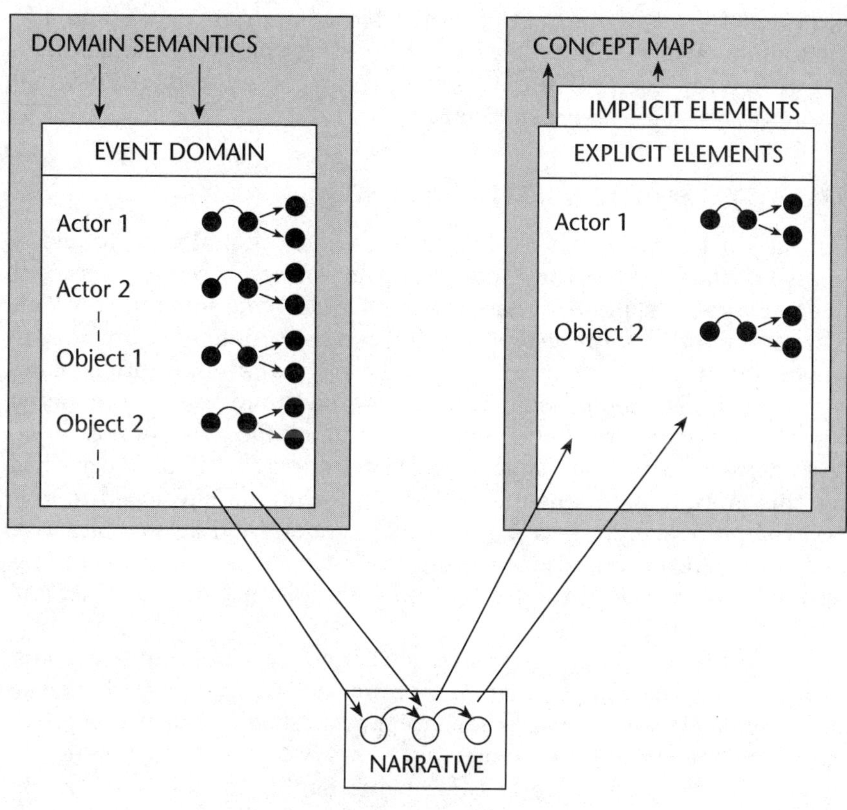

Figure 11.2. Narrative comprehension involves building an elaborate concept map of an event by observing a selected set of specific events (often in the form of a text or dialog). Comprehenders use domain knowledge and narrative comprehension skills to generate inferences and abstractions about the original event.

Like a scenario, a narrative summary contains a subset of the complete information about original actors, objects, states, and events. The narrative has been produced by applying summarization rules, which remove and condense information. (An interesting research topic yet to be explored is what degree of similarity exists between narrative summarization rules and scenario creation rules.) Comprehenders use their knowledge of domain semantics, the narrative event domain, and narrative production strategies to reengineer some of the detail of the original event from the information presented in the narrative summary. Just like analysts elaborating a scenario, story comprehenders build a knowledge representation that is more complete, vis-à-vis the original event, than the narrative summary.

11.3 SYSTEMATIC QUESTION-ASKING

Because of the conventions of narratives and the ability of people to apply knowledge when they understand narratives, the explicit content of a narrative is sparse compared with its underlying semantic content. The content of a narrative or a scenario can be thought of as an *index* to important underlying material about the original event or problem domain. Designers could benefit from a method to expose the unstated information about the problem domain by using the items in the narrative as entrance points to underlying knowledge structures. One method for this is systematic question-asking, a technique developed to give text comprehension researchers a way of understanding the narrative elaboration process and uncovering the knowledge and processes involved. In this section the theory and technique are summarized and applied to a simple story.

Researchers in text comprehension generally agree that textual information can be represented as a network of interconnected concept units called *propositions* [21]. A concept proposition consists of a predicate, which modifies an argument or relates two or more arguments. In natural language, arguments correspond roughly to nouns, and predicates correspond roughly to verbs, adverbs, and adjectives. Thus "John ate a sandwich" is represented by the predicate EAT, which takes JOHN as a subject argument and SANDWICH as an object argument:

```
(EAT, subject: JOHN, object: SANDWICH)
```

The sentence "John ate a large sandwich" is represented by two interconnected propositions. One contains the predicate LARGE modifying SANDWICH; the other contains the predicate EAT, the subject argument JOHN, and an object argument containing the first proposition:

```
(EAT, subject: JOHN, object: (LARGE, subject: SANDWICH))
```

The usefulness of propositional analysis is that complex sentences and phrases can be broken into component-meaning units. Also, the semantics of a predicate are defined in terms of the number and types of arguments it takes and will be constant over all instances of the predicate. This provides a set of rules for representing natural language in a common, propositional notation.

Psychological evidence suggests that when people read text they generate and store a set of propositions [21, 35]. Propositions may be linked to one another according to relational constraints. For example, the phrase "John was hungry so he ate a sandwich" consists of two propositions: one corresponding to John's state of hunger and a second corresponding to his eating. In addition, the two propositions are linked by an intentional relationship, that is, the internal state motivated the action:

```
Internal State: (HUNGER, subject: JOHN)
Action: (EAT, subject: JOHN, object: SANDWICH)
Relation: (MOTIVATE, Internal State, Action)
```

Researchers have been interested in developing a taxonomy of proposition types and the observed relations among them [11, 12, 14, 15].

This explicit representation of narrative text is analogous to a set of state transition diagrams, which specify the behaviors of objects in a scenario. In addition to representing the information that is explicit in a text, people generate inferences that provide coherence and context. Thus it is possible to read a brief narrative and generate an explicit concept map of the information together with related knowledge derived by inference. It is this process that is similar to the problem of deriving a domain model from use-case scenarios.

Researchers have been interested in examining the concept networks that people generate from text. To this end, Graesser and his colleagues [11, 12, 14, 15] have developed a question-asking method for extracting unarticulated knowledge and building concept networks. In order to generate a concept network from a narrative, a natural language text is first simplified by breaking it into propositions. The network of linked propositions reflects the explicit semantics of the text. Next, questions are asked about each proposition and the answers are added to the concept map as new propositions. A new proposition is connected to the original proposition that generated it, with the type of connection being dependent on the type of question asked and the types of propositions being connected.

More than one question can be asked of each proposition. Why-questions tend to generate causal, intentional, and precondition information about a proposition. How-questions tend to generate procedural details and elaborations on the manner in which a proposition was carried out. What-questions tend to generate category information.

Verification questions generate affirmative or negative responses. A single round of questions about each of the propositions in a narrative can increase the size and complexity of a concept map.

At this stage a brief example would be useful in understanding how systematic questioning of a narrative can be used to build a concept map. Consider the following very sparse narrative:

```
John went to the store.
He bought some milk.
John went home and put the milk in his coffee.
```

This brief narrative consists of the four propositions listed as P1–P4 in Table 11.1. The middle layer of Figure 11.3 shows P1–P4 as a simple series of propositions. This series represents the explicit *text base* of the narrative. Questions about each proposition create material for new nodes that are linked to the queried propositions, creating the more elaborate concept map in Figure 11.3.

A complete understanding of the narrative requires the construction of new propositions and the addition of some semantics to the temporal linkages in the text base. It is assumed that readers construct this information by inference. This can be derived empirically by researchers, however, by asking questions about each proposition. Table 11.2 shows the answers to why-questions and how-questions about each of the four propositions in Table 11.1. Under each question category is a list of proposition-answer pairs along with text of possible answers. For example, the first pair under the Why heading is P1–A1. P1 refers to the first proposition in Table 11.1, thus the question is "Why did John go to the store?" An answer, identified as A1, is that "He wanted some milk." When an answer refers to an already-stated proposition the prior proposition is indicated in place of the answer. For example, one answer to "Why did John go home?" (why-P3) is "to put milk in his coffee." This is indicated in Table 11.2 as a P3–P4 pair under the Why heading.

As Table 11.2 shows, asking "why" about P1 and P2 reveals that a

Table 11.1 Propositional Analysis of a Brief Narrative

P1.	John goes to a store.
P2.	John buys milk.
P3.	John goes home.
P4.	John puts milk in his coffee.

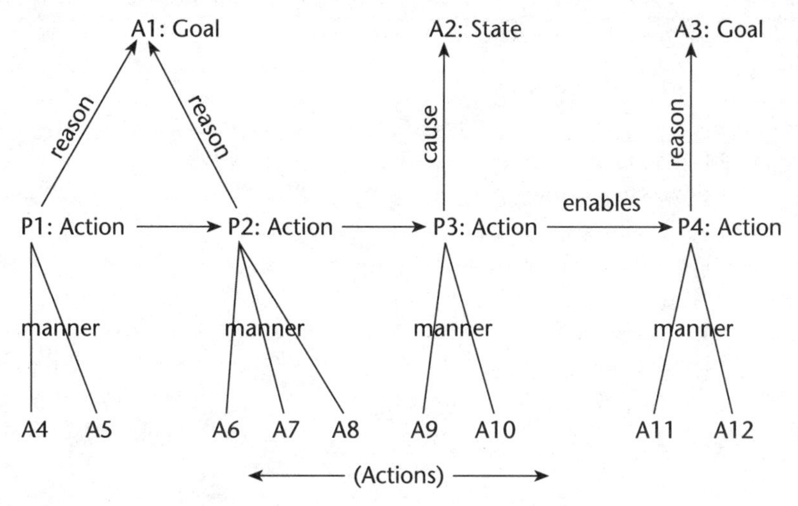

Figure 11.3. Concept map of a simple narrative. The explicit propositions from Table 11.1 appear as P1–P4. Elaborations derived from systematic question-asking (Table 11.2) are shown as A1–A12.

goal is present that motivates both of these actions. This common goal is represented in Figure 11.3 as a node called A1 and labeled *goal*. Asking "why" about P3 reveals an *enablement* relation between P3 and P4. This relation is indicated as a label on the link between P3 and P4 in Figure 11.3. Asking "why" about P3 also uncovers a state that is implied by the story but not actually stated explicitly. This is shown in Figure 11.3 as *state* node A2. Asking "why" about P4 reveals a fact about John that is not stated in the narrative. This fact is indicated in Figure 11.4 as *goal* node A3.

Pursuing the question technique further, asking how-questions about each of the original four propositions yields two of three new propositions, which are procedural details of how each action was carried out. The answers to these questions (A4–A12) are shown under the How heading in Table 11.2, and the propositions appear in the lower layer of Figure 11.3.

The surface structure of the narrative contains only four propositions described as occurring in sequence. However, after asking two questions about each proposition we have developed a concept map with three times as many propositions and richer semantic links.

Table 11.2 Answers to Why- and How-Questions about the Brief Narrative

Why:		
P1	A1.	He wanted some milk.
P2	A1.	He wanted some milk.
P3	P4.	So he could put milk in his coffee.
	A2.	The coffee was at home.
P4	A3.	He liked it that way.
How:		
P1	A4.	He got in the car.
	A5.	He drove to the store.
P2	A6.	He got a carton from the shelf.
	A7.	He took the carton to the register.
	A8.	He paid for it.
P3	A9.	He got in his car.
	A10.	He drove home.
P4	A11.	He opened the carton.
	A12.	He poured it into the cup.

11.4 APPLICATION OF QUESTION-ASKING TO OBJECT-ORIENTED DESIGN

It was argued above that the problem of deriving a concept map from a narrative summary is similar to deriving a domain model from a use-case scenario. One reason for the similarity is the fact that a use-case scenario is a summary of one aspect of a larger set of potential interactions. Even when many scenarios are collected from users, the scenarios contain primarily procedural information about what happened, not design specifications. Systematic question-asking enriches the information available to analysts and designers by filling the gaps that exist in natural-language summaries and by providing the causal relations, conditions, and object interactions that are important to system builders.

The application of systematic question-asking follows closely the methods used in narrative text studies. First, a user scenario is generated or collected. The scenario might be generated by end users, system analysts, designers, or maintainers. In fact, the initial scenario could be a combination of scenarios from multiple sources. The scenario is next analyzed into the propositions that are contained in the explicit text base. An initial round of object extraction and analysis of object interactions can occur at this stage. Next, questions are asked about each of the propositions in the text base. Why-, how-, and what-questions are likely to yield the richest information, but other questions can also be asked. Answers to these questions contain new objects that were not mentioned in the original user scenario, but that played a role anyway and that, therefore, need to be modeled. The object set and object interactions can then be augmented with the new objects and behaviors. Questioning and object description can proceed iteratively on the initial and subsequent answer sets. This approach to scenario-based design is depicted in Figure 11.4.

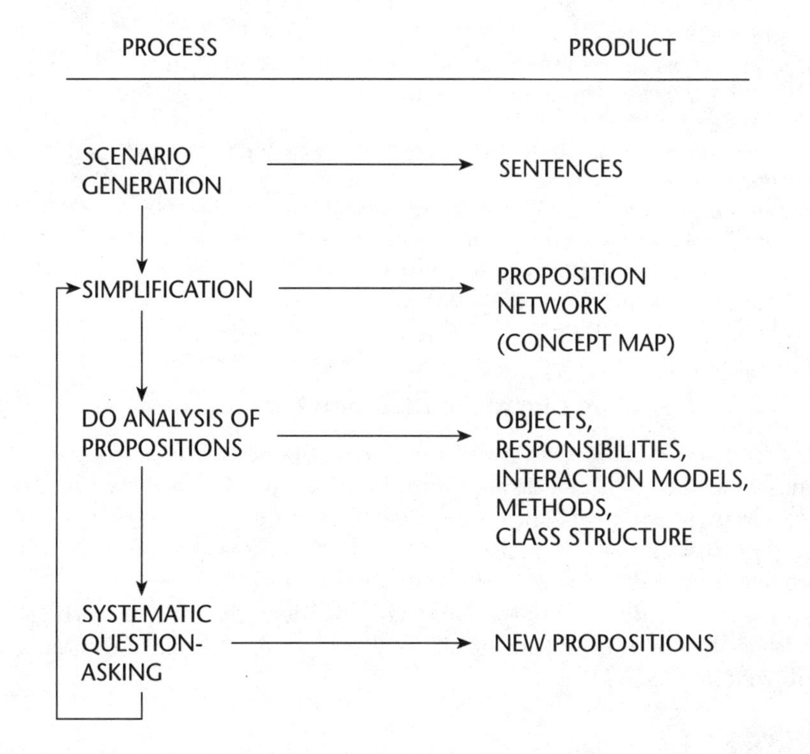

Figure 11.4. Scenario-based design joined with systematic question-asking.

11.4.1 An Example Scenario

The analysis in this section consists of a question-asking session in an example scenario. In the example the analyst's goal is to create an object-oriented analysis for a system that manages an automobile service shop. Because of the familiarity of the domain, the answers to many of the questions will seem obvious and the reader may wonder why the analyst shouldn't just use prior knowledge and intuition to derive much of the material in the analysis. The point of the example is to show how the method works in a familiar context. The reader should keep in mind that the real usefulness of the question-asking method is in domains that are not well understood by the analyst.

Our example scenario is as follows:

The Car Scenario

```
Bob noticed that his new car had 32,000 miles on it.
He decided to get a 30,000-mile checkup.
He called the car dealer to schedule it.
The service manager took down Bob's name and
found Bob's car on the computer.
He told Bob that the checkup would cost $100.
The service manager checked the calendar and found an
open day.
He asked Bob if Tuesday would be okay.
On Tuesday Bob took the car in and left it.
He signed a paper agreeing to the $100 fee.
The car was given a checkup.
When Bob returned he got a bill, paid it, and left.
```

11.4.2 Initial Object Identification and Definition

The first analytic step is simplification of the scenario sentences. The car scenario can be partitioned into the 24 propositions shown in Table 11.3. Most of the propositions represent a single action performed by a single actor. A few propositions represent connections between other propositions. For example, P6 connects P5 and P3.

Candidate design objects can easily be identified as either the subjects or objects of the propositions in Table 11.3. There are five unique subjects in Table 11.3:

car,
Bob, the *customer*
service manager
car record

Table 11.3 Propositional Analysis of the Car Scenario

P1.	Car has 32,000 miles.
P2.	Bob notices P1.
P3.	Bob will get a checkup.
P4.	Bob decides P3.
P5.	Bob calls dealership.
P6.	P5 is in service of P3.
P7.	Service manager takes Bob's name.
P8.	Service manager finds car record.
P9.	Car record is on the computer.
P10.	Checkup costs $100.
P11.	Service Manager tells Bob P10.
P12.	Service Manager checks the calendar.
P13.	Service Manager finds an open day.
P14.	P12 is in service of P13.
P15.	Service Manager asks Bob about Tuesday.
P16.	Bob takes car to garage.
P17.	Bob leaves car at garage.
P18.	P16 and P17 occur on Tuesday.
P19.	Bob signs a contract.
P20.	Contract amount is $100.
P21.	Car gets a checkup.
P22.	Bob returns to the dealership.
P23.	Bob gets a bill.
P24.	Bob pays the bill.
P25.	Bob drives his car away.

checkup,
contract.

Of these five, only three are involved in more than one proposition: the *customer*, the *service manager*, and the *car*.

The objects of the propositions contain a few more candidate design objects:

miles,
dealership,

```
car record,
computer,
dollars,
calendar,
day,
Tuesday,
garage,
bill.
```

A total of 16 candidate design objects have been identified in the scenario. While an analysis of nouns in the text might have yielded the same list, the proposition list shows object interactions and clearly distinguishes objects that are active from those that are acted upon. The proposition list also serves as a guide to the interrelations among objects and contains some information about the properties of objects. P12, for example, shows that the *service manager* interacts with the *calendar*, and P21 shows that the *car* is what gets the checkup.

11.4.3 Extending the Object Analysis by Question-Asking

The propositional analysis yields a considerable amount of information that will be helpful for design. However, scenarios are narrative summaries and so there is much more information behind the surface analysis. Systematic question-asking can be used to elaborate the proposition list in Table 11.3. In this section we will focus on two question types: why-questions and how-questions. Why-questions yield both intentional and causal information. How-questions yield procedural, causal, and enablement information.

For our analysis it will be useful to group together questions about all of the propositions that involve a particular actor. Each question might yield several answers, or an answer that is composed of many propositions, so that a single questioning pass results in a tremendous multiplication of the information derived from a scenario. In our analysis we will generate one or two answers per question for simplicity, although in practice a single question may generate many answers.

Table 11.4 shows answers to questions about the customer, Bob. The answer to "Why did Bob sign the contract?" (Why-P19) reveals the fact that the customer signature enables the checkup (A9), a fact that would be important in the design. This information is not explicit in the scenario and would only be available by the analyst's inference. The question process makes many such inferences explicit.

Additionally, the answers to why-questions about P22, P23, and P24 reveal the fact that paying is a prerequisite to having the car re-

Table 11.4 Answers to Why- and How-Questions about Bob's Role in the Car Scenario

Why:		
P2	A1.	Because he read the odometer.
P3	A2.	To keep the warranty in effect.
P4	A2.	To keep the warranty in effect.
P5	A3.	To schedule a checkup.
P6	A4.	So he'd only have to go there once.
P16	A5.	To get a 30,000-mile checkup.
P17	A6.	So they could work on it.
P18	A7.	Because Tuesday was the open day.
P19	A8.	To guarantee the price
	A9.	and approve the work.
P22	A10.	To get his car.
P23	A11.	So he could make sure everything was done
	A12.	and find out the cost.
P24	A13.	So the dealership would let the car go.
P25.	A14.	Because the deal was done.
How:		
P2	A1.	By looking at the odometer.
P3	A15.	By scheduling an appointment
	A16.	and taking the car in to the dealership.
P4	A17.	By thinking about it.
P5	A18.	He picked up the phone
	A19.	and pressed the right keys.
P6	A20.	It lets the dealership know you're coming
	A15.	so they can schedule an appointment.
P16	A21.	He got in,
	A22.	started it up,
	A23.	and drove it there.
P17	A24.	He parked it in the lot
	A25.	and gave the key to the service manager.
P18	??	
P19	A26.	By writing his name on the bottom line.
P22	A27.	By cab.

Table 11.4 *(Continued)*

P23	A28. The cashier handed it to him.
P24	A29. By giving his credit card to the cashier
	A30. and signing the credit slip.
P25	A31. Happily.

turned. Again, this important fact is available from the scenario only by inference, but can be easily derived through questioning.

How-questions about Bob's actions result in the generation of several subscenarios: A15–A16 in response to "How did Bob get a checkup?" A18–A19 in response to "How did Bob call the dealership in order to get a checkup?" A21–A23 in response to "How did Bob take his car to the garage?" A24–A25 in response to "How did Bob leave his car at the garage?" and A29–A30 in response to "How did Bob pay?"

The answers in Table 11.4 contain ten new candidate design objects:

```
odometer
warranty
appointment
phone
parking lot
key
cashier
cab
credit card
credit slip.
```

Each of these objects participates in some interaction with the customer, Bob. Each object has associated with it at least one behavior or responsibility. In many cases it is possible to find message-passing interactions between objects. For example, P2 told us that Bob learns that his car has gone 32,000 miles. In asking "Why did Bob notice that the car had 32,000 miles on it?" (Why-P2), we find that the odometer provided this information. Thus we can begin to build a model of this interaction like that shown in Figure 11.5. We can consider whether Bob should have a *read* method and whether odometer should have a *tell-32,000-miles* method (the issue of generality of methods will be treated in a later section). Similar object interaction models can be built from all of the new object pairs. Objects may have many interactions within a scenario or across a series of scenarios.

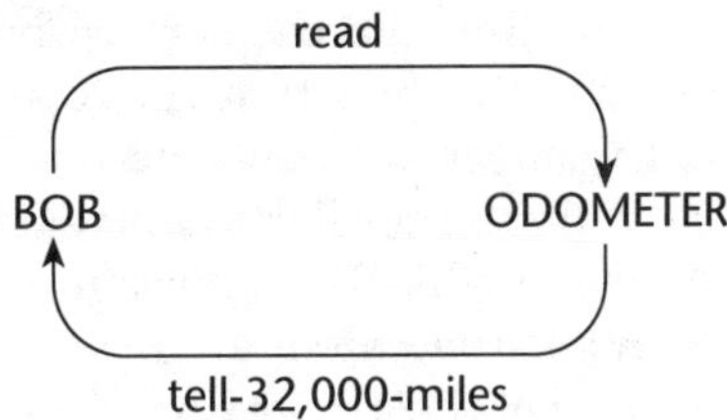

Figure 11.5. A message-passing interaction between two objects in the car application scenario.

Answers to why- and how-questions about the service manager's actions are listed in Table 11.5. The answer to "Why did the service manager take Bob's name?" (Why-P7) reveals that P7 and P8 are related. In designing a car application it is likely that this information

Table 11.5 Answers to Why- and How-Questions about the Service Manager's Role in the Car Scenario

Why:		
P7	P8.	So he could find the car record.
P8	A32.	So he could see what kind of car Bob had,
	A33.	get the price of a checkup,
	A34.	and update the record.
P11	A35.	To get Bob's approval.
P12	A13.	To find an open day.
P13	A3.	So he could schedule the checkup.
P14	A36.	The calendar shows what cars are scheduled at what times.
P15	A37.	He wanted to find out if Bob could come in on Tuesday.
How:		
P7	A38.	By asking Bob for it.
P8	A39.	By entering it into the computer.
P11	A40.	He just said so.
P12	A41.	He looked at each day until he found one with empty space.
P13	A42.	When there is nothing written on a day, it is empty.
P15	A43.	He said "How is Tuesday?"

will be important. The answers to "Why did the service manager ask Bob about Tuesday?" and "How did the service manager find an open day?" (Why-P15 and How-P13) show that the "open" quality of a day is related to the availability of service bays and mechanics.

The answer to "Why did the service manager check the calendar in order to find an open day?" (Why-P14) shows a design object that was formerly being acted upon, the calendar, in a more active role. The answer is phrased in terms of the properties of the calendar. By forcing the answer to explain how the calendar imparts information, the question technique encourages the important skill of anthropomorphizing. The analyst might add a behavior to the calendar to tell a requester about the schedule for the day. The answer to "How does the sales manager check the calendar?" (How-P12) suggests an iterative procedure for querying the calendar.

Table 11.6 shows answers to why- and how-questions for propositions involving the car. Note that the answers to questions about P21, "Why/how did the car get a checkup?" are rich sources of further scenario information. In particular, the how-question results in the generation of another subscenario (A45–A50). Five new candidate design objects are introduced in this subscenario:

```
service bay
oil change
```

Table 11.6 Answers to Why- and How-Questions about the Car's Role in the Car Scenario

Why:		
P1	A44.	Bob drove it a lot.
P21	A1.	Bob looked at the odometer.
	A2.	To keep the warranty in effect.
How:		
P1	A44.	Bob drove it a lot.
P21	A45.	First it went to a service bay
	A46.	where it got an oil change.
	A47.	While it was there the tire wear was checked
	A48.	and the tires were rotated.
	A49.	Then it went to another bay
	A50.	where it got a tune-up.

```
tires
tire rotation
tune up
```

Each new interaction can be added to the model, and iterative question-asking in this scenario would further define the new objects and fill in the overall design.

11.4.4 Iterative Question-Asking

A narrative is a summary of a larger problem space, and questions expose some of the content of the problem space. However, a single round of questions may not be adequate for understanding the problem in enough detail to support a good system design. In particular, the first round of questions will tend to be about the main actors in the scenario. The roles and responsibilities of secondary actors may only be exposed by another round of question-asking. Subsequent questions are applied to the answers that were derived previously.

As an example of the value that can be derived from iterative question-asking, consider P8: "The service manager finds a car record." Answers to why-questions about this item (A32, A33, and A34 in Table 11.5) reveal that retrieving the car record enables the sales manager to get the make of the customer's car, find the price of a checkup, and update the record. The answer to the how-question (A39 in Table 11.5) shows that the sales manager entered the customer's number into a computer in order to retrieve the record. Why- and how-questions might be asked about each of the answers in order to generate more material about the problem space. Consider a why-question about A32: "Why did the sales manager find out what kind of car Bob had?" Since the make of a car has to be determined in order to find the price of a checkup, a reasonable answer is "In order to find the cost of the checkup," which corresponds to another answer, A33. Thus A32 and A33 are related by an enablement link—information that is derived from the iterative questioning.

Now consider a how-question about A33: "How did the sales manager find the price of a checkup?" A reasonable answer is "The sales manager looked it up in the service catalog." This answer introduces a new object, a *service catalog*, which is likely to be very important in the final design. Further iteration on this answer, "How did the sales manager look up the price of a checkup in the service catalog?" would reveal how the service catalog was indexed and provide information about the type of data structure that could be used to model it. Figure 11.6 shows a concept map derived from initial and iterative questioning of P8. Simi-

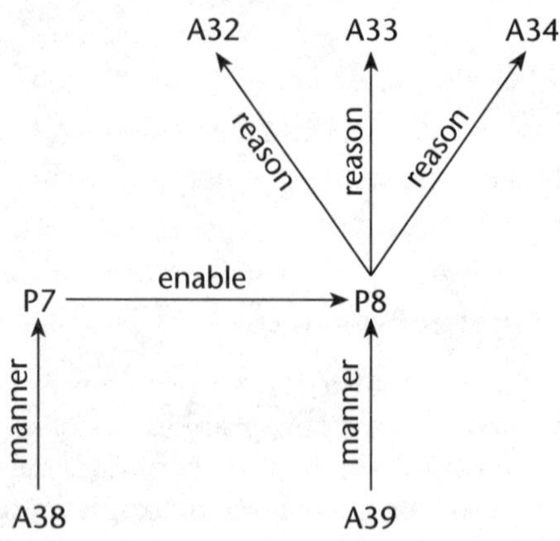

Figure 11.6. Concept map of propositions associated with P8 ("The service manager finds a car record").

lar component parts of the model can be generated by iterative question-asking about all of the material.

11.4.5 Generalizing Classes within a Scenario

Scenarios are phrased in terms of instances, and some of the objects mentioned may be described at a level of specificity that is inappropriate for a design. For example, while "Bob" is a player in the domain model derived from the car scenario, he is too specific for a design object in a car service application. After identifying candidate design objects and their behaviors, analysts who are working from scenarios must next generate classes. This involves identifying prototypical information about the behaviors of objects like the ones in the scenario, grouping similar objects together, and finding class hierarchy information.

What-questions are a vehicle for obtaining information about subclass–superclass relationships and for getting property information about objects in a scenario. What-questions can also reveal object groupings and extract class descriptions. An analyst might ask a what-question about each of the objects that appeared in the initial propositional analysis and as the result of the initial why- and how-questioning phase. In this section, a few examples of what-questions are presented.

The type of answer that is derived from a what-question depends on the level of abstraction of the object being queried. For example, what-questions about the *car* and the *car record* might produce the following answers:

```
What is a car?

A car is a vehicle that carries people around.
It usually has four tires and room for 2-5 people
inside.

What is a car record?

A car record is an information record that contains the
year, make, model, and some identification number for a
car.

It also has the service history of the car.
```

In both cases the answers begin with a class, *vehicle,* and *information record*, respectively, and continue by describing the specialized qualities that make the query objects a subclass. This is exactly the information that an analyst needs in order to create class definitions and organize the class hierarchy for the application. Note also that the answers contain new objects:

```
tires
identification number,
```

which are associated with the queried objects.

An answer to a what-question may lead to the discovery that an object is a unique instance of a class as opposed to being a subclass. Consider, for example, the following:

```
What is Bob?
Bob is a customer.
He's the one who is getting his car fixed.
```

Bob is an instance of *customer*, not a subclass of *customer*. In this case the specialized qualities of the subclass are not described. Instead, the role of the customer is explained in more detail. If a what-question yields a description of a class instead of an explanation of why an object is a subclass, then the analyst should consider modeling the object at the class level. While a *car* and a *car record* should probably become classes in the design, *Bob* should not. Instead, the model should contain a *customer* class.

Whenever a what-question is answered with a class and no description of why the object is a subclass, a second what-question will help the analyst to define its properties. For example, after receiving the answer about Bob, the analyst might ask about a customer.

```
What is a customer?
A customer is a person who comes into a store and buys
things.
```

This answer has the same form as the answers about *car* and *car record*. Specifically, it names a class (*person*) and then explains how a customer is a specialization of the *person* class.

Note that answers to what-questions may show that an instance belongs to more than one class and may also reveal a class hierarchy. For example, equally plausible answers to "What is Bob?" are "He is a car owner," and "He is a person." Because a car owner is also a person (as a what-question will reveal), there is a three-link hierarchy: *Bob* to *car owner* to *person*. Similarly, *Bob* to *customer* to *person* forms a second hierarchy. *Car owner* and *customer* are orthogonal classes because a what-question about one will not yield the other as an answer. The hierarchy in Figure 11.7 can be generated by asking a series of what-questions. A what-question about a node can be sensibly answered by referring to any superordinate node, but never to subordinate or sibling nodes.

It is important for analysts to identify different objects within the scenario that can be grouped together as instances of a class. This allows the objects to inherit from the class. What-questions are also useful for this purpose. Consider the following questions about the objects that were identified in a subscenario (A45–A50):

```
What is an oil change?

An oil change is a service performed on a car.
Old oil is removed and new oil is put in.

What is a tire rotation?

A tire rotation is a service performed on a car.
The positions of the tires are switched from front to
back and from right to left.
This results in more even tire wear.

What is a tune-up?

A tune-up is a service performed on a car.
Several engine components are adjusted and replaced so
that the car runs more smoothly and gets better
mileage.
```

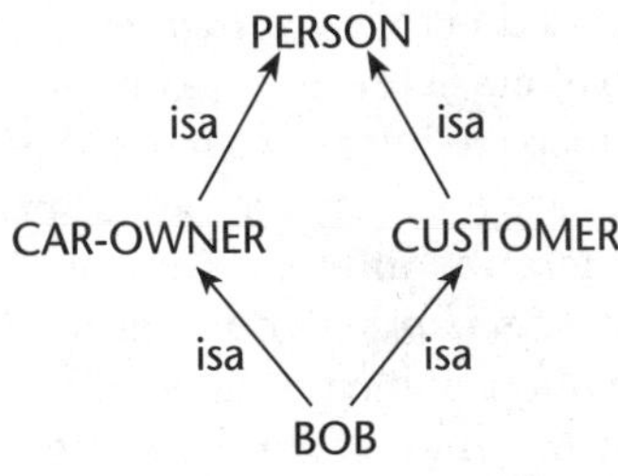

Figure 11.7. A class hierarchy derived from a series of what-questions starting with *Bob*.

In this case three objects are shown to be types of a new class called *service*. Answers to the iterative question "What is a service?" will yield information that can be inherited by the three objects (e.g., that a service has a cost, parts, and time specifications) and, therefore, defined at the level of the service class.

11.4.6 Generalizing and Positioning Methods

Determining the level at which to assign properties and methods is an important task. Recall from the example in Figure 11.5 that we gained the knowledge that the odometer told Bob that his car had gone 32,000 miles. The interaction was modeled with very specific methods. Consider how questions about the details of that message-passing interaction can help clarify the scope of this object's behavior:

```
What is an odometer?
An odometer is a gauge that tells mileage.

What is 32,000 miles?
In this case it is a measure of mileage.
```

These answers, coupled with the earlier discovery from a what-question that *Bob* is an instance of *customer*, allow us to generalize the *tell-32,000-miles* method depicted in Figure 11.5 and to elaborate on our representation by adding a *gauge* class. The answer to "What is an odometer?" explicitly tells us that an odometer's responsibility is to tell mileage, and the answer to "What is 32,000 miles?" tells us that 32,000 is one possible value of a property called *mileage* that cars have. Figure

11.8 updates Figure 11.5 by showing that an odometer is a gauge and that its associated method is to *tell-mileage*.

An important role of class hierarchies in object-oriented systems is to provide an inheritance path for methods. Verification (yes/no) questions can be used to locate a method at the appropriate level in a class hierarchy. In the odometer example in Figure 11.8, the *read* method is associated with *Bob* and *tell-mileage* is associated with *odometer*. By systematically asking about a particular message and receiver in association with an ascending chain of senders, the appropriate level of the message can be determined. For example, Figure 11.9 grafts together the hierarchies from Figures 11.7 and 11.8, adding some superordinate nodes above *gauge* (which would have been generated by what-questions) and sibling nodes at each level of the new *tool* hierarchy. In order to locate the appropriate level for the *read* method, the analyst might ask verification questions about each item above *Bob*:

```
Can Bob read an odometer?              Yes
Can a car owner read an odometer?      Yes
Can a customer read an odometer?       Yes
Can a person read an odometer?         Yes
```

In this sequence it is apparent that the *read* method may be associated with the highest node, *person*, and that all nodes below *person* can inherit this method's behavior.

The legal recipients of a read message can also be determined by ascending the receiver hierarchy with verification questions:

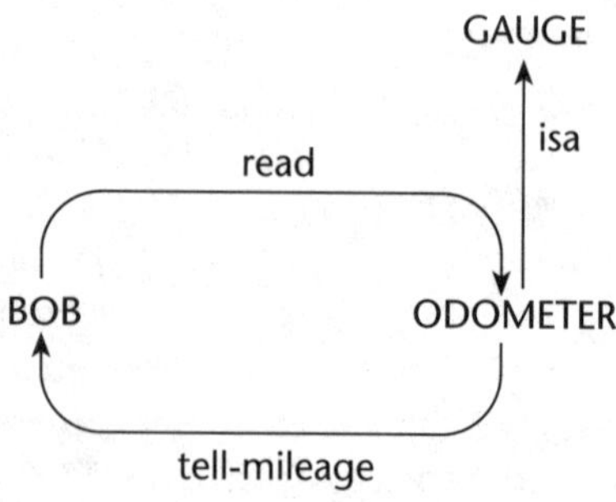

Figure 11.8. A more general analysis of the message-passing interaction between *Bob* and the *odometer*.

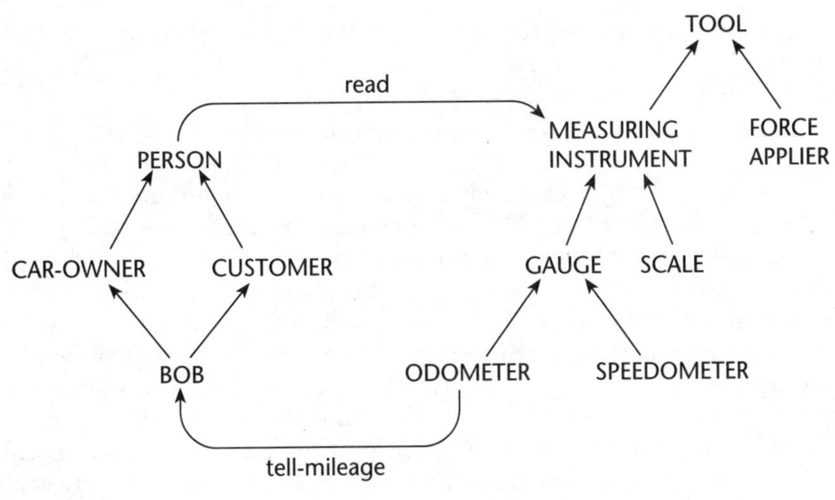

Figure 11.9. A refactoring of the message-passing interaction between *Bob* and the *odometer* after considerable question-asking.

```
Can a person read an odometer?                  Yes
Can a person read a speedometer?                Yes
Can a person read a gauge?                      Yes
Can a person read a scale?                      Yes
Can a person read a measuring instrument?       Yes
Can a person read a force applier?              No
Can a person read a tool?                       Some
```

Note that affirmative answers are given all the way up the hierarchy to *tool*, however not all tools can be read. In fact, the *force-applier* example results in a negative answer. This tells that analyst that *read* is a generalizable method to the level of *measuring-instrument*. If the analyst wishes to examine the specifics of how various objects respond to a *read* message, he or she might ask a series of why-questions in which the method is paired with the receiver objects in the hierarchy:

```
Why does a person read a speedometer?
To learn the speed that the car is moving.

Why does a person read an odometer?
To learn the number of miles a car has gone.
```

Why does a person read a gauge?

To get the measure of whatever the gauge is sensitive to.

Why does a person read a scale?

To get the measure of whatever the scale is designed for.

The answers show that speedometers and odometers return different types of information. The vagueness of the answers at the gauge and scale levels suggests that these are not the appropriate levels at which to define details of the objects' behaviors. Note that this explanation is moving the analyst away from the scenario, and possibly away from the problem domain. Since pursuing a question series can be like pulling a sweater thread, the analyst needs to stay aware of when a line of questioning begins to be uninformative with regard to the problem domain. Sometimes a line of questioning runs out with a nonsensical question (i.e., Can a person read a tool?), but other times it may continue to be productive long after it has become irrelevant.

A similar method-generalization analysis can be applied for the *tell-mileage* method:

Can an odometer tell mileage?	*Yes*
Can a speedometer tell mileage?	*No*
Can a gauge tell mileage?	*Yes*

In this case the very specific method, *tell-mileage*, must be located low in the hierarchy, at odometer. Figure 11.9 shows a refactored analysis developed from questions about the interaction between Bob and the odometer.

11.5 CONCLUSIONS

In this chapter the use of systematic question-asking was explored as a technique for aiding analysts and designers of object-oriented software systems to work from scenarios to a domain concept map. The chapter treated a single scenario in detail in order to illustrate the amount of information that can be derived from the question-asking approach. The approach is advocated especially in situations where analysts and designers do not have strong intuitions about the domain.

Initial simplification of scenario sentences yields a set of propositions that can be subjected to object-oriented analysis. The analysis yields a few objects, some of their responsibilities and properties, and some of their interaction patterns. Why- and how-questions about the propositions generate a new set of sentences in the form of answers. These answers can be iteratively subjected to simplification and question-asking to further expand the information derived from an initial scenario. Why-questions can uncover ordering dependencies, constraints, and rules of behavior for objects. How-questions often result in production of new subscenarios. What-questions are useful for abstracting classes from instances and, when applied iteratively, for developing class hierarchies. The location of a method in a class hierarchy can be achieved by systematic application of verification questions, pairing each sender object and each receiver object with a method.

In actual analysis of a problem domain, analysts would collect several scenarios covering a range of situations. Question-answering about the events in all of these scenarios would reveal the common elements of the scenarios and aid even further in the production of a general design. Also, analysts would ask the same questions of several domain experts in order to gather a larger amount of information about each aspect of the system. A *consensus concept model* would provide a more complete representation of the problem domain. A direction for future work includes understanding how answers from different scenarios and various informants might be integrated.

There is a tension between the specificity and instance-bounded nature of scenarios on the one hand, and the generality of application designs that support the scenarios on the other. The systematic question-asking technique helps with this problem by creating a bridge between the specific scenario events and the general situations that enable, cause, or explain the events. Answers to questions make these behind-the-scenes operations more visible to analysts and can also take analysts and designers into knowledge realms that surround and influence the domain specifics, for example, class hierarchies, social conventions, and past histories. In future work, computer-assisted software engineering (CASE) tools for supporting systematic question-asking and a more articulated theory of the relations between scenario events and answers to questions about them will be developed.

REFERENCES

[1] Adelson, B. (1981). Problem solving and the development of abstract categories in programming languages. *Memory and Cognition, 9,* 422–433.

[2] Adelson, B. & Soloway, E. (1985). The role of domain experience in software design. *IEEE Transactions on Software Engineering, 11,* 1351–1360.

[3] Black, J., Kay, D. & Soloway, E. (1987). Goal and plan knowledge representations: From stories to text editors and programs. In J. Carroll (ed.), *Interfac-*

ing Thought: Cognitive Aspects of Human-Computer Interaction. Cambridge, MA: MIT Press, pp. 36–60.

[4] Booch, G. (1991). *Object-Oriented Design with Applications.* Redwood City, CA: Benjamin/Cummings.

[5] Carroll, J. M. & Rosson, M. B. (1990). Human-computer interaction scenarios as a design representation. In *Proceedings of HICCS-23: Hawaii International Conference on System Sciences.* Los Alamos, CA: IEEE Computer Society Press, pp. 555–561.

[6] Carroll, J. M. & Rosson, M. B. (1992). Getting around the task-artifact cycle: How to make claims and design by scenario. *ACM Transactions on Information Systems, 10,* 181–212.

[7] Coad, P. & Yourdon, E. (1991). *Object-Oriented Design.* Englewood Cliffs, NJ: Prentice Hall.

[8] Detienne, F. & Soloway, E. (1990). An empirically-derived control structure for the process of program understanding. *International Journal of Man-Machine Studies, 33,* 323–342.

[9] Ehrlich, K. & Soloway, E. (1984). An empirical investigation of tacit plan knowledge in programming. In J. Thomas & M. Schneider (eds.), *Human Factors in Computer Systems.* Norwood, NJ: Ablex.

[10] Graesser, A. C. (1981). *Prose Comprehension Beyond the Word.* New York: Springer-Verlag.

[11] Graesser, A. C. & Clark, L. F. (1985). *Structures and Procedures of Implicit Knowledge.* Norwood, NJ: Ablex.

[12] Graesser, A. C. & Franklin, S. P. (1990). QUEST: A cognitive model of question answering. *Discourse Processes, 13,* 279–304.

[13] Graesser, A. C. & Goodman, S. M. (1984). Implicit knowledge, question answering, and the representation of expository text. In B. Britton & J. Black (eds.), *Understanding Expository Text.* Hillsdale, NJ: Lawrence Erlbaum.

[14] Graesser, A. C. & Murachver, T. (1985). Symbolic procedures of question answering. In A. C. Graesser & J. B. Black (eds.), *The Psychology of Questions.* Hillsdale, NJ: Lawrence Erlbaum, pp. 15–88.

[15] Graesser, A. C., Robertson, S. P., & Anderson, P. A. (1981). Incorporating inferences in narrative representations: A study of how and why. *Cognitive Psychology, 13,* 1–26.

[16] Guindon, R. (1990a). Designing the design process: Exploiting opportunistic thoughts. *Human-Computer Interaction, 5,* 305–344.

[17] Guindon, R. (1990b). Knowledge exploited by experts during software system design. *International Journal of Man-Machine Studies, 33,* 279–304.

[18] Guindon, R. & Curtis, B. (1988). Control of cognitive processes during software design: What tools are needed? In *Proceedings of CHI'88: Human Factors in Computing Systems.* Reading, MA: Addison-Wesley, pp. 263–268.

[19] Jacobson, I. (1992). *Object-Oriented Software Engineering: A Use-Case Driven Approach.* Reading, MA: Addison-Wesley.

[20] Jeffries, R., Turner, A., Polson, P. & Atwood, M. (1981). The processes involved in designing software. In J. R. Anderson (ed.), *Cognitive Skills and Their Acquisition.* Hillsdale, NJ: Lawrence Erlbaum, pp. 225–283.

[21] Kintsch, W. & vanDijk, T. A. (1978). Toward a model of text comprehension and memory. *Psychological Review, 85,* 363–394.

[22] Malhorta, A., Thomas, J., Carroll, J. & Miller, L. (1980). Cognitive processes in design. *International Journal of Man-Machine Studies, 12,* 119–140.

[23] Meyer, B. (1988). *Object-Oriented Software Construction.* Englewood Cliffs, NJ: Prentice Hall.

[24] Pennington, N. (1987). Stimulus structures and mental representations in expert comprehension of computer programs. *Cognitive Psychology, 19,* 295–341.

[25] Rau, L., Jacobs, P. & Zernik, U. (1989). Information extraction and text summarization using linguistic knowledge acquisition. *Information Procedures and Management, 25,* 419–428.

[26] Rist, R. (1986). Plans in programming: Definition, demonstration, and development. In E. Soloway & S. Iyengar (eds.), *Empirical Studies of Programmers.* Norwood, NJ: Ablex.

[27] Rist, R. (1990). Variability in program design: The interaction of process with knowledge. *International Journal of Man-Machine Studies, 33,* 305–322.

[28] Robertson, S. (1990). Knowledge representations used by computer programmers. *Journal of the Washington Academy of Sciences, 80,* 116–137.

[29] Robertson, S. & Yu, C. C. (1990). Common cognitive representations of program code across tasks and languages. *International Journal of Man-Machine Studies, 33,* 343–360.

[30] Rolland, C. & Proix, C. (1992). Natural language approach to conceptual modeling. In P. Loucopoulos & R. Zicari (eds.), *Conceptual Modeling, Databases, and CASE: An Integrated View of Systems Development.* New York: Wiley, pp. 447–463.

[31] Rumbaugh, J., Blaha, M., Premerlani, W., Eddy, F. & Lorensen, W. (1991). *Object-Oriented Modeling and Design.* Englewood Cliffs, NJ: Prentice Hall.

[32] Shlaer, S. & Mellor, S. (1988). *Object-Oriented Systems Analysis.* Englewood Cliffs, NJ: Prentice Hall.

[33] Soloway, E., Adelson, B. & Ehrlich, K. (1988). Knowledge and processes in the comprehension of computer programs. In M. Chi, R. Glaser & M. Farr (eds.), *The Nature of Expertise.* Hillsdale, NJ: Lawrence Erlbaum.

[34] Soloway, E. & Ehrlich, K. (1984). Empirical studies of programming knowledge. *IEEE Transactions on Software Engineering, 5,* 595–609.

[35] vanDijk, T. A. & Kintsch, W. (1983). *Strategies of Discourse Comprehension.* New York: Academic Press.

[36] Velardi, P., Pazienza, M. T. & Magrini, S. (1989). Acquisition of semantic patterns from a natural corpus of texts. *SIGART Newsletter, 108*, 115–123.

[37] Visser, W. (1990). More or less following a plan during design: Opportunistic deviations in specification. *International Journal of Man-Machine Studies, 33,* 247–278.

[38] Wirfs-Brock, R., Wilkerson, B. & Wiener, L. (1990). *Designing Object-Oriented Software.* Englewood Cliffs, NJ: Prentice Hall.

CHAPTER 12

The Use-Case Construct in Object-Oriented Software Engineering

Ivar Jacobson
Objectory AB
Box 1128
Torshmnsgatan 39
S-164 22 Kista
Sweden

12.1 INTRODUCTION

System development is a process of model building. This is true also for object-oriented development, which typically begins with a requirements model and ends with an implementation model. Object models include details such as the internal structure of the objects, their associations to each other and how the objects dynamically interact and invoke behavior of one another. This information is, of course, necessary to design and build a system, but it is not enough in order to communicate requirements. It does not capture task domain knowledge and it is difficult to verify that an object model really corresponds to the system that should be built.

The very first system model you build must therefore be comprehensible by people both inside the development organization—analysts, designers, implementors, and testers—and outside—customers, users, and salespeople. Object models are too complex for this purpose: A real but still rather small system (one that takes two to five man-years to build) consists of about 100 objects. A larger system (10 to 100 man-years) consists of several hundred or several thousand objects. And some systems have 10,000 to 100,000 objects!

We therefore do not think the very first model of a complex system should be an object model. Instead, it should be a model that describes the system, its environment, and how it and its environment are related. In other words, it should describe the system as it appears from the outside; that is, a black-box view.

Use cases are a way to structure this black-box view. A use case is just what it sounds like: It is a way to use the system. Users interact with a system by interacting with its use cases. Taken together, a system's use cases represent everything users can do with it. For a more comprehensive presentation of use cases see [14]. We advocate that developers model use cases explicitly at the very start of a software development project. In every project, no matter what method, use cases must be identified—sooner or later, more or less clear—if the project is to be successful. At the latest they are identified during integration testing or when the user manual is written—activities that are, by nature, use-case oriented. However, by identifying them early, during system specification, the entire development will benefit.

Use cases are the "things" a developer sells to customers. It is essential that the buyers and builders of a system agree on this black-box view. If you can identify early on all the ways the system will be used and then control development so that the system offers these ways, you will know you are building the right system.

In this chapter, we describe the use-case construct and different modeling techniques associated with use cases during different activities in the development work. The description is general in the sense that the techniques are applicable to most object modeling techniques and not delimited to a particular object-oriented design method.

12.2 USE CASES

Use cases have two important roles:

1. They capture a system's functional requirements.

A *use-case model* defines a system's behavior (and associated information) through a set of use cases. The environment of the system is defined by describing the different users. The different users then use the system through a number of use cases.

A use-case model does not replace object models—one or more object models is developed orthogonal to the use-case model. The use-case model is an external view of a system; the object model is an internal view of the same system.

2. They structure each object model into a manageable view.

Although it is easy to build object models for toy systems, object models for real systems are unavoidably complex, as mentioned above. We have seen hundreds of examples of how object modeling can be applied to systems such as cruise control, conference management, and home heating systems. The problem with all these examples is that they don't reveal the complexity of real system development such as applications for banking, insurance, defense, and telecommunication. Methods that may seem to work well for these simple applications do not neccessarily scale up.

In order to manage the complexity of a real system it is practical to present its object models in a number of different views. In our approach, one view is drawn for each use case, and for each view you model, only those objects that participate in that use case. A particular object may, of course, participate in several use cases. This means that a complete object model is seen through a set of object model views—one per use case. You can now find all the responsibilities [17] of an object by looking through all use cases where this object has a role. Every role of an object means a responsibility for the object. The total responsibility of an object is received by integrating all its responsibilities. If the model is a design model then you can implement the responsibilities of each object straightforwardly. In the simplest case a design object will be a class coded, for example, in C++.

In this chapter we also have to use a simple application—an automated teller machine (ATM)—as an example to describe how to capture its functionality in a use-case model.

12.3 AN EXAMPLE

At an ATM, a customer can perform simple banking transactions, such as withdrawing money, without visiting a cashier. To accomplish this, the ATM must communicate with a central bank system to update the account balance before it dispenses cash (Figure 12.1). The central bank system stores all the information about customers, their accounts, and the personal identification number (PIN) associated with each card. When a customer performs a transaction at the ATM, the central bank system has control over verifying the PIN code and updating the account balance.

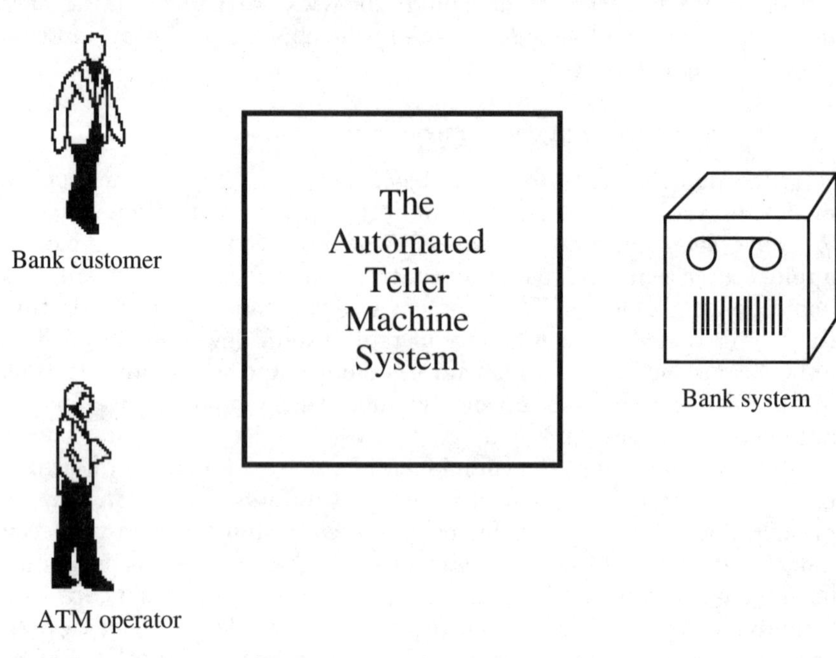

Figure 12.1. Overview of the ATM.

Customers can also deposit money or transfer funds between accounts at an ATM. In both cases, the ATM must inform the central bank system so it will know the correct balance of all accounts.

When the ATM must request some information, for example, the PIN, from the customer, it displays a message on a screen. The customer answers the request through a keypad. Finally, at the end of any transaction, the customer receives a receipt with the information about the transaction and his or her account balance.

(We realize that security is a very important issue in a system like this, but we will not address this aspect so as to simplify the explanation of the system.)

12.4 USE-CASE MODELING

In this section, we present the constructs used to build a use-case model. We will interleave precise definitions of their syntax and semantics with their application to the ATM example.

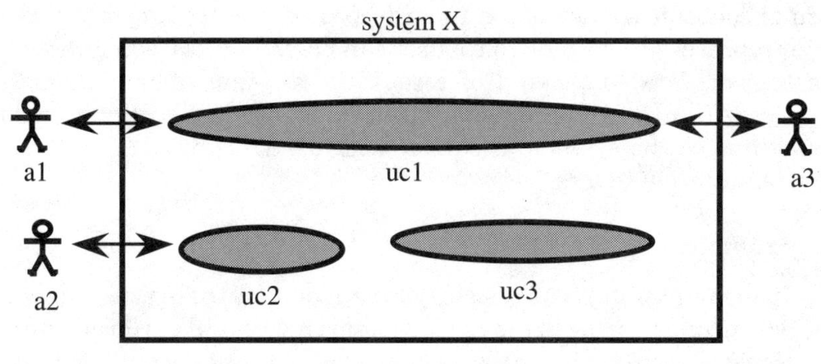

Figure 12.2. A use-case model (a1–a3 are actors and uc1–uc3 are use cases).

A *use-case model* is a graph with two types of nodes, *actor* nodes and *use-case* nodes. It has a name—the system name. See Figure 12.2 for a schematic example.

Attached to each actor node is a *name* and an *actor class*. Actor node names are unique.

Attached to each use-case node is a *name* and a *use-case class*. Use-case node names are unique within the scope of the system.

An actor node has an arc to at least one use-case node, and a use-case node has an arc to at least one actor node. These arcs are denoted *communication* arcs.

An instance of an actor can create instances of use cases (actually of use-case classes)—a use-case instance obeys its class. A communication arc between an actor node and a use-case node means that stimuli can be sent between instances of the actor class and instances of the use case or the use-case class itself. The latter case is relevant when new use-case instances are created.

12.4.1 Actor Pragmatics

Actors are objects that reside outside the modeled system; use cases are objects that reside inside the system. Actors are what interact with the system and are created outside the control of our modeling tools. They represent everything that has a need to exchange information with the system. Nothing else outside the system has any impact on the system. Actors may be implemented both as humans and as other systems.

We make a difference between actors and users; users are not a formal concept. A user is a human who uses the system, whereas an actor represents a specific role a user can play. Actors are instances of a class; users are some kind of resource that "implements" these instances. An instance of an actor class exists only when the user does something to the system. The same user can thus act as instances of several different actors.

Example:

In modeling our ATM system, you can identity three types of actors. The primary actor is the bank customer, who will perform transactions; you are building the system for this type of actor. Then there is the operator, who will maintain and support the system. Finally, there is the bank computer, which must be informed of transactions that bank customers perform.

Thus, there are three different actors:

- Bank customer
- ATM operator
- Bank system

12.4.2 Use-Case Pragmatics

When an actor uses it, the system performs a *use case*. The collection of use cases is the complete functionality of the system. In the same way as with actors, the use case is a class that can be instantiated. When a use case is performed, this is a class instance, which exists as long as the use case is operating.

What Is a *Good* Use Case? A *good use case* when instantiated is a sequence of transactions performed by a system, which yields a measurable result of values for a particular actor. Let us look more closely at two of the keywords here:

- *A measurable result of values*—The keyword is important in obtaining use cases that are not too small. A use case shall make sure that an actor can perform a task that has an identifiable value. It can be considered possible to put a price or a value on a successfully performed use case. In certain circumstances, it is possible to use a use case as a planning unit in the organization that includes the actor. For example, a user of a CASE tool for method support can be offered the use cases Identify Object Model and Specify an Object.

- *A particular actor*—The keyword is important in obtaining use cases that are not too large. It is important to begin with individual (human) actors, that is, instances of actors. A good hint when determining suitable actors is to name at least two different people, who would be able to perform as the individual actor. Assume that you are developing a CASE tool. It can be seen that an actor, in this example the user, is really two different actors. It can be a developer, someone who develops systems using the CASE tool as a support. It can also be a system administrator, someone who manages the CASE tool. Each of these two actors will have their own demands on the system, and therefore require their own set of use cases.

Thus you can look at use cases as long transaction objects with states that you can manipulate by communicating with them. The main difference between what you usually think of as an object and a use case is that objects can communicate with other objects within the same system, whereas a use case can communicate only with actors outside the system, not with other use cases.

Where Do Use Cases Come From? Use-case modeling is preceded by an envisioning activity in which users participate to find the use cases and the associated user interfaces. It is very appropriate to carry out the envisioning work as a series of workshops in which user interface designers are observers and users are the center of interest. Users are observed in the workplace, they are interviewed and asked to describe in an episodic way different use scenarios (use-case instances). As a means to better understand the users' needs, sketches of the user interface evolve and, when these have become stable and not before, prototypes can be developed. This kind of use-oriented design (usability testing and so on) is very important in understanding the envisioning work.

Example:

There are three actors and four use cases shown in Figure 12.3. "Cash withdrawal" is an example of a use case for a bank customer. A bank customer must be able to withdraw money from his or her account. Other use cases that might be interesting are "transfer funds" and "deposit funds." Are these use cases not too small? Should these all be one single use case? Probably, but in this example you have to treat them as separate use cases to demonstrate use-case modeling for real systems.

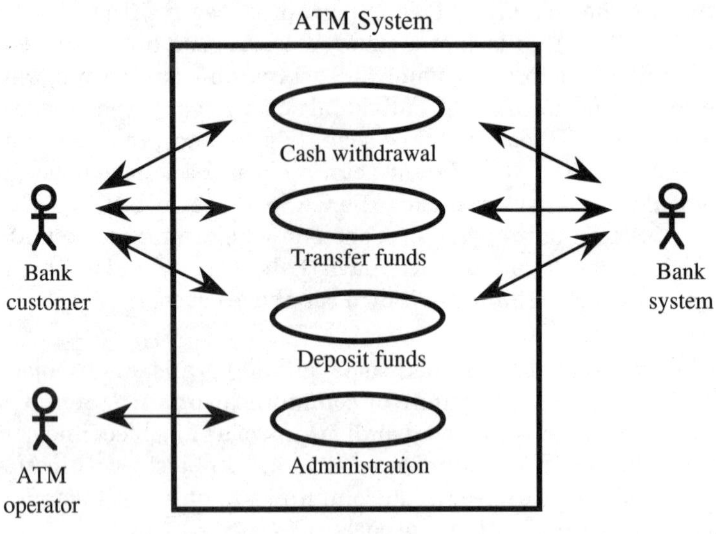

Figure 12.3. Example of a use-case model.

The ATM operator wants to perform the use case "Administration."

The bank system must interact with the first three use cases, which also interact with the bank customer.

How Are Use Cases Different from Scenarios? Use cases resemble use scenarios as used by some authors in the object-oriented world. However, there are several differences, syntactic as well as semantic. Scenarios normally mean use-case instances and there is no equivalent to use-case classes. Use cases are treated more formally, and described in a model of their own, as well as in interactions between objects in different object models. Scenarios are normally described as interactions between objects only.

12.4.3 Use-Case Classes

A *use-case class* can be modeled as a state machine. An instance of a use case traverses states of this machine during its lifetime. A state represents here the potential of the use case (instance). Which continuation the use case will follow from its current state is dependent on which stimulus it will receive. A received stimulus from an actor (instance) will cause the use case to leave its current state and perform a transaction; which one depends on the state-stimulus combination. The transaction includes manipulation of internal attributes of the use case and outputs to actors. These can be the ones that created the use case or other actors that have been involved during the course of the use case. The transaction is finished when the use case again has entered a state (possibly the same one) and awaits another stimulus from an actor.

Traditional information systems have use cases that are simpler and are usually not modeled as state machines. If these use cases can be viewed as having only one state, then the state machine model may seem unnecessarily complex. In these cases a simpler model could be used.

Hence, the use-case model is represented by several actors and use cases. When the system is in operation, instances are created from the classes in this model. Each use-case class has a description, which is crucial for understanding the system requirements and for finding the actual objects in the system. For the time being, we recommend that you describe the behavior of use cases informally, in structured English.

Example:

So the Cash withdrawal use case is as follows:

A normal course

A greeting message is waiting on the display:
The customer inserts his or her card into the ATM (see Figure 12.4).
The ATM reads the code from the magnetic tape on the card and checks if it is acceptable.
If the card is acceptable, the ATM asks the customer for his or her PIN code.

Waiting for PIN code:
The customer enters his or her PIN code.
If the PIN code is correct, the ATM asks the customer to select a type of transaction.

Waiting for transaction type:
The customer selects the cash withdrawal function, and the ATM will send the PIN code to the bank system and ask the bank system for the customer's accounts.
The account numbers that are received will be displayed to the customer.

Waiting for the customer to decide:
The customer selects an account and keys the amount to be withdrawn.

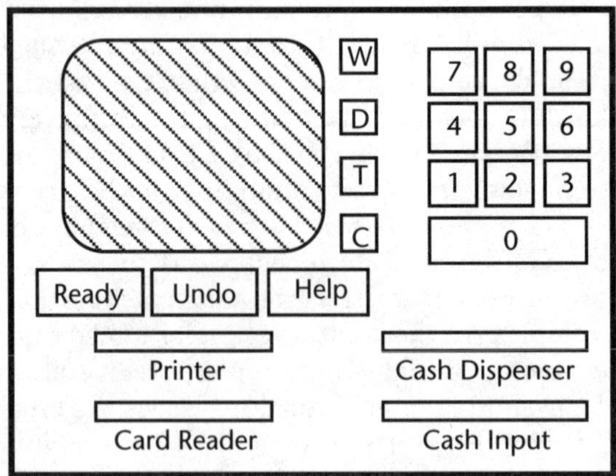

Figure 12.4. The bank customer user interface.

The ATM sends a request to the bank system for the withdrawal of the amount from the specified account.
The bills are prepared to be dispensed.
The card is ejected from the ATM to the customer.
The receipt is printed and given to the customer.
The bills are dispensed to the customer.

Alternative courses

The card is not acceptable:
If the card is not acceptable because the magnetic tape on the card is not readable or if it is of the wrong type, then the card is ejected with a bip.

Incorrect PIN code:
If the PIN code is incorrect, a message will be displayed to the customer, who is given a chance to enter the correct code.

Not allowed to withdraw:
If the bank system does not accept the withdrawal, a message informing the customer is displayed in 10 seconds and the card is ejected.

Cancel:
The customer can always cancel the transaction at all times when he or she is asked for some information. This will result in an ejection of the card and the end of the transaction.

As seen above, a use case has a number of alternative courses that may carry the use case through a different flow. As many as possible of these alternative courses, often erroneous courses, should be noted when the use case is specified.

12.5 USE-CASE INTERACTION—WHAT CAN AND WHAT CANNOT BE MODELED?

Because the use-case model should express only an external view of the system, we made several important decisions about what can and cannot be expressed in the model:

1. Internal communication among occurrences inside the system must not be modeled. So use-case instances that are the only objects in this model must not communicate with one another. Otherwise, you would have to specify interfaces among use cases.
2. Conflicts between use-case instances must not be expressed in the model. In the implemented system, instances of use cases will obviously affect one another. These relations are certainly very important, but they are internal details that should not to be expressed here. These could be expressed in an object model of the entire system, realizing the whole set of integrated use cases.
3. Use-case models will not express concurrency. Instead, we assume that use cases are interpreted one instance and one transaction at a time; you may say that the system is sliced into use cases and that use-case transactions are atomic and serialized.
4. The use-case model can express only class associations.

In this way you get a use-case model, which can be used to understand the requirements of the system and for agreement between people who order the system and people who develop the system. In some cases it would be very interesting to simulate the system at an early stage. With the above stipulations made, the use-case model cannot be used. Instead we suggest an early object model for this purpose. In *Object-Oriented Software Engineering—A Use-Case Driven Approach* [14] we suggest use of the analysis object model.

12.6 ASSOCIATIONS BETWEEN USE CASES

Now we will continue to present the basics of use-case modeling. In particular, we will present class associations between use cases. (These ideas were first introduced in [11] and further elaborated on in [14].)

Real systems may contain a large number of use cases. From our experience, a smaller system (two to five man-years) might include something like 3 to 20 use cases. A medium-sized system (10–100 man-years) might include 10 to 60 use cases. Larger systems such as applications for banking, insurance, defense, and telecommunication may contain hundreds of use cases.

To produce an intelligible use-case model, you need a way to relate the use cases to one another, avoid redundancy between use cases, and describe use cases in a layered way.

We do this with association arcs: Use-case nodes can be interconnected with arcs of two types: *uses* arcs and *extends* arcs.

12.6.1 The Uses Association

When developing real applications with several use cases it is normal to find use cases with similar descriptions. In order to avoid redundancy and to enhance reuse you need means to extract the similar descriptions and to share these between different use cases. We say that these shared descriptions are descriptions of abstract use cases and that the original use cases—those that share descriptions—are concrete use cases. The numbers we gave above all refer to concrete use cases.

> ***Example:***
>
> In the ATM example, it is obvious that several use cases will share the sequence that checks the card and the PIN code. In the "Cash withdrawal" use case, we see this sequence in Initialization steps 1 to 4. It will also show up when the bank customer transfers or deposits funds.

We call that part of a use case extracting an *abstract* use case because it will not be instantiated on its own, but is meaningful only to describe parts shared among other use cases. Use cases that really will be instantiated are *concrete* use cases.

> ***Example:***
>
> Here you might identify an abstract use case that checks the card and its PIN code. This abstract use case, called Card transaction, is used by concrete use-case sequences as a subsequence.

Formally, a uses arc between two use cases, for instance, Cash withdrawal and Card transaction, means that a use-case instance, which is created and obeys the concrete class Cash withdrawal, will, as instructed by this class, obey an abstract class Card Transaction. Only concrete use cases can be instantiated, whereas abstract ones cannot.

You break out abstract use cases like the one in Figure 12.5 so that you design them only once and then reuse them in other use cases. Experience shows that you should wait to identify abstract use cases until you have described several concrete use cases. Abstract use cases should evolve from concrete use cases, not the other way around.

We describe abstract use cases as we do other use cases, such as the previously described Cash withdrawal. The modified use case class Cash withdrawal will then specify how it uses Card transaction. It will also describe what it uses of the abstract use case's class.

The uses association is very close to an inheritance association, but because the semantics of this kind of inheritance have not been formally defined, we give it another denomination. Uses between use cases can also be multiple uses (compare with multiple inheritance). Several common parts may have been extracted out of a concrete use case into a number of abstract use cases since several use cases share these parts. In other words, a specific concrete use case can then use all these abstract use cases.

In use-case sharing, the entire abstract use-case class is always used. The shared use-case class need not be one single transaction description or part of a transaction description, although this is often the case. Instead, you may have a situation where the uses association means that the shared transaction descriptions are interleaved into a concrete use-case class (see Figure 12.6).

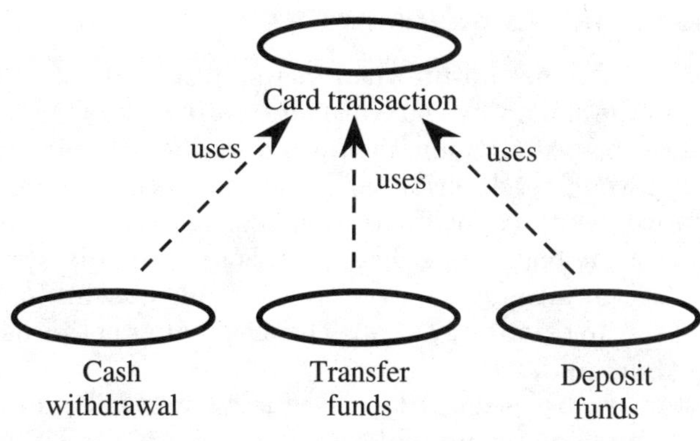

Figure 12.5. The uses association to describe sharing between use cases.

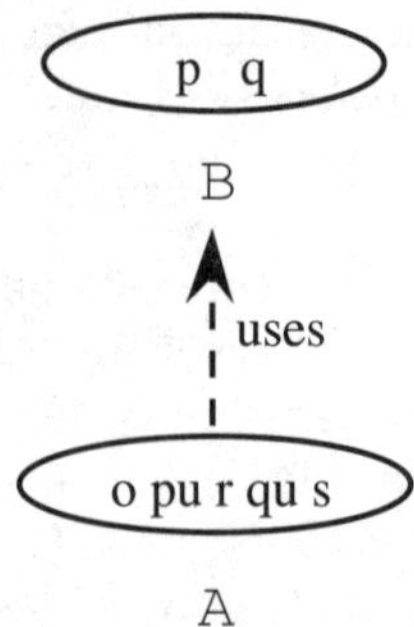

Figure 12.6. The concrete use case A uses an abstract use case B and decides how to interleave the parts from B.

For example, in the description of the abstract use case B, p and q are parts of transaction descriptions that will be interleaved with r and s in describing the concrete use case A. The notation pu and qu means "use" p and q, respectively.

So an instance of the use-case class A will, during its obeyance of A (after obeying o), be instructed to use p and then continue to follow A's part r, and so forth. Within a use-case description there may be several different atomic sequences like o p_u r q_u s, where o normally is initiated by the reception of an input stimulus.

12.6.2 The Extends Association

The extends arc lets us capture the functional requirements of a complex system in the same way you learn about any new subject: First you understand the basic functions, then you introduce complexity. In use-case modeling, you first describe the basic use cases and then describe how to enhance them to allow more advanced use cases, some of which may depend on the basic ones. The extends arc not only supports the development of an intelligible structure, it is also useful to introduce new use cases to an existing system. (The pragmatics of this association are discussed in [10].)

The use-case class where the new functionality should be added should be a complete, meaningful course of events in itself. Hence, its description is entirely independent of the extended course. In this way, the description pays no attention to any courses that can be inserted, and this complexity is thus avoided. You describe the first basic use-case classes totally independently of any extended functionality. Similarly, you can add new extensions without changing the original descriptions.

Example:

Suppose you want to collect statistics on how often Cash withdrawal is used. To do this, you could extend the use case Cash withdrawal (Figure 12.7). Every time you execute Cash withdrawal, another use case counts and accumulates the number of times this transaction has been used.

In this way you gain two things. First, the original use-case description is easy to understand because it is not loaded down with the extension. Second, the extension is very clearly separated from other behavior descriptions.

An extends arc from one use case to another, for instance, from Gathering withdrawal statistics to Cash withdrawal, means that a use-case instance that obeys class Cash withdrawal will, as instructed by the other class, interrupt the interpretation of Cash withdrawal and instead obey Gathering withdrawal statistics. Later, the instance can once again obey its original class.

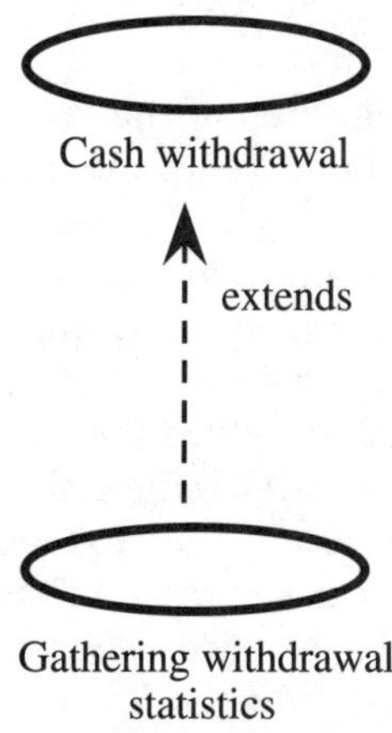

Figure 12.7. A common situation is having one use case collecting statistics regarding another use case, thus extending the other use case.

Thus, extends is used to model extensions to other, complete use cases. You use extends to model:

- Optional parts of use cases
- Complex and alternative courses
- Subsequences that are executed only in certain cases
- The insertion of several different use cases into another use case, for example, Card transaction or a menu system with options

To get an appreciation for the extends association, we would like to present some experimental use of it. We studied a very large application (more than 100 man-years), which had been designed using an object-based approach. The existing design consisted of a number of objects interconnected through well-defined interfaces.

We studied two alternatives:

1. Redesigning the system without the extends association. In this case, we had to first design about 80 percent of all known functional requirements in the first release and were then able to add the remaining 20 percent without having to modify the first release.
2. Redesigning the system with the extends association (and its corresponding programming language support and tools, as indicated in [10]). In this case, we had to first design about 20 percent of all known functional requirements in the first release and were then able to add the remaining 80 percent as extensions, without changing the first release. With the right programming tools, it would be possible to add more than half of the extensions without even having to test that they did not cause any damage to the first release.

This experiment shows that using extends gives us an opportunity to reduce software-development costs dramatically since it allows us to add even larger increments to a system without changing what already exists. In other words, you can reduce the complexity of maintaining a software system and thus greatly reduce the costs for the continuous development of the system. Even if the extends association is not supported in the programming environment but is used only in analysis, it gives us a more structured (the word used in its normal sense) way to understand a system's requirements. To a much greater degree than would otherwise be possible, extends lets us introduce requirements in layers: first basic functionality and later more advanced functionality, without having to modify the basic functionality.

12.6.3 The Uses versus the Extends Association

As with the uses association the extends association may also be viewed as a type of inheritance association. But there are important differences between the uses and extends associations.

Suppose you have three use-case classes: Cash withdrawal, Gathering withdrawal statistics, and Supervising withdrawal behavior. You have introduced a new extended use case, Supervising withdrawal behavior, which allows the designers of the ATM system to learn more about how people really use their system.

Only Cash withdrawal will be instantiated. The other two classes include extends associations to Cash withdrawal. An instance of Cash withdrawal will, during its lifetime, obey behavior as specified by its class and extend it as specified by the other two classes. These extensions may be conditional—inserted only when a specific condition is valid (Figure 12.8).

Why not employ uses associations instead of extends associations? There are two ways to do this:

1. Cash withdrawal uses Gathering withdrawal statistics and Supervising withdrawal behavior (Figure 12.9). That would mean that Cash withdrawal had references to the extensions, which would spoil the whole extensibility idea—that Cash withdrawal can be understood and developed independent of Gathering withdrawal statistics and Supervising withdrawal behavior.

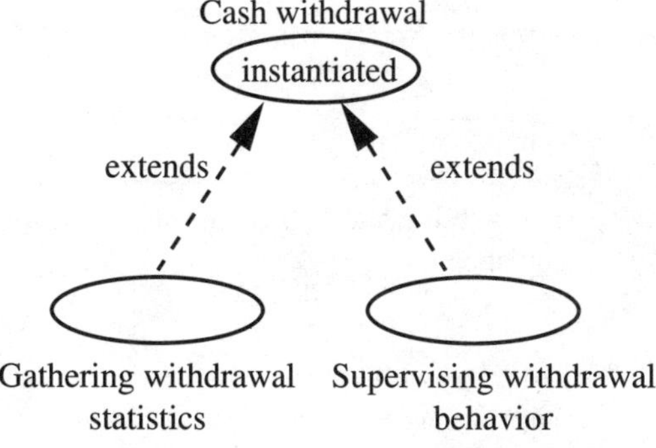

Figure 12.8. Only cash withdrawal will be instantiated.

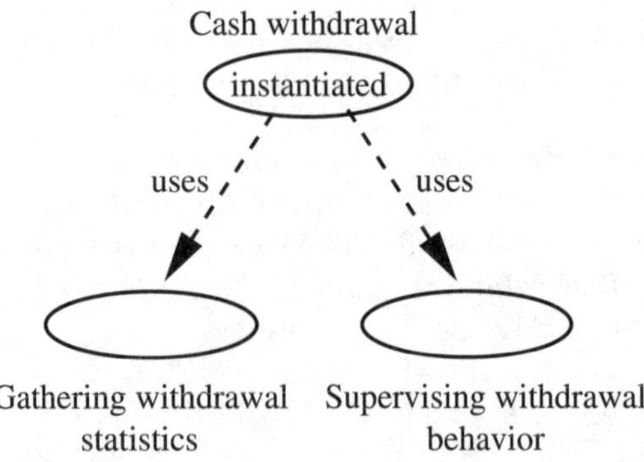

Figure 12.9. Uses instead of extends association—alternative 1.

2. Gathering withdrawal statistics and Supervising withdrawal behavior uses Cash withdrawal. This would not only require the use cases Gathering withdrawal statistics and Supervising withdrawal behavior but also a use case corresponding to a combination of these (Figure 12.10).

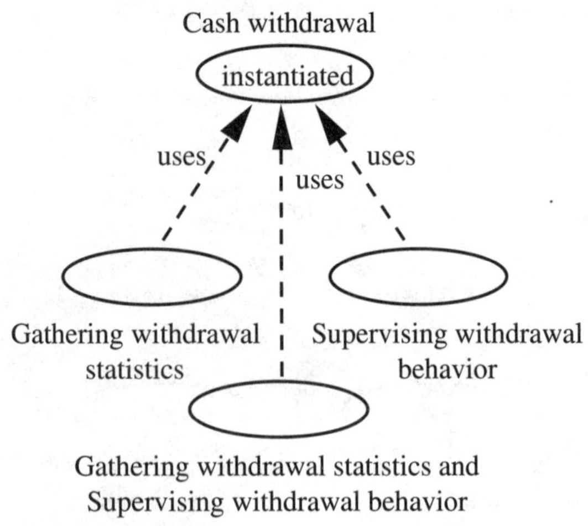

Figure 12.10. Uses instead of extends association—alternative 2.

> This is necessary in order to express the flexibility offered by the extends association, namely that Cash withdrawal can be extended by any combination of Gathering withdrawal statistics and Supervising withdrawal behavior. With many extensions this would be an unmanageable technique.

In fact, in most cases the choice between uses and extends is quite obvious and causes no problems. Uses are found through extraction of common sequences from several different use cases, whereas extends are found when new courses are introduced, or when there are extensions to an existing use case that the user wishes to perform in some specific cases.

12.7 THE USE-CASE MODEL VERSUS OBJECT MODELS

Use cases are used to communicate the requirements of a system and to drive the development of the system through different models, here object models, down to code. Each one of these models has its own particular role and is intended for its own interested parties. In *Object-Oriented Software Engineering—a Use-Case Driven Approach* (OOSE) [14], five different models are described: a use-case model intended for people who order the system and people who develop it, an optional ideal object model (an analysis model) for analysts, a real object model (a design model) for designers, an implementation model for programmers (and compilers), and a testing model for system testers.

The use cases capture the functional goals of the system. As design proceeds, designers eventually flesh out the use cases in terms of specific implementation techniques. You may describe design as a process of *hypothesis generation and validation*. That is, given a use case, you generate (as a hypothesis), using, for instance, the design principles of OOSE, one or more possible objects, and then in some way *validate it* against the original use case to determine if it is a good implementation with respect to some criteria. There is a *gap* between a use case, in the use-case model, and its actual design and implementation in terms of interacting objects. This gap is filled with details of how conflicts between use cases are solved, how concurrency is dealt with, and at the lowest level, how use cases are implemented in code.

Here we will not deal with the actual design process. We will assume that one way or the other you will identify the objects you need to realize your use cases, and we will describe how these use cases then can be represented in terms of your objects.

12.7.1 Traceability between Different Models

We will not discuss the different object models any further; it is enough to know that there are several object models. The associations among these models are important, of course, and add another dimension to the complexity in software development. To maintain the system, there must be support for *traceability*: You must be able to trace objects in one model to objects in another model.

The obvious way to do this is to simply relate an object in one model to its corresponding object(s) in the other model. Generally, it is not that simple to map an object in one model to exactly one object in another model. The target model may have been restructured because of issues such as the choice of an implementation language, database or computer architecture, or because of reuse of existing objects, and so forth.

However, by stipulating that you structure the object model one use case at a time, you can express traceability in a much more understandable way: For each use case there exists exactly one object view in each object model and these object views are related to one another. You reduce the problem of relating two object models to one of relating each use-case object view in one model to the same use-case object view in the other model. The total object model is the set of use-case object views *superimposed* on one another. We use two types of notations to map use cases to object models—object diagrams and interaction diagrams.

12.7.2 Object Diagrams

For each use case you prepare an object diagram, which shows the objects participating in the use case and their interdependencies. Use use-case description and your selected design method to identify candidate objects and their interaction to realize the use case. Then use an object diagram to describe the result.

Example:

Assume that the use case *Cash withdrawal* has arrived at an object diagram (using a strongly simplified notation for an OOSE real object model)—see Figure 12.11. (We discuss only the normal flow of events, not the exception handling.) The nodes in the object diagram are objects—classes or instances—and the arcs are associations.

As you can see, eight objects participate in (perform the behavior of) this use case. The first three—Bank Card Reader, Card Transaction, and Customer Panel—are the objects that participate

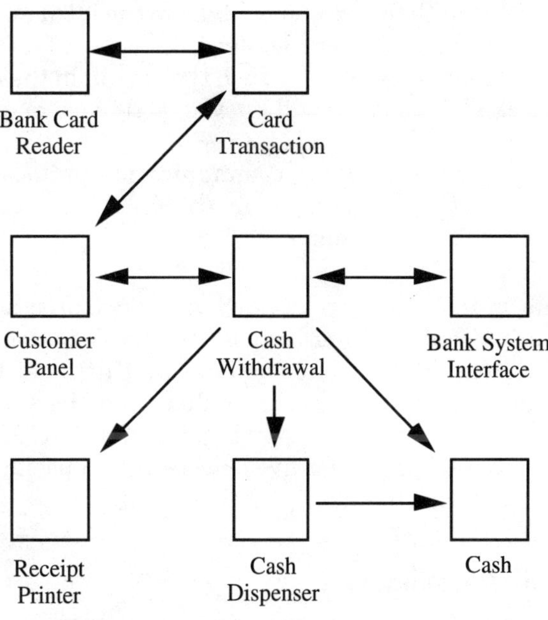

Figure 12.11. Object diagram for the use-case Cash withdrawal.

in the Card transaction use case, which is used by the Cash withdrawal use case. Here is a brief description of the eight objects. The descriptions are not complete, but they will give you an idea of what each object will do.

- Bank Card Reader will implement the card driver, a mix of hardware and software, for reading bank cards.
- Card Transaction will perform all the operations on the card information, initialize the Customer Panel, and perform all communication with the Customer Panel.
- Customer Panel will perform all communication with the customer; that is, display messages from the ATM and receive information entered by the customer.
- Receipt Printer will print receipts for the customers.
- Cash Dispenser will perform all operations on the real bills; that is, count and dispense money to the customer.
- Cash Withdrawal will coordinate the withdrawal transaction. It will initiate all the necessary communication with the cus-

tomer as well as the Bank system. It is also responsible for checking that there are enough bills in the ATM and a sufficient balance in the customer's account.

- Cash will hold a counter for each type of bill in the ATM. In this way, Cash Withdrawal will know exactly how many bills there are of each type in the ATM.
- Bank System Interface, a communication protocol, will transform the internal messages in the ATM to electrical signals sent to the Bank system.

In this system, you have decided to use two processes. The first will handle objects that interact with the Bank customer— that is, Bank Card Reader, Card Transaction, and Customer Panel. These objects will be able to receive stimulus from the Bank customer even if there is a transaction going on inside the ATM. The second process will handle the other five objects, which perform the transaction and dispense the money.

12.7.3 Interaction Diagrams

An interaction diagram shows how participating objects interact to offer the use case; one is required for each concrete use case.

Interaction takes place when objects send stimuli to one another. As you draw the interaction diagrams, you also define all the stimuli sent, including the parameters. The main purpose of this activity, which we call use-case design, is thus to identify the protocols of the objects.

Interaction diagrams have been used for many years in the telecommunications world to describe communication among hardware units. The author introduced these diagrams in 1968 for object-based design of software systems and in 1987 to the object-oriented community [11].

Example:

We will now look at the design of the use case *Cash withdrawal*. You distribute the text associated with the use case over the objects participating in the use case. The resulting interaction diagram is shown in Figure 12.12. How we arrived at this diagram is in itself a very interesting story, but we will not cover that here. Here we will assume that your method has helped you to do that work and we will show how you can represent your design.

In the interaction diagram you see that almost all events are directly triggered from an operation on the window. You thus have no complex sequences in this diagram. In this diagram you have only described the normal course of events. All error and exception handlings are shown in other interaction diagrams.

At the left edge of the interaction diagram, to the left of the system border, you describe the sequences—what is happening in precisely this part of the use case. This description is textual, either structured text or pseudocode, depending on the type of object model. If you are in the design process and use pseudocode, you should use constructs that exist in the current programming language, to ease migration to the actual implementation later. Parts of use cases are called *operations* (function, method, etc.). You also mark the column to which the operation belongs with a rectangle representing the operation. The textual description consequently belongs to the object where the operation takes place and where it later shall be refined, and whose column therefore is marked at the place of the operation.

You can also describe parallel sequences, for example, when several processes participate in a use case, in an interaction diagram by using caselike constructs.

The interaction diagrams are controlled by events. A new event gives rise to a new operation. These events are *stimuli,* which are sent from one object to another and initiate an operation. There is an alternative to interaction diagrams to describe how a use case is performed in terms of object interactions. That technique was introduced in [8] and means that you in principle annotate the associations in the object diagram with stimuli names and the order in which these stimuli are being sent. That technique is particularly useful for simpler use cases, but it does not scale up to describe larger use cases.

Generally, the concepts used here are generic terms. When we specialize to a specific implementation environment, we use its concepts. For example, when working in Ada we could talk about rendezvous messaging instead of stimuli.

12.8 BEST USES FOR USE CASES

Use cases play many different roles in modeling real, complex systems. Complex systems are software systems for financial applications, geographical-information systems, process-control systems, telecommunication systems, CAD/CAM, and more traditional information systems. Complex systems are also enterprise models for banks, manufacturers, insurance companies, and telecommunication administrations.

For what kinds of development work are use cases particularly well suited? We have already mentioned the following uses of use cases:

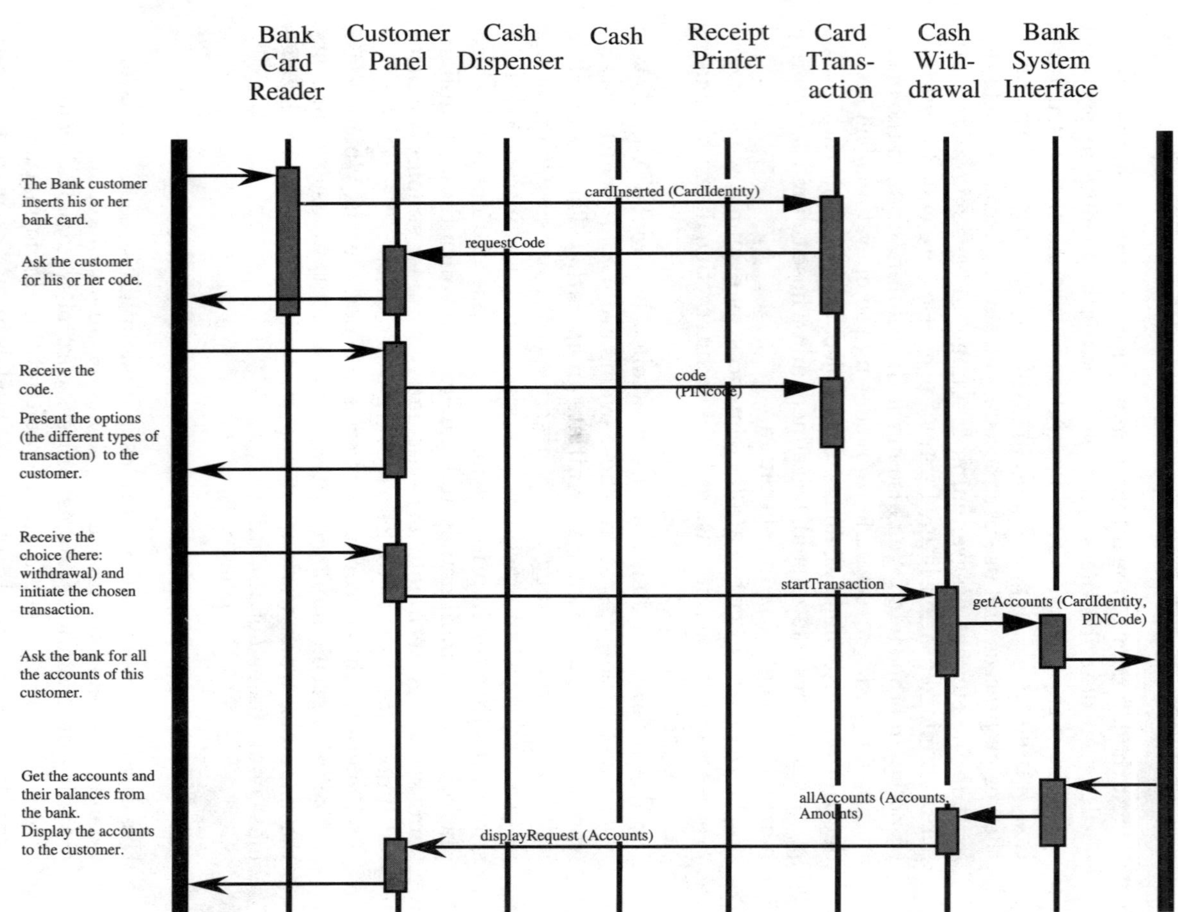
Bank Card Reader
Customer Panel
Cash Dispenser
Cash
Receipt Printer
Card Transaction
Cash Withdrawal
Bank System Interface
The Bank customer inserts his or her bank card.
cardInserted (CardIdentity)
requestCode
Ask the customer for his or her code.
Receive the code.
code (PINcode)
Present the options (the different types of transaction) to the customer.
Receive the choice (here: withdrawal) and initiate the chosen transaction.
startTransaction
getAccounts (CardIdentity, PINCode)
Ask the bank for all the accounts of this customer.
Get the accounts and their balances from the bank.
Display the accounts to the customer.
allAccounts (Accounts, Amounts)
displayRequest (Accounts)

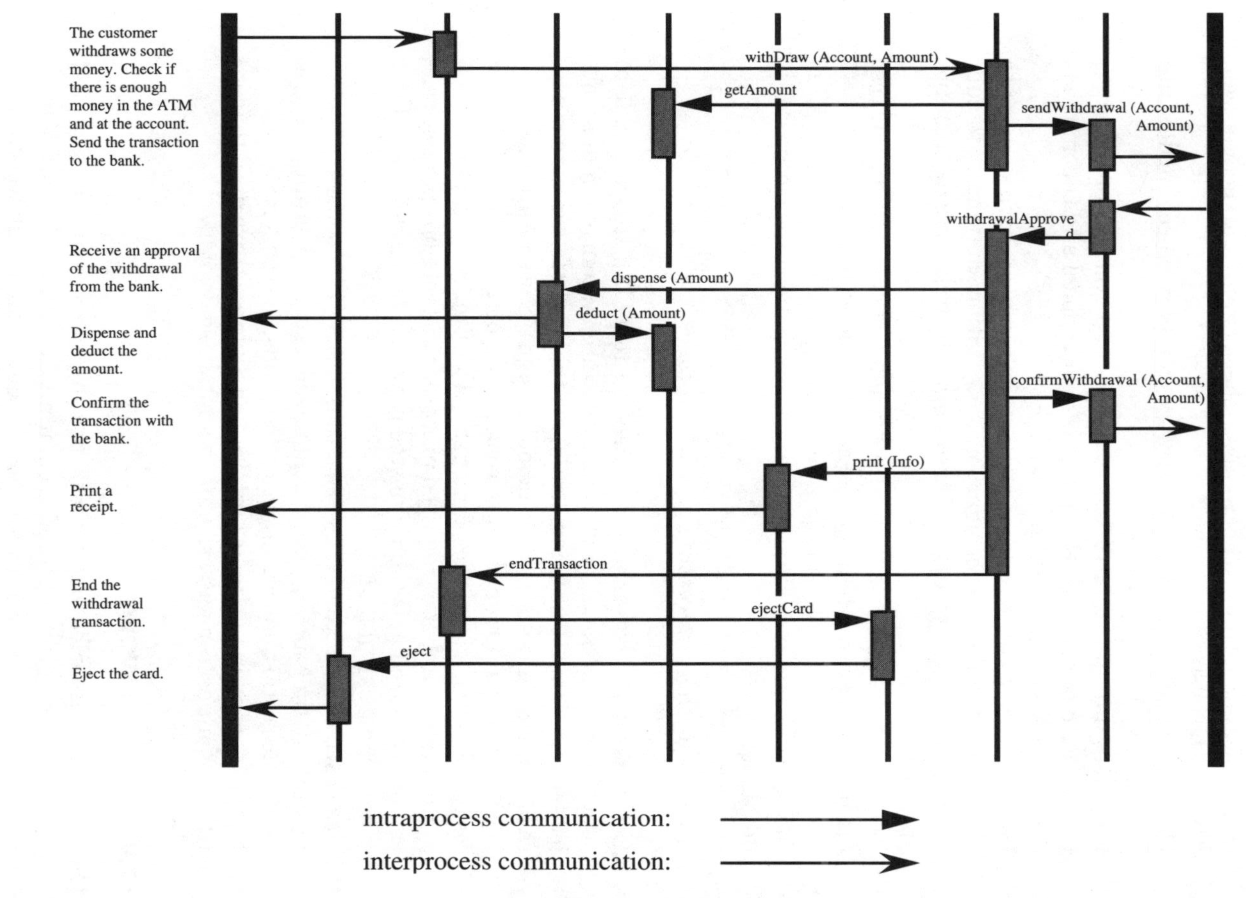
The customer withdraws some money. Check if there is enough money in the ATM and at the account. Send the transaction to the bank.
Receive an approval of the withdrawal from the bank.
Dispense and deduct the amount.
Confirm the transaction with the bank.
Print a receipt.
End the withdrawal transaction.
Eject the card.
withDraw (Account, Amount)
getAmount
sendWithdrawal (Account, Amount)
withdrawalApproved
dispense (Amount)
deduct (Amount)
confirmWithdrawal (Account, Amount)
print (Info)
endTransaction
ejectCard
eject
intraprocess communication:
interprocess communication:

Figure 12.12. The interaction diagram for the use case Cash withdrawal.

- Use cases are a tool to model the system from an external viewpoint, a black-box view. This view is essential for the sake of agreement between people who request the system and people who develop the system.
- Use cases can be used to structure a complex object model into manageable views.
- Use cases bind together different models of a system, for instance, the use-case model with the analysis object model and the analysis object model with the design model.
- Use cases are a tool to organize the developer's work, from sales to requirements analysis, design, implementation (optionally including the operating system and the computer architecture), testing, and operation.
- Use cases are test cases in the integration test of a system. The test planning can start when the use cases are identified.
- Use cases are also the source when writing the user manual. Thus the work with the manual can start when the use-case model is developed.

These are other interesting uses of use cases:

- Use cases are a powerful reengineering tool [12]. It is difficult to capture the functionality of an old software system, even of an object-oriented one. But it is normally rather easy to recreate a use-case model and map it onto the old design. (Several projects have been carried out using this approach as reported in [13].)
- Use cases can be used to dimension the processor capacity of a system. The number of required processor instructions per use case can be measured and the requested capacity for a given mix of use cases can be calculated.
- Use cases can be treated as execution objects in a software implementation, they may be atomic change objects in a running system, or atomic restart objects at error situations, and so forth.
- Use cases (and in particular interaction diagrams) are used to identify efficient access patterns for the database design.

12.9 RELATED WORK

The use-case construct has been in use for many years. It was first presented to the object-oriented community in 1987 [11], but it (or a similar construct) has been used for the development of object-based systems since 1967. (See [7, 8, 9] for earlier papers on this topic.)

The CRC-card approach in Beck and Cunningham [6] uses a similar idea, called *execution scenario,* in a refreshingly informal way. A system's design evolves by going through a number of execution scenarios and identifying classes participating in each scenario. Each class gets a card, on which is written the name of the class, its responsibilities, and its collaborators. This approach is excellent for teaching object-oriented thinking, but in our view it is too simple to develop and maintain real systems—even if some people use it for that purpose today.

Responsibilities [17] of the system (viewed as an object) are close to use cases. A particular responsibility of a specific object within the system is that part of a use case that is requested by the specific object.

Scenarios in Rumbaugh et al. [16] are intended to serve as use-case instances. The definitions, however, are very loose. Scenarios are described by event traces, which are similar to interaction diagrams (presented in [11]). This is a more practical notation than timing diagrams as sketched in Booch [1]. Use scenarios in Rubin and Goldberg [15] are also use-case instances, and scripts in the same reference are an alternative concrete syntax for interaction diagrams.

Threads [4] can be viewed as a generalization of use cases. Interesting work is being done on threads, particularly a notation for threads that is being developed [3].

Others [1, 2, 5] have introduced similar ideas—threads of execution, mechanisms, and scenarios—but the definitions, when they exist, are weak. Booch [2] now has adopted use cases and interaction diagrams but objects are found first and use cases as fixed object interactions later.

By now it may be clear why we have chosen the term *use case* instead of a term like *use scenario*. The term use case is more precise, like test case. We want to discuss all the ways a system is going to be used and we want to do that in a more and more formal way as we proceed to develop more and more detailed models of the system. When the system is implemented we want to be able to track a use case down to the code that implements it. Even in an operating system we want to be able to associate a use-case instance to executed instructions.

12.10 SUMMARY

Use-case modeling is an important tool to develop an outside view of a system. Combined with other techniques for human-computer interaction, it will help us to build systems with high usability. Furthermore, it is a powerful means of communication between different kinds of people participating in the development work, such as orderers, users, requirement analysts, designers, and testers.

Use cases play an important role in driving the whole development work and simplifying the traceability between different object models.

REFERENCES

[1] Booch, G. (1991). *Object-Oriented Design with Applications.* Redwood City, CA: Benjamin/Cummings.

[2] Booch, G. (1994). *Object-Oriented Analysis and Design with Applications.* 2d ed. Redwood City, CA: Benjamin/Cummings.

[3] Buhr, R. J. A. & Casselman, R. S. (1992a). Notations for threads. *Technical Report SCE-92-07,* Department of Systems and Computer Engineering, Carleton University, Ottawa, February.

[4] Buhr, R. J. A. & Casselman, R. S. (1992b). Architectures with pictures. *In Proceedings of OOPSLA'92,* October.

[5] Coad, P. & Yourdon, E. (1991). *Object-Oriented Analysis.* 2d ed. Englewood Cliffs, NJ: Prentice Hall.

[6] Beck, K. & Cunningham, W. (1989). A laboratory for teaching object-oriented thinking. In *Proceedings of OOPSLA'89,* Special Issue of *SIGPLAN Notices, 24,* 10(October): 1–6.

[7] Jacobson, I. (1983). On the development of an experience-based specification and description language. In *IEEE Proceedings of Software Engineering for Telecommunication Switching Systems,* July.

[8] Jacobson, I. (1985). *Concepts for Modeling Large Real Time Systems.* Department of Computer Systems, The Royal Institute of Technology, Stockholm, September.

[9] Jacobson, I. (1986a). FDL: A language for designing large real time systems. *In Proceedings of IFIP'86,* September.

[10] Jacobson, I. (1986b). Language support for changeable large real time systems. *In OOPSLA'86.* New York: ACM Press. Special Issue of *SIGPLAN Notices, 21,* 11(November).

[11] Jacobson, I. (1987). Object-oriented development in an industrial environment. In *Proceedings of OOPSLA'87,* Special Issue of *SIGPLAN Notices, 22,* 12 (December): 183–191.

[12] Jacobson, I. (1991). Industrial development of software with an object-oriented technique. *Journal of Object-Oriented Programming,* (March/April): 30–41.

[13] Jacobson, I. & Lindström, F. (1991). Re-engineering of old systems to an object-oriented architecture. In *OOPSLA'91.* New York: ACM Press, pp. 340–350.

[14] Jacobson, I., Christersson, M., Jonsson, P. & Övergaard, G. (1992). *Object-Oriented Software Engineering—A Use-Case Driven Approach.* Reading, MA: Addison-Wesley.

[15] Rubin, K. & Goldberg, A. (1992). Object behavior analysis. *Communications of ACM, 35,* 9(September): 48–62.

[16] Rumbaugh, J., Blaha, M., Premerlani, W., Eddy, F. & Lorensen, W. (1991). *Object-Oriented Modeling and Design.* Englewood Cliffs, NJ: Prentice Hall.

[17] Wirfs-Brock, R., Wilkerson, B. & Wiener, L. (1990). *Designing Object-Oriented Software.* Englewood Cliffs, NJ: Prentice Hall.

CHAPTER 13

Designing Objects and Their Interactions: A Brief Look at Responsibility-Driven Design

Rebecca Wirfs-Brock

Digitalk, Inc.
7585 S.W. Mohawk Street
Tualatin, OR 97062
USA

13.1 INTRODUCTION

The approach one takes to define and describe objects has profound impacts on the resulting software design. This chapter describes some important principles of the object modeling technique called *responsibility-driven design* [1, 2]. This approach draws upon the experiences of a number of very successful and productive SmallTalk designers. The concepts and motivation behind responsibility-driven design were initially formulated when several of us developed and taught a course on object-oriented design to Tektronix engineers [3]. These engineers were working on object-oriented projects, which would be implemented in SmallTalk, C++, and other non-object-oriented programming languages.

Since the early days at Tektronix, our design notions and modeling techniques have evolved to meet needs of developers from a variety of backgrounds. We developed several significant object designs ourselves and reviewed numerous designs for batch processing, interactive client/server, and even embedded hardware control applications. We have taught design to hundreds of business system analysts and programmers from dozens of companies. Our modeling techniques have been used in many different contexts.

Responsibility-driven design places great emphasis on informal techniques for describing objects, their roles, responsibilities, and interactions. We focus on describing what objects *do* and *how they behave* first, then address other object model aspects. The central idea behind responsibility-driven design is to develop a model of cooperating, communicating objects. Our focus is in sharp contrast to object design methods that emphasize formal descriptions of object structure and internal state. Responsibility-driven design focuses on the dynamics of an object design. In contrast, the OMT method [4] emphasizes static, structural models and constraints between objects, while the Booch method [5, 6] offers extremely rich notations for modeling object state, messaging, and real-time communication models.

Novices find responsibility-driven design techniques to be readily approachable and a good way to ease into *object think*. Experienced designers, as well, benefit from our focus on objects and how to appropriately distribute responsibilities [7]. Other methods that emphasize object behavior include Object Behavior Analysis [8] and Object-Oriented Role Analysis and Software Synthesis [9].

Our method provides a conceptual framework for building an initial model of interacting, cooperating objects. This model is purposefully vague about certain aspects of the design. For example, we view precise, formal descriptions of internal object structure and storage as more properly deferred to later in design or even during application construction. Once object roles and collaborative behaviors are understood, many different design perspectives can be detailed.

13.1.1 Goals for the Design Process

Initially we had several goals for describing an object-oriented design process. We wanted to encourage exploring alternatives early on, while providing guidelines and design strategies for improving upon initial decisions. We wanted designers to first develop a high-level view of how key objects in their application interact, before filling out precise details for individual classes of objects. We wanted them to concentrate on the dynamics of their model. In our experience, we found it all too easy for engineers to focus in on minute technical design details and lose sight of why they are developing their applications and even what good design practices to follow. As a practical matter, it is much easier to consider, refine, and even discard ideas up front before major investments in detailed design or coding have been made. With each new refinement comes further insights and change. It is important, in our view, not to force design decisions before there is enough knowledge to make intelligent tradeoffs. Getting a design to gel involves making assumptions, seeing how they play out, adjusting one's ideas or perspective slightly, and reiterating. Design is a difficult, involved task. It is inherently nonlinear. Yet, developers must be able to trace their work products back to some statement of system requirements. Given these objectives, let's examine the central activities in our approach.

13.2 SETTING THE STAGE: DESCRIBING SOFTWARE FROM THE OUTSIDE LOOKING IN

Developing an object-oriented software application entails identifying and creating a model of software objects. Before designers can delve into object modeling, they need to understand what their software is required to do. They can then expand upon that understanding to produce an implementable solution. Historically, the gap between the language of the software developer and software user has been wide. Users describe systems in nontechnical, task-oriented terms while developers think in terms of software algorithms and data representations. This is even true for object-oriented software. An object-oriented design describes a model of real-world objects, which reside in the physical realm of the user and are modeled in the software designed by a developer. However, a user's notions of a physical or conceptual *object* differs from our synthetic view that we model in our software. There still is a semantic gap between these two worlds. We have developed a conceptual map for describing our software from an external perspective and then evolving these descriptions into a working application (see Figure 13.1). In this chapter, we will focus on exploratory design tasks, steps 3 through 7 in the figure, that complement other collaborative design techniques.

Software developers need practical techniques for bridging the gap between descriptions meaningful to software users and descriptions that contain sufficient technical details to build a model of interacting software objects. Ideally, developers, interface designers, users, domain experts, and software specialists all need to work together to drive out detail from their different perspectives during the entire software development process. In our experience, software designers are active, involved participants in developing system requirements.

Task	Goal	Document
1. Determine the software system Determine the system boundaries and scope Identify the actors Identify the system "interfacers" to the actors Develop first-cut subsystem partitioning	Establish the limits of the system being modeled	Context diagram, Updated requirements document
2. Stereotype the actors Determine if the actors are active or passive Describe the actors' roles	Identify sources of external stimuli and external resources	List of actors identified by stereotype
3. Determine system use cases Use existing requirements, system descriptions, or scenarios as input Identify and describe units of actor-level interaction	Decompose system into discrete chunks meaningful to both businesspeople and developers	Use Cases
4. Construct conversations Identify name, actor, and overview Describe the context Identify sequence of actor actions and model responses Identify alternatives Identify key constraints and considerations	Capture the sequence of interactions between the actors and the system for each use case	Conversation Worksheet
5. Identify candidate objects Spot nouns in written requirements and user's concepts Identify more objects from required attributes Capture name, stereotype, and utility on cards	Establish an initial set of design objects	Design Cards (CRC cards)

Task	Purpose	Output
6. Identify responsibilities of candidate objects Extract from requirements and use cases Add as verb phrases to design cards Find new objects	Determine what each object knows and can do	Design Cards
7. Design collaborations Determine a system control style Construct object interaction diagrams for each conversation and significant alternatives Refine responsibilities Add collaborators to design cards	Capture the dynamic behavior of the system	Object interaction diagrams, Design Cards
8. Design class hierarchies Create a classification hierarchy, adding new classes to represent common abstractions Identify abstract and concrete classes Factor common responsibilities into superclasses	Determine inheritance relationships between classes and identify class hierarchies	Class hierarchy diagram
9. Fully specify classes Define the class interface (public and private responsibilities and message formats) Detail methods (pseudocode or algorithms) Design attributes Establish class contracts	Complete the class design	Class specifications
10. Design subsystems Group related classes Identify interfaces between subsystems Analyze and simplify subsystem collaborations	Design subsystems to manage complexity	Collaboration Graph

Figure 13.1. Responsibility-driven design tasks.

Scenarios have been useful tools for envisioning software systems. Jacobson [10, 11], however, made the keen observation that a use case can be treated as a refineable, extensible, and reusable specification of system requirements. We have found use cases and other informal descriptions useful in providing a focus and meaning to our software development efforts. Use cases are textual descriptions of interactions between an *actor* (e.g., a user or another system playing a specific role) and our software. Use cases provide boundaries and constraints on the system to be built. Use cases in some sense form a contract between developers and users of the system. In the spirit of cooperative, incremental development, however, they must be developed to meet the needs of all interested parties. We have found the tasks of building, refining, and amplifying meaningful use cases to require a blend of art, teamwork, and experimentation. There are a number of questions we ask about using them, in conjunction with other descriptive forms:

- What are good ways to build them?
- How should they be recorded?
- How do they evolve?
- Who should look at them? and from what perspectives?
- How detailed should they be?
- Are there different levels of detail?
- When are we done finding and describing them?

A similar set of questions crops up when we consider the design of software objects. It isn't surprising that these themes recur, since people who build and describe software systems want to know how much they should describe before they have an adequate understanding of what they are building. Many of the answers to these questions depend on how these descriptions are applied. Answering the question "What's a good use case?" in our own consulting practices meant realizing that one format cannot fit all purposes. Instead it is reasonable to formulate different descriptions from a common base. On the other hand, if we were careful not to get too arcane or jargon-laden, high-level descriptions could be understood by a wide audience. We are perfectly content to ascertain real needs of various contributors to a development effort before coming up with a practical way to describe our software from an external view.

13.2.1 An Example: Our First Use-Case Description

To illustrate, let us describe at a high level a use case for a hypothetical Automated Teller Machine, which is designed to support interactive financial services. One of the actors is the customer who walks up to the machine and wishes to make one or more financial transactions.

Use Case: Performing a Financial Transaction
Actor: Bank Customer

A bank customer can select a financial service from several available transactions. These transactions include cash withdrawal or deposit, inquiring about an account balance, and transferring funds between accounts. Once a customer has selected a financial service, he or she will be prompted to enter information necessary for performing the financial transaction. Upon completing a transaction, the customer may choose to perform additional transactions or indicate that he or she wishes to terminate this session at the ATM. When a session terminates, the customer will be presented with a paper record of the financial transactions.

This description is so nonspecific that we could present any design (a human teller might satisfy these requirements . . . or a fairly ridiculous design that had users entering their bank account numbers or cash amounts in Morse code!) and argue that it met these requirements. This obviously isn't our intent. To fill in the gap between this description and what is needed to produce an object design model we must add more detail.

13.2.2 Our Next Refinement: Describing a Conversation between the Actor and Our System

We have found it useful in both our consulting practices and teaching to clearly separate what the system does from what the user communicates to our software. We like to demarcate actor actions and system responses or activities. This allows us to add more to both parts of this description, and to describe in high-level terms a *conversation* between an actor and our system. There are two central parts to this actor/system conversation: a description of the actor's requests or inputs to the system, and a corresponding description of the high-level responses or actions taken by our software system.

Together, these side-by-side narratives capture a dialog between an actor and our system. Eventually, our software will support the system side of each conversation. We also list alternatives to the main course of each conversation and expand alternative descriptions, if they significantly alter the flow of the conversation. Alternatives represent a reasonably complete, but not exhaustive, list of conditions that the software must be able to detect and handle. Here's our next level of detail, an actor/system conversation:

Conversation: Performing a Withdrawal Transaction
Actor: Bank Customer

Overview: Bank customers can perform any number of financial transactions once they've presented the system with an unexpired, not-known-to-be-stolen bank card and entered their valid personal identification number. The typical customer performs a single transaction before terminating a session at the ATM.

Actor Action	**System Response**
1. Indicate desire to withdraw cash	
	2. Present customer with a list of his or her accounts
3. Select an account	
	4. Prompt customer for cash amount
5. Indicate amount	
	6. Validate available funds on hand in machine Update account balance Log transaction record Prepare receipt information Dispense cash Sense when customer has taken cash Ask customer if another transaction is desired
7. Indicate he or she is finished	
	8. Print and eject receipt Eject user's bank card

Alternatives:

1. Insufficient funds on hand
2. Insufficient funds in customer account
3. Customer has exceeded daily withdrawal limit
4. Customer wishes to perform an additional transaction

We have found that conversations can be readily constructed by knowledgeable experts from diverse backgrounds. Conversations can either be developed by a team or drafted by an individual and then reviewed, explained, and revised by a small group. It is important that teams developing conversations blend the talents of developers, users, and other specialists. Each contributor has a unique and valuable perspective. No perspective should dominate, yet a certain interest may take center stage during a working session. It is important that side concerns be recorded and worked through, perhaps as an outside activity. Respect and appreciation for the concerns of others is important; teamwork and a spirit of joint development is crucial. For example, in one working session, I recall diving into technical design details for several minutes, backing up to reexamine whether the flow of the conversation we had proposed was still workable, then summarizing what issues were solved and what new ones were raised by a single decision. Technical, user interface, and business issues were all discussed in a single session while holding everyone's attention.

One key to building a good conversation is to preserve the dual purpose of guiding developers who will be creating an object design model and recording the important events and information conveyed between the user and the system. In order to fill both these objectives, conversations must be written at a fairly high level. Actions and responses should be kept to short, simple verb phrases. It often is the case that sequencing of system responses (for example, the details of processing a withdrawal transaction, step 6 in the example above) is not an accurate reflection of the tasks that the system must do. Yet, this need not be early on. What is important is that an interdisciplinary team is sketching out how they expect their software system to work.

We've found it preferable to illustrate specifics of how information might be presented or interchanged between system and user through user interface mockups or rough prototypes. For this reason, we tend to leave out potentially misleading user interface constraints from our conversations. For example, we would rather state that our system "presents transaction choices" instead of stating that our system "presents a menu of allowable transactions." We pin down details of our user interfaces by quickly developing and evaluating a number of rough working prototypes as a parallel activity. Conversations capture the flow of communication between actor and system. If the nature or the amount of information changes significantly, we have found that the demands of our object model change as well.

This implies that descriptions of system responses must contain sufficient detail, and reflect changing interaction and interface design if they are to accurately guide our object model design. Walking this fine line between capturing sufficient detail and bogging down in too much detail requires practice. The sample conversation we wrote still needs more detailed descriptions before most designers could build a working system, but might contain useful information for constructing user interface prototypes. System responses can readily be expanded to include:

- A description of necessary information, which must be supplied by the actor, and reasonable defaults, if any, for information not supplied.
- Descriptions of any important data validation or business constraints that must be checked before performing critical system actions.
- Descriptions of information that needs to be assembled for reports that are generated.
- Timing and contents of any significant system feedback.

Conversations and supporting information can be captured in a word processing document, be handwritten, or, in less formal situations, might be directly placed into descriptions of our objects. We developed a worksheet for briefly capturing additional constraints and use it in the classroom. Effective ways to capture additional details depend on team dynamics. In practice, we find it easy to record information, and easier to keep it relevant if we don't cram too many details into either side of a conversation. Conversations have value in their simplicity and sparseness.

Users and software interface designers also need visual artifacts such as screen mockups or storyboards. New object designers prefer more detailed system responses whereas experienced designers are comfortable with leaving out details that can be inferred from other conversations or design documents. Teams transitioning from traditional, formal, structured software analysis and design tend to record supplementary information to complement basic use cases and conversations. Large, multiyear, multiperson projects often generate additional guiding documents ranging the gamut from user interface guidelines, to detailed business process descriptions, regulations, and business policy descriptions. All this supporting information needs to be distilled into comprehensible forms and fed into our object design activities. We can always refer to the wealth of supporting requirements; we do not want to be overwhelmed by them. We use conversations to guide our design activity, and other material to provide more detailed explanations.

We wrote our above conversation for a concrete situation, withdrawing cash. We could have written it more abstractly, describing a conversation that could encompass any permissible customer transaction. If we wrote at this more abstract level, we would either have to remove a fair amount of detail from both the actor and system dialogs or add constraints. For example, since not all transactions involve cash amounts specified by the customer, we might restate that the "user is prompted for additional information, if required," or that the "bank customer enters appropriate information." We would also have to describe situations under which certain alternatives apply. For example, daily limits are checked for withdrawals only.

Writing *abstract conversations* feels uncannily like the process we go through when we refactor object responsibilities and tidy up our object model. Typically, this refactoring occurs only after we have initially assigned responsibilities to objects that handle specific situations. We typically make several passes over our initial design, reformulating responsibilities and designing consistent ways to accomplish things. The refactoring can significantly alter our objects. It is at this point that we also look for ways to exploit class inheritance to fit similar objects into some classification hierarchy and specify inherited responsibilities. If this cleanup activity is done too early, we won't have enough concrete situations to extrapolate from.

Likewise, we find it useful to keep conversations at a fairly concrete level for another reason. They are intended to be understood by potential users, business analysts, and developers. The purpose of abstraction is to aid in building consistent software. This goal conflicts with our initial need to understand how a user ideally wants to interact with our system for a specific situation.

13.3 OBJECT STEREOTYPES

Once we have described a sufficient number of conversations, we like to build an object model that supports them. We first develop and describe a list of candidate design objects, then show how they collaborate to support each conversation. We start by trying a variety of schemes to discover a natural and reasonable way to abstract our system into objects. Objects in a design can either be involved, active participants in many conversations, or be docile, responding only when asked, taking a more supportive role. In between these two extremes are many shades of behavior. We find it useful to initially classify objects according to their primary purpose, their modus operandi, and their general utility. There are several ways we characterize object utility.

Business or Domain Objects model necessary aspects of a concept that would be familiar to a user of the software we design. If we were designing an Automated Teller Machine for a bank, we might have Bank Customer, Bank Account, and Financial Transaction objects. If we were designing an oscilloscope we might model Triggers, Waveforms, or Timebases. These objects correlate directly with concepts in the user's domain.

Application Objects, while also business related, intentionally are limited to the scope of a single application. Sometimes objects crafted to work in a single context can be reworked and generalized to work in numerous related applications. For example, we could choose to design Financial Transaction objects that could be reused in other banking applications rather than be specialized to work in just the Automated Teller application. Objects designed to work within a single context are certainly simpler to conceptualize. They also potentially carry around less baggage than if they were designed to work in several applications, and may be easier to use and maintain. Yet reuse of an object across an entire suite of business-specific applications is a compelling goal. Broad reuse of domain objects ensures consistency across a suite of applications. However, it takes significantly more design work to adequately model business objects.

Utility Objects are generally useful, non-application-specific objects. For example, SmallTalk programming environments come with many generically useful classes. Classes for structuring other objects, such as Set, Array, Dictionary, and classes representing numbers or strings fall into this category. There are compelling reasons for application developers to create additional utility objects. It is extremely useful to design new utility objects that explicitly support system policies or common application programming practices. For example, we have created classes that stylize error handling and sequencing of processing steps; classes that model ranges of settable values, increments, and units of measurement; and classes that monitor detectable external conditions.

13.3.1 Stereotyping Object Behaviors

We task certain objects by prodding others to do the detail work and others to hold onto facts, perform calculations, and interface to other systems. As a starting point, we stereotype objects as controllers, coordinators, structurers, information holders, service providers, or interfacers. These objects can be generally useful, application specific, or useful in several business-specific applications. When we architect our application's control style, we need to focus our attention on those objects that *coordinate*, *initiate,* or *monitor* major application activities. Let's look at these behavioral stereotypes in more detail.

Controllers are active, vital centers of influence. Often, these objects can be identified in an existing design by their name. Having "Manager" or "Controller" or "Handler" or "Driver" is common for controlling objects. These objects are responsible for controlling a cycle of action. This cycle can either be repetitive, with conditional branching logic, or be initiated and executed once on detection of a certain set of events or circumstances. Control and coordination tasks are often placed in multiple objects in an application. Controlling objects might initiate an ongoing systemwide activity, or iterate over a minor application task.

The original SmallTalk-80 user interface presented a stylized three-way collaboration between Model, View, and Controller objects. Controller objects were responsible for responding to user directives, such as mouse clicks or keystrokes, and initiating appropriate responses. Views displayed the current state of the application, and model objects were application-specific objects. We use a broader definition than that implied by SmallTalk-80 controller objects. Controlling objects need not be spurred to action only on behalf of user directives. Controllers can be found and created for many parts of an application where a cycle of activity is initiated, sequenced, and sometime later completed.

For example, in the design of an Automated Teller Machine, an ATM object might have responsibility for initializing and sequencing system activities at a high level. A further design refinement can add the concept of a Session Manager, which controls the sequence of activities of a single bank customer wishing to carry out one or more financial transactions. At a lower level, there may be a Network Controller responsible for handling network traffic between the application and the communication network.

Coordinators are the managers and delegators within a system. Coordinators often pair client requests with objects performing a requested service. A coordinator may respond to a request by briefly establishing an appropriate context, and then delegating a request to one or more objects within its sphere of influence. For example, in the Automated Teller Machine design, we could design a Session Manager that had more of a coordination role, and be less controlling, by slightly shifting intelligence between objects. A Session Coordinator could first determine which transaction the bank customer wished to perform, then create and delegate responsibility to the appropriate Financial Transaction object to carry out the detailed transaction tasks.

Structurers primarily maintain the relationships between application objects. In many applications, business objects have very complex structural relationships. Consider a simplistic real-world example of a file cabinet, which contains folders that hold documents. In this real-world example, the file cabinet provides some structure for its contents, but it doesn't have very interesting responsibilities. The cabinet just holds folders that may be tabbed and labeled. Folders simply hold their contents. It is the documents that are of interest.

In contrast, with an object design we can embellish our objects with responsibilities to suit our personal design tastes. We can design software File Cabinet objects that do more than organize their contents. A File Cabinet object could know when any folder was last referenced, how much room is left in the cabinet, or even maintain a history of who looked through its contents. When we classify an object as primarily being a structurer, we think first and foremost about what relationships it should maintain between objects it knows about, and secondarily what additional useful responsibilities might be appropriate.

Information Holders keep values that can be asked about. At times it can be useful to create objects that are responsible for yielding information. In procedural programming languages we have the ability to declare constant values. In object designs, information holders are an equivalent concept.

Service Providers are typically designed to perform a single operation or activity on demand. A well-designed service provider has a simple interface to a clearly defined operation. It should be simple to set up and use. Pure service objects often are the products of a highly factored design. Such a design consists of many classes of objects with highly specialized behaviors. One reason to create service objects is to facilitate optional or configurable software features. Also, as more responsibilities are added to a class, it can become complex to integrate new responsibilities with existing ones. Creating a service provider can reduce complexity.

For example, we could design our ATM Financial Transaction objects to know precisely how to print information about the transaction on a receipt. Alternatively, we could create a Report object that provides printing and formatting services for transactions and other kinds of objects.

Interfacers are found at the boundaries of an object-oriented application. They can be designed to support communications with users, other programs, or externally available services. Interface objects come in many sizes, shapes, flavors, and at many conceptual levels. Interface objects are responsible for bridging between the nonobject world and the object world of messages and objects. When we think about designing interfacer objects, we focus on those objects that define the boundaries between our objects and the external, non-object-oriented world. Many low-level details can and should be encapsulated within these objects. For example, in the Automated Teller Machine Application we have a number of physical devices such as the Receipt Printer, Cash Dispenser, and the Card Reader. In our design, all these devices would have interface objects that define a high-level interface to the services they provide. A Cash Dispenser object might be responsible for dispensing cash, knowing the cash balance, and adjusting the balance.

Interfacers can translate external events or requests into messages fielded by interested application objects. For example, many external events need to be handled by the ATM system—to name a few: jamming of cash in the Cash Dispenser, failure of the deposit door to close, running out of paper to print receipts on, and so on. Responsible objects, the most likely candidates being the appropriate interface objects, need to be assigned the responsibility for detecting and responding appropriately.

13.4 RESPONSIBILITIES AND COLLABORATIONS

Identifying and stereotyping central classes in an application is just a first step. We next need to describe which actions must get accomplished, and how our objects will work together to accomplish them. A responsibility is a cohesive subset of the behavior defined by an object. An object's responsibilities are high-level statements about the actions it can perform as well as the knowledge it maintains and provides on demand. An analogy between designing objects and writing a report can clarify our intent. An object's responsibilities are analogous to major topic headings in a report outline.

```
An Object's Responsibilities

Publicly Available Services
Responsibility #1
 a message
 another message
 yet another message
 ...
Responsibility #2
 some other message
 and another message
 ...
Private Responsibilities
 some other message
 and yet even more messages
...
```

The purpose of developing an outline (and then a detailed outline) before writing a report is to map out the topics to be covered in the report and their order of presentation. Similarly, the purpose of outlining an object's responsibilities is to understand its role in the application before fleshing out the details, which include the messages it understands and the internal storage it encapsulates.

A good way to determine an object's responsibilities is to answer these questions:

- What does this object need to know in order to accomplish each goal it is involved with?
- What steps toward accomplishing each goal should this object be responsible for?

Objects do not exist in isolation. Object-oriented applications of even moderate size consist of thousands of cooperating objects. A collaboration is a request made by one object to another. An object fulfills some responsibilities itself. Most responsibilities likely require collaboration with a number of other objects. Object collaborations can be modeled as interactions between clients and service providers. A client makes a request of a server to perform operations or acquire knowledge. The service provider responds with information or performs an operation upon request. Clients and servers are dynamic roles objects assume during execution. Modeling client/server interactions helps reinforce the good design practice of information hiding. A client shouldn't care how a service provider performs its duties, only that it responds appropriately. On the other hand, a service provider is obligated to respond to any request, regardless of who makes it.

Relationships between clients and servers can be formalized in a contract. A contract is a set of related responsibilities defined by a class. A contract describes the ways in which a given client can interact with a server. It lists requests that a client can make of a server. Both client and server must uphold the terms of their contract. The client fulfills its obligation by only making those requests specified in the contract. The server must respond appropriately to those requests.

Later, with a more complete understanding of our design, we fill in the fine print of each contract. This can involve specifying details of client requests, including message names and arguments, preconditions that must be met before making a request, and postconditions that will be true after the server has performed the requested operation [12]. For objects with distinctly different clientele, or objects that fit multiple behavioral stereotypes, the notion of further organizing their public interface is essential. For many kinds of simpler objects presenting simple interfaces, this activity is not necessary.

If we wish to construct class hierarchies that clearly and simply exploit inheritance, we need conceptual tools that allow class hierarchy designers to precisely state the permissible ways for subclasses to *extend* a contract. In early stages of design, we talk about inheriting superclass responsibilities. In more detailed design we need to be able to cleanly extend inherited responsibilities by providing different implementations and even by offering new public services [9]. In early stages of design, however, it is enough to understand contracts stated in simple terms.

13.4.1 A Simple Tool

Given an initial set of candidate objects, a designer can elaborate object responsibilities and collaborations by testing how the model responds to a variety of requests. Conversations can initially guide our object modeling. Patterns of collaboration required to handle each important system response can be traced. Running through a number of typical conversations rapidly points out gaps in understanding. It is common to find new objects, discard ill-conceived ones, elaborate and reassign responsibilities, or fabricate new design objects. It is also a time when missing or conflicting system requirements surface and can be resolved.

Kent Beck and Ward Cunningham [13] initially developed the concept of using 3-by-5-inch index cards to teach object-oriented concepts. The idea behind CRC cards (for Class-Responsibility-Collaboration) was to provide a quick, effective way to capture the initial design of an object (see Figure 13.2). This technique was first used to teach object design concepts to our students at Tektronix. This technique, however, has far broader applicability than just as a teaching aid. Since its inception, the

Class: Withdrawal Transaction Superclass: Financial Transaction	
Knows account	
Knows amount to withdraw	
Performs withdrawal transaction	
Logs transaction results	Transaction Logger
Initiates dispensing of cash to	Cash dispenser
customer	

Figure 13.2. The face of a design card. On the left side responsibilities are listed, on the right side are collaborations with other objects. Collaborators are objects used to fulfill a specific responsibility.

use of CRC cards in group design sessions has been widely used in informal settings and embellished [14].

The name of each class is written on the front of an index card. Each identified responsibility is succinctly written on the left side of the card. If collaborations are required (and as they become known) to fulfill a responsibility, the name of each class that provides necessary services is recorded to the right of that responsibility. Services defined by a class of objects include those listed on its index card, plus responsibilities inherited from its superclasses. Subclass-superclass relationships and common responsibilities defined by superclasses can also be recorded on index cards. In fact, the intrinsic value of index cards lies in their simplicity and the ease with which their contents can be modified or customized on the spot. On the back of the card, we briefly describe why the object exists in our design and identify initial stereotypes we think it fits (see Figure 13.3). Writing and reviewing these brief descriptions can readily point out differences in design ideas.

The cards can be easily arranged on a tabletop and a reasonable number of them viewed at the same time. They can be picked up, reorganized, and laid out in a new arrangement to amplify a fresh insight. They facilitate team interaction. They are great for hand-simulating collaborations to test the object model. Individuals can pick up cards and physically walk through a design scenario, simulating the sending of a message by moving one card toward another. A designer can hold onto a card and role play an object during a design session. Designers can group and organize cards in imaginative ways looking for patterns and drawing analogies between objects and sets of objects that cut across inheritance, composition, aggregation, or collaboration perspectives. Design is an inherently messy process. Design cards let designers explore ideas in a nonthreatening, free-form environment.

	Withdrawal Transaction
Purpose:	Withdraws cash from a customer account and dispenses it
Stereotypes:	Service object, coordinator, business object

Figure 13.3. The back side of a design card. Initial notions about what an object's role is, and how it is stereotyped, are recorded on the reverse side of the card. As our designs evolve, these early notions are often revised.

Developers often modify and customize information on cards. By personalizing their cards, teams make them suit their modeling needs. One developer shared how he had come to model attributes and encapsulated state on the reverse side of his cards. He asked me "What shouldn't be seen from outside an object?" The answer he was looking for was, "things hidden inside an object, namely its encapsulated data." He placed information about things that should remain private (e.g., should be hidden from view when a card was face up) on the reverse side, to reinforce the good design practice of concealing these details.

When a card fills up with too many important responsibilities it needs factoring into several simpler objects. The limits to what can be written on a card help us express the design object it represents at the right level of abstraction and complexity. Fixing overly full cards requires experimentation. A student in a recent object design class told me that whenever a card for a controller grew to have too many responsibilities, he felt compelled to look for ways of delegating control. Several well-defined centers of control worked their way into his design over a two-day period. It required time and background mental activity, as well as brainstorming sessions with his design partner. In this fairly short gestation period, however, he came up with several meaningful new classes.

Subdividing the responsibilities of a large, complex class into a number of simpler classes requires deeper understanding of the system and a strategy for distributing responsibility among objects. Each newly created class needs a clearly stated role. There already may be identified classes that can fulfill part of the responsibilities of the rather large concept. Most likely, this isn't the case. A hypothesis must then be formulated on how to partition the vague concept into several distinct roles. Each role will be assigned to a new class.

A key designer of a large successful application told me that his design team subdivided responsibilities according to when, what, and how. These subresponsibilities were then assigned to separate classes that were responsible either for knowing when, knowing what, or knowing how to perform an operation. Sounds simple in theory, but his design team found they spent lots of time debating whether a particular responsibility was actually a *when,* a *what,* or a *how*. One object's what is another object's how. It all depends on your design perspective. The debates they had about placing responsibilities helped clarify object roles in their emerging model.

Cards can fill up for other reasons too. Information holder objects often are responsible for knowing lots of facts. Enumerating each small fact can quickly fill an index card. For example, it is preferable to write that a Customer object knows its address rather than recording that it knows a street address, city, state, and zip code. Cards force us to record information at a fairly abstract level.

It is fairly easy to shuffle and manipulate a couple dozen cards. A couple hundred cards is obviously impractical. Following the detailed interactions of a couple hundred objects is beyond comprehension, no matter what medium is used. Index cards are effective for exploring small, focused scenarios. They are compact, easy to manipulate, and easy to modify or discard. A designer doesn't feel that there's a lot invested if the design is merely recorded on thirty or forty index cards. It is easier to take more risks, tossing out unwieldy designs if they aren't expected to work.

Several developers [15, 16, 17] have built software tools that manage basic Class-Responsibility-Collaborator information. Putting CRC design cards on-line alters the fluidity of the design process. Most of these tool developers, however, have been sensitive to the exploratory nature of our approach. They have added ways to capture and assist works in progress. For example, in Intersolv's Execelerator II, designers can drop unassigned responsibilities onto a background screen. Later these responsibilities can be placed on the right object once it is created. Other tools let users flip cards from front to back by pushing a button, and even print freshly updated card decks to be used during hands-on modeling sessions.

There is a mysterious phenomenon that occurs once a design is entered into a computer. It often takes on a life of its own. Because it has been recorded in a polished-looking format, it becomes much harder to consider alternative objects, roles, and distribution of responsibilities. Fairly soon designs need to be entered into a more permanent record in order to communicate and review ideas with a larger audience, or even to develop much more detail. Index cards are not a substitute for detailed modeling, nor are they the only medium we use to explore initial design ideas.

13.5 EXPERIMENTING WITH OUR MODEL

We cross-check our design ideas by walking through a picture of object collaborations for a particular conversation. We check that each object is responsible and knows enough to handle the messages it receives. We use whiteboards a lot during the development of our index card designs. We draw and redraw alternative collaboration sequences, wave our hands, and run through consequences listing pluses and minuses and looking for better ways to distribute object responsibilities. If we can show how our objects collaborate to support a conversation, we've succeeded in simulating our object model. On the other hand, Rosson's Scenario Browser [18] provides a context in which designers explore ideas and record design rationale within an executable application. Designers who use Rosson's Scenario Browser are building and testing their designs while they work out proper distribution of object responsibilities and collaborations.

Neither the static description of object responsibilities and stereotypes on a card, nor a diagram showing collaborations for a particular conversation provide a complete picture. Judging the soundness of this model requires examining how objects work together in more detail, summing up the roles and responsibilities of each participant, and examining the larger patterns of communications and information flow that have developed.

To understand any single object's role, it must be looked at in the context of others with which it interacts. It is much harder when an object participates in a number of relationships. In this case, it is essential to build an understanding of the dynamic behavior of the object. Performing design walkthroughs, tracing a chain of object collaborations in response to a stimulus, is a good way to understand object interactions. The more situations that are modeled, the better.

As simple as this sounds, it takes an acquired skill to effectively elaborate object interactions. The goal is to first develop a *big picture*, dive into some detail, then try out alternatives while pushing toward a thought-out, justifiable design. A way to start this is to trace object collaborations between objects that are at either the same or the next conceptual level in the design. First we work to develop an overall, high-level view of key object interactions, then elaborate and subdivide roles and object responsibilities. This breadth-first-then-depth exploring approach avoids modeling classes at widely differing conceptual levels, which indeed is difficult.

We need to develop a dominant pattern for distributing the flow of control and sequencing of actions among collaborating objects. A class may incorporate more or less intelligence according to how much it knows or does, and how many other classes of objects it affects. Control strategy decisions have a strong influence on how responsibilities are distributed among objects. As we consider alternatives, we seek out ways to distribute control between business objects. We prefer a model with moderately intelligent, collaborating objects over one that concentrates intelligence into just a very few objects.

Delegating responsibilities enables us to design participants in a collaboration sequence that is less complex to build and easier to understand. Following a distributed control strategy, each object typically knows about a small number of collaborators. In contrast, a more centralized control strategy concentrates knowledge and visibility of many objects in one central object. This is a very procedural style of object design. When responsibilities are distributed, it can be harder to see the overall control and sequencing; a chain of collaboration must be followed to see how our model responds to a particular situation. Changes to a design, however, are typically localized and fairly easy to accommodate, and have minimal impact on other objects.

Designers often try too early to overconstrain objects to fit a specific behavioral profile. If designers start with objects from the user's vocabulary, they typically only have a set of information holders and what they contain and are missing any notion of how the application should work. We need to work out how various objects might perform required tasks. We need to construct a model of how each responsibility will be accomplished. This requires experimentation. There's no one right design solution; there are many reasonable solutions and a few very good solutions. In the early stages of design, responsibilities typically aren't cleanly separated. We have objects with multiple roles, rather than many different objects, each with a singular purpose.

We find it useful to ask whether an object is assuming too much responsibility, and whether it would be more appropriate to create new classes of objects to share the load. It is also judicious to distinguish how a design choice causes an object's behavior to shift one way or the other on a behavioral continuum. Has an object become too active or passive? Is it perhaps taking on too much responsibility by both assuming a coordinating role as well as performing a useful service? Would it simplify our design to subdivide an object's responsibilities into smaller, simpler concepts? What would be an appropriate pattern of collaboration between that object and a newly defined service provider?

The more experience we gain, the more we have learned to create designs with highly specialized classes of objects having simple roles. Classes are inexpensive conceptual tools. We use them to divide and conquer modeling problems. If we find out, as we work out more details, that a class adds unnecessary complexity, we simply collapse its behavior into its clients. On the other hand, we often find that it is easier to rework smaller concepts more easily so as to be usable in several places within a single application. An admirable aspect of many seasoned object designers is their intolerance for complexity. Throughout design and implementation, they seek to simplify. They frequently refactor design objects during implementation, spawning new objects with well-defined, simpler roles. They build new service providers and create new abstractions to hold meaningful implementation information. They seem to refactor effortlessly. In actual fact, they mull over refactoring ideas as a background task while busily spending most of their time building and implementing their current design. When their ideas finally gel, they consciously fix up the design rather than go with the current flow.

13.6 SUMMARY

The end product of software design is a model of how our software should work. In this chapter we presented a number of informal techniques for describing our software and building upon those descriptions to develop an object-oriented software model. Our software model describes how objects, each with distinct roles, collaborate to perform software tasks. Just as our software model consists of cooperating objects, our software is often designed by a collaborative team. Each participant brings to this team a set of unique skills, talents, and concerns. Our modeling techniques are intended to enhance collaborations and to facilitate communication. Conversations derived from use cases describe our software in terms relevant to both programmers and users. Object stereotypes provide a common vocabulary for describing design objects, enabling developers to discuss alternative design ideas. Design cards are used to collaboratively develop a description of object responsibilities and collaborations. We have found that the design process can be significantly enhanced when tools and techniques are adapted to fit the needs of design participants. To this end, we constantly look for ways to improve the process of software development and firmly believe that responsibility-driven design has a natural fit with other collaborative design techniques.

ACKNOWLEDGMENTS

I would like to acknowledge the valued insights and contributions from my Digitalk consulting and training colleagues: Craig Brandis, Sharon Collins, Alan McKean, Jon Marshall, Mary Wells, and Mike Yinger. They always provide me with a ready ear and constructive criticisms. Craig initially derived the responsibility-driven task list from our course material; I have been tinkering with it ever since. Mary and Alan synthesize my new ideas, add their own insights, and work hard to make our methods teachable. Jon Marshall always has fresh ideas about the dynamic nature of software design. Sharon and Mike have shared valuable insights from their encounters with client teams building large applications on tight schedules. And, finally, I would like to acknowledge the constant support from my treasured object designer, manuscript reviewer, and friend, Allen Wirfs-Brock.

REFERENCES

[1] Wirfs-Brock, R. & Wilkerson, B. (1989). Object-oriented design: A responsibility-driven approach. In *Proceedings of OOPSLA'89, SIGPLAN Notices, 24*(10), 71–76.

[2] Wirfs-Brock, R., Wilkerson, B., & Wiener, L. (1990). *Designing Object-Oriented Software*. Englewood Cliffs, NJ: Prentice Hall.

[3] Wirfs-Brock, R. (1991). Responsibility-driven design. *The SmallTalk Report, 3*(1).

[4] Rumbaugh, J. et al. (1991). *Object-Oriented Modeling and Design*. Englewood Cliffs, NJ: Prentice Hall.

[5] Booch, G. (1991). *Object-Oriented Design with Applications*. Redwood City, CA: Benjamin/Cummings.

[6] Booch, G. (1994). *Object-Oriented Design with Applications* 2d ed. Redwood City, CA: Benjamin/Cummings.

[7] Sharble, R. C. & Cohen, S. (1992). The object-oriented brewery: A comparison of two object-oriented development methods. *Boeing Technical Report*.

[8] Rubin, K. & Goldberg, A. (1992). Object behavior analysis. *Communications of the ACM*, September, *35*(9): 48–62.

[9] Wirfs-Brock, R. & Johnson, R. (1990). Surveying current research in object-oriented design. *Communications of the ACM*, September, *33*(9), 104–124.

[10] Jacobson, I. et al. (1992). *Object-Oriented Software Engineering: A Use-Case Driven Approach*. Reading, MA: Addison-Wesley.

[11] Jacobson, I. (1995). *Chapter 12 in this volume.*

[12] Meyer, B. (1988). Programming as contracting. *Interactive Software Engineering,* Technical Report.

[13] Beck, K. & Cunningham, W. (1989). A laboratory for teaching object-oriented thinking. In *Proceedings of OOPSLA'89, SIGPLAN Notices, 24*(10), 1–6.

[14] Wrangler, M. & Hansen, P. (1992). Visualizing objects: Methods for exploring human computer interaction concepts. *SIGPLAN Notices*, *27*(10), 146–153.

[15] *Excelerator II OOA&D for OS/2 Reference Manual.* Intersolv, Inc.

[16] *Object System CRC.* Palladio Software.

[17] *Getting Started with HOMSuite*. Hatteras Software, Inc.

[18] Rosson, M. B. & Carroll, J. M. (1995). *Chapter 10 in this volume.*

CHAPTER 14

Discussion: Scenarios as Engines of Design

Robert L. Mack
IBM Watson Research Center
30 Saw Mill River Road
Hawthorne, NY 10532
USA

14.1 INTRODUCTION

This book has made a thorough case for and analysis of the role of scenarios in the design and development of software technology. That scenarios play a role in design is not new. What is new is the claim for centrality of the role for scenarios in all stages and activities of design and development, the depth and specificity of experience and lessons learned using scenarios in design, and perhaps the beginning of a more theoretical foundation for scenarios that might lead to better understanding of how to use scenarios in design. In this discussion chapter, I would like to provide a brief summary of these three claims, emphasizing a practitioner's perspective.

14.2 CENTRALITY OF SCENARIOS IN DESIGN

The experiences reported in all chapters of this book make a convincing case for the role of scenarios throughout design. This role changes with different stages of the design process, but the use of scenarios remains a unifying thread throughout. Several chapters, beginning with

Carroll's introduction, provide explicit and useful taxonomies (Figure I.1; see also Chapters 3 and 5) of the various roles of scenarios through design. (From this point on, I will use the term *design* as shorthand to cover all phases of development, including implementation. Also, the terms *user* and *users* will be shorthand for customers, workers, clients, etc., as users of computer systems being designed.) Scenarios can express broad goals for a vision of a project, which may be especially important in the beginning for building a cohesive team or obtaining management support. More specific scenarios may capture specific work practices and goals, contributing directly to concrete requirements and design possibilities. Still more specific scenarios, expressed in terms of implementation actions may be used to guide user or product testing, and may be part of a functional specification for the resulting product.

These taxonomies, coupled with the concrete case studies of design discussed throughout the book provide many useful examples of the role of scenarios, and provide a basis for more or less explicit guidelines for practitioners regarding their use. Practicing usability and software engineers should find familiar claims, as well as useful new claims, perspectives, and examples.

In usability engineering practice, for example, as described in Gould [1], and the first half of Whiteside, Bennett, and Holtzblatt [2], scenarios of use are used to help set overall design objectives, especially usability objectives, and for guiding various aspects of design and the evaluation of design implementations. The utility of these roles for scenarios is largely taken for granted in this book (see Nielsen, Chapter 3, for a useful summary). In *addition* to these roles, the discussions of scenario use in this book focus on two larger roles. The first is the use of scenarios to represent the broader cognitive, social, and contextual aspects of work. This analysis contrasts to task analysis focused on narrower ergonomic considerations and behavioral analysis [3]. Kuutti (Chapter 1) discusses the historical and conceptual background for understanding the relevance of this social and work context to the development of computer technology aimed at supporting it.

The second larger role for scenarios discussed in this book is that of influencing design more directly and broadly, by having scenarios serve a design role traditionally reserved for functional specifications, and using scenarios to drive design activities, which generate and evaluate design possibilities and play a role in documenting design decisions. These uses of scenarios contrast to the more indirect role in usability engineering, where scenarios are used to establish usability and functional objectives, and design is influenced through the analysis of the results of empirical evaluation of systems in relation to those objectives. The chapters in this volume advocate and provide case studies of a closer relation between scenarios, detailed design, and prototyping.

Usability engineering, of course, is not the only approach to user-centered software design. Participatory design approaches have emerged, which focus on more radical approaches to understanding users, and involving them directly in the design process. Participatory design methods, and the role of scenarios in them, are well-represented in this volume, notably in Kyng (Chapter 4), Kuutti (Chapter 1), and Muller, Tudor, Wildman, White, Root, Dayton, Carr, Diekmann, and Dykstra-Ericson (Chapter 6). Muller et al. (see also Muller, Kuhn, Wildman, and White [4] and Schuler and Namioka [5] provide a useful introduction to the diversity of Participatory design techniques various practitioners and researchers have developed. Participatory design approaches are based on philosophical world views that provide motivation for specific practices advocated by these methods. Participatory design methods discussed in this volume, for example, by Muller et al., and Kyng, focus on involving users in the process of detailed design, including actual prototype development, in addition to working with users to understand their existing work practices. Cooperative design is not only technically valuable in this approach for guiding design, but is considered a social and political requirement for users' acceptance of technology.

Another user-centered design approach, Contextual design, similarly advocates cooperative design with users, beginning with deep immersion in the users' context of work, not as an objective scientific observer but as a sympathetic partner, open to the possibility of radical transformation of work, beyond automating existing work processes with specific technological solutions [2, 6, 59]. Contextual design adapts ethnographic methods of understanding human behavior in context (e.g., the workplace), and extends these methods to function within traditional software and usability engineering practices.

Using scenarios will not necessarily be new to advocates of Participatory and Contextual design. However, the specific techniques discussed in this volume (especially in Chapters 4 and 6) should be welcome additions to a growing body of experience and methodology. In turn, these design approaches emphasize two issues regarding the use of scenarios that I believe are important for understanding their role in design.

The first is the need for keeping the design process thoroughly grounded in users' work context. As I will argue (reflecting claims of chapters in this volume), the development of scenarios, and their effective use requires extensive interaction with both the ultimate end users and software designers, in more than one context, an interaction that is also an evolving, iterative process. The second issue is acknowledging and managing the tension between semiformal expressions of designers' understanding of users and their tasks, as expressed in scenarios of use, and more formal design representations typical of software engineering. Working with users and developing scenarios creates a more open-ended understanding of technology than focusing only on technical and implementation software engineering concerns. Both perspectives are necessary, but it can be difficult to manage both. Doing so requires attention to supporting communication among all interests involved in design (Introduction and Chapter 2).

The discussions in this volume also have implications for software engineering. What is central to software engineering is to develop software that achieves several objectives, of which meeting users' needs is key but pragmatically not the only one. Other goals are to meet development schedules, create a maintainable and extendible implementation, and do all this within typical constraints on time and resources. The main contrast to the use of scenarios advocated in this book is to functional specifications. The heart of the functional specification is a relatively formal and systematic description of specific functions, that is, *what* the system does (or is supposed to do). Traditionally, if scenarios played a role as expressions of user tasks, it was to motivate and perhaps illustrate functional specifications, or to serve as test cases for evaluating conformity of software implementations to the functional specifications. In contrast to this traditional role for scenarios, the discussions in this book describe a deeper and wide-ranging role, where scenarios become the functional specifications, and the driving force for design.

This larger design role for scenarios is illustrated in certain approaches to object-oriented (OO) software engineering, discussed in four contributions to this volume, by Rosson and Carroll, Robertson, Jacobson, and Wirfs-Brock (Chapters 10, 11, 12, and 13). In these approaches, OO design begins as problem identification and problem analysis. Scenarios of use (or use cases in Jacobson's approach) are the vehicle for representing tasks and user roles in this analysis process. The first cut at defining programming objects is directly related to the conceptual entities identified in object models derived from these scenarios. In Jacobson's use-case methodology (Chapter 12; see also [7]), scenarios become more formal and procedural, especially in later stages of software implementation. At a very general level, however, I believe that a use case is a type of scenario (Jacobson might not agree on this point, and the reader should consult Chapter 12). The methods discussed in Rosson and Carroll and Wirfs-Brock (Chapters 10 and 13) also encourage iteration in problem analysis and domain modeling, as well as in later design and implementation process. These methods contrast with a staged, *Waterfall model* of software development, a model that is becoming increasingly untenable on many grounds [8]. Scenarios are much more closely connected to specific software engineering methods, not just to validate that an implementation meets some functional specification, but to drive the design of a coherent domain model for users' tasks. Software engineers at large, and OO software engineers in particular, should benefit from the examples and discussions of methods for involving users seriously in requirements gathering and design.

14.3 GUIDELINES AND PRACTITIONERS' PERSPECTIVES ON SCENARIOS

One of the distinctive features of this volume is the number and depth of concrete design case studies that demonstrate the role of scenarios in design. Every chapter presents at least one specific case study of design, in the context of which is discussed the role of scenarios. The case studies discussed in this book tend to focus on early design phases, although there are examples and certainly discussion of a role later in design. Carey and Rusli (Chapter 7), for example, use scenarios to document the results of user experiences with software, and MacLean and McKerlie (Chapter 8) propose to use scenarios to help document design decisions in the Questions, Options, and Criteria (QOC) design rationale framework. We will organize our discussion around three questions—How to:

- Develop scenarios by working with users.
- Use scenarios effectively in design through group design activities.
- Establish the completeness of scenarios as specification of design.

Most broadly, scenarios are intended to express an understanding of the intended users' tasks and needs to a sufficient level to guide design of new software, which enables those tasks to be completed using that software with greater facility than can be done with existing software or work practices. In this section we will highlight guidelines, techniques, and tools discussed in this book that attempt to address these issues.

14.3.1 Develop Scenarios by Working with Users

Several chapters in this volume, most notably Kuutti, Kyng, and Karat (Chapters 1, 4, and 5), discuss techniques for eliciting user requirements in the form of scenario descriptions of their tasks, needs, preferences, and problems. These chapters also discuss techniques and issues involved in crafting scenarios into representations for guiding design (also see Chapters 7 and 9 by Carey and Rusli and Johnson, Johnson, and Wilson). General user task goals and specific work practices can be discovered through observation of users in the field (workplace), interviews with users, conversations and less formal hanging out with users, specialized focus groups or workshops (Chapters 4 and 5), and direct design exercises and role-playing (Chapter 6). To choose an approach to identifying user requirements obviously requires understanding the objectives for the software development project. That is, the range and depth of the activities with users depends on many factors, including resources available, type of software system under development, experience with that software, and knowledge of the users. Methods for understanding users and their tasks can also be found from a usability engineering perspective in Gould [1], Nielsen [9], Rubenstein and Hersh [10], Shneiderman [11], and the first half of Whiteside et al. [2]; Schuler and Namioka [5], from a participatory design perspective (see also Chapters 4 and 6); and, from a contextual design perspective, the second half of Whiteside et al. [2] and Holtzblatt and Beyer [59].

Scenarios can have varying levels of generality and completeness. Typically, the scenarios that are initially obtained from working with users are selective and not complete with respect to some ideal of completeness. Scenario descriptions can begin as relatively raw narratives of current practice derived from observation and interview of users in their work situation, or they can be quite focused, and based on more formal or empirical evaluation of existing or similar systems that support these tasks (Chapter 7). Narratives of existing practice can include observation and interpretation by designers or human-computer interaction (HCI) specialists of specific work practices and associated artifacts (forms, documents, tools). They can be general war stories, which capture some broad generality about users and some target set of tasks. Erickson (Chapter 2) provides an example in a story of how professionals organize work-related paper documents. Computer support for business executive users (so-called executive support systems) has been largely driven by high-visibility stories of executives whose access to corporate information via computers has resulted in enormous business advantages for their companies [12]. These stories can capture the essence of some task domain, and some particularly salient requirement, in a way that can provide a compelling and common focus for all members of a design team even though they may have quite different specific responsibilities with respect to developing that system.

Scenarios can also point beyond existing practices and technology support. They can include, or be entirely focused on, modifications and extrapolations of existing practice, which users believe would be useful. Adaptations of traditional brainstorming techniques are often used to conduct these interactions. Examples of techniques can be found in Kyng's discussion of future workshops (Chapter 4), Nielsen's discussion of the role of scenarios in "feature brainstorms" (Chapter 3), Karat's discussion of focus groups (Chapter 5), and Holtzblatt and Beyer [59]. Scenario descriptions may be coupled with preliminary design, where users are invited to do paper-and-pencil design themselves (Chapter 6). Scenario descriptions may be distilled into a sequence of concrete subtasks and actions, as exemplified in use of scenarios in usability engineering to drive laboratory test procedures [1, 2], the use of scenarios in structured usability inspections such as Cognitive Walkthroughs [13], or in use cases for developing object models in the object-oriented software analysis and design methods discussed in this volume (Chapters 10, 12, 13).

These examples of scenario generation demonstrate that scenarios are themselves a product of design as much as discovery. Several tools and methods discussed in this volume are aimed at supporting early design activity closely coupled to scenario development. These tools range from recommendations for using paper and pencil to sketch designs or to generate interface mockups (Chapter 4), perhaps with specialized design tools like PICTIVE and CARD (Chapter 6), to task description schemes like those under development by Johnson et al. (Chapter 9). PICTIVE and CARD are techniques intended to be used in group design activities involving end users, and are aimed at developing early design prototypes in close collaboration with users. These techniques not only provide a concrete medium in which to express existing work practices, but designers, working with actual users, can transform them into scenarios expressing new implementation possibilities of software technology. Additional discussion of the form and content of scenario representations in a software design context can be found in Karat and Bennett [14], Carroll and Rosson [15, 16], and Tetzlaff and Mack [17].

14.3.2 Use Scenarios Effectively in Design through Team Design Activities

The tools and techniques referred to in the preceding section as ways to discover and develop scenarios also point to what it takes to effectively use the scenarios in the *process* of design. As we discussed earlier, scenarios are relevant to, and used differently in, different aspects or phases of design. Selected scenarios may be used to define testable usability objectives within a usability engineering framework. Objectives guide user testing, and can provide benchmarks for evaluating usability. Scenarios can be used in the context of other design activities to help infer general functions a software system should provide in order to enable users to accomplish general task goals, and to infer what specific user interface elements or styles might be appropriate for implementing that function for a specific class of users. And they can be used in design walkthroughs to structure the analysis and evaluation of design issues such as the integration and flow of functional capabilities, and presentation techniques for some level of prototype or implementation. Nearly all discussions in this book describe the context for these activities as involving the design team, and possibly end users, in various forms of design review driven by scenarios, and the application of user-centered perspectives.

Karat (Chapter 5, also personal communciation) provides an example of usability-focused and scenario-driven design reviews, and pointers to other case studies (e.g., [14, 18]). In this volume, Karat illustrates the role of scenarios in the design of a quick reference guide for a speech recognition interface for OS/2 (the IBM VoiceType Dictation System). On the one hand, this exercise was intended to begin developing a real user guide. On the other hand, engaging the whole design team in this discussion was also a useful way of encouraging an early focus on the usability issues of key elements for the speech recognition interface. The development team already had initial ideas about how they thought various interfaces should look (e.g., for dealing with speech recognition failures, or adding customized voice commands to the system). These interfaces reflected a mix of technical considerations and knowledge of similar systems (competitive products existed), but little obviously not first-hand experience with users using such systems. Walking through the user guide forced the entire team to be explicit about, and to constructively question, the assumptions about how intuitive elements of the interface were likely to be for new users.

Designing the Quick Reference materials encouraged the design team to be explicit about the product goals. For example, at one point the team realized that there were too many pages for a *quick* reference guide, and too many of those pages were about handling speech misrecognition error conditions. This was not consistent with the claims the product would make about increasing user productivity. Playing out user tasks against the paper-and-pencil interface design proposals led to clarification of specific functional and usability objectives, and it contributed to a shared vision on the part of the team about these objectives and design ideas.

This case study is a good example of the often-cited recommendation in usability engineering that an effective early design strategy is to "develop a user guide before a line of code is written" (cited in Gould [1]). Examples of scenario-driven iterative design, often with design teams, are discussed in several contributions to this volume, especially Chapters 4 and 6. Several features of this general design process deserve discussion.

First, we can characterize the overall process as one of "generating and testing" of design ideas. A set of user tasks in the form of concrete step-by-step scenarios can provide hypotheses about what software functions are needed, and possibly aspects of how function might be implemented (Chapters 4 and 12). The technology available, or committed, to factors in additional constraints and possibilities, for example, an interface style. The initial design is then played out against scenarios. New problems, issues, or even possibilities with some technical implementation may evolve. This process is not automatic, of course, but involves skill, creativity, and discussions based on diverse kinds of expertise, discussions that are most effectively carried out in the give-and-take of a team design review.

A second characteristic of this overall process is iteration. The design process is not a linear or top-down unfolding of design, but an iterative cycle of design [1, 2]. Generating a design based on synthesizing requirements in the form of scenarios and design objectives may result in a deeper understanding and possible revisiting of other aspects of design. Scenarios evolve with design, or, perhaps more accurately, multiple sets of scenarios evolve. Initial scenarios express existing task goals and procedures for accomplishing them, and end up expressing new ways of accomplishing those tasks (Chapter 4). The overall task goals may be the same at the end, but the means and methods for accomplishing them change.

A third feature of the design process is that the analysis of design issues often involves walkthroughs of some level of design specification by a design team. Walkthroughs are typically scenario-driven, and proceed by asking questions about the potential utility and usability of design elements. Bennett [19], for example, has long advocated using cognitively motivated questions and user task scenarios to organize usability-related walkthroughs of designs. Questions like "What do users see?" "What are users likely to know?" and "What do they need to do?" asked in relation to task goals expressed in scenarios, on the one hand, and screen layouts and specified actions, on the other, can lead to insights about the intuitiveness of interface elements and interactions. Muller et al.'s use of PICTIVE and CARD with end users (Chapter 6) is also a type of walkthrough design and evaluation of software design concepts.

Usability-related walkthroughs are also called *usability inspections* and are relatively common in applied settings. Practical usability inspection methods such as heuristic evaluation and cognitive walkthroughs are discussed in Nielsen and Mack [20]. Inspection techniques tend to be oriented toward *evaluation* of software *interface* design implementations, but larger issues about how to support user tasks in software *function* design and implementation follow closely from evaluation in these methods. Walkthrough-style inspections in the context of a design team appear especially effective. These teams can involve design specialists and software engineers, and may also involve end users. More discussion of the dynamics and rationale for team design reviews can be found in Karat (Chapter 5) and Muller et al. (Chapter 6; see also [4, 5, 14, 18]).

How does this user-centered design process compare with traditional software engineering program reviews? These reviews typically evaluate how well an implementation actually matches a design (or functional) specification, and generally in terms of software engineering issues such as the completeness of implementation with respect to meeting look-and-feel specifications, and covering error and boundary conditions. As detailed design and implementation take place, other kinds of design analysis and review may be necessary, as well as focusing on design and implementation issues quite different in nature from usability-related issues [21, 22]. These reviews are important, of course, in software engineering [21]. In scenario-driven design, however, evaluation of design possibilities is not simply assessing this kind of fit of implementation to specifications, but involves a potentially more open-ended evaluation of fit to users' needs and task goals, and the possibility of user problems.

What drives user-centered and scenario-driven design processes to converge on useful results? This is, of course, largely an empirical question, in the sense that we cannot guarantee results, and one whose answer depends on a variety of other factors including product management skill. Three observations are worth making. First, the result that is obtained may be a compromise driven by the need to take into account other development objectives. Time, skill, resources, and technological constraints (e.g., a required choice of hardware or operating system) may force trade offs in achieving functional and usability goals. Often, requirements generation and design become fixed because of development schedules (what Waltz, Elam, and Curtis [23] call *shutdown*). Second, the process, while iterative, should be guided by usability objectives that ideally provide concrete means for determining how designers can know that the objective has been achieved (for example, some level of facility for using the system to accomplish some key task).

Finally, design requires more or less open-ended, creative application of design methods by various members of the design team, including end users. Currently, the best techniques appear to involve creating and facilitating group review. As Nielsen (Chapter 3) notes in a somewhat more specific context, but one more generally applicable to several aspects of the preceding discussion:

> The scenario-building exercise utilized the fact that the human imagination is the cheapest multimedia prototyping system around. Just a few words serve to call up reasonably vivid pictures and imagined interfaces. Of course, reliance on human imagination as a prototyping tool leaves the system even more under specified than more traditional prototyping, so the different participants in a scenario-building session may have somewhat different understandings of the system that is being discussed. These differences emerge over time as more detail is added, and more examples are discussed.

The role of HCI specialists throughout design is both technical (bringing knowledge of users and of usability considerations into the design process), and to facilitate team interaction. HCI specialists do not have a monopoly on such skills, but increasingly assume this responsibility of acting to organize and manage the different technical perspectives and interests that are brought together in team design (see [14, 18, 59]; Chapter 4).

14.3.3 Establish the Completeness of Scenarios as Specification of Design

There are at least two pragmatic design goals against which we might want to assess the completeness of scenarios: We want to specify general requirements for what user tasks to support (i.e., what functions to implement), and we want to specify concrete ways to implement tasks in terms of sequences of user interactions with the software. That is, we want to make sure we have started with or end up with scenarios most representative of what our target users do and need. This may be difficult to know at the outset. Indeed, the completeness of scenarios with respect to representing what must be implemented may evolve through the design process itself. Missing scenarios or gaps in scenario descriptions can probably only be discovered through analysis and probing design ideas and prototypes with users, as the design develops into a specific implementation. Scenarios become complete as they become implemented in the function of more or less complete prototypes or developing product software. The completeness of the functions with respect to user needs can be assessed, in turn, by having users evaluate the system.

What is needed to drive completeness in both areas—specifying function, and specifying specific implementation possibilities—is interaction with users, on the one hand, and playing scenarios out against the design on the other hand. We discussed specific methods in the previous section (see Chapters 4 and 6). Of course, these observations vary in pertinence with task domain and software being developed. There may be task domains where all tasks can be enumerated and specified with much less user interaction, and where the usability of user interface techniques can be assessed analytically or via laboratory testing. An example might be telephone operator service interfaces (see [57]; but see Chapter 6 for examples of more open-ended design even in this domain). In other cases, there may be a history of software releases, and the new software to be developed may be a more or less routine extension of the existing system. In the general case, however, scenarios are more open-ended, and as scenarios are developed, and used to design, new questions emerge, which can be answered only by returning to users. A practical implication here is that effective use of scenarios implies continual elaboration and revitalizing, in both work context and in the context of an emerging design.

Software engineering poses the question of completeness in terms of the availability and completeness of a functional specification for the software to be developed. A functional specification describes what to do and how to do it in terms of specific technical elements. Functional specifications claim to provide a complete description of what the technology in question is supposed to do. The specification also typically assesses how complete the implementation is with respect to standard software quality issues like error and boundary conditions on actions.

However, functional specifications are problematic in at least two ways. First, they focus on the technology of the computer software, and do not express the psychological or work context for the technology in use. As a consequence, functional specifications can become divorced from users' needs and requirements. They can devolve into checklists of functions, narrowly defined, without a context of use that embeds simple actions in a larger flow of user actions, goals, and expectations, which could make those actions meaningful or problematic. Second, and related, functional specifications may provide a misleading sense of closure on design. It is too easy to simply declare functional specifications as complete *by definition*, and beg fundamental questions about whether an implementation conforming to those specifications meets users' needs.

Of course, ultimately, there can be a role for describing the software artifact in static, functional terms, outside a context of use. A complete description of that design in purely software technology terms is an important design representation as well. However, that context of use is essential in design, especially in early phases. Scenarios are problematic also. As Carroll discusses in his introduction (see also Chapter 15), scenario descriptions, even when expressed at the level of implementation detail, can be relatively redundant, and certainly informal with respect to describing a specific implementation for supporting the tasks underlying the scenario descriptions. For example, a specific software function or feature may appear as part of several scenarios. It is important to understand these different contexts for that feature. However, it is also appropriate in other situations to simply describe that feature or function in self-contained terms (see also Tetzlaff & Mack [17]). Traditional functional specifications and scenario-oriented design representations are both needed and should complement each other.

The relevant consideration in my view is to make sure that design, is open at any level to serious question about its fit to users' needs, and, hence, open to serious iteration as long as possible (as long as other objectives, like development schedule or cost permit iteration). Traditional functional specifications do not provide a context that allows for evaluation against user goals, and that allows for iterative design, at any level of the design process. That is, it is important to maintain a perspective on design where it is possible to discover that an implementation may conform well to a specification, but is not what users need. Evaluating design against user needs and expectations expressed in scenarios provides just this perspective.

14.4 THEORETICAL PERSPECTIVES ON THE USE OF SCENARIOS IN DESIGN

For my purposes a theoretical perspective means systematic analysis and reflection about the generality and principles underlying methods and practices, to improve understanding of those principles and methods, to drive further research, and ultimately improve the application of those principles and methods. In the HCI domain such reflection often tries to exploit a connection to existing research in Cognitive Science, which can include Artificial Intelligence, Linguistics, and Anthropology, among other disciplines. In this respect, all the chapters in this volume are examples of researchers and practitioners reflecting on the practice of using scenarios in software design, and attempting to develop principled understanding of their use. For example, the work on design rationale discussed in MacLean and McKerlie (Chapter 8) or Rosson and Carroll (Chapter 10) attempts to create an explicit methodology out of less formal and perhaps unreflective design activities observed in software engineering practice. Similarly, the scenario-driven walkthrough methods discussed in the preceding sections arose, in part, out of attempts to turn cognitive models of human-computer interaction into practical methods for evaluating interfaces.

The practical guidelines discussed in the previous section are subjects of ongoing reflection and analysis, particularly in the HCI community. Many of the methods and ideas discussed in this volume are also being developed in application contexts—in the marketplace—which introduces pragmatic objectives that can complicate interpretation even as they provide opportunity for real-world relevance and validity from the outset. This section highlights several theoretical perspectives, based largely on connections to research topics familiar to Cognitive Science researchers. (Further discussion of Cognitive Science research pertinent to scenarios in object-oriented design practice can be found in Carroll, Mack, Robertson, and Rosson [24].) We will focus discussion in terms of the same three issues around which we organized our preceding discussion of practical guidelines

14.4.1 Develop Scenarios by Working with Users: Facilitating Interactions with Users

The research questions here have to do with how we can more effectively create contexts for learning what users do, need, and prefer. As we noted earlier, simply observing overt behavior as in classical time-and-motion studies and behavioral task analysis is not sufficient. We need to understand not only what tasks are done, but why tasks are done the way they are, which may require deeper probing of the social, historical, and cognitive rationale for what people do. Interest in ethnographic methods in an HCI context (e.g., Suchman [25]) is motivated by the belief that these methods will provide more effective ways to do this probing. Discussions in this book take for granted this background of concepts and methods for interacting with users, and the value of developing rich, qualitative descriptions of what people do and think as they engage in meaningful activity. The research opportunities here lie in at least two related directions.

First, there is need for better understanding how to converge as quickly and confidently as possible on a set of representative task scenarios that capture high-level goals and tasks. In particular, we need to solve the first-order problem of making sure that the scenarios cover a coherent and complete set of tasks. Traditional methods like observing and interviewing require skill and effort on the part of specialists in knowing how to observe, ask questions, and interact with users. There may be an opportunity to make these methods more efficient, both in application and in learning them in the first place, and perhaps supported by tools. There may also be opportunities to make structured interventions, like focus groups, effectively stand in for longer-term observation, interviewing, and "living with users" in their work environment.

A useful research focus for scenario generation methods may be in exploring systematic question-asking. Of course, effective questioning of users in the workplace is already an acknowledged skill for HCI specialists in requirements gathering and task analysis. However, research might be directed at identifying principles and methods for more effective question-asking. Robertson's proposed question-asking techniques (Chapter 11) may play a role here, although they seem oriented to more procedural elaboration of scenarios once they are obtained in some form, rather than generating scenarios in the first place. Question-asking may help flesh out the task space, but a good sampling of scenarios in the first place seems a crucial starting point. Carroll and Rosson [27] have proposed a framework of initial, generative questions for driving the development of scenarios. These are not yet tied to methods for interacting with users outside the design team (see also their discussion of the role of questions in design in Chapter 10).

Identifying conceptual frameworks for motivating questions (or other forms of inquiry about work practices and rationale) is a related area of research. What questions are asked, and how they are asked reflects assumptions about what is important to focus on in a work situation, and what kinds of information are relevant to the questioner's purpose (e.g., contributing to design). Question-asking frameworks we have already discussed—including Robertson's (Chapter 11) and those underlying usability inspection methods like Cognitive walkthroughs—are largely based on models of human cognitive skills underlying human-computer interaction. These models use the concepts of goals, subgoals, and actions to analyze human-computer interaction, and analyze complexity and likelihood of user problems in terms of the complexity of goal and subgoal structures, and difficulties mapping goal structures to actions in the interface. This cognitive framework has proven very influential in HCI research [26, 28, 29], and in a qualitative way in practical HCI methods such as usability inspection methods (see, e.g., [13, 20, 33]).

A different conceptual framework for understanding work and, in this context, structuring questions about work content and flow is the language/action framework as it has been developed by Winograd and Flores [36] (see also Winograd [30]). This framework focuses much more on the social and communicative dimensions of human activity. Purposeful activity is analyzed in terms of conversational structures composed of the language of negotiation, promises and commitments, conditions of satisfaction, breakdowns in communication, and repair activities. The framework has been used to develop software applications (e.g., the Coordinator (R), discussed in Flores, Graves, Hartfield, and Winograd [31], and methodologies for analyzing business processes in terms of communication models of human interaction [32]). It shares intellectual roots, concepts, and methods for analyzing work content used in Participatory and Contextual design approaches to designing computer technology [2, 34, 35, 59]. The questions a designer asks and the scenarios developed would have a different focus than those motivated by, for example, traditional task analysis methods that might only focus on information or data flow in an organization, and explicit procedures for using that information. The language/action framework may be better able to represent new forms of business and work interaction more dependent on negotiation and the "politics of social networking," than task representations based on management practices derived from traditional hierarchical business organizations [37].

In my judgment, identifying the "best," most representative set of scenarios will largely remain an empirical process of working with users in their context of work. Furthermore, developing requirements, particularly in the form of scenarios, is in practice an iterative process that requires an interweaving of data gathering involving users in the work context, and analysis and summarization in more reflective design context that may or may not also involve users. All the chapters in this volume discuss the need to create a closer, more efficient synergy between these processes. Developing requirements, generating scenarios, and doing design can reinforce each other, and tools for facilitating the interaction of these activities would be valuable. Participatory design methods discussed by Kyng (Chapter 4) and Muller et al. (Chapter 6) are examples of techniques that have been used, and are currently subject to reflection and analysis. Holtzblatt and Beyer [59] provide a concrete case study of design from a Contextual design perspective, which exemplifies approaches to analyzing user requirements from multiple perspectives, and in an iterative process, which supports design directly and concretely.

14.4.2 Use Scenarios Effectively in Design through Team Design Activities

A related direction for research is understanding the dynamics of, and factors that contribute to, successful group design, especially involving end users. Research opportunities here lie in at least two directions. The first is more study of the software design process, and the factors or practices that contribute to effective design. This is an active area of empirical research (e.g., see *Communications of the ACM*, October 1993—particularly, Walz et al. [23]; also Grudin [60]; Olson, Olson, Carter, and Storrøsten [38]) and theoretical reflection (e.g., Carroll [39]; Carroll, Kellogg, and Rosson [40]; Carroll and Rosson [41]; Henderson [42]; Karat and Bennett [14]). The research issues here include more than the role of scenarios, but do address the technical and social context in which scenarios are relevant.

The second research direction focuses on developing or improving tools that substantially, if not radically, accelerate the process of visualizing, implementing, and iterating on design possibilities. The evolution of PICTIVE and CARD (Chapter 6) are examples of tools and methods that not only can elicit descriptions of work from users, but do so in the context of explicitly generating design alternatives to how that work might be done. Research is needed to explore the generality of these techniques to other domains of software development.

Other techniques include cognitive and usability walkthroughs, to which we have alluded in earlier sections [13, 14, 18, 19, 20, 43]. These techniques use scenarios and questions about the fit of user goals and expectations to the interface techniques intended to achieve user goals, to drive analysis and evaluation of design ideas. As we noted earlier, these questions probe goal and action relationships, and are based on a more or less formal cognitive model of human-computer interaction, to which we have alluded earlier [26]. Skilled use of these techniques can interweave evaluation of specific design issues, as well as stimulate the generation of new design ideas [20]; [44].

Design analysis methods, also discussed in this volume, should lend themselves to supporting scenario-driven design. These techniques are intended to facilitate the development of design representations for documenting and analyzing design decisions. The examples discussed in this volume include MacLean and McKerlie's QOC (Question, Option, and Criteria) method of design analysis (Chapter 8), Rosson and Carroll's claims analysis (Chapter 10), and Johnson et al.'s ADEPT software tool for task modeling and software design (Chapter 9) (ADEPT stands for Advanced Design Environment for Prototyping with Task models). QOC and claims analysis both provide a scheme for making design decisions explicit, and analyzing them in relation to user needs, and possible tradeoffs among potentially conflicting design implications. MacLean and McKerlie allude to applications of QOC in their own work and that of others. Carroll and Rosson provide an example of how scenario development, problem domain analysis (*requirements analysis* in another parlance), and detailed design and implementation interrelate, and can be supported in tools, at least in the domain of object-oriented software design. Johnson's ADEPT tool provides a way to represent task goals, analyze them into subgoals and actions, and use these task representations to guide the design of user interfaces appropriate to users' experience and expectations.

All these techniques are aimed at identifying the knowledge and reasoning underlying good design, and turning this understanding into methodologies accessible to more designers. (See [45], introducing a special issue of Human-Computer Interaction, devoted to design rationale analysis methods, including QOC and claims analysis.) All these techniques are promising, and capture aspects of what good designers appear to do spontaneously. They have been applied in various projects, mainly by the researchers who have developed them, and their general utility remains to be established.

14.4.3 Establish the Completeness of Scenarios as Specifications of Design: Support for Modeling and Inference

As we have already discussed, completeness of scenarios means specifying goals and subgoals for tasks in the problem domain sufficient to guide design of useful function, and resolve goals and subgoals into specific software implementation techniques. Scenarios are necessarily incomplete with respect to design objectives, at least initially, because they are not expressed in terms of the software system to be designed. Scenario goals and subgoals are either high-level, without specifying specific actions, or specific actions express methods based on existing technology. We have already alluded to empirical approaches described in this book for driving scenarios toward completeness: We can evaluate the design with users, as a prototype or running implementation, identify gaps in what the system lets users do, and modify the system.

There is potential for research to improve this empirical process of completion. Another research direction is to develop more analytical methods for driving scenarios toward completeness.

Robertson's chapter (Chapter 11) suggests a possible approach, at least scenarios that describe user tasks in the original problem domain. Robertson's approach is to apply question-asking techniques to derive inferences about implicit aspects of the goals and action expressed in scenario descriptions. For example, given an initial description of a user task (a scenario), questions about *how* some goal might be achieved can elaborate methods and procedures in some domain of means and mechanisms. Asking questions about *why* some action might be carried out has the potential for elaborating on goals and subgoals for the initial task description.

The technique is motivated by Cognitive Science research into the role of questions in understanding and learning from discourse (two useful collections of research on the psychology of questions are Graesser and Black [46], and Lauer, Peacock, and Graesser [48]; the latter specifically addresses HCI issues). Scenario descriptions share similarities with stories, as several chapters (especially Chapter 2) in this volume have noted. Scenarios are generally more procedural and not expressive (or fictional, of course), but the content of scenarios need not be narrowly procedural or descriptive. Cognitive scientists have developed many concepts about how to represent the expressive discourse of stories, and the descriptive discourse of procedures and tasks. One key concept is that the surface form of discourse is not complete in essential ways. The surface form of most discourse, especially but not only stories, leaves out motivations, and details of actions and events. Filling in these elements becomes part of what readers must infer in normal comprehension. Indeed, a quality of good storytelling is the intentional crafting of story elements to require readers to make inferences about them [47].

As a potential design specification, of course, we want to recover or generate this underlying, but implicit *deep structure* of scenarios. Robertson's suggestion for generating this deep structure of task content via *how* and *why* questions shares similarities with question- and scenario-driven approaches to design walkthroughs advocated in usability inspections and walkthrough methods such as cognitive walkthroughs, as discussed in Section 14.2. Note, however, that simply elaborating scenarios is not enough; in a design context, we want scenarios to be as complete as possible. But not all elaborations are of comparable usefulness in design: We still need some way to focus on what is relevant to design. The elaboration process must be coupled with an evaluation or analysis process aimed at deriving design-relevant information from the elaborated scenarios.

A second research direction would explore how to facilitate the mapping of scenario descriptions of goals, subgoals, and actions into a specification of usable software. Scenarios would better support design if they more directly contributed to useful inferences specifically about how to implement tasks in a usable way in terms of available software and interface technology. Team design activities and usability walkthroughs as we have discussed them are effective *empirical* approaches to deriving design implications from scenarios. Object-oriented software engineering methods can bring systematic analysis and modeling methods to this mix (Chapters 10, 12, and 13). But fundamentally the approaches are empirical in the sense that they depend on designer skill, experience, and user feedback.

The Holy Grail of HCI research is to model design expertise and human-computer interaction characteristics effectively enough to build more or less intelligent design tools for inferring effective design from a set of requirements. Several attempts have been made to build such systems (see Barnard [49]; Barnard, Wilson, and MacLean [50]; Blatt and Knudson [51]; Fischer et al. [52, 53]; Johnson et al. (Chapter 9); Kieras and Polson [28]; and case studies in Sullivan and Tyler [54], Section IV: "Knowledge-based tools for interface design"). In Chapter 11, Robertson touches on the possibility. Johnson et al.'s ADEPT project describes a set of tools intended to aid designers in representing user task requirements in terms of goal and subgoal descriptions, applying rules and guidelines to select possible user interface techniques and elements whose usability attributes match task needs and user strengths and limitations, and building user interface prototypes based on these decisions. These tools are intended to at least augment intuitions of designers, and perhaps ultimately automate many of these decisions.

Building intelligent software design tools as Johnson proposes to do in ADEPT, and as others have attempted, remains an ambitious, unfilled goal of HCI research. Is it possible to really capture in a system of representations and inference rules what is important and salient about cognitive skill, problem solving, and reasoning in the use of computers? Other attempts at serious formalizing of the knowledge and rules underlying skilled and novice human use of computers have been carried out in modeling schemes like GOMS or Cognitive Complexity theory [28, 55]. Opinions vary on the relative success of these efforts (see Kieras [33] and Olson and Olson [29] for review and an optimistic assessment of the state of the art; see Gray, John, and Atwood [57] for a recent successful application). Certainly, it seems fair to assert that these schemes have not tackled the scope or depth of analysis for work content at issue in the discussions in this book.

It is more likely that tools like ADEPT will be useful in helping to structure and guide aspects of the kinds of empirical design team analysis and walkthrough methods we described earlier. Even if these modeling schemes were effective, they would need to be turned into practical tools for HCI specialists, if not for software engineers at large. So far, evidence for the practical applicability of these tools, especially for complex task domains, is modest. As Karat notes (workshop communication; see also Karat [56]), GOMS-based analyses, perhaps the most mature of the cognitive theories in HCI, have yet to be turned into broadly applied, practical tools whose ease of learning and using are justified by the benefit of using them, except in some more or less narrow task and design domains [57]. More generally, formal task representation schemes and design analysis methods all entail more or less complex tools and methods in their own right that have to be learned, and used productively. This observation also applies to design rationale schemes we have discussed, such as QOC and claims analysis, and further discussion can be found in Shum and Hammond [58].

14.5 CONCLUSIONS

The three issues we used to organize this discussion are, of course, highly interrelated, in that the issues pertaining to generating scenarios, using them effectively, and building complete scenario-based represenions overlap considerably. Moreover, the distinction between practical, proven methods and research is ultimately artificial, especially in the domain of HCI research and application. Finally, this discussion has emphasized the *processes* that I believe are essential to effective use of scenarios. Every aspect of scenario development and use involves interactions with *users* whose tasks we are trying to support with technology, and with the *designers* building that technology. The specifics of this interaction, and the respective roles and methods HCI specialists and software designers apply can vary considerably because the demands of the task domains and technology can vary widely. Put another way, there are no recipes: The experiences and reflections compiled in this volume are good starting points, but obviously require creative application in different development circumstances.

Whether the reader accepts some of the strong claims about the potential for scenarios to transform software development—for example, that scenarios can replace functional specifications—there should be no doubt about the importance of using scenarios for effective software design. A serious commitment to the use of scenarios in design provides an essential counterpoint to the strong potential for the demands and imperatives of software technology and project management practices to dominate the design process. Scenarios provide a common ground of communication for all parties with a stake in the development of a software system (Introduction and Chapter 2). Users can understand them as stories about their work practices and assumptions. Software engineers can understand them in these terms, as well as more procedural versions that resolve higher-level goals into specific actions and dependencies among actions. Scenarios are the way in which the *what* and *why* of user needs and preferences can be held in the foreground of design, constantly challenging but also informing the technological *how* aimed at meeting user requirements.

Of course, bringing these multiple groups together, and managing these multiple roles and perspectives, creates new challenges for managing the design process. Software engineering practices understandably try to turn scenarios into specifications that focus on what concretely needs to be implemented. Usability engineering, although no less committed to results, nonetheless questions implementations as deeply (and often) as possible with respect to their adequacy in meeting user needs and task requirements.

As such, it seems inescapable that use of scenarios will be surrounded by creative tensions and ambiguities of the kind laid out in Carroll's introduction (see Figure I.2). On the one hand, we do not want design to ossify into rigid functional specifications, and scenarios to become rote action scripts. We want to keep them connected or grounded in the complexity of human thought and emotion that is involved in the work processes that they represent. On the other hand, design is taking action, making choices and tradeoffs, and therefore necessarily full of compromise. We do not want to paralyze design process either. What we need is better management of this dialectic from both sides. We want to bring design representations closer to the richness of scenario descriptions, and also find ways to converge on a design solution to the task requirements expressed in scenarios. The contributions to this volume provide effective starting points for managing these difficult software design processes.

ACKNOWLEDGMENTS

I would like to thank Jack Carroll for the opportunity to participate in the Kittle House Workshop, and to contribute a chapter to this volume. I also thank Jack, Beth Maier, and Bonnie Nardi for careful readings, which greatly improved this chapter.

REFERENCES

[1] Gould, J. (1988). How to design usable systems. In M. Helander (ed.), *Handbook of Human-Computer Interaction.* Amsterdam: Elsevier Science, pp. 757–790.

[2] Whiteside, J., Bennett, J. & Holtzblatt, K. (1988). Usability engineering: Our experience and evolution. In M. Helander (ed.), *Handbook of Human-Computer Interaction.* Amsterdam: Elsevier Science, pp. 791–818.

[3] Drury, C., Paramore, B., Van Cott, H., Grey, S. & Corlett, E. (1997). Task analysis. In G. Salvendy (ed.), *Handbook of Human Factors.* New York: Wiley, pp. 225–256.

[4] Muller, M., Kuhn, S., Wildman, D. & White, E. (1993). Guest editors with taxonomy of participatory design practices: A brief practitioner's guide. *Communications of the ACM, 36*, 24–28.

[5] Schuler, D. & Namioka, A. eds. (1992). *Participatory Design: Perspectives on System Design.* Hillsdale, NJ: Lawrence Erlbaum.

[6] Wixon, D., Holtzblatt, K. & Knox, S. (1990). Contextual design: An emergent view of system design. In *Proceedings of CHI'90: Conference on Human Factors in Computing Systems,* Seattle, April 1–5. New York: ACM Press, pp. 329–336.

[7] Jacobson, I. (1992). *Object-Oriented Software Engineering: A Use Case Driven Approach.* Reading, MA: Addison-Wesley ACM Press.

[8] Brooks, F. (1987). No silver bullet: Essence and accidents in software engineering. *IEEE Computer* (April): 171–195.

[9] Nielsen, J. (1993). *Usability Engineering.* New York: Academic Press.

[10] Rubenstein, R. & Hersh, H. (1984). *Human Factors: Designing Computer Systems for People.* Bedford, MA: Digital Press.

[11] Shneiderman, B. (1993). *Designing the User Interface: Strategies for Effective Human-Computer Interaction.* 2d ed. Reading, MA: Addison-Wesley.

[12] Rockart, J. & DeLong, D. (1988). *Executive Support Systems: The Emergence of Top Management Computer Use.* Homewood, IL: Dow-Jones/Irwin.

[13] Polson, P., Lewis, C., Rieman, J. & Wharton, C. (1992). Cognitive walkthroughs: A method for theory-based evaluation of user interfaces. *International Journal of Man-Machine Studies, 36*, 741–773.

[14] Karat, J. & Bennett, J. (1991). Using scenarios in design meetings: A case study example. In J. Karat (ed.), *Taking Software Design Seriously: Practical Techniques for Human-Computer Interaction Design.* Boston, MA: Academic Press.

[15] Carroll, J. & Rosson, M. B. (1985). Usability specifications as a tool in iterative development. In R. Hartson (ed.), *Advances in Human-Computer Interaction.* Norwood, NJ: Ablex, pp. 1–28.

[16] Carroll, J. & Rosson, M. B. (1990). Human-computer interaction scenarios as a design representation. In *Proceedings of HICSS-23: Hawaii International*

Conference on System Sciences. Los Alamitos, CA: IEEE Computer Society Press, pp. 555–561.

[17] Tetzlaff, L. & Mack, R. (1991). Discussion: Perspectives on methodology in HCI research. In J. Carroll (ed.), *Designing Interaction: Psychology at the Human-Computer Interface.* New York: Cambridge University Press, pp. 286–214.

[18] Karat, J. & Bennett, J. (1991). Working within the design process: Supporting effective and efficient design. In J. Carroll (ed.), *Interfacing Thought: Cognitive Aspects of Human-Computer Interaction.* Cambridge, MA: MIT Press, pp. 269–285.

[19] Bennett, J. (1984). Managing to meet usability requirements: Establishing and meeting software development goals. In J. Bennett, D. Case, J. Sandelin & M. Smith (eds.), *Visual Display Terminals.* Englewood Cliffs, NJ: Prentice Hall, pp. 161–184.

[20] Nielsen, J. & Mack, R. (eds.). (1994). *Usability Inspection Methods.* New York: Wiley.

[21] Yourdon, E. (1989). *Structured Walkthroughs* 4th ed. Englewood Cliffs, NJ: Yourdon Press.

[22] Gilb, T. (1988). *Principles of Software Engineering Management.* Reading, MA: Addison-Wesley.

[23] Walz, D., Elam, J. & Curtis, W. (1993). Inside a software design team: Knowledge acquisition, sharing, and integration. *Communications of the ACM, 36*(10), 63–77.

[24] Carroll, J., Mack, R., Robertson, S. & Rosson, M. B. (1994). Binding objects to scenarios of use. *International Journal of Human-Computer Studies, 41,* 243–276.

[25] Suchman, L. (1987). *Plans and Situated Actions: The Problem of Human-Machine Communication.* Cambridge, MA: Cambridge University Press.

[26] Norman, D. (1986). Cognitive engineering. In D. Norman & S. Draper (eds.), *User Centered System Design: New Perspectives on Human-Computer Interaction.* Hillsdale, NJ: Lawrence Erlbaum, pp. 31–62.

[27] Carroll, J. & Rosson, M. B. (1992). Design by question: Developing user questions into scenario representations for design. In T. Lauer, E. Peacock & A. Graesser (eds.), *Questions and Information Systems.* Hillsdale, NJ: Lawrence Erlbaum, pp. 85–130.

[28] Kieras, D. & Polson, P. (1985). An approach to the formal analysis of user complexity. *International Journal of Man-Machine Studies, 22,* 365–394.

[29] Olson, J. & Olson, G. (1990). The growth of cognitive modeling in human-computer interaction since GOMS. *Human-Computer Interaction, 5,* 221–266.

[30] Winograd, T. (1988). A language/action perspective on the design of cooperative work. *Human-Computer Interaction, 3,* 3–30.

[31] Flores, F., Graves, M., Hartfield, B. & Winograd, T. (1988). Computer sys-

tems and the design of organizational software. *ACM Transactions on Office Information Systems, 6*(2), 153–172.

[32] Scherr, A. (1993). A new approach to business processes. *IBM Systems Journal, 32*(1), 80–98.

[33] Kieras, D. (1988). Towards a practical GOMS model methodology for user interface design. In M. Helander (ed.), *Handbook of Human-Computer Interaction.* Amsterdam: Elsevier Science, pp. 135–158.

[34] Greenbaum, J. & Kyng, M. (1991). Introduction: Situated design. In J. Greenbaum & M. Kyng (eds.), *Design at Work: Cooperative Design of Computer Systems.* Hillsdale, NJ: Lawrence Erlbaum.

[35] Kyng, M., & Greenbaum, J. (1992). Participatory design. Tutorial notes from *CHI'92, ACM Conference on Human Factors in Computing Systems,* Monterey, CA, May 3–7. New York: ACM Press.

[36] Winograd, T. & Flores, F. (1986). *Understanding Computers and Cognition: A New Foundation for Design.* Norwood, NJ: Ablex.

[37] Peters, T. (1992). *Liberation Management: Necessary Disorganization for the Nanosecond Nineties.* New York: Knopf.

[38] Olson, G., Olson, J., Carter, M. & Storrøsten, M. (1992). Small group design meetings: An analysis of collaboration. *Human-Computer Interaction,* 7(4), 347–374.

[39] Carroll, J. (ed.). (1991). *Designing Interaction: Psychology at the Human-Computer Interface.* Cambridge, MA: MIT Press.

[40] Carroll, J., Kellogg, W. & Rosson, M. B. (1991). The task-artifact cycle. In J. Carroll (ed.), *Designing Interaction: Psychology at the Human-Computer Interface.* New York: Cambridge University Press, pp. 74–102.

[41] Carroll, J. & Rosson, M. B. (1992). Getting around the task-artifact cycle: How to make claims and design by scenario. *ACM Transactions on Information Systems, 10,* 181–212.

[42] Henderson, A. (1991). A development perspective on interface, design, and theory. In J. Carroll (ed.), *Interfacing Thought: Cognitive Aspects of Human-Computer Interaction.* Cambridge, MA: MIT Press, pp. 254–268.

[43] Mack, R. (1992). Questioning design: Toward methods for supporting user-centered software engineering. In T. Lauer, E. Peacock & A. Graesser (eds.), *Questions and Information Systems.* Hillsdale, NJ: Lawrence Erlbaum, pp. 101–130.

[44] Wharton, C. & Lewis, C. (1992). The role of psychological theory in usability inspection methods. In J. Nielsen and R. Mack (eds.), *Usability Inspection Methods.* New York: Wiley.

[45] Carroll, J. & Moran, T. (1991). Introduction to this special issue on design rationale. *Human-Computer Interaction, 6*(3–4), 197–200.

[46] Graesser, A. 7 Black, J. (eds.). (1985). *The Psychology of Questions.* Hillsdale, NJ: Lawrence Erlbaum.

[47] Olson, G., Mack, R. & Duffy, S. (1981). Cognitive aspects of genre. *Poetics, 10,* 283–315.

[48] Lauer, T., Peacock, E. & Graesser, A. (1992). *Questions and Information Systems.* Hillsdale, NJ: Lawrence Erlbaum.

[49] Barnard, P. (1991). Bridging between basic theories and the artifacts of human-computer interaction. In J. Carroll (ed.), *Designing Interaction: Psychology at the Human-Computer Interface.* Cambridge, MA: Cambridge University Press, pp. 103–127.

[50] Barnard, P., Wilson, M. & MacLean, A. (1988). Approximate modeling of cognitive activity with an expert system: A theory-based strategy for developing an interactive design tool. *The Computer Journal, 31*(5), 445–456.

[51] Blatt, L. & Knudson, W. (1994). Interface design guidance systems. In J. Nielsen & R. Mack (eds.), *Usability Inspection Methods.* New York: Wiley, pp. 351–384.

[52] Fischer, G., Lemke, A., McCall, R. & Morch, A. (1991). Making argumentation serve design. *Human-Computer Interaction, 6*(3-4), 393–420.

[53] Fischer, G., Grudin, J., Lemke, A., McCall, R., Ostwald, J., Reeves, B. & Shipman, F. (1992). Supporting indirect collaborative design with integrated knowledge-based design environments. *Human-Computer Interaction,* 7(3), 281–314.

[54] Sullivan, J. & Tyler, S. (eds.). *Intelligent User Interfaces.* Reading, MA: Addison Wesley (ACM Press). (Section IV: Knowledge-based tools for interface design).

[55] Card, S., Moran, T. & Newell, A. (1983). *The Psychology of Human-Computer Interaction.* Hillsdale, NJ: Lawrence Erlbaum.

[56] Karat, J. (1988). Approximate modeling as an aid to software design. *Human Factors Society Bulletin, 31,* 1–3.

[57] Gray, W., John, B. & Atwood, M. (1993). Project Ernestine: Validating a GOMS analysis for predicting and explaining real-world task performance. *Human-Computer Interaction, 8,* 237–309.

[58] Shum, S. & Hammond, N. (1994). Argumentation-based design rationale: What use at what cost? *International Journal of Man-Machine Studies, 40,* 603–652.

[59] Holtzblatt, K. & Beyer, H. (1993). Making customer-centered design work for teams. *Communications of the ACM, 36,* 92–103.

[60] Grudin, J. (1991). Interactive systems: Bridging the gaps between developers and users. *Computer* (April): 59–69.

CHAPTER 15

Some Reflections on Scenarios

Bonnie A. Nardi
Apple Computer
Advanced Technology Group
Intelligent Systems Program
1 Infinite Loop
Cupertino, CA 95014
USA

As the chapters in this volume surely testify, scenarios are a protean tool adaptable to a wide variety of uses. Scenarios figure in methodologies ranging from tightly focused means of modeling constrained dialogs for simple systems such as ATMs (Wirfs-Brock, Chapter 13) to multiperson, multiyear projects involving elaborate user participation in complex projects (Kyng, Chapter 4). The range of possible inputs to scenarios is vast: Nielsen (Chapter 3), in keeping with his discount philosophy, offers "microscenarios" consisting of single bullet items ("Make friends," "Influence people," while Kyng, sparing no expense, advocates "in-depth studies of the workplace" envisionment workshops, and an insistence that actual users participate materially in design because "marketing people, HCI specialists, ethnographers and . . . managers" are insufficient!

Readers of this volume will undoubtedly seek out the scenario methodologies that best fit their needs. Karat (Chapter 5) points out that scenarios can be used successfully in many ways; one of their advantages is their adaptability to different styles of working. Strict by-the-book usage, such as has been recommended for GOMS, isn't necessary (Karat, Chapter 5). A refreshing breeze of laissez-faire informality blows along with the scenario technique, and is undoubtedly an aspect of its success.

Mack (Chapter 14) provides an excellent overview and categorization of the chapters in this volume. The chapters themselves demonstrate what can be done with scenarios in many practical settings. Anyone who wants to utilize the scenario technique has a wealth of information from this text. The present chapter will develop a critique of the scenario technique considering some questions: How might we go wrong with scenarios, what are the limits of scenarios, and where are they leading us? I examine these questions by exploring issues centered around the quality of data used to create scenarios; situations in which scenarios are insufficient; scenario reuse; and using scenarios effectively within an organization.

15.1 DATA QUALITY

One way we might go wrong with scenarios is if they do not faithfully represent users' tasks and contexts. Scenarios are intended to provide information on the context in which users work (Kuutti, Chapter 1), as well as some sense of user perspective ("[the] user's view of what happens, how it happens, and why," Carroll, Introduction). Scenarios should reflect "social reality" (Carroll, Introduction). If scenarios do not reflect some genuine social reality, then we are not serving real user needs; rather, we are merely doing what seems interesting and claiming user centeredness by virtue of the use of a specific literary form. Coming up with valid descriptions of social reality is no easy task. Let's look at the chapters that deal with data collection (Johnson et al., Chapter 9; Kyng, Chapter 4; Carey and Rusli, Chapter 7; Muller et al., Chapter 6) to see how the authors propose to generate such descriptions. The problem is to find a set of techniques that produces good data reflective of users' experiences, yet is practical enough to deploy in everyday settings.

Johnson and his team designed a system for use by radiographers in a London hospital. They worked closely on a day-to-day basis with the radiographers, which enabled them to obtain good results tailored to the specific needs of radiographers in a particular setting. The team did extensive background work in order to understand their users' tasks, including "interviews, observations . . . and enactments of activities, which included the designers themselves going through the radiographers' tasks". The design team was careful to establish "a strong communication relationship" with the customer.

In many ways, this is an ideal solution to the problem of scenario input; users and designers work closely together so that users can communicate to designers what they need to know to produce useful, usable systems. For the consulting situation in which a custom system is commissioned and designers have free access to users, the use of scenarios is a very good tool with which to promote communication and anchor system design, as evidenced in Johnson et al.'s work (Chapter 9).

However, often the circumstances enjoyed by Johnson and his colleagues do not apply. Time is short and it is difficult to gain access to users to get the kind of input that Johnson and his colleagues received. Many systems are off-the-shelf, built under the immense pressure of a hectic product schedule, to meet the needs of a large, varied pool of users. Even for custom work, designers often lack good access to the actual users, who are too busy or too remotely located to participate over time in system design.

Kyng's (Chapter 4) cooperative design approach as described in this book is rich in careful data collection techniques (going well beyond scenarios) and is a kind of guiding ideal for HCI practice. Cooperative design is especially suited to research environments. But at the present time, the use of cooperative design in nonresearch environments is just an ideal; its actual use is beyond the means of most everyday work in industry (at least outside of Scandinavia). Kyng describes a project in which software was designed to support the activity of building the world's largest suspension bridge. The cooperative design work spanned a two-year period and involved the ongoing participation of twenty users. The development team included a Danish university and a state-owned company. A veritable treasure trove of resources was expended on this project. While I am very much in sympathy with (and in awe of!) Kyng's commitment to user participation, the oft-heard criticism that Scandinavian methods of cooperative design do not export easily must be sounded yet again [2]. The reality in most countries and companies is that of a complete lack of the infrastructure and philosophy necessary to support Scandinavian-style cooperative design. The time and money involved across designers, managers, and users is far beyond what can be expended in ordinary industrial projects. (The techniques proposed as "cheap" alternatives to more extensive field research in Kyng's "Designing for a dollar a day" [5] are not particularly "cheap" by U.S. industry standards, techniques including workplace visits, workplace discussions, future workshops, mockup simulations. The problem is often one of time, due to tight development schedules, more than money. It is not unusual for a design team to have only six or eight weeks in which basic product decisions are made.)

But perhaps I am overstating things. Muller and his colleagues, inspired by cooperative design methods, have attempted to adapt them for use in the United States. They call their methods "participatory design" (although there are other versions of participatory design as well). They advocate the use of low-tech materials (colored pens, paper cards, and so forth) to act as props in design discussions to help users open up and actively discuss their work. A skilled facilitator to run meetings in which designers and users come together is essential. While Kyng might not recognize these methods as "cooperative design" with some interpretive latitude they can be construed as a relaxed version adapted from the classic techniques.

Low-tech methods are cost-effective and accessible. They are capable of producing subtle results, such as Muller's discovery that telephone operators are "knowledge workers" who spend much of their time problem solving, not simply supplying telephone numbers to customers. Seeing operators in this light leads to a different set of technologies for their use, as well as aiding the humanistic goal of recognizing operators' resourcefulness and their importance to the success of the telephone company.

It would be nice to see Muller's methods supplemented by at least some ethnographic study of the type Kyng advocates, to gain a perspective on the actual situation in which users work. The use of CARD involves preprinted cards in which task flow is already determined (though new cards can be created during the design sessions), which implies previous understanding of users' work. As in many of the other papers, Muller and colleagues seemed to take as unproblematic the generation of these critical baseline data. Probably the baseline data collection is being done by conscientious social scientists, but it would be helpful to have some discussion on this point. People reading this book who consider adapting a particular methodology need to understand the full ramifications of the methods, including allocation of sufficient time and appropriate personnel.

Muller et al.'s style of participatory design seems best suited to fairly procedural tasks in which flowchart-like representations (such as CARD) are adequate design representations. The extent to which a highly trained facilitator with extreme tact and flexibility is key to the method is unclear; it would seem that the lack of such a person might be a showstopper in some settings.

Perhaps what we can work toward in the future for everyday development in industry is a happy medium between extensive, lengthy projects involving many person-years of effort, as described by Kyng, and the much more restricted methods such as CARD, which are applicable only for certain kinds of very well defined tasks.

15.1.1 The Superficiality of Scenarios

While scenarios are clearly a useful design representation, their utility is somewhat hampered by their superficiality. This problem was noted by Robertson (Chapter 11), who sought methods by which to expand and deepen scenario content. Another means of going beyond the superficiality of a short narrative is to provide fuller ethnographic description, as Kyng (Chapter 4) advocates. This description becomes background to scenarios, to be used by those who wish to dig beneath the surface of a short scenario. Carey and Rusli (Chapter 7) discuss ways to preserve "interpretive scenarios" which embody ethnographic interpretation, for reuse, making data collection more cost effective than Kyng's thorough but expensive "in-depth studies of the workplace" for each new project. Scenarios, as well as the background information that informs them, can be placed in reusable case libraries.

15.1.2 Sampling

Another way in which scenarios can go very wrong is if they do not represent the users of interest. Three of the chapters in the volume mentioned the problem of sampling raised by the use of scenarios (Chapters 7, 10, and 11). For custom systems designed for a specific set of users known to designers (as in Chapters 4 and 9) sampling is not a problem. But for everyone else, it is a problem. Scenarios, being short narrative descriptions of concrete activities, practically beg to be abused from a statistical point of view. What class of users does a scenario represent? If we have a set of scenarios, have we achieved coverage for our population of users? How do we know? Rosson and Carroll (Chapter 10) note that "... spurious factors from one case can provoke design decisions felt throughout the design." A literary form that embodies brevity and concreteness, as scenarios must in order to communicate effectively (Introduction and Chapters 2, 5, 7, and 9), has no way to reveal whether it is or is not representative of some user population. It does not wear its statistical validity on its sleeve.

Thus there is a need for background work to establish that a particular scenario represents the users the designers want to design for. In other words, a designated group of users must be studied before a scenario is constructed from the data they supply. Alternatively, a set of scenarios, each representing an individual, can be constructed, so long as the study participants are known to be representative of the larger population of interest.

We are all aware of the situation in which researchers and engineers design for themselves and are then surprised when other classes of users, with different needs, do not like the technology they produce. Scenarios that are not grounded in the actual experiences of a well-chosen sample of users can exacerbate this problem. Scenarios that are "stories" invented by engineers (Erickson) or imaginary envisionments (Karat: "we argued about whether the scenario was 'correct' . . . whether people would want to use such a system") must be used with extreme caution.

15.2 WHEN WOULDN'T YOU USE SCENARIOS?

Scenarios are so flexible and take so many forms, as we see from the range of ways they are used in this book, that they would seem to rise to almost any occasion. But scenarios are short, crisp depictions of sequences of particular events embedded in some context. A short, crisp depiction (or even a set of them) does not always substitute for a full-blown task analysis, or an ethnographic description of the complexities of the workplace, or a carefully researched list of user requirements, or an exhaustive set of specifications, except perhaps in the case where designers are working so closely with the prospective users that gaps in the scenarios are made up in everyday interaction. Raeithel and Velichkovsky [8] point out that "the scenario method doesn't seem to be of use for the design of general-purpose software for desktop publishing, drawing illustrations, authoring hypertext media, etc., because there isn't just one traditional task structure to copy from. Rather there are so many of them that listing, analyzing, and reproducing all those styles of using materials and tools seems a hopeless and never-ending endeavor. Designers of such applications cannot really know the multitude of objects beforehand that will be built with their new tools, and with the materials they provide for." Indeed, it is hard to imagine a set of scenarios comprehensive enough to use to design, say, Microsoft Word.

But Karat (Chapter 5) did use scenarios to develop a general-purpose dictation and speech command system. Is this a counterexample to the claim of Raeithel and Velichkovsky? It seems that Raeithel and Velichkovsky are talking more about general-purpose *collections of tools* rather than changing a general input modality, so this is not a counterexample. There is a straightforward way to use a speech system; it is not a matter of a multitude of unpredictable ways of combining fine-grained tools as, say, drawing is. Some of Karat's scenarios provide information that bears on very basic features of a dictation system, rather than the minute particulars of combining tools to achieve a goal. For example, one scenario centered on dictation showed that someone other than the creator of a document may be doing proofreading and correction. This kind of information is invaluable in generating very high level features that are critical for the basic function of a dictation system.

So it may be that Raeithel and Velichkovsky [8] are right: Building a large general-purpose tool that can be used in many ways is not well supported by scenarios or, at best, it is supported in a limited way. But perhaps we need a scenario to describe every feature a system could have? And scenarios to describe the ways users combine tools, as, so often, that is when problems occur, as testers know well. Would this be a good use of scenarios?

The answer to that question depends on how much latitude you allow the word "scenario." My own view is that a scenario's scenarioness derives from two things: (1) the inclusion of some user context and (2) a narrative format, as in a text narrative or storyboard or video. If these characteristics are missing, then the term "scenario" can seem very similar to "user requirement," or "feature," or "test pattern," or "system configuration," or "error recovery mechanism," or a variety of other terms. Karat, for example, uses the term "scenarios" in many senses. He describes some context/narrative scenarios and some "scenarios" that seem to fall into more traditional software engineering categories. As an example of the former we have: "The doctor will dictate his or her report onto a tape, give it to the secretary for typing, proofread it, return it for corrections, and then send it out. This process can take a week for nonurgent reports" (Chapter 5).

This seems a "bona fide" scenario. And it feels like a different beast than "change font size to 18," another scenario Karat offers, which is essentially a test pattern. (The variable binding, size 18, is really not relevant; the test pattern is "change font size using speech"). Some of Karat's other examples also map to traditional concepts, for example, "Change the background color of the icon for the communication folder to red" (a test pattern and Karat describes it as "testing"); "tak[e] away the keyboard and mouse . . . and do . . . everything through voice commands" (basic system configuration); "what will happen if the system misrecognizes a command?" (error recovery). The important point about these latter examples is that they would have been generated in any conventional software design environment. Having a design representation called "scenario" would not have made any difference; the engineers would most certainly have delimited a hardware configuration and thought about basic mechanisms of error recovery and worked out some simple tests. These examples raise the question: Does a scenario, if it lacks context and narrative, really buy anything more than, say, the concepts of test pattern or task requirement or error recovery? Is it perhaps wise to reserve the word for more specialized uses, which incorporate context and are formulated as narratives? Rosson and Carroll (Chapter 10) say that ". . . scenarios offer . . . a rich view of the goals, actions, and experiences of users," and this seems a good general orienting perspective on scenarios.

15.3 SCENARIOS: LET'S PRESERVE THEM

Scenarios are already a successful design representation, as evidenced by the chapters in this volume. But where are scenarios heading? Kuutti (Chapter 1) views scenarios as a "preliminary vocabulary," symptomatic of an awakening desire to "articulate the importance and independence of the work-process level in design, and, to some extent, demand that it should get a dominating voice in guiding the process." But are scenarios a stopgap, a dead end, or an evolving form in this process of articulation?

They might be any of the above, depending on how we use them. One way for scenarios to evolve beyond their present state is for them to develop into reusable narratives that can be cataloged and retrieved to inform a broad-based scientific approach to design (Introduction and Chapter 7). In order to be reusable, scenarios must describe the experiences of a designated sample of users and be constructed from valid user data. Ideally then, scenarios would combine the crisp narrative form, which has made them popular, with content based on carefully collected data.

Carey and Rusli (Chapter 7) are concerned with scenario reuse. The goal of their "retrospective scenarios" is to "enable other designers to find, absorb, and apply the design insights from a library of cases." They find that scenarios are "an effective way to encapsulate the richness of user behavior in a complex discretionary task." Carey and Rusli embrace scenarios as an interpretive form in which user meanings, and not just atomic actions, are of value to designers. They argue that it is not enough simply to observe a behavior, but it is important to know why, from the user point of view, the behavior was chosen. Carey and Rusli note that anthropologists have long experience with constructing interpretive accounts, and their expertise will be useful as we try to push scenarios along an evolutionary path to greater utility.

Carey and Rusli's approach to reusable scenarios is important because it is often organizationally impossible to invest in extensive baseline data collection for a particular project. It might be argued that it is more expensive in the long run *not* to invest in this kind of data collection because the costs come later down the line when the system fails to meet user needs. There is some truth to that, but it is also wasteful, in terms of time and money, to do a lengthy study when past work can be leveraged. The need to reduce time-to-market is one of those brutal competitive realities that will not go away, no matter how much we would like to take the time to get it right. If we can adhere to short product schedules *and* infuse designs with rich, insightful material from carefully conducted user studies, so much the better. Sometimes it is possible to conduct a small study at the outset of a project. If that study is supplemented by material from the case libraries Carey and Rusli propose, a much richer understanding of users will develop.

Of course, an endeavor such as reusable case libraries implies a belief in the possibility of generalizing across situations.[1] A radically situated view of things [6, 12, 13] would dictate against reusable case libraries, but approaches mentioned by Kuutti (Chapter 1) such as distributed cognition [3, 11] and activity theory [4, 7] could accommodate the development of reusable scenarios.

It may be that scenarios will continue to be used as a sort of "live theater," a powerful but ephemeral medium in which the production needs to be staged anew each time a performance is to be given. Scenarios will be much more useful, however, if we can preserve them for future use, as suggested by Carey and Rusli (Chapter 7). Ideally we should be working toward taxonomies of user activities and technical solutions that support those activities, as proposed by Brooks [1]. Scenarios could be a part of such taxonomies. While the development of taxonomies is a daunting prospect, the work of Rasmussen, Pejtersen, and Schmidt [9] and Rasmussen and Pejtersen [10] provides a model of how this can be done. Rasmussen and his colleagues argue that guidelines do not really help designers; designers need to understand work systems so they can build appropriate computer systems to support the work. Rasmussen and his colleagues have compiled "prototypical classes of work systems" to which design solutions can be related. They do not incorporate scenarios in their work, but scenarios could easily be part of their libraries. I would not argue that the work of Rasmussen et al. is the last word in taxonomies, but it is suggestive of what might be done. Useful information that could go into a taxonomy would be annotated

---

[1]Carey and Rusli lose their nerve a bit at the end of their chapter when they hedge with, "Interpretive scenarios [contain] insights about 'certain individuals, in certain situations, under certain circumstances.'" If true, this would completely undermine their approach, so I am going to assume they were merely trying to make the point that predicting human behavior is not easy.

interface designs along with scenarios: Designers would have user context encapsulated in scenarios and matching designs, with annotated explanations, to show how previous designers attempted to meet needs derived from scenarios (see Rosson and Carroll, Chapter 10). Scenario/design pairs would also provide a laboratory in which to continue scrutinizing and evaluating designs.

15.4 SCENARIOS IN THE ORGANIZATION: REACHING OUT

HCI is very engineering oriented. The engineering orientation is reflected in many of the chapters in this volume in which scenarios are a tool for designers who are either engineers themselves or one step removed from engineers. In some of the chapters scenarios are very close to the code, almost like code browsers or version managers (e.g., Chapters 12 and 13), rather than a more broadly conceived means of embodying and communicating user experience. While the engineering side of scenarios is clearly vital, scenarios might also provide a means of reaching out to a key part of the organization with whom we now have rather distant and often chilly relations, that is, *marketing*.

Erickson's (Chapter 2) discussion of scenarios as a medium of communication in an organization provides a perspective on scenarios that emphasizes the social nature of design and the heterogeneous audience to which a scenario may play. He underscores the need to see scenarios, or any design representation, not as isolated technical artifacts, but as part of a larger social process in which work gets done. An opportunity for HCI, which we all seem to be missing, is to work more closely with those in marketing groups, rather than thinking of ourselves only as partnering with engineering. Marketing folk often drive design as much as, if not more than, engineers. They are concerned with users and often are the ones in an organization who actually define "the user experience."

However, the methods by which HCI people and marketers go about their work are quite different. Marketers work with information from a variety of sources: professional market forecasters, whose information is usually based on survey data (though some of it is outright guesswork); company-generated statistical data on market behavior; and direct contact with customers. Marketing people are very good at the numbers part of the game and often have an excellent overview of the market. When designing new products, it is well worth knowing what is selling and where and to whom. Marketers know this. HCI professionals are much closer to the experience of individual users, or groups of users. They study this experience more systematically, in the fuller context of work. As we develop scenarios based on the social reality of designated users, we capture valuable information about how users actually go about doing their work, information that we then use to *infer* technical solutions. Marketers on the other hand, are, in my opinion, rather too fond of asking direct hypothetical questions to get their information ("Do you think you would like wearing these virtual reality goggles?"), which tends to yield problematic data. Their sampling techniques may be haphazard as they conduct relatively unstructured interviews and sometimes overgeneralize the results of unsystematically asked questions. Marketers are often aware of the problematic nature of their data, but are unsure of what to do about it.

Is there some way to bridge the HCI-marketing gap, to draw upon the differing strengths of HCI professionals and marketing professionals? One possibility would be for marketers to define market segments, using their knowledge of the overall market, and to then work with HCI professionals who would develop scenarios representative of those market segments. Marketing people do not have the time to collect the in-depth information on work practices that should go into scenarios, but they can appreciate the results. At least one of the statistical problems we noted for scenarios would be alleviated by careful consideration of who the scenarios are supposed to represent, as defined by marketing. In this way, a potential weakness of scenarios can be overcome, by drawing on marketing's strengths. Data can be put into a form—the scenario—that marketers will find useful. Marketers can participate in the interviews and observations done by HCI professionals, at least to some degree, to get a feel for how the data are being generated. Thus a collaboration between HCI and marketing, with scenarios as a core technique, might be effected, with better technology being the ultimate outcome.

15.5 BEYOND SCENARIOS

Part of the appeal of scenarios is that they are short and fun and vivid. But if used uncritically, without due attention to data quality and representativeness, scenarios will be no more expressive of the needs of real users than the musings of engineers or researchers unaided by a representation of user experience. It is easy to feel that one has caught user experience because it is represented in a narrative or storyboard; but these accessible representations can easily be inflated into more than they really are. We want to be careful to distinguish the form that the information is packaged in from the quality of the content therein. As we attempt to design for broader and broader classes of users who are less and less like designers themselves, it is critical that we find a way to pipe stimulating input to designers that faithfully captures users' needs and problems. In that way we will foster design efforts grounded in a rich foundation of genuine user experience.

Scenarios have proven their mettle, and have potential as part of reusable case libraries. However, they are not likely to be the last word in design representation. Scenarios, by themselves, are insufficient tools with which to think about larger issues such as: How do we navigate the Internet? How does a user build a multimedia document? What tools are needed to manage a distributed team? How should technology be used in the classroom? As we attempt to use computers for more complex and/or more inherently social tasks, it will be helpful to find design representations that allow us to address problems of larger scope. In particular, tools such as microscenarios (Chapter 3), use cases (Chapters 12 and 13), scenario browsers (Chapter 10), while very useful, are tied to the production of code rather than to the exploration of the means by which we will be able to define broad new classes of new technology and make them accessible to a wider range of users—issues that Carroll (Introduction) flags as critical.

The strengths of scenarios—brevity and concreteness—are weaknesses when we move toward larger problem spaces. A challenge for the future, as Kuutti (Chapter 1) points out, is to find a standard language in which to talk about work and technology with a rich, precise vocabulary. The language in which scenarios are couched is completely ad hoc. While this flexibility makes scenarios accessible, it also limits the scope of what we can do with them. Making progress on taxonomies, reuse, generalization will require a standard vocabulary, as Kuutti observes. Activity theory and distributed cognition are potential choices here.

Scenarios will undoubtedly remain a part of our design repertoire as we push forward toward more theoretical means of predicting and explaining user experience (Chapter 1). Scenarios are a preliminary vocabulary—informal, ad hoc, but lively—in which to speak to one another as we attempt to rise to C. Wright Mills' challenge, recalled in this volume by Carroll, to meet our obligation to "provide effective guidance for the development of social practices"—of which the design of technology is surely one of the most important.

REFERENCES

[1] Brooks, R. (1991). Comparative task analysis: An alternative direction for human-computer interaction science. In J. M. Carroll (ed.), *Designing Interaction: Psychology at the Human-Computer Interface.* Cambridge, MA: Cambridge University Press.

[2] Grudin, J. (1990). Obstacles to participatory design in large product development organizations. In *Proceedings of Participatory Design Conference'90,* Seattle, April, pp. 14–21.

[3] Hutchins, E. (1994). *Cognition in the Wild.* Cambridge, MA: MIT Press.

[4] Kuutti, K. (1991). Activity theory and its applications to information systems research and development. In H.-E. Nissen (ed.), *Information Systems Research.* Amsterdam: Elsevier Science, pp. 529–549.

[5] Kyng, M. (1989). Designing for a dollar a day. *Office: Technology and People, 4,* 157–170.

[6] Lave, J. (1988). *Cognition in Practice.* Cambridge, MA: Cambridge University Press.

[7] Nardi, B. A. (ed.). (1995). *Context and Consciousness: Activity Theory and Human Computer Interaction.* Cambridge, MA: MIT Press.

[8] Raeithel, A. & Velichkovsky, B. (1995). Joint attention and co-construction of tasks. In B. A. Nardi (ed.), *Context and Consciousness: Activity Theory and Human Computer Interaction.* Cambridge, MA: MIT Press.

[9] Rasmussen, J., Pejtersen, A. & Schmidt, K. (1990). *Taxonomy for Cognitive Work Analysis.* Roskilde, Denmark: Riso National Laboratory.

[10] Rasmussen, J. & Pejtersen, A. (1993). *Mohawc Taxonomy Implications for Design and Evaluation.* Roskilde, Denmark: Riso National Laboratory.

[11] Rogers, Y. & Ellis, J. (1994). Distributed cognition: An alternative framework for analyzing and explaining collaborative working. *Journal of Information Technology, 9,* 119–128.

[12] Suchman, L. (1987). *Plans and Situated Actions.* Cambridge, MA: Cambridge University Press.

[13] Winograd, T. & Flores, F. (1986). *Understanding Computers and Cognition: A New Foundation for Design.* Norwood, NJ: Ablex.

Index